D0856859

THE ESSENTIAL ARTICLE SERIES

Bernard N. Schilling
University of Rochester
General Editor

Donald G. Adam
Chatham College
Assistant General Editor

Harry G. Rusche
Emory University
Assistant General Editor

Volumes Available

ESSENTIAL ARTICLES FOR THE STUDY OF ENGLISH AUGUSTAN BACKGROUNDS

Ed. Bernard N. Schilling

ESSENTIAL ARTICLES FOR THE STUDY OF ALEXANDER POPE. Revised and enlarged edition.

Ed. Maynard Mack

ESSENTIAL ARTICLES FOR THE STUDY OF JOHN DRYDEN

Ed. H. T. Swedenberg, Jr.

ESSENTIAL ARTICLES FOR THE STUDY OF OLD ENGLISH POETRY

Ed. Jess Bessinger and Stanley J. Kahrl

ESSENTIAL ARTICLES FOR THE STUDY OF FRANCIS BACON

Ed. Brian Vickers

Essential Articles for the study of Francis Bacon

Edited by **Brian Vickers**

SIDGWICK & JACKSON London

297

192.1
V637e

157827

Copyright 1968 by The Shoe String Press, Inc.
Hamden, Connecticut, U.S.A.

First published in Great Britain 1972 by
Sidgwick and Jackson Limited
1 Tavistock Chambers, Bloomsbury Way
London, W.C.1

ISBN 0.283.97816.3
Printed in the United States of America

CONTENTS

FOREWORD vii

PREFACE ix

INTRODUCTION xi

I. BACON THE SCIENTIST

R. F. JONES
The Bacon of the Seventeenth Century 3

VIRGIL K. WHITAKER
Francis Bacon's Intellectual Milieu 28

C. W. LEMMI
Mythology and Alchemy in *The Wisdom of the Ancients* 51

GEOFFREY BULLOUGH
Bacon and the Defence of Learning 93

MARY HESSE
Francis Bacon's Philosophy of Science 114

MOODY E. PRIOR
Bacon's Man of Science 140

II. BACON ON LAW, POLITICS AND HISTORY

PAUL H. KOCHER
Francis Bacon on the Science of Jurisprudence 167

KARL R. WALLACE
Discussion in Parliament and Francis Bacon 195

LEONARD F. DEAN
Sir Francis Bacon's Theory of Civil History-Writing 211

GEORGE H. NADEL
History as Psychology in Francis Bacon's Theory of History 236

III. BACON THE WRITER

JOHN L. HARRISON
Bacon's View of Rhetoric, Poetry, and the Imagination 253

RONALD S. CRANE
The Relation of Bacon's Essays to His Program for the Advancement of Learning 272

R. TARSELIUS
"All colours will agree in the dark": A Note on a Feature in the Style of Francis Bacon 293

ANNE RIGHTER
Francis Bacon 300

ADDITIONAL ARTICLES FOR FURTHER STUDY 322

FOREWORD

Immense resources are now available for literary study in England and America. The contributions to scholarship and criticism are so numerous and often so valuable that the student preparing himself for a career in literary teaching and study may be embarrassed, not to say overwhelmed. Yet from this mass of commentary certain titles have emerged which seem to compel attention. If one offers a seminar in one of the standard areas or periods of English literature, the syllabus will show year after year some items which cannot be omitted, some pieces every serious student should know. And with each new offering of the course, one must face the task of compiling a list of these selections for the seminar's reserve shelf, of searching out and calling the the library's copies, and reserving space for the twenty or thirty or forty volumes the list may demand. As if this were not enough, one must also attempt to repair or replace the volumes whose popularity has had the unfortunate side effects of frequent circulation and the concomitant wear, abuse, and general deterioration.

We propose an alternative to this procedure. We propose to select from the many learned journals, scholarly studies, and crtical books the best selections available, the selections which consistently reappear on graduate seminar shelves and on undergraduate honors program reading lists. Let us choose from those articles which time has sanctioned, those too from the best of more recent performances, and let us draw them into a single volume of convenient size. This offers a clear gain in simplicity and usefulness. The articles chosen make up a body of knowledge that cannot fail to be valuable, and they act as models of the kind of contributions to learning which we are training our students to make themselves. And if we can have ready to hand a concentration of such articles for each of the standard areas, and several individual authors, we may conduct the study of these subjects with greater confidence, knowing more fully the extent and kind of reading we can take for granted. And, while we benefit our classes and students, we can also allow the library to keep the original editions of the articles on its shelves and so fulfill its proper and usual function.

We must add, finally, that each book in the series, and therefore the whole series, is the result of unselfish help from contributors and editors from all of Great Britain and the United States. We wish to acknowledge their help and the help of the Bowdoin College Research Fund in rendering this useful service.

B. N. S.	Rochester, N. Y.
D. G. A.	Pittsburgh, Pa.
H. G. R.	Atlanta, Ga.

PREFACE

All references to Bacon have been regularized to conform to the standard edition by James Spedding, R. L. Ellis, and D. D. Heath (London, 1857–74), consisting of Works, 7 vols., and Letters and Life, 7 vols. These are here numbered consecutively and quoted in abbreviated form, e.g. Vol. 3, p. 217: III, 217; XIII, 24 etc. I am grateful to Dr. George Nadel of the Warburg Institute, London, for the loan of his copy of the American version of Spedding's text, which (confusingly) reproduced the Works in 15 vols. (Boston, McTaggart and Brown, 1860–4); the loan has greatly aided the correction of page-references for four of the articles. The Spedding edition has been reprinted (Friedrich Frommann Verlag, Stuttgart-Bad Canstatt, 1962), but in an unfortunately reduced photo-copy: happily, it has now been re-issued in a handsome and readable format by the Garrett Press (New York, 1968).

INTRODUCTION

After a long period of neglect and abuse it is a pleasure to report that the last thirty years have seen a great revival of interest in Bacon, a revival that has produced informed and detailed criticism both at the general level[1] and as more specialized studies, the best of which are included in this volume. Comparing this interest in Bacon with that of the nineteenth century, we note first a welcome decline in the genre of incriminating biography, that which tries to minimize Bacon's achievements as a writer, historian, politician, lawyer, philosopher, and psychologist by seizing on his dismissal for bribery or alleged irregularities in his private life—a type of biography most notoriously represented by Macaulay but revived in a shrill and feverish way by Lytton Strachey (Elizabeth and Essex, 1928). Macaulay's prejudices were exposed by James Spedding in his patient, thorough demolition, Evenings with a Reviewer (1848), and Strachey's are not worth discussing—Fulton Anderson has vigorously exploded these and many other misconceptions in the opening chapter of his recent biography.[2] But although we applaud the decline in this type of activity, we must sadly recognize that the world continues to produce otherwise sane and responsible people who devote much energy and money to trying to prove that Bacon was an illegitimate son of Queen Elizabeth and/or wrote the works of Shakespeare, Spenser, the Authorized Version of the Bible, and anything else outstanding, even apparently as far as Carlyle. This is a laughable insanity, but it has its serious side, for no other great writer has been so pestered by eccentrics as Bacon has.

Sanity reigns elsewhere, however, and in addition to the general accounts mentioned earlier there have been a number of important full-length studies of Bacon. Two complementary expositions of his philosophy are those by F. H. Anderson and Benjamin Farrington.[3] Anderson gives a straightforward analysis of Bacon's thought from the standpoint of "pure" philosophy, while Farrington stresses the technological element. They are both valuable contributions, but are less good when it comes to the analytical evaluation of Bacon's scientific theories or to the historical sources for them. The latter approach has been best explored by Paolo Rossi,[4] and he provides further evidence that Bacon the scientist does not conform to our modern idea of a physicist, say, but draws many of his assumptions and some of his experimental method from what seems to us a jumble of hocus pocus, Renaissance alchemy and magic (similar conclusions are reached in the works by Fisch, Haydn, and Thorndike listed in note 1, and by Lemmi in this volume). Bacon drew freely on the past, but succeeded in passing his ideas on to the future in a much more modern-looking form, the apparatus of apparently exhaustive scientific method in the Novum Organum, and it is perhaps for this reason that it has taken us so long to recognize those medieval and Renaissance elements in his thought which are best described as "pre-scientific." Certainly the seventeenth century took him as the first of the Moderns, not the last of the Ancients, and Bacon's influence on the Royal Society continues to excite discussion[5]—the last thirty years have also seen a recognition (possibly excessive) of the importance of that body.

Studies of Bacon's scientific theories and influence are to be expected, but the range of other work is surprising. Although we do not yet have an adequate modern account of Henry VII, Bacon's theory of history has been treated in two general books,[6] and in the articles by Dean and Nadel reprinted here. His relationship to seventeenth-century scepticism has been well studied,[7] and together with the work of Hiram Haydn we can now see that Bacon was not simply an iconoclast but belonged to a very serious reaction against authority and certainty: the paradox is that in his own scientific programme Bacon was an incurable optimist, even when the support that he so badly needed was not forthcoming, and here as so often Bacon's thought reveals what seems at first to be a contradiction but which turns out to be a union of complementary extremes. In his attitude to rhetoric he is both a traditionalist and an innovator, as Karl Wallace has shown,[8] and similarly in his use of the legal maxim Peter Stein has demonstrated[9] a dual process whereby Bacon first makes himself fully aware of the accepted function of the maxim in legal argument and then reshapes it to his own uses. The interplay between tradition and experiment may continue to be one of the most fruitful approaches to Bacon.

The articles presented here pursue more specialized topics, and all do so with an accuracy and care for detail that set a challenging standard for future workers in these fields. We begin with the classic work of R. F. Jones which established for the first time the historical framework within which Bacon's scientific ideas permeated the seventeenth century: in this chapter from Ancients and Moderns we have what is still the clearest exposition of Bacon's ideas about the reform of science; the rest of the book (which will always be essential reading for anyone interested in the seventeenth century) shows the enormous impact of those ideas. The next three articles move from what Bacon produced to what influenced him. Virgil Whitaker reconstructs an important part of Bacon's intellectual milieu, namely his debt to Renaissance encyclopedists, and both the general framework and the individual details give scope for future work (Professor Whitaker also represents the healthy independence of modern Bacon critics in castigating him for uncritically accepting facts and theories). C. W. Lemmi's pioneering study of the iconographical symbolism of The Wisdom of the Ancients is represented here by a substantial excerpt. Lemmi began by demonstrating Bacon's considerable knowledge of classical and Renaissance mythography, but seems to have realized while analysing this strand that Bacon's eclectic mind was also drawing on a very different medieval-Renaissance tradition, the mysteries of alchemy. His exposition of the union of the two streams of thought in the De Sapientia Veterum is a fine piece of detective work with important consequences, supporting Whitaker's conclusions as to the traditional, "old-fashioned" element in Bacon's thought and thought-processes: significantly, both writers place him alongside Spenser. Geoffrey Bullough takes a perspective closer in time to Bacon, the sixteenth-century dispute about the nature and value of humanist learning, a controversy in which the best-known and the most violent voice is that of Cornelius Agrippa (whose influence on Bacon is also discussed by Professor Whitaker). But the controversy ranged from the concentrated scepticism of Agrippa and Montaigne to much more mundane attitudes to the scholar in society (an unemployable person, or a pedant), and by wide reference to contemporaries such as Nashe, Raleigh, Daniel, Greville and others Professor Bullough sets Bacon against the whole social and literary background, and if he underestimates Bacon's debt to alchemy this is easily corrected by work already referred to. The Advancement of Learning is now rightly seen as a triumphant "rampart for true learning," a justification of the whole humanist tradition.

From the influences and circumstances behind the work we move to evaluations of the work itself. Mary Hesse brings to her re-appraisal of Bacon's philosophy of science the training of a scientist and historian of science, and if the results are at times difficult for the lay reader he should persevere with this authoritative assessment—one that (after the many disparaging reviews of modern scientists and philosophers) is surprisingly sympathetic to Bacon. Dr. Hesse brings out well the inconclusive, evolving nature of Bacon's thought, and her final paragraph is a judicious balance-sheet of his errors and achievements as a philosopher and scientist. Moody E. Prior is concerned with a different but related topic, Bacon's new vision of the nature of the scientist. He shows first how Bacon embraced some of the theoretical tenets of scepticism but grafted on to these an optimistic vision of the eventual discovery of certainty and truth; to this optimistic vision is joined a sincere belief in the ability of science to relieve "man's estate" and an essentially compassionate view of human life: an almost symbolic expression of this attitude is the description of the perfect scientist in the New Atlantis, who "had an aspect as if he pitied men." As R. L. Ellis put it in 1857, "Herein we see the reason why Bacon has often been called an utilitarian; not because he loved truth less than others, but because he loved men more" (I, 58). Professor Prior goes on to stress the ethical and Christian basis which is a constant in Bacon's work, his scorn for selfishness and his plea for philanthropy and charity, his use of Christian symbols and Biblical myths (true science could help man to overcome the Fall), his attacks on pride. Bacon in fact urged that the scientist has an ethical responsibility to society, and time increasingly shows that he was right.

The second part of this volume is devoted to Bacon's activities in the professional spheres—law, politics, historiography. Paul Kocher's detailed account of Bacon's theory of jurisprudence is a valuable complement to the work of Peter Stein. In this sphere as in every other he entered, Bacon reveals the same penetrating intellectual qualities—a sharp evaluation of extant systems is followed by an impatient and compelling scheme to improve their theoretical and practical potentialities. Here he finds the laws both voluminous and disorganized, proposes a briefer, more coherent system and, most important, tries to establish the principles which govern the law, the legal maxims which are as important here as the aphorism is in his general methodology.[10] In the second part of his article Professor Kocher moves from theory to practice, with Bacon's attempts to have his proposals accepted by James I and others (attempts which unhappily came to nothing) and in the third section he joins Whitaker, Prior, and other writers such as Harold Fisch in stressing the religious elements in Bacon's thought. Parts of this article may seem too technical for the general reader but it is important to see how Bacon's ideas and methods develop across the various disciplines (here we find the aphorism, induction, and the ever-present religious basis)—for him they were not separate and watertight, and for us they should not be so either. Karl Wallace demonstrates the flexibility needed by the student of Bacon, for he moves from the theoretical basis of rhetoric to the practical oratory of the parliament chamber, another sphere in which Bacon's gifts were soon recognized and respected. From contemporary records he displays the variety of procedures available in the Jacobean parliament (such as the distinction between a "committee" and a "conference") and shows Bacon's connection with both the matter and manner of parliamentary discussion.

The continuity of approach that Bacon employed throughout his work can be seen from other angles in Leonard Dean's wide-ranging study of his theory of civil history writing. Here again Bacon made some penetrating criticism of extant methods and evolved theories that would improve them, and here too he showed a rare detachment from the assumptions of his age, seeing the historian's real difficulty in attaining a true historical perspective. In the content of his proposals there are connections with his views on other subjects: Professor Dean points out that Bacon stressed that the historian's task is not merely to collect facts but to evaluate them, and we are reminded of Dr. Hesse's dismissal of the "frequent misinterpretation of Bacon as a mere fact-collector"—here too the facts are only the "materials on which his method was to work." Similarly Professor Prior's demonstration of the important place of ethics in Bacon's concept of the scientist is supplemented by this discussion of his plea for a more detailed and realistic treatment of ethics and psychology in historical writing. Here too are the faults that are found elsewhere: surprising lapses at the primary level of written evidence, for just as in the scientific work he accepted uncritically the fabulous material of classical encyclopedias, here he neglected to consult important original documents on Henry VII. Bacon did not always practise what he preached, but at least he preached persuasively. His interest in the psychology of history is treated in more detail by George Nadel, who gives further evidence of the continuity of Bacon's thought by his impressive demonstration that the basic methodological tool of Bacon in the sciences, induction based on axioms, is present in his theory of history (and in his theory of jurisprudence, as shown by Professor Kocher). Thus Bacon in his own work goes a long way towards establishing that *philosophia prima*, common to all the sciences, which he celebrated in the *Advancement of Learning* and elsewhere. Dr. Nadel discusses Bacon's "insistence that the subject matter of history is individual and social psychology," shows the close connection in Bacon's work between ethics and psychology (an interest that might be called "moral psychology"), and points to the inevitable discrepancies and contradictions. Above all is the stress that history, like philosophy, should be in accord with the "actual nature of things," and we can endorse Dr. Nadel's conclusion: "That learning should be 'true to life' is the overarching inspiration behind all Baconian thought."

The last section of this volume deals with Bacon the writer, and might seem to be concerned with persuasion rather than truth, except that Bacon would have called it "persuasion in the service of truth." As he figures importantly in other fields in the early seventeenth century so he comes into English literature too, and as elsewhere both in theory and practice. His discussion of the nature and function of poetry in Book Two of the *Advancement* has aroused much ill-informed controversy, and it is the success of John Harrison's paper that by approaching the question with a sound grasp of two topics which the objectors have notably lacked (namely Renaissance rhetoric and poetic and Bacon's full range of reference to literature, not one or two remarks taken out of context), he can present a very different picture to that of the hard-headed, anti-imaginative scientist. After what we have learned from the most informed studies of Bacon's scientific sources and thought-processes it is no surprise to find him described here as a traditionalist lover of allegory and myth (Lemmi and Whitaker placed him with Spenser), and Mr. Harrison easily proves that Bacon's concept of poetry's illuminative power is religious rather than "scientific" and that in his respect for the creative power of the imagination he deserves to be ranked with Sidney and Shakespeare. (Nevertheless one must take issue with that section of Mr. Harrison's argument [pp. 263–4 below] which describes Bacon as "prosaic-minded" and makes him responsible for destroying the "multi-analogical conception of the micro-macrocosm": Bacon used that analogy often and responsively.)

INTRODUCTION

If Bacon "comes into" English Literature it must be as a great prose-writer in a great age, for he produced few if any works whose intention is purely literary: the New Atlantis and The Wisdom of the Ancients are obviously vehicles for his scientific ideas, but not until Ronald Crane's article of 1923 was the true nature of the Essays perceived. This has always been the most misunderstood of Bacon's works, its form being confused with that of the discursive, whimsical tradition (from Montaigne to Charles Lamb and beyond) and thus pronounced cold or sterile; the Machiavellian element in its content being crudely attached to Bacon's own character and dismissed as cynical or immoral. Professor Crane demonstrated simply that the Essays were designed to fill the gaps in the study of man noted in Book II of The Advancement of Learning (it can be shown that the first edition of 1597 is an embryonic version of the same concern), deficiencies in "moral" and "civil" knowledge, presenting as remedy an outline of human psychology—the passions, heredity, environment—and even an elementary form of sociology. Here Bacon did practise what he preached, and the Essays contain some of his most perceptive analyses of the human condition: each is in effect a set of notes or aphorisms towards a psychological casebook, say. Once this simple truth is grasped a better appreciation of the Essays' content as indeed of the whole range of Bacon's moral psychology can be foreseen. Appreciation of their manner has been notably lacking in recent years (I have tried to remedy this in my study of Bacon as a writer), but one successful demonstration of the connection between scientific and imaginative modes in Bacon's style has come from Miss Ruth Tarselius, who shows how Bacon often tends to base an imaginative analogy on either a predictive grammatical form or on some natural phenomenon: "For all colours will agree in the dark." It is another way of achieving certainty, and Miss Tarselius has cast light on the force and conviction with which Bacon wrote. Finally Anne Righter contributes the best short account of Bacon in existence, sympathetic and sensitive, with a rare grasp of his essentially imaginative modes of thinking and writing.

From a range of disciplines almost as wide as Bacon's own the contributors to this volume provide the insights for a fresh assessment of his work. They independently agree on many points —his integrity in the dedicated search or pilgrimage for truth; his flexible application of some central types of method (observation, expressed in aphorisms; experiment leading to the formation of axioms which become the poles in an inductive system) across several intellectual fields—science, law, history, psychology; his curiously anomalous position as a herald of the new scientific age who is also an incorrigible addict of modes of thinking which his expressed programme would replace: allegory, myth, iconographical symbolism, alchemy. This general agreement may point the way to new approaches to Bacon, or may reveal omissions thus far. Having in this Introduction tried to survey the extant body of modern scholarship and criticism, perhaps I may be allowed to suggest in an equally summary fashion what can be hoped for from the future. The great biographical and historical work of James Spedding will never be superseded, but the time may soon be ripe for supplementary studies. Spedding relied on the pioneering Stuart histories by S. R. Gardiner, and one would imagine that several revolutions in historiography since then may produce new information and new ways of evaluating it. Certainly Bacon's role in Parliament can already be re-assessed with the help of the great editions of seventeenth-century parliamentary diaries inspired by Wallace Notestein.

On the scientific side we can predict that studies of Bacon's inductive method are perhaps sufficient, but more needs to be done to evaluate his concept of the hypothesis and its relation to his theory of aphorisms. Thanks to the great work of R. F. Jones on Bacon's influence on the seventeenth century this topic may be left for a while (although the repercussions of the programme for a new "scientific" prose style have not yet been fully explored)— his effect on the eighteenth and nineteenth centuries, in England, Europe, and indeed America is such a vast topic that only a polymath or series of full-time researchers could handle it. As for the sources of Bacon's scientific ideas and methods, this is of all topics the most important and urgent. Something has been done on alchemy, but not enough, and perhaps the recent revival of interest in Neo-Platonism, the occult, the cabbala and other hermetic traditions (most notably by Dr. Frances Yates[11]) augurs well for this topic. The debt of Bacon to several sixteenth-century scientists needs close study, and again the recent survey by Paul Kristeller[12] which includes Telesio and Patrizi may increase interest. Indeed Bacon's awareness of his immediate stimuli is virtually unstudied, and among the major figures to be considered one would list Vives, Erasmus, and Agrippa.[13]

In more general philosophical fields Bacon would certainly profit from the rigorous but imaginative application of the History of Ideas approach. His interest in scepticism has been considered by Hiram Haydn, H. G. Van Leeuwen, and Geoffrey Bullough, but it may be taken further, and his knowledge of Stoicism and Neo-Platonism might be significant. Most pressing in this area would be an analytical and historical study of Bacon's moral thought, his frequent separation of ethics from expediency (touched on here by Professor Kocher), which might be related to his position in the great Renaissance debate over the Active and Contemplative lives (briefly handled by Professor Bullough, but certainly of wider ramifications). Perhaps when a number of such studies have been published the time would be ripe for an approach which has a remarkable potential, the development of Bacon's thought across several fields and the interaction between them. A similar study is needed of the development of Bacon's style, his increasing use of the expressive resources of language, and more work is needed on his use of allegory, perhaps along the lines laid down by C. W. Lemmi and John Harrison. Bacon as poet might have seemed to be the last refuge of article-writers, were it not for the recent splendid demonstration by Paul Fussell[14] of the rhythmic and metrical subtleties of his poem In vitam humanam ("The world's a bubble"). And there may soon be a need for a new edition of his works: a certain amount of manuscript material has turned up,[15] although as far as I know no systematic searches have been made, and it would be immensely valuable to have sound texts and translations with detailed annotation by a team of scholars learned in Renaissance philosophy, science, literature, law, and politics, possibly with the great Yale edition of Sir Thomas More as an example.

These have been one man's suggestions for new work, but perhaps it is safest to say that the future range of Bacon studies is unpredictable, although its growth will continue. For the sustained mental energy with which he reviewed so many intellectual and social disciplines, attacked the sterile elements and pointed the way to new growth, expressing criticism and construction in language which is penetrating, imaginative and emotionally moving—this combination will surely attract many to study one of the most remarkable minds of the Renaissance.

INTRODUCTION

NOTES

1. Important general accounts of Bacon include the following: H. Craig, The Enchanted Glass (Oxford, 1936, 1950); H. Fisch, Jerusalem and Albion (London, 1964); N. W. Gilbert, Renaissance Concepts of Method (New York, 1960); H. Haydn, The Counter-Renaissance (New York, 1950); D. G. James, The Dream of Learning (Oxford, 1951); E. Sewell, The Orphic Voice (London, 1961); L. Thorndike, A History of Magic and Experimental Science Vols. V–VIII, (New York, 1941, 1958); Karl Wallace, Francis Bacon on the Nature of Man (Illinois, 1967); Basil Willey, The Seventeenth Century Background (London, 1934) and The English Moralists (London, 1964); F. P. Wilson, Elizabethan and Jacobean (Oxford, 1945).
2. F. H. Anderson, Francis Bacon, His Career and Thought (University of South Carolina, 1963).
3. F. H. Anderson, The Philosophy of Francis Bacon (Chicago, 1948); B. Farrington, Francis Bacon, Philosopher of Industrial Science (London, 1951); Farrington has expressed his views further in the context of a volume presenting useful translations of several minor scientific works, The Philosophy of Francis Bacon (Liverpool, 1964).
4. Paolo Rossi, Francesco Bacone: Dalla Magia Alla Scienza (Bari, 1957); English translation (with slight revisions) by Sacha Rabinovitch, Francis Bacon: From Magic to Science (London, 1968).
5. See T. Sprat, History of the Royal Society, ed. J. I. Cope and H. W. Jones (London, 1959), and R. F. Jones, Ancients and Moderns (2d ed., Washington University Press, 1961). Two recent studies are complementary in that they each take extreme positions: Christopher Hill, in his Intellectual Origins of the English Revolution (Oxford, 1965), overstresses the Puritan element in the growth of scientific research, while Marjorie Purver, The Royal Society: Concept and Creation (London, 1967), overemphasizes the purely Baconian influence and undervalues the other research groups in Oxford and London. The truth lies somewhere between these accounts.
6. F. S. Fussner, The Historical Revolution: English Historical Writing and Thought, 1580–1640 (London, 1962) and W. H. Green-

leaf, Order, Empiricism and Politics: Two Traditions of English Political Thought (London, 1964).

7. H. G. Van Leeuwen, The Problem of Certainty in English Thought, 1630–90 (The Hague, 1963).

8. Karl Wallace, Francis Bacon on Communication and Rhetoric (Chapel Hill, North Carolina, 1943); "Imagination and Bacon's View of Rhetoric," Dimensions of Rhetorical Scholarship (Norman, Oklahoma, 1963).

9. Peter Stein, Regulae Irsuis: From Juristic Rules to Legal Maxims (Edinburgh, 1966).

10. I have analysed the methodological and stylistic role of the aphorism in Francis Bacon and Renaissance Prose (Cambridge, 1968), chapter 3. In my own account I unfortunately neglected to mention Professor Kocher's article, which I found very helpful, even though I was treating the aphorism along rather different lines.

11. F. A. Yates, Giordano Bruno and the Hermetic Tradition (London, 1964); and The Art of Memory (London, 1966), which contains an expert analysis of Bacon's theory of memory.

12. Paul Kristeller, Eight Philosophers of the Italian Renaissance (Stanford University Press, 1964).

13. C. G. Nauert, Jr., Agrippa and the Crisis of Renaissance Thought (Urbana, Illinois, 1965) considers some details of the influence on Bacon.

14. Paul Fussell, Jr., Poetic Meter and Poetic Form, chapter 8 (Random House, New York, 1965), pp. 182–3.

15. It was stated at the time that the Ellis and Spedding edition was not complete, for it did not include all the Legal Works by Bacon known to exist. D. D. Heath, the editor of this section, was not granted permission even to inspect works in the Stowe collection, then the property of Lord Ashburnam (VII, 305). This contained Bacon's first legal work, his Reading on Advowsons, made at Gray's Inn in 1587, and two other manuscripts of uncertain nature. Heath knew of two more unpublished manuscripts, one in Cambridge University Library on the Sutton Hospital Case, in Law French and one in the British Museum (Harleian MSS. 7017 no. 43) in Bacon's hand,

which he thought to be merely a commonplace book. R. G. Usher has described what seems to be the same manuscript (in the B. M. volume ff. 179 et seq.:) which, he argues, shows considerable skill in handling Law French (Modern Language Notes Vol. 24 p. 28 ff.). The Office of Alienations was omitted by Heath as being spurious, though I think that a strong case could be made, on stylistic grounds if nothing more, for Bacon's authorship. Another work which was regarded as doubtful but included in the Spedding edition is the Letter, written out of England, which C. Rickert now claims to be authentic (Modern Language Review, Vol. 51, p. 72 ff.). Three manuscripts have been found and printed: the original "Licence to travel the seas" granted for Bacon in 1576 (by R. L. Eagle, Notes & Queries, Vol. 195, p. 334 ff.); still earlier is a letter written by the thirteen-year-old Bacon at Trinity, which antedates by seven years the earliest hitherto known to exist (by E. R. Wood, Notes & Queries, Vol. 196, pp. 248–9). More important than these is the discovery by V. F. Snow in the Public Record Office (State Papers 14/59 Fol. 451b) of the original manuscript for the letter of advice to Fulke Greville; Snow reports that there seem to be other letters by Bacon in this collection (see under "Articles for Further Study" at the end of this volume). Several letters were discovered in the Guildhall and printed as long ago as 1869, and it is odd that they should have escaped Spedding's careful eye. (See Illustrations of Jack Cade's rebellion . . . Together with Some Newly-Found Letters of Lord Bacon, &c., by B. Brogden Orridge [London, 1869].)

A number of manuscripts have been discovered but not yet printed. In S. de Ricci's impressive compilation, A Census of Medieval and Renaissance Manuscripts in the United States and Canada (New York, 1946–50, Supplement, 1962), are listed more than thirty Bacon manuscripts, mainly letters, some of them being copies, but many original and so far unpublished, the majority being in the Folger and Huntington Libraries. The largest haul went to Chicago, however, as announced in a letter to the Times Literary Supplement (February 11th, 1926) consisting of the Bacon family archives, a vast collection of "several thousand items," still to be catalogued, but including documents, deeds, and letters, from the twelfth to the seventeenth centuries. An even more exciting prospect is that some forty-seven commonplace books said to be in the hand of Bacon's secretary, William Tottel, including it seems extracts from books marked by Bacon and with notes in his hand, were announced for sale in 1943 (Times Literary Supplement, February 3, 1943) and then disappeared from view. They were successfully traced by Mr. Stuart Clark, Assistant Lecturer in History, Swansea University (whom I have also to thank for information about current work on Bacon as historian) to the collection of C. K. Ogden, now acquired by the library of University College, London. Mr. Clark is studying the collection, but his first reports indicate that the presence of Bacon's annotation has been exaggerated. Another case of erroneous ascription seems to be the list of books sold to the Folger Shakespeare Library in 1927 (MS. M.a. 276) by N. M. Broadbent, claimed to contain annotations in Bacon's own hand, for which no sound evidence exists. But it is likely that some of Bacon's books are preserved in the world's major libraries, and as scholars have recently become more conscious of the significance of a writer's book-owning more might still be discovered.

Thus no major manuscripts have yet come to light, but perhaps there is already enough for at least a supplementary volume.

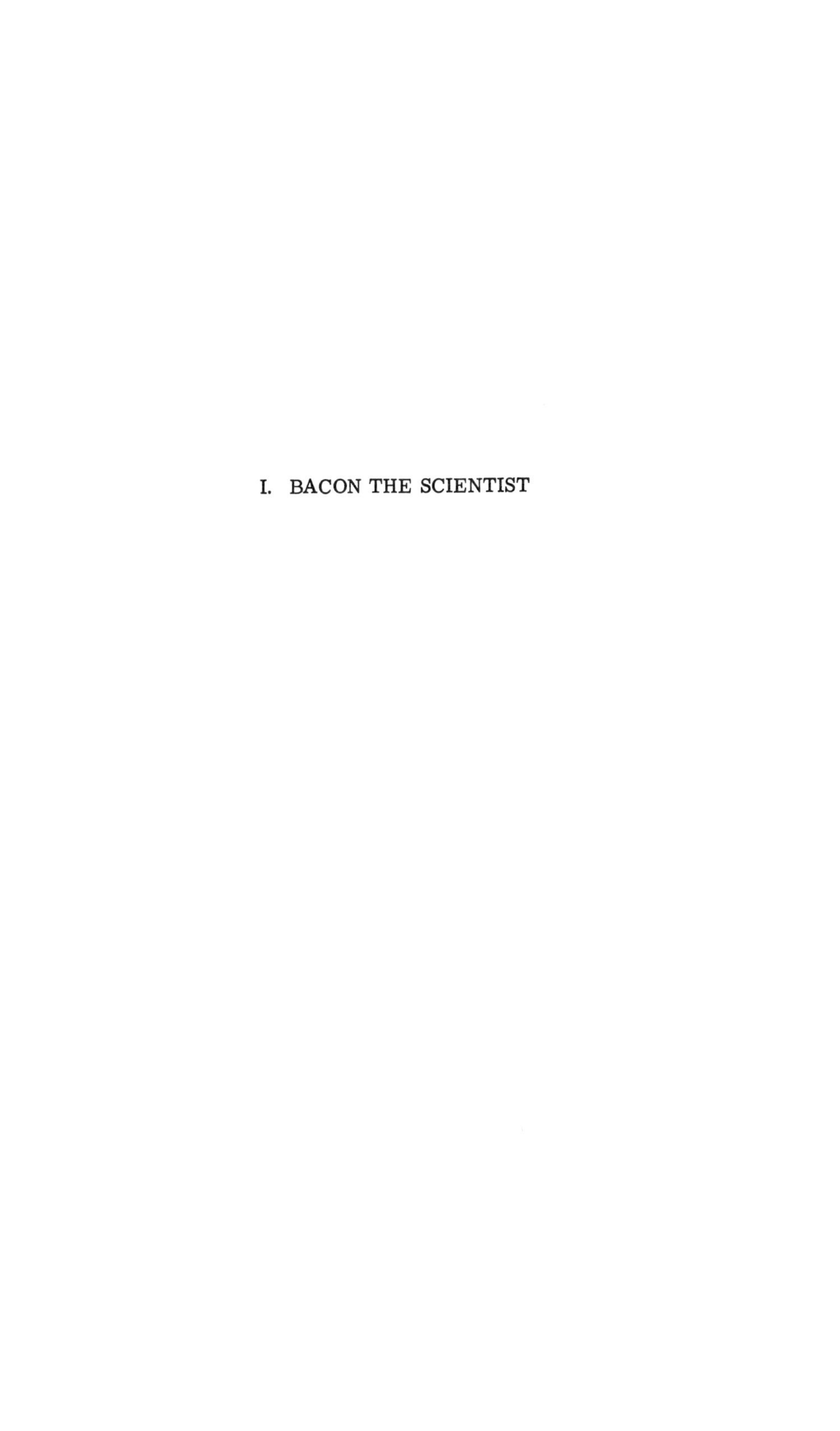

I. BACON THE SCIENTIST

THE BACON OF THE SEVENTEENTH CENTURY

R.F. Jones

> Wherefore since I have only taken upon me to ring a bell to call other wits together, it cannot but be consonant to my desire to have the bell heard as far as can be. And since they are but sparks which can work but upon matter prepared, I have more reason to wish that those sparks may fly abroad, that they may the better find and light upon those minds and spirits that are apt to be kindled.
>
> Sir Francis Bacon's letter to Dr. Playfere. (X, 300–1)

It would hardly be possible to give in a book, much less in a chapter, a satisfactory discussion of the philosophy of one who took all learning for his province, and did much to encompass it. There were, however, certain elements in Bacon's philosophical conceptions and attitudes which were especially influential in the development of the scientific movement in seventeenth-century England. Some of these have received due notice from historians of ideas; others have been too slightly treated. In fact, the true measure of the part that Bacon played in the early development of scientific thought has never been taken. It is the purpose of this chapter to throw into relief those ideas of his which inspired and stimulated the progressive minds of the second and third quarters of the century, which indeed determined the scientific complexion of the century. A knowledge of them is essential to a satisfactory understanding of the subsequent chapters of this book, by no means the least purpose of which is to make clear the remarkable domination which Bacon maintained over human thought.

Bacon's ideas concerning the reformation of learning fall roughly into three groups: the recognition of the inadequacy of existing

Reprinted from Ancients and Moderns (Washington University Press, 1961), pp. 41–61, by permission of Mrs. R. F. Jones and the Washington University Press.

knowledge, and of the need and possibility of its advancement; the hindrances that prevented this advancement; and the means by which it might be secured. The dissatisfaction which Bacon felt over the state of learning in his own day was of great importance. Insisting that men overestimated their store of knowledge, he points out the evil of their believing that all truth had been discovered, an attitude which was as "pillars of fate" set in the way of science.[1] This discontent he continually manifests in pointing out those branches of learning which were incomplete. The inventory of knowledge contained in the Advancement of Learning revealed such deficiencies that it could not but tend to change a complacent into a critical attitude toward it. Down through the century we hear this indictment of undisturbed satisfaction with imperfect or erroneous ideas preferred by those eager to supply the deficiencies. But even more important than the realization of the inadequacy of science was the view implied in the title, Advancement of Learning, and necessitated by the very fact of his exposing the deficiencies in knowledge; namely, the appreciation of the need of progress and faith in its possibility. All Bacon's writings are, in fact, animated by the desire and confident hope of pushing forward the frontiers of learning. The influence of this spirit was to turn men's faces from the past to the future. It was as if a bar had been taken down and a door opened on a new vista. In this view was born the idea of progress, not yet, it is true, the vision of a future limitless in time and improvement, but certainly the foundation of such a conception. In every stage of the subsequent development of science, this progressive attitude, emphasized by the frequency with which the word "advancement" is used, appears, and at no time more conspicuously than during the Commonwealth.

The importance of inspiring men with faith in the possibility of progress is disclosed in Bacon's recognition of despair as the greatest of all the hindrances to the progress of science (IV, 90, 103). The obscurity of nature, the vastness and difficulty of the task of discovering truth, the weakness of the judgment, the deceitfulness of the senses, all conspired in Bacon's eyes to impress men with the hopelessness of their condition. Likewise, the belief that there was nothing new to be discovered, that the best had come down to us from the past, a view which finds frequent condemnation later in the century, discouraged man from attempting anything new. The received philosophy, also, because of the erroneous nature of many of its tenets, imposed upon men a deliberate and factitious despair, and effected an unfair circumscription of human power (III, 249; IV, 86). For the most part Bacon attributed this feeling of hopelessness to the fact that men underrated their power and were ignorant of their own strength. He felt especially called upon to give them a higher opinion of their ability and resources, and to encourage them in their conflict with nature. In fact, he lays modesty aside sufficiently to offer himself as an example of what a single man, though occupied with multifarious duties, could do toward advancing science, in order to suggest how much could be achieved by the joint labors of many men continued through many ages.[2] Like Hakewill, he issues a rallying call to mankind to know their own abilities and bestir themselves from the slough of despond. His call echoes throughout the century.

Perhaps the most significant obstacle to the advancement of science was reverence for antiquity, and in combating this evil Bacon helped to establish an essential attitude of the new science, for scientific progress depended primarily upon a favorable outcome in the controversy between the moderns and the upholders of antiquity, in which science was and continued to be the central issue until the end of the century. Bacon's condemnation of antiquity, though not extreme, is quite apparent. His chief objection to the Greeks was that they relied more on reason than on direct observation of nature. The ancients, he says, took experiments upon credit, and built great matters upon them; knowledge derived from them is talkative, not generative, full of controversies rather than works, and of contentions rather than fruit. Had there really been any life in ancient philosophy, learning would not have stagnated for such a long time, but some profitable results would have come from it. He contrasts the progress of the mechanical arts, in which philosophy and authority did not figure, with the corruption of ancient philosophy; one develops with time and the other degenerates.[3] He praises Aristotle's Problems, from which he took much himself, and admits that the Stagirite possessed wonderful acuteness of mind, but his desire to conquer made his philosophy dogmatic and magisterial, and destroyed the more significant atomic philosophy of the ancients. For the most part he speaks disrespectfully of Aristotle, whose philosophy he considered "contentious and thorny" (IV, 59, 69, 88, 344–5, 357).

Upon subserviency to the authority of the ancients Bacon engaged in repeated attacks, perceiving, as he did, how it militated against all intellectual advancement. How long, he exclaims, will men let a few accepted authors stand up like Hercules' Pillars, beyond which there can be no sailing or discovery! More than once he employed this figure of speech, the popularity of which in the seventeenth century is striking, and which he did much to make popular (IV, 81–2, 283). He urges men not to be dazzled by the great names of ancient philosophers, nor the huge volumes of their modern followers, for though they may be large in bulk and manifest the great diligence of the authors, they shrink to pitiful proportions when they are stripped of fables, antiquities, quotations, idle controversies, philology, and ornaments which are fitted for table-talk rather than for the advancement of learning. He laments that the sciences are confined to a few prescribed authors who are imposed upon the old and instilled in the young, teaching them to affirm or deny, but not to explain or satisfy themselves, with the result that all progress is precluded and dominion over nature forfeited. Since new discoveries, he points out, must be sought from the light of nature and not brought back from the darkness of antiquity, little hope can be entertained of men who are enslaved to established opinion, itself full of verbal contentions and barren of works (IV, 14, 16, 109, 299; V, 132).

Bacon took due notice of the influence which the idea of nature's decay exerted upon the worship of antiquity, to which idea, however, he does not return an emphatic denial. Men, he says, fear that time is past children and generation, a fear which he seeks to allay with his paradox, Antiquitas sæculi, juventus mundi:

> As for antiquity, the opinion touching it which men entertain is quite a negligent one, and scarely consonant with the word itself. For the old age of the world is to be accounted the true antiquity; and this is the attribute of our own times, not of that earlier age of the world in which the ancients lived; and which, though in respect of us it was the elder, yet in respect of the world it was the younger. And truly as we look for greater knowledge of human things and a riper judgment in the old man than in the young, because of his experience and of the number and variety of the things which he has seen and heard and thought of; so in like manner from our age, if it but knew its own strength and chose to essay and exert it, much more might

> fairly be expected than from the ancient times, inasmuch as it is a more advanced age of the world, and stored and stocked with infinite experiments and observations (IV, 82).

Bacon seems not to deny the superiority of the ancients in genius, but finds the same comfort in his paradox which others derived from the figure of the giant and dwarf. In knowledge the moderns should be superior, for they are the heirs of all that has been discovered, and because knowledge grows by increments, those who come last are more fortunate than their predecessors. In speaking of the great extent to which reverence for antiquity had prevented progress he repeats his paradox and stresses the greater stock of information possessed by the moderns owing to geographical discoveries (IV, 82). Whether he really believed that the ancients were superior to the moderns in genius, or whether he thought it best to make such a concession to his age, it is true that he repeatedly insists that he is not matching ancient and modern wits, but is pitting his method against ancient wits. The ancients, he grants, were wonderful in matters of wit and meditation; he does not disagree with the estimate put upon their genius but with their method. Again and again he insists that he is opposing to the ancients only a new method, "by them untried and unknown" (III, 546; IV, 41, 52, 62). It is also possible that Bacon in emphasizing the fact that no unusual mental qualifications were requisite for his method was partly making a concession to the wide-spread belief in modern deterioration in order to encourage his age. The idea of circular progress, or what Bacon calls the ebb and flow of sciences, which Hakewill later was to advance against the theory of decay, Bacon deliberately rejects as causing men to despair of progress beyond a certain point, and also, perhaps, because it contradicted his idea of the incremental advancement of learning (IV, 90).

In spite of his aversion to the philosophy of the ancients and his emphatic condemnation of servility to their authority, Bacon goes as far as he can toward conciliating the supporters of antiquity. The ancients, he says, deserve reverence; modernity should take its stand upon them before determining the best way to proceed. He does not wish to eradicate the received philosophy, but concedes its use for disputation and ornament. There is no doubt, however, that he considered the moderns superior to the ancients in learning, partly because of the addition to knowledge made by the geographical discoveries of the preceding century. He bases his faith that his era will surpass any period of antiquity on the number of modern wits, the monuments of ancient writers, printing, and the multitude of experiments unknown to the ancients which have been revealed by the discovery of new lands (IV, 73, 312; V, 110). Although he staunchly upholds the moderns in the controversy with antiquity, it is the possibilities of the future which arouse his keenest enthusiasm. The circumnavigation of the globe, he says, the privilege and honor of his age, has brought it about "that these times may justly bear in their motto. . . plus ultra—further yet—in precedence of the ancient non ultra—no further" (IV, 311).

In characterizing ancient philosophy and its later versions as contentious, erroneous, and barren of works, in denouncing the enslaving of minds to authority as derogatory to the dignity of the human mind and as an effectual bar to intellectual progress, in exalting his own times over antiquity, as well as in his optimistic view of the future, and in opposing his inductive method to whatever the past could boast, Bacon was outlining the campaign which the moderns relentlessly carried on against the ancients throughout the next half-century. Gilbert had previously opened the campaign, and his influence is pronounced during the first generation of the seventeenth century; but with the ascendency of the Puritans into power, Bacon rapidly becomes the chief inspiration in the revolt from the past. His followers, however, express fainter praise for antiquity and denounce with more virulence the ancients and their upholders, probably because it became increasingly evident that subserviency to authority presented the greatest obstacle to the growth of science, and because the growing number of discoveries and the wider popularity of the experimental method rendered progressive minds more certain of their faith and more confident that the conservatives in science were hopelessly wrong.

Some of the hindrances to the advancement of learning which Bacon pointed out seem to have made little impression upon the century. In fact, one of these impediments, specialization in research, constitutes a virtue in modern eyes. The basis of his own method was a true, universal natural history, and he looked with suspicion upon any endeavor which sought to encompass only a small field. He finds fault with investigators' confining themselves to some one subject as an object of research, such as the magnet, the tides, and the heavens (he undoubtedly had Copernicus and Gilbert in mind), because he thinks it is unskilful to investigate the nature of anything in itself, since the same nature is also manifested in other things. He maintains the same attitude toward the arts and professions, which, he insists, draw their strength from universal philosophy, and which, when studied individually, retard the progress of learning (IV, 87, 286; III, 324).

Bacon makes a great deal of the injury to learning which derives from men's relying more on mind than on nature, so that they withdraw from the observation of nature and seek truth through the operations of the intellect. They desert the senses for reason, and are more eager to build systems than to understand the physical universe (III, 292). This antithesis between mind and the senses, which is more fully developed in the discussion of his method, is one of the most characteristic scientific attitudes of the seventeenth century. The same may be said of the injury to science which Bacon finds in men's not proposing a utilitarian goal for knowledge, which failure, indeed, he styles the greatest error of all (III, 294). Though he condemns the seeking for experiments of fruit only and the unseasonable eagerness to grasp benefits, he does so because such a procedure interferes with the greater material good for man, which will follow a patient and uninterrupted searching out of the laws of nature and the proper utilization of them. Another hindrance, which later Baconians constantly combat, Bacon describes as the deceitful and hurtful opinion of long standing, that the dignity of the human mind is impaired by long and close intercourse with experiments and particulars, with material things subject to sense (IV, 81, 296). It is amusing to listen to the ardent advocates of experimentation in the Commonwealth and Restoration jeering their opponents for withholding their hands from material things, and at the same time glorying in their own commerce with low and common objects.

Bacon was particularly concerned over those psychological factors which, as he expresses it, render the understanding a false mirror of the external world, and to which he gave the name of Idols. He seems to call attention to them in the hope that men being warned of them will be on their guard, or at least can reckon with them. The Idols of the Tribe are those mental characteristics common to all men: proneness to suppose more order and regularity in the world than exist; the tendency of mental prepossessions to bend all things into conformity to themselves; and the influence which the will and affections, such as pride, hope, impatience, and the like have upon the mind, but particularly the part which desire plays in determining thought. Finally, the greatest hindrance to learning associated with the mind is the dullness, incompetency, and deception of the senses, which without the proper aids are infirm and erring, and instruments can do little to assist them. The defects inherent in the senses can be remedied only by the senses themselves assisted by experiments. Of these mental imperfections, it was the last which later scientists stressed.

The Idols of the Cave, or of individual men, refer to the bias which education and environment impose on the variable and erratic spirit of man, and later are frequently cited as the reason for the obstinacy with which many men still cling to the past. The Idols of the Theater represent the circumscription of the mind by philosophical dogma and received systems, which represent nothing real in nature because they are based upon insufficient observations and experiments, as with Aristotle's philosophy, which he calls sophistical, or are based upon too highly specialized fields of experimentation, as with the theories of the alchemists and Gilbert, which he calls empirical.

The Idols which Bacon considered the most troublesome of all, and which in his eyes had rendered philosophy sophistical and inactive were those of the Market-place. These refer to the reaction of the understanding to words, and Bacon's recognition of them marks the beginning of a movement that is one of the characteristic features of early English science. Bacon believed that words filled the understanding with misapprehensions, because, being invented to accommodate vulgar minds, they were defective. He cites as evidence the fact that when superior wits engage in argument the discussion often becomes a mere dispute over words. He did not have the faith in definitions which Hobbes later professed, because in natural and material matters, definitions consist only of words, which beget other words, and so the problem is not solved. The express fault which he finds with words is that they either represent things which do not exist in nature, or else convey very confused ideas of things. In short, language does not impart to the mind a true or accurate picture of material reality, but fills it with more or less fantastic ideas of nature. That he particularly had traditional philosophy in mind is revealed in the remedy proposed for this evil, namely, that all theories be dismissed and recourse had to individual instances, or direct observations. He reveals the same linguistic attitude in his discussion of syllogistic logic. Syllogisms consist of propositions, and propositions of words, which in turn are only "marks of popular notions of things" (cf. Hobbes's definition of words as the marks of things), so that if these notions have no, or only a confused, relation to the material world, the whole logical edifice crumbles (IV, 411). This linguistic view had two marked effects upon later scientists. First, it determined the most consistent charge which they brought against the philosophy of the past, namely, that it was merely verbal, with no counterpart in reality; and second, it influenced them to consider a reformation in language and style as essential as one in science, to formulate their linguistic and stylistic ideals, and to try to make them operative. The effort to construct a more satisfactory language received its most complete expression in John Wilkins' _An Essay towards a Real Character and Philosophical Language_, 1668, and the stylistic views, which played a great part in the simplification of English prose style in the seventeenth century, are clearly expressed in Sprat's _History of the Royal Society_.[4]

Bacon firmly believed that progress in knowledge was possible only when the ground had been completely cleared and a new foundation laid. Men must begin, he says, from the very foundations and effect a total reconstruction of all sciences. Especially must the mind be freed from every opinion or theory, and proceed straight to nature. He exhorts men "with unpossessed minds" and "with minds washed clean from opinion to study it [nature] in purity and integrity." Much, he claims, may be expected of men of well-purged minds, who apply themselves directly to experience and particulars (IV, 8, 52, 53; V, 132). This insistence upon sweeping the mind clear of all opinions is very suggestive of the procedure which Descartes in the _Discours de la Méthode_, 1637, tells us he adopted, but there is a significant difference between the two methods. The French philosopher started with the simple principle, _Cogito, ergo sum_, upon which, by means of reasoning and clear ideas, he sought to construct a sound edifice. The English philosopher, on the other hand, though insisting just as emphatically upon the necessity of purging the mind of all notions, proposed a sensuous and material basis for man to build his ideas of nature upon. Reason, or logic, says Bacon, has for so long been divorced from facts that it has fixed errors rather than discovered truth, and, therefore, the important step is to return to a purely sensuous knowledge of natural things, and from that foundation to work slowly upward, constantly guiding and controlling the mind by observations and experiments. As we shall see later, this difference is reflected in the distinction drawn in the Restoration between the experimental and mechanical philosophies, between Bacon's experimental learning and Descartes' rationalism.

Bacon's realization of the nature of the received philosophies, in which logic played a much greater part than fact, and his emphasis upon direct contact with nature made him depreciate the understanding and exalt the senses, suspect reason and trust direct observation. The intellect, he says, is far more subject to error than the sense, which at once apprehends the appearance of an object and consents to its truth. By itself the mind can effect little and is not to be trusted. Thus it stands in constant need of being directed and assisted by the senses in order to cope with the subtlety of nature.[5] More than anything else Bacon stresses the material object, the concrete fact, and the necessity of using one's eyes. Careful and severe examination and visual evidence are the fundamental tests of truth (IV, 19). But the senses themselves, though more trustworthy than the mind, are deceptive. "To the immediate and proper perception of the sense therefore I do not give much weight," he says in apparent contradiction of other opinions which he has expressed (IV, 26. Cf. IV, 428). Therefore, it is necessary to examine the evidence of the senses and rectify it where necessary. The remedy for the defects of the senses, as for the defects of the understanding, lies in sense itself assisted by experiments which produce and urge things too subtle for the sense to some manifestation which may be comprehended by it. As he expresses it, "the office of the sense shall be only to judge of the experiment, and . . . the experiment itself shall judge of the thing." He sums up the whole matter by saying that he does not take away the authority of the senses, but supplies them with help; does not slight the understanding, but governs it (IV, 26, 112, 412). The importance which this idea accords experimentationa does much to explain the all-embracing value ascribed to it later in the century.

Perhaps the most important service which Bacon contributed to the cause of science lies in this very fact, that he forcefully called men's attention back to the physical world, made them distrust the sheer operations of the mind divorced from material reality, and taught them the value and necessity of sensuous observation of nature as a *sine qua non* of scientific knowledge. More than once he calls attention to the fact that he himself dwelt constantly among the data of nature, withdrawing his intellect from them no farther than was necessary to perceive them properly, and this continual conversancy with the external world, he claims, possessed more value than his wit, for truth was to be sought not in the mind but in the world (IV, 19, 21, 31). This high valuation of the importance of observation and experiment, together with a sceptical attitude toward the more ambitious operations of the reason, became the chief value of seventeenth-century science in England.

A corollary of this emphasis upon the importance of sense-observation and the corresponding distrust of the understanding unless securely tied to the physical world is disclosed in his attitude toward systems, to which he maintained an abiding aversion, because they represented to him the unlawful operation of reason upon an insufficient physical basis. He mentions a dozen ancient philosophers, including Aristotle and Plato, and a half-dozen modern writers, including Gilbert, who invented systems after their own fancy to no good effect (III, 293; IV, 15, 63; V, 131). This opinion explains his view of the great discoveries of his age. The Copernican system he regarded as only a contrivance by which celestial phenomena could be explained mathematically,[6] and not as necessarily being true in nature. In this case, as in others, he objects to a system which depends more upon reason than upon physical data. The Ptolemaic and Copernican systems, he held, were equally supported by the phenomena, which other theories might be invented to explain. In short, they are only hypotheses devised for calculations and the construction of tables (III, 716; V, 511). One of the investigations which he proposes is to find out whether the Copernican theory is to be found in nature, or whether it was merely invented for the convenience of calculation (IV, 183). He admits that the theory of the earth's rotation, which, he says, was prevalent in his own day, cannot be refuted by astronomical principles, for it explains the phenomena, but believing that it is essentially false, he holds that it may be refuted by the principles of natural philosophy.[7] In astronomy, just as in science in general, hope for discovery does not lie in invented systems, but in a deeper and wider investigation into the nature of things.

> . . . it is not merely calculations or predictions that I aim at, but philosophy: such a philosophy I mean as may inform the human understanding, not only of the motion of the heavenly bodies and the period of that motion, but likewise of their substance, various qualities, powers, and influences, according to natural and

> certain reasons, free from superstition and frivolity of traditions; and again such as may discover and explain in the motion itself, not what is accordant with the phenomena, but what is found in nature herself, and is actually and really true.[8]

While he believes that astronomical theories, invented to explain phenomena, have corrupted natural philosophy, he at least concedes that the findings of the latter should be reconcilable with the phenomena. He raises the rather shrewd question, fully in keeping with his belief that the mind of man is prone to see more order in nature than exists, as to whether there is any system at all, or whether man has merely imposed his own invented scheme of things upon nature. In short, in astronomy, as in other sciences, his injunction is to abjure theories and find out by observation and experiment what is actually in nature. His attitude toward the Copernican theory is in full accord with his attitude toward science in general.[9]

The same is true of his opinion of Gilbert, for whom he had a high regard. He appreciated his countryman's laborious employment in the study of the loadstone, speaks of his collecting observations "with great sagacity and industry," and approves of a question raised "by Gilbert, who has written upon the magnet most laboriously and after the experimental method" (IV, 59, 185, 323). But he objects to his making a philosophy out of his observations on the magnet and to his constructing an entire system in accordance with his favorite subject. In other words, Gilbert let his mind go beyond his data, inasmuch as he confined his experiments to a field too narrow for his philosophy. Furthermore, Bacon believed that to understand a subject, a larger field of inquiry than the subject itself was necessary (IV, 65). He maintained the same attitude toward the chemists: their theories, which only confuse their experiments, he rejects, but he grants that a number of discoveries and useful inventions have come from their experiments.[10] This was exactly the opinion of them later entertained by Boyle and other members of the Royal Society.

Associated with Bacon's hostility to systems was his insistence upon the necessity of suspended judgment, or a critical attitude. The mind, he explains, is constitutionally hasty in framing and asserting notions, much to the hindrance of learning. One should always maintain a sceptical attitude towards systems and writers, taking nothing on faith and authority and without examination, and one should also be very slow in forming ideas or reaching conclusions about things. The understanding must not be allowed to fly from sense and particulars to the most general conclusions, the practice prevalent in his day and the chief fault he finds with syllogistic logic, which is based upon general principles hastily devised from the scantiest data (III, 247, 293; IV, 24–5, 50, 97). The raising of doubts guards philosophy against errors and attracts an increase in knowledge, so that "he who makes too great haste to grasp at certainties shall end in doubts, while he who seasonably restrains his judgment shall end in certainties."[11] He distinguishes, however, between his suspension of judgment and philosophical scepticism, which denies the certainty of the senses and understanding, on the ground that his view maintains only that nothing can be known except in a certain way and course which bring the proper aid to the mind.[12]

The method which Bacon stresses so heavily, and which he claimed was new and untried, falls into two parts. The first was "a Natural and Experimental History," such as would serve for the foundation of a true philosophy, and perhaps was considered by him the more important of the two. He insists that such a history is essential to an interpretation of nature, is, indeed, the foundation of all, "for we are not to imagine or suppose, but to discover, what nature does or may be made to do." Without it, he says, his Organon, or inductive method, would be of little use, though the history by itself would much advance science. He even goes so far as to claim that when this history has been satisfactorily established, the investigation of nature and all the sciences will be the work of but a few years (IV, 28, 127, 251, 252; V, 211, 507). To its neglect he attributes the unreal philosophies, barren of works, against which he never tires of inveighing. The purpose of this natural history, as he defines it, is twofold: to furnish knowledge of particular things; and to supply the primary materials of philosophy. He was especially interested in the second, which, he says, had never been taken in hand. Thus in his eyes, the noblest end of natural history is not pleasure or profit, but to be, as it were, the nursing mother of philosophy, to furnish the stuff and matter of true lawful induction, and thus become a solid and eternal basis of true and active philosophy (IV, 254, 298; V, 507–8). The history was to be a most comprehensive collection of experiments and observations, gathered over the whole field of nature, to furnish data from which the mind could construct a universal philosophy by means of Bacon's inductive method.

Bacon stresses the importance to his history of observations collected from the widest sources. The experiments of natural magic were to be diligently sifted for any authentic material. Even superstitious stories of sorceries, marvels, witchcraft, charms, dreams, and divinations were not to be altogether excluded, if they could show any clear evidence of fact (IV, 255, 296). But he was particularly impressed with the contribution which a mechanical and experimental history could make to his natural history, material which had been scorned as low by other natural historians, and which was to be gathered from the mechanical arts, the operative parts of the liberal arts, and experiments not yet grown into an art. The greatest diligence, he says, must be bestowed upon this history, "mechanical and illiberal as it may seem, (all fineness and daintiness set aside)," and he enumerates, as examples of the arts which might contribute to the history, agriculture, cookery, chemistry, dyeing, glass, enamel, gunpowder, and paper.[13] The importance of experimentation loomed large in his eyes. As we have already seen, it provided the means of correcting the defects of the senses, and so of governing the reason. Furthermore, he believed that experiments take off the mask from natural objects, and disclose the struggles of matter, for nature reveals herself under vexations. Mechanical experiments also do not vanish in speculations but lead directly to operations to relieve the inconveniences of man's estate (IV, 257, 297).

Bacon a second time divides his natural history into the speculative, or the search for causes, and operative, or the production of effects. It is the second in which he is interested, for all true fruitful natural history ascends from experiments to axioms, or principles, and descends again to new experiments, at each stage rising to more general principles (IV, 343). Speculation is justified on the ground that it makes possible other effects. Though Bacon was more concerned with the final philosophy to be drawn from his natural history, he was not blind to the benefits to be derived more directly from observations and experiments. He denies that he despises the benefits which will accrue to the various arts from experiments, and calls attention to the immediate good which will be gained in the discovery of new commodities through the transfer of the observations of one art to the use of others (IV, 258, 297).

His conception of natural history necessitated two other ideas: the need of co-operation, and the fact that no unusual intellectual ability is required of those who would compile it. Certainly the immense amount of data required by his conception was so great that men could very well despair of ever achieving it.[14] He himself realized that the proposed goal necessitated much labor and expense, was, in fact, a "royal work," but he insists that all difficult works can be overcome by amplitude of reward (which he hoped the King would furnish), soundness of direction (which he would supply), and conjunction of labors (IV, 101, 251; III, 322). "For the last," he says, "touching impossibility, I take it that all these things are to be held possible and performable, which may be done by some persons, though not by one alone; and which may be done in the succession of ages, though not in one man's life; and lastly, which may be done by public designation and expense, though not by private means and endeavour."[15] As another move toward co-operation, Bacon proposed the establishment of a college of natural history.[16] Since his plan required a great number of men, the question of ability naturally arose, for geniuses are rare. Bacon solves the problem by insisting that the compilation of his history does not require men of unusual abilities: "But the course I propose for the discovery of sciences is such as leaves but little to the acuteness and strength of wits, but places all wits and understandings nearly on a level." And again, "For my way of discovering sciences goes far to level men's wits, and leaves but little to individual excellence; because it performs everything by surest rules and demonstrations" (IV, 62–3, 109). In one case he compares his method to a compass, and in another to a machine, both of which require little of their operators. In stressing the fact that his method would more than compensate for the limited abilities of his followers, he was really seeking to remove the despair effected by the theory of nature's decay, which bestowed upon the moderns a necessary intellectual inferiority to the ancients.

Bacon lays down some general rules for his history. Particulars should be carefully entered, and in doubtful cases the reader should be warned by some such expression as "It is reported." Sometimes the name of the observer should be given. In all cases, the manner of conducting the experiment should be clearly described so that men may judge and verify it, and especially that others may be stimulated to improve it, since natural history is open to every man's industry (IV, 260–1; V, 135–6, 509).

More than any other element in his philosophy Bacon's conception of natural history and its importance influenced the seventeenth century. As will be seen, the most prevalent motive animating scientists in the third quarter of the century was the desire to contribute data to such a history. Boyle repeatedly claims this as his motive; Sprat says that the aim of the Royal Society was the accumulation of a vast pile of experiments, complains that the ancients did nothing toward this end, and prefers the joint labors of many men to those of individuals no matter how significant. The multifarious activities of individual scientists and of the Royal Society as a whole can best be explained on this basis. Later the need of co-operation is not only emphasized in words, it is also met in practice by the various groups of experimenters out of which developed the Royal Society, itself the final embodiment of the co-operative plan in Bacon's philosophy. The faith in, and hope of, a comprehensive natural history, based on experiments and observations, were responsible for much of the enthusiasm with which later English scientists entered into their work. But they were not, any more than Bacon, indifferent to the immediate good which might arise from the materials of this history, especially as regards the so-called mechanical arts, which received from them the same emphasis accorded by Bacon.

Bacon did not conceive of his natural history as a haphazard collection of unorganized observations and experiments. In fact, he says that little is to be expected from the intellect unless particulars are apt, well arranged, drawn up, and marshalled in some order. He also states that a greater abundance of experiments is to be sought according to a fixed law and in regular order, and he elaborates upon this order and direction in conducting experiments, which he explains under the terms of Variation, Production, Translation, Inversion, Compulsion, and Chances of experiments (IV, 95, 96, 413 ff.) When, however, experiments and observations of all arts have been collected, digested, and brought into one man's knowledge (IV, 96), his own inductive method is to be applied. There are three distinctive features of the latter. The first has to do with the various stages of the process of establishing general principles, in which he contrasts his logic with the syllogistic logic of the day. Whereas the latter merely glances at experiments and particulars, and at once establishes the highest generalities, abstract and useless, his induction dwells duly and orderly among particulars, and rises gradually to general principles (IV, 50). In fact, this gradual and unbroken ascent from sense and particulars to the most general principles Bacon stresses as the true but untried way. The understanding, he asserts, must not be permitted to jump from particulars to remote axioms, but must rise by successive steps from particulars to lesser, to middle, to greater axioms. The lowest axioms, he explains, differ little from bare experience, and the highest, are notional and abstract; the middle, are the true, solid, living axioms upon which depend the affairs and fortunes of men (IV, 97). In another passage he says that one is not to extract works from works, or experiments from experiments, but to extract principles from them, and from these principles new works and experiments (IV, 96, 104). In short, the interpretation of one experiment furnishes a principle which suggests other experiments, and these in turn lead to higher principles.

The second unique feature of his induction is found in his conception of form, which is more clearly understood in connection with his attitude toward atomism. Bacon based his science upon a purely physical foundation, though he frequently found it necessary to employ current terminology, which may sometimes be misleading. Spirits, for instance, which figure frequently in his writings, are nothing but natural rarified bodies. What he styles the original passions or desires of bodies, or the primary elements of nature, are only the qualities of dense and rare, solid and fluid, hot and cold, heavy and light (IV, 29). He used the word "form," because it was familiar, though he considered the forms of the received philosophy mere figments. His dictum that bodies are not acted upon but by bodies suggests a purely materialistic basis for his philosophy (IV,179; V,500). There is also little doubt that in a way he accepted the atomic philosophy.[17] He asserts that his purpose is not to resolve nature into abstractions, but "to dissect her into parts; as did the school of Democritus, which went further into nature than the rest." Matter rather than forms should be the object of our attention, "its configuration and changes of configuration, and simple action, and law of action or motion."[18] Force, or motion, was implanted by God in the first particles, from the multiplication of which all variety proceeds. He declares that the motion and virtue of the atom are the beginning of all motions and virtues. In one passage he compares solid bodies to machines, which from their configuration admit innumerable variations, and in another maintains that the diversity of things is due to the magnitude, configurations, and positions of one fixed and invariable substance (V, 463,464,472,469). All this, though rather far from the mathematically elaborated mechanical philosophy of Descartes, indicates that Bacon leaned to the theory of atoms.

There is nothing in nature, Bacon says, but individual bodies performing individual acts according to fixed laws, the discovery and explanation of which are the foundation of knowledge and operation. This law he calls form. And again he defines forms as those laws and determinations of absolute actuality which govern and constitute any simple nature such as heat, light, and weight in every kind of matter that is susceptible of them. His own observations and experiments led him to the conclusion that the nature of which heat is a particular case appears to be motion (IV, 120, 146, 150). If we combine these ideas, we arrive at the conclusion that the form of heat is the law governing the particular motions of individual bodies (certainly his particles), which produce the nature of heat. Bacon believed that the forms, or laws, of simple, or abstract, natures are few in number, but that they may be seen in nature (III, 243). They are like the letters of the alphabet, which, though not numerous, can be variously combined to form any number of words. If, then, one understands these forms, he will be able to combine them at will to achieve any result of which nature is capable, and thus command her.

His induction, the explanation of which he did not complete, was his method of arriving at a knowledge of these fundamental forms. He is careful to distinguish his particular inductive logic from the common one of simple enumeration, which he calls childish, because being based on too small a number of such facts as lie at hand its results are precarious and likely to be contradicted by a single instance (IV, 25). What chiefly distinguishes his method is his conception of rejection or exclusion. In the process of exclusion, he declares, are laid the foundations of true induction (IV, 149). He further explains that the principle of exclusion operates in cases where several natures are not found when the nature under investigation is present, or are found when the given nature is absent (IV, 145). Thus his process is essentially one of elimination, though he says that conclusions can be reached only on affirmative instances, which, after proper exclusion, are solid, true, and well defined. Perhaps a simple example may clarify this explanation. Flames produce both heat and light, but the moon, according to Bacon, gives forth only light. Therefore, in investigating the form, or law, of heat, exclude light. Bacon looked upon his method as insuring absolutely certain results, as finally making the understanding of man a match for nature (IX, 97, 146).

His ideas of forms and exclusion did not influence the seventeenth century very much. In fact, his influence on the scientific movement was general rather than specific. He impressed upon his followers the importance of experimentation and inspired them with confidence in the certainty of its results, but he cast little light upon the proper method of experimentation. This fact, together with his failure to appreciate the great discoveries of his day and to make any himself, is responsible for the present depreciation of his importance in the history of science.[19]

Bacon proposed for the most part a utilitarian end for science. He believed that the greatest error men had made in learning was in mistaking the end of knowledge, which to him was the relief of man's estate (III, 294; IV, 79). He proposed his method to enable men to secure dominion over nature, "to endow the condition and life of man with new powers and works" (III, 498; IV, 24, 104, 114). In his eyes, human learning and human power were one and the same. It is true that he warns men not to seize too soon the fruits of their experiments and observations, but only because he believed that by pursuing their investigations to a knowledge of more general principles, they could so command nature that fruits would come "in clusters" (IV, 29, 71). He classifies experiments as "experimenta fructifera" and "experimenta lucifera," "either of use or of discovery" (II, 501; IV, 95), terms which are constantly employed throughout the century, but the experiments of light are of value because ultimately they lead to the securing of greater benefits. One justification of this utilitarianism is seen in his humanitarian spirit. He seems to have been deeply impressed with the wretched condition of the human race, and cherished the hope that out of the marriage of mind and things there might spring "a line and race of inventions that may in some degree subdue and overcome the necessities and miseries of humanity" (IV, 27. See also IV, 21, 32, 91). Certainly he is one source of the humanitarianism and social-mindedness which are so conspicuous in the period of Puritan domination. Bacon firmly imposed the utilitarian spirit upon seventeenth-century science in England.

A few other views of Bacon's played their part in the later development of science. His emphatic separation of science and religion (III, 219; IV, 342; V, 112) certainly made scientific progress easier and enabled the Puritans to embrace his philosophy. The great value he placed upon inventions (III, 223; IV, 99, 113, 114) long survived him, and he is frequently cited in the praises of them. His criticism of the schools and universities and the reforms he would introduce are sufficiently close to those later published by the Puritans as to suggest that he influenced the latter either through Comenius or directly. The more important are: that children come too early to the study of logic and rhetoric, when they should be taught matter rather than ornaments; that the universities are too much committed to certain authors as authorities; that no liberty of thought is permitted; that readings, disputations, and other scholastic exercises should be abolished; and that correspondence with European universities should be established (III, 323 ff., 326, 327, 502; IV, 89, 288, 289).

Bacon impressed upon his age the need of advancement and held out to it the hope of scientific progress. His own unfailing assurance in his philosophy supported the encouragement which his optimistic spirit offered men. He did more than anyone else to break the fetters which bound his age to servile submission to the authority of the ancients, and he inspired his followers to face the future rather than the past. His repeated insistence upon experiment and observation as indispensable for the discovery of scientific truth, his reiterated injunction to learn the appearance of things and find out what really is in nature called men from mind to matter, and from libraries to laboratories. His conception of a universal natural history and all it entailed was mostly responsible for the comprehensive and varied experimentation carried on by individuals or by groups with the assiduity and indefatigability which characterized the scientific temper of the third quarter of the century. In the material welfare of man he found for his age an impressive sanction for his scientific program, and thus furnished a social motive for a materialistic and utilitarian enterprise. His was a stimulating and vitalizing influence hardly to be overestimated. Without it science would have moved forward, but in England scientific activities would have been retarded to no inconsiderable extent. The bell he touched rang with increasing intensity throughout the years.

NOTES

1 See the preface to the Magna Instauratio in Works IV, 13. In commenting on the idea entertained by some, that all sciences

had reached their full perfection, Bacon exclaims, "Would it were so! But the truth is that this appropriating of the sciences has its origin . . . . in the confidence of a few persons and the sloth and indolence of the rest," a criticism which later echoes through most of the attacks on antiquity.

2 III, 249; IV, 13, 102. "If there be any that despond, let them look at me."

3 II, 354; IV, 14. This contrast is employed again and again in the second and third quarters of the century.

4 For a discussion of this matter see the articles by R.F. Jones collected in The Seventeenth Century (Stanford, 1951). In his undertaking Wilkins was evidently inspired by the first chapter of the sixth book of The Advancement of Learning, in which Bacon speaks of the "real characters" used in the Far East. (See, however, Dorothy Stimson's "Dr. Wilkins and the Royal Society," Jour. Mod. Hist., III [1931], 543.) Sprat (History of the Royal Society, p. 113) describes the plain, simple style demanded by the Society of all the scientific communications of its members, a requirement which seems to go directly back to Bacon. The latter criticizes the natural histories of his day for being full of fables, quotations from the ancients, disputes, philology and ornaments, as if setting up a treasure-house of eloquence rather than a sound and faithful narrative of facts (V, 508). So when he came to describe the proper way in which a natural history should be drawn up, it is not strange that he should wish to banish all the evils mentioned above: "And for all that concerns ornaments of speech, similitudes, treasury of eloquence, and such like emptinesses, let it be utterly dismissed" (IV, 254).

5 IV, 17, 27, 47, 50, 428. Bacon remarks that it is strange that no one has laid out a road for the human understanding direct from the senses (IV, 80). Of course, Bacon's method gave an important function to the understanding, but he stressed more heavily the part the senses play, because of their neglect. He defines his purpose as "a true and lawful marriage between the empirical and rational faculty, the unkind and ill-starred divorce and separation of which has thrown into confusion all the affairs of the human family" (IV, 19). During the Restoration this stress upon sense and distrust of reason was carried to greater lengths. In the same way in which imagination was

to be controlled by reason, reason was to be controlled by the senses.

6 This characterization of the Copernican theory was amply supported by the spurious preface to Copernicus' De Revolutionibus Orbium Coelestium. Bacon's failure to appreciate the importance of mathematics, a deficiency lamented by his later followers, can be explained in the same way as his rejection of the Copernican theory. To mathematics he attributes the function of giving definiteness to natural philosophy, and thus as physics advances and develops new axioms, it will require fresh assistance from mathematics in many things (IV, 93, 371). For mathematical systems he entertains less regard. The science, he says, has been more acutely inquired into than other matters, because it is "the nature of the human mind, certainly to the extreme prejudice of knowledge, to delight in the open plains . . . . of generalities rather than in the woods and inclosures of particulars," with the result that logic and mathematics, which should be the handmaidens of science, exercise dominion over it (IV, 370). The fact that mathematics, like syllogistic logic, is deductive, proceeding from general principles to particulars, was repugnant to Bacon's whole philosophy, and so mathematics takes its place with other systems in which reason plays too great a part in proportion to observation (IV, 411).

7 IV, 229, 373. For instance, he says we must know the nature of spontaneous rotation, before we can decide whether the earth or the heavens move (IV, 123). In short, in our astronomical theories we should seek for truth in physical nature and not in mathematics.

8 V, 511. In another passage he says that in astronomy all theories should be suspended, because natural philosophy should embrace only "pure and separate" phenomena, as if nothing whatever had been settled by the art of astronomy. Only the observations and experiments of the latter, accurately collected, and perspicuously described, are of use.

9 V, 524, 515 ff., 557. Though Bacon thought the value of the microscope was distinctly limited, he did appreciate the importance of the telescope in astronomical observations, and of the discoveries made with it, which he calls noble endeavors,

worthy of the human race and performed by men who should be praised highly for honesty, boldness, and clear explanations and descriptions of their proceedings. He adds that all that is needed is "constancy and great severity of judgment, to change the instruments, to increase the number of witnesses, to try each particular experiment many times and many ways," and to consider every possible objection that can be raised (IV, 192–3; V, 512–3).

10 IV, 74, 84; V, 205. In similar manner Bacon condemned magic and astrology because they were full of superstition and contained too much of the merely imaginative and credulous, but he wished them purified rather than destroyed, for he thought there was a certain amount of physical knowledge in them which would be a contribution to natural history. In fact, he says that the experiments of magicians and astrologers have frequently proved useful (III, 289; IV, 349, 366–7). Later in the century all three of the pseudo-sciences called upon Bacon for justification.

11 III, 250; IV, 357, 429. Bacon is usually careful to advance his own conclusions as tentative.

12 IV, 32, 53. This sceptical view became a typical attitude of seventeenth-century science in England.

13 IV, 257; V, 506. Bacon believed that "on account of the pernicious and inveterate habit of dwelling on abstractions, it is safer to begin and raise the sciences from those foundations which have relation to practice, and to let the active part itself be as the seal which prints and determines the contemplative counterpart" (IV, 120–1).

14 "For since all Interpretation of Nature commences with the senses, and leads from the perceptions of the senses by a straight, regular, and guarded path to the perceptions of the understanding, which are true notions and axioms, it follows of necessity that the more copious and exact the representations of the senses, the more easily and prosperously will everything proceed" (IV, 192).

15 The same idea is repeated elsewhere (III, 328). This passage removes to the distant future the fulfilment of his design. It

is his natural history that represents the difficulty in his method, for, as we have seen, he believed that after it had been completed, the acquiring of the knowledge of nature would be the work of only a few years (IV, 252). That Bacon had in mind governmental support for his scheme is revealed not only in this passage, but also in his New Atlantis, in which the model of his co-operative plan, Solomon's House, is clearly a function of the government. In various works, Bacon's protégé, Thomas Bushell, makes it plain that Bacon made some headway in realizing his Solomon's House.

16 III, 323. As further encouragement to his age, Bacon proposed himself as an example of what one man, though busied with many things, could do to advance knowledge. What, he then asks, may not be hoped from leisure and co-operation through many ages, one man taking charge of one thing, and another of another?

17 In one passage Bacon seems to repudiate the atomic philosophy: "Nor shall we thus be led to the doctrine of atoms, which implies the hypothesis of a vacuum and that of unchangeableness of matter (both false assumptions); we shall be led only to real particles, such as really exist" (IV, 126). He rather clearly indicates here that he considered the atoms of Democritus unreal, probably an hypothesis to explain phenomena. This interpretation is borne out by another passage in which he says, "The doctrine of Democritus concerning atoms is either true or useful for demonstration" (V, 419). The difference between the atoms of Democritus and Bacon's particles may probably be explained by the fact that Bacon did not believe his particles were infinite or perpetually divisible. For a more complete discussion of Bacon's atomic philosophy, see C. T. Harrison, "Bacon, Hobbes, Boyle, and Ancient Atomists," Harvard Studies and Notes in Philology and Literature, XV (1933), 191–218.

18 There is ample evidence of Bacon's high regard for Democritus and his philosophy. See V, 419, 421, 465, 466.

19 According to Bacon's plan, there were two stages in the scientific process: the construction of a natural history, and the employment of induction upon the materials thus afforded. So scientists may be divided into two classes: theorizers, and observers and ex-

perimenters. Of the latter no unusual ability was demanded; the field was open to the joint labors of many men. But Bacon implied that the former must be men of superior intellects. He bemoaned the fact that he had to engage in the low task of laying the foundation, when he deserved to be the architect of the building (II, 335).

FRANCIS BACON'S INTELLECTUAL MILIEU

Virgil K. Whitaker

Too many years ago I first made the acquaintance of Francis Bacon in a seminar under the late William Dinsmore Briggs, of which Professor Paul Kocher was also a member. Subsequently I wrote my doctoral dissertation upon Bacon. That dissertation was undoubtedly a contribution to knowledge, because it taught me that I did not know what I was talking about. So I deferred Bacon to the future, hoping that in the meantime I might acquire a better knowledge of the language he spoke—a vocabulary that derived its essential meaning from the thought and practice of his times. But always I have wanted to get back to Bacon, and I accepted an invitation to appear before this distinguished gathering as a first step towards that end. This paper might therefore be described as remembrance of things past and a hope of things to come. My pursuit of Bacon may confirm, however, his famous dictum that the final cause does not contribute to human knowledge.

When we turn to Bacon's works, however, we encounter a difficulty inhering in the material causes, for his steps are extremely hard to trace. No doubt annoyed by the endless pedantic quotation and quibbling in the polymaths upon whom he leaned, Bacon laid down in the Parasceve ad Historiam Naturalem et Experimentalem a rule which he unfortunately followed himself:

> First then, away with antiquities, and citations or testimonies of authors; also with disputes and controversies and differing opinions; everything in short which is philological. Never cite an author except in a matter of doubtful credit: never introduce a controversy unless in a matter of great moment (IV, 254, 260).

An address delivered at a meeting at the William Andrews Clark Library, Los Angeles, 18 November 1961, celebrating the 400th anniversary of Bacon's birth. Reprinted from W. A. Clark Memorial Library, University of California, Los Angeles, Paper (1962), pp. 27, by permission of the author and the publisher.

The practical result of this rule is that Bacon gives us very little guidance as to the writers who formed an important part of his intellectual milieu. Occasionally he lists various categories of writers or mentions a source with approval, the most obvious example being his praise of Telesio's psychology. More often we must assume that, when Bacon mentions a writer to dissent, he has been silently indebted to the same man. Most often we must depend upon the industry of scholars, especially that of Ellis, Spedding, and Heath, whose edition, though now a hundred years old, is still a monument of learning.

Granted these severe limitations in my knowledge and in Bacon's method, my thesis will be simply that Bacon is much more a man of his times than has often been supposed. This is not to discredit Bacon or his achievement, for we would all agree that the times were glorious, if not for philosophy in the narrower sense, at least for the human mind in ferment. But the fact remains that Bacon's limitations and even his strengths were largely derived from his milieu. It would be impossible, of course, to cover all Bacon's thought in a discussion of this length. I will try, rather, to establish his general position as I see it, which is that he is one of a group of Renaissance encyclopedists, and then to suggest three respects in which he shows the influence of his times: namely, his eclecticism and indifference to precision of thought, his retention of a large body of conventional ideas concealed beneath a surface novelty of approach, and the distrust of human intelligence which is so marked a characteristic of his thinking.

Arguing that Bacon was fundamentally an encyclopedist will require a brief preliminary discussion of his background. The Middle Ages inherited from classical times a tradition of works which attempted to survey large areas of human knowledge. The corpus of Aristotle was itself the first and greatest example, but Lucretius' _De Rerum Natura_ or Pliny's _Natural History_ were lesser variants. Christian writers, taking their pattern from nine homilies _On the Hexaemeron_ of St. Basil the Great, Bishop of Caesarea (370–379), early began to organize all knowledge in terms of the six days of creation.[1] The work in this tradition that I know best is the _Liber de Proprietatibus Rerum_ of Bartholomew of England (thirteenth century), which was widely printed during the Renaissance and three times published in an English version by John Trevisa in 1495, 1535, and, with additions by Stephen Batman, in 1582. But the greatest of the medieval encyclopedias was undoubtedly the group of _Specula_ written by Vincent of Beauvais (died 1264). Since we shall be concerned primarily with the part of encyclopedic learning which included natural philosophy or what we should call simply science, what Vincent has to say as to the organization of his Speculum Naturale will be of interest. He writes:

> This work contains knowledge in compendium: first, a short tractate concerning God the triune and single creator of all things; then one about the fiery heaven and the nature of the angels; also one about the state and order of the good and the reign and malice of the proud. After this it treats of formless matter and the production of the world according to the order of the works of the six days, and of the nature and properties of the single things in order; then of the creation of the first man; of the nature and strength of the soul and the senses, parts, and properties of the human body.[2]

The works of God in the six days of the creation are divided as follows: the first, separation of light and darkness; second, the firmament and the multifold heaven together with fiery space and the airy heaven; the first work of the third day, the gathering of the waters, the earth and earthy bodies, and the bodies contained in the bowels of the earth (stones, etc.); the second work of the third day, plants and trees; the fourth day, the luminous bodies of heaven and the seasons; the fifth day, birds, fish, and marine monsters; the sixth day, terrestrial animals of all sorts, man, the vegetable and the sensible soul, the parts of the human body, the generation and varieties of man, and places suitable for human habitation. Nor is the work a mere catalogue of the things created by God. As the creation of each item is mentioned, all the extant knowledge about it is summarized.

Similar, though less extended, works in the hexaemeral tradition were attempted in the Renaissance. One thinks of The French Academy of Pierre de La Primaudaye, which appeared in an English version at intervals from 1586 to 1618, and especially of the third part; La Sepmaine of the Huguenot poet Guillaume de Salluste, seigneur du Bartas, which appeared in 1578, and between 1592 and 1604 was translated into English verse by Joshua Sylvester as The Divine Weekes and Workes (the second week is a history of the world);

and the Universae Naturae Theatrum of the great French jurist Jean Bodin, published in Latin in 1596 and never, so far as I know, translated into English. Bodin's work, though it retains the hexaemeral organization, is a dialogue. It belongs in this category in that its material is conventional; in discussing problems it verges on the third category to be discussed presently. With Bodin we come to a man of Bacon's intellectual stature and a similar range of interests in law, history, and science.

Another work, published in 1503, which reduces the current school learning to the simple dimensions characteristic of the new "methods," belongs in the same encyclopedic tradition but illustrates an alternative scheme of organization furnished by the seven liberal arts—grammar, rhetoric, logic, arithmetic, geometry, astronomy, and music—and the three philosophies—natural, moral, and rational—which constituted the medieval curriculum. It is the Margarita Philosophica of Gregorius Reisch (died 1525). I mention it primarily because of its organization.

The second category of encyclopedic works which I will distinguish for my purposes includes only one book, the De Incertitudine et Vanitate Omnium Scientiarum et Artium of Henry Cornelius Agrippa von Nettesheim, written in 1526. He had earlier written a work, De Occulta Philosophia, in which he showed particularly his leaning toward the New Platonism and his interest in the Cabala. Repenting of these follies, he wrote on the vanity of the arts and science. The work, which was translated and published in England in 1569 and 1575, is a bitter attack on the learning of the day, with its pedantry and subservience to Aristotle. In plan it is an encyclopedic survey of knowledge organized like Reisch's humbler work, in terms of the seven liberal arts and three philosophies. Its method is to demonstrate that various received opinions are contradictory and to infer, therefore, that all knowledge, except the Holy Scriptures, is worthless. Agrippa's complete sincerity may be doubted. Both his own swashbuckling temperament and the tradition of Pyrrhonism may have led him to exaggerate his pose of complete skepticism. But his work was undoubtedly an important factor in revivifying the skeptical tradition of classical philosophy and illustrates its common alliance with fideism, which we will notice in Bacon.

It is simple and reasonably accurate to label Agrippa a skeptic; but I badly need a term for the third, and for our purposes most important, category of encyclopedic writers. Bacon himself, in his exposition of the fable of Cupid and heaven (III, 114), calls Telesio "novorum hominum primum"; and perhaps we may take our cue from him and call them the innovators, especially since another term that he uses for them—the Empirical school—implies almost the reverse of the facts. But his description of the school is substantially accurate:

> There is also another class of philosophers, who having bestowed much diligent and careful labour on a few experiments, have thence made bold to educe and construct systems; wresting all other facts in a strange fashion to conformity therewith (IV, 64).

The influence of Lucretius seems to me apparent in the work of these men, as in Bacon himself. I mention this point because, in my opinion, the influence of Lucretius needs further investigation, especially during the period between the great edition of Dionysius Lambinus (Denys Lambin) in 1564 and the work of Pierre Gassendi upon Epicurus beginning in 1647.

Bacon himself supplies two lists of philosophers who fall into this category. That in the Novum Organum (IV, 103) includes only "Telesius, Patricius, Severinus"—that is, the Italians Bernardino Telesio (1509–1588) and Francesco Patrizzi (1529–1597), and the Danish physician Peter Severinus (1542–1602). In remarking that digests of philosophers are needed, Bacon supplies another list:

> Neither do I exclude from this calendar of the dogmas of the old philosophers modern theories and doctrines; such as that of Theophrastus Paracelsus, eloquently reduced into a body and harmony by Severinus the Dane; or that of Telesius of Consentium, who revived the philosophy of Parmenides, and so turned the weapons of the Peripatetics against themselves; or of Patricius the Venetian, who sublimated the fumes of the Platonists; or of our countryman Gilbert . . . (IV, 359–60).

Of these Paracelsus (c. 1490–1541), who wrote under the compulsion of his medical theories, Telesio, and Patrizzi, whose Nova de Universis Philosophia attacked Aristotle from a Platonist-Christian point of view, were true encyclopedists. To them should be added Jerome Cardan (1501–1576), whom Bacon mentions in several other passages, at least once with Telesio (III, 571), and the English

Paracelsan Robert Fludd (1594–1637), who belongs to a later generation.

All these writers attacked Aristotle and the received view of the universe, and each of them felt compelled to set up a new cosmological system of his own and therefore to survey all knowledge. I should confess at this point that, whereas I have read carefully all the encyclopedic works mentioned in the first two categories except for Vincent of Beauvais, here I have read only De Subtilitate Rerum and De Rerum Varietate of Cardan and the De Rerum Natura of Telesio. I would not pretend, furthermore, that I understood long sections of Telesio, who seems to me very obscure. Cardan, though he does not mention the six days of creation, follows the traditional arrangement of knowledge. He argues that the dominant factor in determining the nature of anything is its "subtility," posits Hyla, uncreated and imperishable (cf. Greek hyle), as the primary substance, and rejects fire as an element. Telesio is far more radical. He builds his universe of a passive matter, earth, and heat and cold as active principles, it being the property of heat to rarify and elevate bodies and produce white, and of cold to solidify, to prevent motion, and to descend. Cold is associated closely with earth, which is immobile and black. On the basis of this trinity he works out a complete and logical cosmological system, even to a brilliant doctrine of psychology to which Bacon was heavily indebted. The organization of the work is as original as the content.

I have described all three categories of encyclopedists, instead of concentrating on the third, because Bacon himself obviously reflects all three. The title that he gives to his scientific foundation in The New Atlantis should put us on our guard. It is called Salomon's House, or the College of the Six Days' Works (III, 127, 146). If one makes an outline of the De Augmentis Scientiarum, as I have done, it will be obvious that, although Bacon has worked out a new scheme for himself, he has been guided to a considerable extent by the older convention in the arrangement of parts. His division of the history of generations is approximately that of the older encyclopedists, particularly in the rather illogical separation of earth and sea from the common masses of matter or elements, which is a direct inheritance from the classification by the days of creation. God separated the earth and waters by a special operation; consequently, Bacon has made a special category, not under the influence of the Bible but under that of the medieval writers. It should be noted, however, that he has reversed the customary order in so far as he intends to treat earth and water ahead of the elements. Similarly, the division of the study of man into that of the body, of the irrational or animal, and of the rational soul is in the encyclopedic tradition.

However, in a catalogue of particular histories appended to the Parasceve ad Historiam Naturalem et Experimentalem (I, 405 -10), Bacon shows his dependence upon the encyclopedic convention much more strongly as he descends to more minute details. This list of subjects is an expansion of the subdivisions of the history of generations. The history of species is in the traditional order (except for the last item) and treats of metals and stones, plants and trees, fish, birds, quadrupeds, and insects and serpents. Similarly, there comes at the end a long list of histories of separate arts, which is very like that in either Agrippa or Cardan and which is similarly placed at the conclusion of the plan.

From the whole encyclopedic tradition, therefore, Bacon inherited the attempt to summarize all knowledge and, in important details at least, a scheme for organizing his material. This is the more significant because, as often, one would not come to this conclusion if guided only by Bacon's explicit statements. In the Novum Organum (IV, 66) he writes, speaking of excessive veneration of authority, "Yet in this vanity some of the moderns have with extreme levity indulged so far as to attempt to found a system of natural philosophy on the first chapter of Genesis." Bacon means, of course, that they had gone farther in doing so than was traditional and customary. Bacon, like other writers, must always be read in terms of assumptions that he makes, so automatically that he forgets them to be assumptions.

To Agrippa Bacon apparently refers only once in the philosophic works. In the Temporis Partus Masculus, one of his innumerable fragments, he describes Agrippa as "neotericus homo . . . sed trivialis scurra" (III, 536). That is, Agrippa is on Bacon's side, but he is a petty buffoon. This same ambiguity of attitude appears in two other passages where Agrippa is not named but must be in Bacon's mind. One of these, from the Preface to the Great Instauration, also contains an obvious allusion to Cardan's De Subtilitate (IV, 15-6). But the other is far more significant in that Bacon is compelled to acknowledge a kinship:

> The doctrine of those who have denied that certainty could be attained at all, has some agreement with my

> way of proceeding at the first setting out; but they end in being infinitely separated and opposed. For the holders of that doctrine assert simply that nothing can be known; I also assert that not much can be known in nature by the way which is now in use. But then they go on to destroy the authority of the senses and understanding; whereas I proceed to devise and supply helps for the same (IV, 53).

That is to say, Bacon also destroys the authority of the senses and understanding, but he provides crutches as well. Here Bacon is at one with the skeptics, or possibly simply with Agrippa, deny it as he may, and familiarity with Bacon's ways leads me to conclude what is sustained by the evidence of content—namely, that Bacon was sufficiently indebted to Agrippa to be at special pains to vindicate his originality.

That Bacon was himself one of the innovators must already be apparent. Like them he sets out to survey the universe—with one all-important difference to which we shall come presently. Like them he equates Aristotle quite uncritically with the received body of knowledge and methodology and berates the poor philosopher at every opportunity. And I feel another curious parallel that I cannot demonstrate, simply because it is a matter of tone. Several of the innovators, and especially Patrizzi, were under strong Platonic influence. In spirit and in method Bacon is, of course, much closer to Aristotle than to Plato. But he seems to manifest a tenderness toward Plato that contrasts strangely not only with his assaults upon Aristotle but with his hostility to all non-empirical philosophers—if I may invent a category. I suspect that for Bacon, as for Patrizzi and others, Plato was primarily the first and greatest anti-Aristotelian and, as such, one of the elect.

But Bacon also has more in common with the methodology of these men than he would care to admit. As one reads their work, one becomes aware of, and then irritated by, a common method. Certain test cases are part of the received body of lore, and they must be proved consistent with the system being propounded. Among the encyclopedists these examples are passed around, and Bacon uses them as uncritically as the rest. This habit deserves illustration.

Cardan, in his discussion of the heights to which winds may rise, gives us the following examples:

> Solinus relates that Mount Olympus in Thessaly is so high that after the sacrifices have been completed on the yearly day, the ashes remain unmoved until the following sacrifice, because during the whole year the crest of the mountain is without winds on account of its height . . . The same will hold for a mountain which is in Teneriffe (this island is one of the seven which Ptolemy calls fortunate, outside the Pillars of Hercules); for if we may believe them [travellers] say that the ascent is sixty miles . . . and in Gaira the tops of the mountains are covered with snow, although it is only ten degrees from the equator. Either province [Gaira and Beregua, mentioned in the omitted portion] is situated near Paria [a province of Peru]. I know for certain from oral report that the air is stirred there. But if the cinders are not disturbed, this condition is possible because the air is very rarified and therefore wholesome; and this agrees with what Solinus tells about Mount Athos, if any confidence can be placed in him.[3]

Bodin also has occasion to mention the limits to which winds may rise, and he does so in these words:

> [Men have concluded that they do not rise higher] because of the highest mountains, on the summits of which ashes are disturbed by no wind and are wetted by no rains, as has been discovered on Mount Olympus in Thessaly and the Peak of Teneriffe, which are hardly three miles high from the top to the bottom on the perpendicular.[4]

We shall not be surprised to find that Bacon has the following to say on the same subject:

> 1. It is said that the priests who offered the yearly sacrifices on the altars at the tops of Mount Athos and Olympus used to find the letters which they had traced in the ashes of the victims the preceding year no way disarranged or obliterated; and this, although the altars did not stand in a temple, but in the open

> air. This fully proved that at that elevation there had been neither rain nor wind.
> 2. It is said that at the top of the Peak of Teneriffe, and also on the Andes between Peru and Chile, snow lies along the cliffs and sides of the mountains; but at the summits themselves there is nothing except a still air, so rarified as almost to stop respiration, and so acrimonious and pungent as to excite nausea in the stomach, and to redden and inflame the eyes (V, 172).

Cardan, it will be noted, has cited one of his sources; the other two have mentioned none at all. Yet this passage is a blend of material taken from Aristotle,[5] Solinus,[6] Acosta,[7] and Purchas.[8] Moreover, the arrangement of examples found in these three passages must have been common property, since Bacon can hardly have borrowed from Cardan.

A final respect in which Bacon seems to me to reflect his backgound in the encyclopedists, I can suggest only dogmatically in passing, since substantiation would require a book. As everyone knows, the Novum Organum is far short of Bacon's original design, but the actual explanation of Bacon's inductive method in the second book is confined to specimens of the way in which instances relevant to a problem under investigation must be presented to the understanding and to a lengthy discussion of prerogative instances—that is, the kind of instances that should be inquired into. In many ways the section on "Learned Experience, or the Hunt of Pan" in the De Augmentis (Book 5, Chapter 2; IV, 413 ff.) is a better guide to Bacon's intentions. But both seem strangely remote from science as we know it or even from what Harvey or Galileo were up to. It is a truism, of course, that Bacon had no notion of the theoretical importance of the hypothesis, although he constantly acted upon a hypothesis himself. But what really amazes the reader is the enormous proliferation of categories under which observed phenomena related to a given problem should be arranged or cross-classified in elaborate and endless tables. My conjecture is that Bacon was really improving the methods and correcting the errors of the innovators rather than of men who were really laying the foundations of modern science. For the innovators did use experiments, though Cardan's boast shows how casual they often were:

> You have in this book, dear reader, the causes, strengths, and properties of more than fifteen hundred various hidden and excellent things, not common but difficult, observed by the author here and there [hincinde] by experiment.[9]

Telesio tells of several interesting experiments. But a surprising number of them are used to demonstrate a principle that we know to be utterly false. For this condition there are, I believe, two reasons. In the first place, it was apparently the universal habit to use one slight experiment to demonstrate a general proposition, where a multitude should have been performed if the truth was actually to be reached; and in the second place, the experiments were performed to demonstrate some belief that operated, in effect, as a hypothesis, and yet the particular trial was seldom performed in such a way as to test the actual truth of the assumption. I shall try to show by examples the two faults that I have in mind.

Consider, for example, the following from Cardan:

> An experiment shows that ice is no less cold than fire is hot. For if you place on a log or on the glowing side of it the same amount of ice, the ice will be no more quickly melted than the fire is wholly extinguished.[10]

Or again examine this passage from Bodin:

> Th. Certainly my sense shows that water and other bodies grow hot by motion, but I do not see whether air is made cold by motion.
> M. This can easily be perceived; for if you blow the air from your hot lungs lightly from your mouth, you will feel it hot; but if you blow violently and with a narrow mouth so that the air rushes violently from the narrow mouth you will perceive that it is cold; and for no other reason if the south wind blows gently from regions burning with heat, it will retain its heat; but if violently, it will be cold.[11]

Granted that Cardan actually performed his experiment, which seems doubtful, neither experiment is adequate for the formulation of the rule laid down, especially because no attempt was made to exclude extraneous factors such as the heat of the room, or the effects of evaporation of moisture It is this kind of haphazard experimenting, I think, that led to Bacon's elaborate tables of instances and his extreme efforts to systematize everything. In fact, several passages in which he is clearly referring to this school charge them briefly with errors which he is at pains to guard against in his own system.[12]

Notwithstanding all that I have said so far, the fact remains that the innovators are largely forgotten or remain, at best, in the survey of specialists in Renaissance thought; but we are gathered today to celebrate the four-hundredth anniversary of Bacon's birth. Why? The answer lies, of course, in what is original in Bacon, and placing him in context may enable us to see some of his unique qualities more clearly.

Despite the mania for categorizing which he shared with Polonius and other Renaissance worthies, Bacon impresses any candid reader with his extraordinary open-mindedness and common sense. I suspect myself that he owes his eminence to the latter quality more than to anything else. For one thing, he realized all too well that he could not encompass all knowledge. He shared the encyclopedic impulse in full measure, but he had the wisdom to concentrate on surveying the state of knowledge in preference to surveying knowledge. He attempted both, of course, though we forget that fact; for the Advancement of Learning or the De Augmentis Scientiarum can still be read with pleasure and profit, whereas those works which he hopefully intended for the fourth and fifth parts of the Great Instauration—the examples of inquiry according to his method and those things which he had himself discovered (IV, 31)—are now almost forgotten. The histories of Winds, Heavy and Light, Life and Death, Dense and Rare; the Inquiry Respecting the Magnet; and so on—how many of you have read these or even know of them?

He also saw the importance of methodology as none of the encyclopedists did. In this he perhaps profited from his breadth of interests, for the contemporary controversy over method raged primarily among those interested in logic and rhetoric as part of the traditional philosophic system. As usual, Bacon both borrowed and modified.

Before I go further, let me once again confess that I am on unsure ground. All I know about Ramism and other discussions of method is derived largely from two recent works—Professor Wilbur S. Howell's Logic and Rhetoric in England and Neal W. Gilbert's Renaissance Concepts of Method. But their findings suggest that

Karl R. Wallace's study of Bacon's rhetorical theories should be regarded as important pioneering but not as definitive.

Of Ramus himself Bacon held no high opinion. He mentions him at least once by name in the De Augmentis, praising him for reviving the rules that propositions should be true, universally, primarily, and essentially, but condemning his uniform method and dichotomies (IV, 453; cf. 448). Ramus's notion that arrangement should proceed from the most general to the specific was, of course, anathema to Bacon. In so far, however, as Ramus sought to eliminate overlapping between logic and rhetoric by including invention and judgment in logic and style and delivery in rhetoric, Bacon was very close to him indeed. For Bacon distinguishes four "rational arts": "Art of Inquiry or Invention; Art of Examination or Judgment; Art of Custody or Memory; and Art of Elocution [that is, style] or Tradition [that is, delivery]" (IV, 407). Ramus, futhermore, divided invention into finding artistic and non-artistic arguments—that is, those based upon dialectical methods and those involving such things as laws, witnesses, contracts, torture, or oaths. Bacon, like Ramus, places topics and syllogistic reasoning under invention, but he reverses Ramus's heavy emphasis upon artistic arguments and devotes almost all his attention to induction as a means of invention. There is certainly implicit in Ramus's rearrangement the notion that invention is concerned with finding truths as well as arguments and that it is a way of increasing knowledge. Bacon explicitly divides the Arts of Discovery into discovery of Arts (that is, useful knowledge) and of Arguments. Ramus's treatment of judging includes the syllogism, induction, and his method of arrangement from the most to the least conspicuous. For Bacon the Art of Judging becomes judgment by induction and by the syllogism, plus the all-important development of detection of fallacies from the perfunctory treatment in traditional logic into an elaborate analysis paralleling that in the first book of the Novum Organum but omitting the Idols of the Theater. The Novum Organum is, in fact, simply a development of the Art of Judging as outlined in the De Augmentis (IV, 428–34), and there seems no question that the Ramist controversy contributed much to Bacon's thinking, even though in his most brilliant achievement—the discussion of fallacies—he went far beyond either the Ramists or their opponents.[13]

Turning to style as a third Rational Art brings us to another excellence that has preserved Bacon's wisdom for the delight of subsequent generations. He is, quite simply, a very great writer, as his contemporary Ben Jonson so generously recognized. Bacon has stated his own goal as a writer on science:

> I have on my own part made it my care and study that the things which I shall propound should not only be true, but should also be presented to men's minds, how strangely soever preoccupied and obstructed, in a manner not harsh or unpleasant (IV, 42).

And anyone who has observed the almost childish interest in personal ornament that appears throughout The New Atlantis will not be surprised by his repeated protests that, in setting up a practical science, he has no intention of eliminating those arts that adorn the intellect. "But yet notwithstanding it is a thing not hastily to be condemned, to clothe and adorn the obscurity even of philosophy itself with sensible and plausible elocution" (III, 284). With respect to the stylistic controversies of his day his attitude was a plague on both your houses. The context in the Advancement of Learning (1605) from which I just quoted contains a vigorous denunciation of Ciceronianism as hunting "more after words than matter." When he came to write the De Augmentis (1623) fashions had changed, so he added a condemnation of "a style in which all the study is to have the words pointed, the sentences concise, and the whole composition rather twisted than allowed to flow: a trick which has the effect of making everything seem more ingenious than it really is." This, too, he found "a kind of hunting after words and verbal prettiness" (I, 452). It is a fair summary of his own practice to say that he wrote at different times both Ciceronian and Stoic prose; but almost always he avoided the worst excesses of either, and almost always he wrote well.

This brings me back to my main argument. Though one with the encyclopedists in so many respects, Bacon excelled them in surveying the deficiencies of knowledge and in seeing the supreme importance of method. Though he could not rise above them far enough to chart the way to the future science, for his inductive logic is radically defective, he could call upon men to attempt the journey and show how it began, and his eloquence gave to him the status of a major prophet.

Bacon is, however, a man of his times in far more than his fundamental position—I say "far more," but I hope to make my case in far less time. I want, however, to make the case, because I find several of these reflections of Renaissance habits of mind of very great interest—not least Bacon's eclecticism and indifference to exactness.

One does not read far into the Renaissance without being struck by the general willingness to pick up interesting ideas from any classical context and to use them without regard to consistency of thought. I recall being amazed, as a young man first working on Bacon, by Du Bartas' inconsistency in lifting from Lucretius long passages that were part of a carefully reasoned argument against any divine order in the universe, using them in an orthodox Christian context, and later on belaboring the Roman poet with sundry charges of atheism and unflattering epithets, one of which Sylvester translated as "sin-sick elf." I published an article on the subject that now seems to me very naïve. Later I encountered that favorite Latin text in English schools, Palingenius' Zodiack of Life, which goes far beyond Du Bartas in its random borrowing without regard to consistency or organization. Such writers, and their betters, wanted simple, usable ideas without regard to refinements of thought. There is much of this in Bacon, but I will select only one example for discussion—his use of the term "form."

In trying to determine what Bacon means by "form" or "forms," we suffer from an excess of definitions. They are, the Novum Organum tells us in the first book, "laws of actions" (IV, 58) or "laws of pure act" (75). The second book complicates matters: "Of a given nature to discover the form, or true specific difference, or nature-engendering nature [that is, natura naturans], or source of emanation (for these are the terms which come nearest to a description of the thing), is the work and aim of Human Knowledge" (119). Forms are the laws which govern individual bodies "performing pure individual acts according to a fixed law" (120). The source and operation of this law is nowhere discussed. And difficulties multiply. The next aphorism tells us that "whosoever is acquainted with Forms, embraces the unity of nature in substances the most unlike . . . From the discovery of Forms therefore results truth in speculation and freedom in operation"; the following that "the Form of a nature is such, that given the Form the nature infallibly follows" (120–1). What was the nature of a thing in the sense of natura naturans has now become, in effect, the nature of that nature. A few aphorisms later "the Form of a thing is the very thing itself" and "no nature can be taken as the true form, unless . . ." (137) We are back where we started, after encountering Stoics, neo-Platonists, Scholastics, and apparently Bacon himself on the journey.

I note that the Forms are nowhere called by Shakespeare's favorite terms: seeds of nature or nature's germens. Perhaps Bacon did not write the plays after all. It seems reasonably clear that Bacon means something analogous to a law of nature that operates at several levels in a hierarchical order ascending from the individual nature of one kind of thing to a more general nature operative in several kinds of things. Furthermore, Bacon's forms, and in this they somewhat resemble Plato's ideas, can operate either in substances or in qualities like heat and cold. But certainly one could wish for, and in either a philosopher or a scientist should expect, more precision of thought and definition. Several of the terms to which Bacon equates "forms" imply an entire philosophic system and cosmology. To these implications Bacon is simply indifferent, as he is to the contradictions involved. I apologize for treating so cavalierly a problem that Ellis has discussed with great learning in his general preface. I feel sincerely, however, that, just as nineteenth-century critics bemused themselves by expecting too much exactness and consistency in Shakespeare, so we may have tried to find precise meaning where it does not exist in Bacon. Certainly Ellis's analysis is ingenious and thorough, but he himself admits to difficulties.

The preceding discussion of forms has incidentally illustrated another characteristic of Bacon's thought that deserves comment. For just as natura naturans, laws of nature, and emanation became involved in Bacon's definition of Forms and must have been at work in his thinking, so at every turn we become aware of Renaissance commonplaces lurking beneath the surface novelty of Bacon's ideas. Several examples can be mentioned briefly.

Though Bacon saw clearly that the collection of a new natural history must extend well beyond his lifetime, he seems, at least in his earlier years, to have expected rapid progress. Certainly he underestimated the undertaking involved. As I recall, he somewhere speaks of the natural history as extending to about four times the bulk of Pliny's. If we couple this kind of optimism with his allusions to laws of nature, it is a fair inference that we are very close indeed to the tidy, ordered world of limited complexity presented by the scholastic philosophers or assumed by Bacon's cosmologically orthodox contemporary, Richard Hooker.

We are even closer to this world when we get beneath Bacon's psychology. The surface differences, which include separating the God-given rational soul from the "sensible or produced soul" and regarding the sensible soul as corporeal, he borrowed from Telesio, as he in effect tells us (IV, 398). But his view of the rational soul itself is thoroughly traditional, though he seems to equate the sensible soul with the spirits which were traditionally its agents. But consider the following from the De Augmentis:

> We come now, most excellent king, to moral knowledge, which respects and considers the will of man. The will is governed by right reason, seduced by apparent good, having for its spur the passions, for its ministers the organs and voluntary motions (V, 3).

Or this from the Novum Organum: "The human understanding is no dry light, but receives an infusion from the will and affections" (IV, 57). Either passage might have been written by Hooker (this is as true of style as of content).

Even when the content is more original, traditional habits of mind intrude. Bacon tells us:

> I have thought it my duty besides to make a separate history of such Virtues as may be considered cardinal in nature. I mean those original passions or desires of matter which constitute the primary elements of nature: such as Dense and Rare, Hot and Cold, Solid and Fluid, Heavy and Light, and several others (IV, 29).

We have passed beyond the traditional organization of all things in terms of the qualities hot and cold, dry and moist; but we have not got beyond a similar series of dichotomies.

Finally, I cannot resist mentioning Bacon's most pregnant apothegm: "We cannot command nature except by obeying her" (IV, 114, 47). This was published in 1620, though variants of the same idea could be found in his earlier writing. In The Winter's Tale (c. 1610) Shakespeare wrote:

> Yet nature is made better by no mean
> But nature makes that mean; so over that art
> Which you say adds to nature, is an art
> That nature makes (IV, iv, 89–92).

I may now be accused, however, of setting up a counter-offensive and suggesting that Shakespeare wrote Bacon.

To turn to a final point in which Bacon seems to me a child not only of his own age, but of his own mother, I well remember that Professor Briggs told me, when I was working on my dissertation, that the real key to Bacon's thought was his religion. Frankly, I did not then know what he was talking about. I think that I do now.

No one can really understand Bacon without sympathy for the man or capacity to respond emotionally to the evangelical fervor which is so large a part of his call to the service of mankind. He was himself dedicated to his mission, which he pursued steadily throughout his life, whether amid the sufferings of disgrace or the more insidious perils of worldly success and a busy career. Many passages, and especially the great prayer which ends the Plan of the Work prefixed to the _Novum Organum_, show that Bacon was, in his own way, a profoundly religious man. Ellis, in his preface, states the case exactly in saying that Bacon "declared with all the weight of his authority and of his eloquence that the true end of knowledge is the glory of the Creator and the relief of man's estate" (I, 64).

So much is obvious, but, even in equating the glory of God and the betterment of man, Bacon betrayed the practical bent of the Calvinistic Protestantism that he absorbed as a boy, not least from his mother, who was a Calvinist of strong piety. I think that the effects of Calvinist views may reasonably be found at the center of Bacon's thought. Our best clue here is the "Treatie of Humane Learning" of his life-long friend Fulke Greville, Lord Brooke. Greville, like many Calvinists, extended the doctrine of human depravity, which Calvin himself carefully restricted to moral acts relative to salvation, to all operations of the human intellect. The "Treatie" is simply a Calvinist epistemology—though it is also, in my view, a very great poem. After surveying the depravity and error of man's intellect and senses, and glancing at Idols—undoubtedly derived from Bacon—that lead men astray, Greville concludes that all human knowledge is illusion. In striving to better the situation man must remember his goal:

> The chiefe use then in man of that he knowes,
> Is his paines taking for the good of all.

> Our chiefe endeavour must be to effect
> A sound foundation, not on sandy parts
> Of light Opinion, Selfenesse, Words of men,
> But that sure rocke of truth; Gods Word, or Penne.

Having in mind these ends, men can only hope that Grace and Faith will implant in the elect a new nature that will enable them to achieve a true wisdom pleasing to God. On this pessimistic note Greville concludes.

Greville's assessment of man's intellectual capacities is exactly that to be found throughout Bacon. In his preface to the Great Instauration he tells us that he tackled the "fogs and clouds of nature" "relying on the divine assistance" (IV, 19). All confidence in the natural human reason must be refuted (IV, 27). Bacon repeatedly asserts as a chief merit of his method that it "leaves but little to the acuteness and strength of wits, but places all wits and understandings nearly on a level" (IV, 62–3). He has even anticipated the obvious rejoinder: What about your own wits? "And therefore I attribute my part in all this, as I have often said, rather to good luck than to ability, and account it a birth of time rather than of wit" (IV, 108). The essence of Bacon's method, then, is to supply the senses with such helps and so to govern the reason (IV, 112) that an elaborate methodology will atone for the worthlessness of man's senses and understanding. This attitude toward human capacity was strong in contemporary Calvinism. It would have been powerfully supported by the revived skepticism of Agrippa. The interaction of Protestantism and skepticism in undermining the traditional reliance upon right reason has, in fact, been thoroughly discussed.

Surely this acute distrust of mental processes, which must be buttressed by endless methodical observation and cataloguing, contributes to two faults of Bacon's methodology that have been constantly noted. Though he repeatedly acted in his own investigations on what amounted to a hypothesis, and though something like an educated guess is several times vaguely implied in his methodology, he nowhere shows the slightest theoretical understanding of the key role that the hypothesis plays in all scientific experiments. Yet a man of his keenness of mind should easily have inferred that role from his own acts; it is one of fate's ironies that the experiment on refrigeration which led to his death was undertaken to test a very sound hypothesis. But use of the hypothesis enables the human intellect to transcend or to shortcut other methodology, and this Bacon on his own showing thought beyond man's clouded wits. His failure to recognize the role of mathematics in science is only a venial sin, if we grant that he was of his own times. He has, in fact, one strikingly farsighted remark: "Inquiries into nature have the best result, when they begin in physics and end in mathematics" (IV, 126). But it is at least a fair conjecture that Bacon's distrust of rational processes was a major barrier to his rising above his age in his general assessment of the role of mathematics in scientific inquiry.

Bacon's religious background was also in large part responsible, I think, for a pronouncement in which he did anticipate another important—and to my mind unfortunate—characteristic of modern science. As one might anticipate from his distrust of human reason, he is a thoroughgoing fideist—not in the specific sense of one who believes that man is saved by faith alone (on Bacon's doctrinal views we have, so far as I know, no direct evidence), but in the larger derived meaning of one who separates problems of salvation from those of man's participation in the knowledge and affairs of this world. Bacon's pronouncements are perfectly specific: "This likewise I humbly pray, that things human may not interfere with things divine, . . . that the understanding . . . may give to faith that which is faith's" (IV, 20). He charges those who try "to deduce the truth of the Christian religion from the principles of philosophers" with "disparaging things divine by mingling them with things human" (IV, 88). "And therefore it were a vain labour to attempt to adapt the heavenly mysteries of religion to our reason" (IV, 342). In this remark we arrive at Sir Thomas Browne's famous "*O altitudo!*"

Granted the tradition in which Bacon was reared—a faith that man's chief end is to glorify God and that in serving man all other things also work toward God as their final cause—it was impossible for him to separate human knowledge and faith without divorcing human knowledge from the final cause and therefore from final causes. The outrageous misuses made of final causes by natural philosophers must, however, have led him to the same view. These final causes, he tells us, "have relation clearly to the nature of man rather than to the nature of the universe; and from this source have strangely defiled philosophy" (IV, 57). "For the inquisition of Final Causes is barren, and like a virgin consecrated to God produces nothing" (IV, 365). I am no biologist, but I suspect that Bacon has been partly falsified, in that any principle of natural selection in effect reintroduces the final cause in another guise. Be that as it may, as soon as one eliminates final causes as a legitimate concern of science, one removes the only basis on which value judgments can be made, and one separates science and morality. The attempt to keep them separate has been made not only by the natural but by the social sciences—but made, I must protest as a humanist, with catastophic results.

To return from this gloomy note once again to my main thesis, I hope that I have presented convincing evidence—overloaded, I grant, with much conjecture—that Bacon was fundamentally a man of his times. To restate my former question, why, then, are we honoring him today? First of all, once more to repeat myself, because they were great times, and they appear at their greatest in Bacon. It is a paradox that, though Bacon set out to describe a philosophy of nature, he is always best in writing about man. It takes, for example, a dedicated student or a professor trying to write a paper to struggle through Book II of the *Novum Organum*, with its endless discussion of Prerogative Instances; but the first book, and especially its Idols, become more enthralling and challenging with each rereading. The paradox is no accident. If Bacon combines incredible insight into human nature in action with almost unique powers of expression, so do Shakespeare and Donne and Sidney and, I would argue, Spenser, with whom he belongs. Then, though Bacon may not have charted the true scientific method, he did recognize the importance of sound methodology beyond any of his contemporaries, whether innovators or true scientists. Moreover, he is never contemptible in writing about the study of nature. His acuteness of intellect and breadth of experience appear even when he goes astray or becomes involved in categorizing. His fellow encyclopedists often descended to triviality, or silliness, or plain superstition. He never does. Finally, he had a great vision, and he followed it, at whatever cost, throughout his life. I am tempted to conclude with the prayer prefixed to the *Novum Organum* to which I referred earlier. It is to my mind one of the most moving passages ever written. Instead, I prefer to let Bacon display his usual acumen and describe quite accurately his true role in the new science, though, in doing so, he will reduce my criticisms to silence. I quote from the opening of the fourth book of the *De Augmentis*:

> If any one should aim a blow at me (excellent King) for anything I have said or shall hereafter say in this matter,

> . . . let me tell him that he is acting contrary to the rules and practice of warfare. For I am but a trumpeter, not a combatant; one perhaps of those of whom Homer speaks:
>
> Χαίρετε κήρυκες, Διὸς ἄγγελοι, ἠδὲ καὶ ἀνδρῶν:
>
> and such men might go to and fro everywhere unhurt, between the fiercest and bitterest enemies. Nor is mine a trumpet which summons and excites men to cut each other to pieces with mutual contradictions, or to quarrel and fight with one another; but rather to make peace between themselves, and turning with united forces against the Nature of Things, to storm and occupy her castles and strongholds, and extend the bounds of human empire, as far as God Almighty in his goodness may permit (IV, 372–3).

Let us echo Homer: "Hail trumpeter, messenger of God, and of men!" The summons was loud and clear.

NOTES

1 See Frank Egleston Robbins, *The Hexaemeral Literature* (Chicago: University of Chicago Press, 1912).

2 Prologus XV; cited from the 2 volume edition of Anton Koberger (Nuremburg, 1485).

3 *De Subtilitate*, ii, 56–7 (Paris, 1551 edition).

4 *Universae Naturae Theatrum* (Hanoviae, 1605), pp. 169–70.

5 *Prob.* xxvi, 39. See notes to Bacon's *Historia Ventorum* V, 172.

6 *Polyhist.* 15.

7 iii, 9, 20, for the Andes.

8 v, 785, for the Peak of Teneriffe.

9 *De Subtilitate*, Epistle.

10 *De Subtilitate*, I, 27.

11 1605 edition, p. 156.

12 Cf. *Novum Organum*, I, lxii, civ (IV, 63–4; 97); *Redargutio Philosophiarum* (III, 571).

13 On Ramus, cf. Wilbur S. Howell, Logic and Rhetoric in England, 1500–1700 (Princeton: Princeton University Press, 1959), pp. 148–62; Karl R. Wallace, Francis Bacon on Communication and Rhetoric (Chapel Hill: University of North Carolina Press, 1943), pp. 35–6.

MYTHOLOGY AND ALCHEMY IN THE WISDOM OF THE ANCIENTS

C. W. Lemmi

In nothing is Bacon more delightful as a writer than in his copious allusions to classical mythology. The myths of Greece and Rome are so familiar to him that they become almost a new, vivid language on his lips, whence they flow in a profusion of apt similes and striking metaphors, or in less obvious comparisons to which he deftly gives point and meaning as he goes, or again in complete allegories which embody whole trains of thought in picturesque and memorable images. Indeed, as we turn the pages of De sapientia veterum we are almost ready to believe, as he would have us, that the myths themselves are his subject, and that from them really emerge the ingenious or sagacious ideas which he wishes to convey to us. In a measure, Bacon doubtless believed this himself; for he was at least of two minds as to the actual existence of a golden age whose wisdom the poets had turned to mystery and song. Certain it is that in these pages he appears to us more than ever as the eager inquirer after truth, and as we follow in his steps we feel with a pleasant excitement that we are sharing in his discoveries.

So disarmingly spontaneous are Bacon's interpretations of mythology that scholars have generally accepted them as entirely original (VI, 608–9). In doing so, however, they have, perhaps, been hasty. The tendency to adopt and adapt so characteristic of the Renaissance is by no means unnoticeable in the Essays; and we have no sooner begun the introduction to De sapientia veterum than we are reminded of Cicero by a remark about Chrysippus and of Julian by a reflection on the significant absurdity of certain myths.[1] Indeed, it would have required no small effort to expound the gods in an entirely new way. Pausanias, Plutarch, Lucian, Cornutus, Servius,

Reprinted from The Classic Deities in Bacon: A Study in Mythological Symbolism (Baltimore, 1933), pp. 46–9, 74–91, 196–213, by permission of the estate of C. W. Lemmi and The Johns Hopkins Press.

Macrobius, Fulgentius, to mention but a few, were familiar to educated men; so were the Neo-Platonists and the Fathers. The treatises of Giraldi, Cartari, Sabinus, counted many readers; the Mythologiæ of Natalis Comes was famous. Numerous emblem-books might also be mentioned. Nor must we forget the strange writings of the alchemists who, extremely active and copiously productive of books throughout the seventeenth century, often used the classic myths for their pseudo-scientific symbolism. Under these circumstances it becomes of interest to investigate Bacon's possible sources, all the more so as the inquiry involves the origin of some of his ideas. I have made such an investigation and will endeavor to show that while all Bacon's interpretations bear the mark of his creative fancy, and while some are practically original, most are, in varying degrees, adaptations of others which preceded them.

Nobody has denied, I take it, that some of Bacon's mythological symbolism was conventional in his time. Even if no special literature had existed, it would have been natural, in an age saturated with classical learning, that classical mythology should be drawn upon for metaphor, and simile, and painted emblem. Therefore, when Bacon refers to "the works of Bacchus and Ceres" (IV, 83), or to those of Dædalus and Vulcan (IV, 287), or when he says that Henry VII wisely sowed Hydra's teeth (VI, 95), he is following a common practice and would probably have been understood even without the brief elucidations which he gives in passing. James I, we may be sure, did not miss the compliment when he was referred to as laboring with the laws, which he had in his head "as Jupiter had Pallas."[2] The reader at large was not mystified by the exhortation to princes and divines that they should damn and send to Hell, "as by their Mercury rod" (VI, 384), violent religious intolerance; nor did he fail to see the point of the comment, in regard to conflagrations considered as cataclysms, that "Phaeton's car went but a day" (VI, 512). Even we moderns understand the remark, on Solomon's regarding all novelty as oblivion, that "the river of Lethe runneth as well above ground as below" (Ibid.). These are but a few examples of what were probably current figures of speech. I think it safe to believe that in a general way Pan was a familiar symbol of nature, Prometheus of the progressive leader and reformer, Paris, in his famous decision, of the man who flings away wealth and wisdom for love. Not only do all three interpretations occur in both Comes's[3] and Boccaccio's works,[4] but the first and second are to be found in Alciati's Emblematum flumen, and the third in Thynne's Emblemes and Epigrames. So, too, in a general way, Tantalus was commonly understood as a symbol of money-greed, the Sirens were held up as a warning to the voluptuous, Scylla and Charybdis as one to the intemperate and rash.

It will be noticed that Bacon applies the myth of the dragon's teeth in his own way. Anybody would have understood him to mean the raising of soldiers, but not necessarily "for the service of this Kingdom." So too, Mercury's task of leading departed spirits to Hades is extended to the conducting of opinions and tendencies. The famous frontispiece of the Instauratio magna, with its ship sailing triumphantly between the Columns of Hercules, doubtless told the beholder that here was promised an excursion into the unknown; but the ship sailed in defiance as well as in high hopes: "For how long," demands Bacon, "shall we let a few received authors stand up like Hercules' columns, beyond which there shall be no sailing or discovery in science?" (IV, 283). No symbol was commoner in a moral sense than that of Scylla and Charybdis; Bacon skillfully refreshes it by making it enjoin moderation on scientific thinking. Even commoner was the symbolism of Tantalus; but we shall presently see how deftly it is made to express the dull palate and stupidly grabbing hands of primitive rapacity in general. Indeed, a subtle gift of transmutation is natural to the man; but for that very reason we must beware lest we come to regard it as exclusively his own. In warning the scientists to forsake Minerva and the Muses "as barren virgins" (IV, 287), he seems to enliven a hackneyed figure with a characteristic quirk; yet Minerva suggests the following comment to Boccaccio: "As for temporal matters, she is barren, for the fruit of wisdom are eternal."[5] The quirk is there, but we may doubt whether it amounts to more than a clever reversal of judgment.

While Bacon's short interpretations are frequently conventional, his elaborate ones are not; and it is here that the question of sources becomes especially interesting. In discussing these passages and essays,. . . I shall first consider the interpretations of a scientific nature; then such as are more an expression of worldly wisdom than of purely scientific doctrine. . . .

I: SYMBOLS OF SCIENTIFIC SPECULATION

Proserpine (VI, 758–61).

Few myths are more famous than that of Proserpine, carried away to Hell, while gathering flowers, by Pluto; long sought, torch in hand, by her mother Ceres; and at last, though the pomegranate seed which she had eaten prevented her complete release, yet granted leave by Jove to return to earth six months every year. The usual interpretation of this myth, which Bacon might have found in Cicero[6] and elsewhere, is that Prosperine symbolizes the seed of all plants, and that her yearly return stands for the sprouting of all green things. Bacon, however, offers an explanation of his own, —one of the most peculiar and interesting in his repertory. Let him speak for himself:

> The fable relates, as I take it, to Nature, and explains the source of that rich and fruitful supply of active power subsisting in the under world, from which all the growths of our upper world spring, and into which they again return and are resolved. By Proserpine the ancients signified that ethereal spirit which, having been separated by violence from the upper globe, is enclosed and imprisoned beneath the earth (which earth is represented by Pluto), as was well expressed by those lines:
>
> > Whether that the Earth yet fresh, and from the deeps
> > Of heaven new-sundered, did some seeds retain,
> > Some sparks and motions of its kindred sky.

We have here, then, a symbol not merely of the forces of vegetation but of all the creative energies of the earth. Of this Bacon leaves us no doubt when further on in the essay he discusses "the spirit which is contained in metals and minerals" (760). These energies are one in essence and, as we presently learn, quite distinct from the matter they give life to. Proserpine is well named the queen of the subterranean world,

> for the spirit does in fact govern and manage everything in those regions, without the help of Pluto, who remains stupid and unconscious (759).

Indeed, the creative power would escape to the upper regions and leave the world a dead mass behind it; but it is nourished and thus detained, even as Proserpine was (760).

The peculiar Hylozoism set forth above is of exceptional interest because of its importance in Bacon's philosophy. The essay on Proserpine is in fact an allegory of his theory of spirits. In his Sylva sylvarum he tells us so himself:

> For spirits are nothing else but a natural body, rarified to a proportion, and included in the tangible parts of bodies, as in an integument. And they be no less differing one from the other than the dense or tangible parts; and they are in all tangible bodies whatsoever, more or less; and they are never (almost) at rest; and from them and their motions principally proceed arefactions, colloquation, concoction, maturation, putrefaction, vivification, and most of the effects of nature; for, as we have figured them in our Sapientia veterum, in the fable of Proserpina, you shall in the infernal regiment hear little doings of Pluto, but most of Proserpina: for tangible parts in bodies are stupid things; and the spirits do (in effect) all (II, 381).

Bacon implies the same identification in much else he says about the spirits, and in some of these passages throws further light on his interpretation of Proserpine. Thus in Historia vitæ et mortis.:

> No known body in the upper parts of the earth is without a spirit, whether it proceed by attenuation and concoction from the heat of the heavenly bodies, or by some other way. . . . Now the grosser parts of bodies, being of a sluggish and not very movable nature, would last for a long time, if this spirit did not disturb, agitate and undermine them, and prey upon the moisture of the body, and whatever else it can turn into fresh spirit; after which both the pre-existing and the newly formed spirit gradually escape together (V, 321).

The spirits prey on matter, but by their expansion create bodies out of it:

> Generation or vivification is likewise the combined work of the spirit and the grosser parts, but in a very different manner. For the spirit is entirely detained, but swells and moves locally; and the grosser parts are not dissolved, but follow the motion of the spirit, which as it were inflates and thrusts them out into various figures (V, 322).

Whence did Bacon derive the curious doctrine embodied in the essay on Proserpine? The lines which he quotes occur in Ovid's account of the first appearance of man (Book I, 80–5), and the ideas expressed in them are mentioned by Lucretius (Book V, 906–8) in an obvious allusion to Empedocles's theory of the first appearance of living beings in general. His "ethereal spirit," too, which he describes as "enclosed and imprisoned beneath the earth," answers more or less to Empedocles's imprisoned fire or ether, whose yearning to its native upper regions, whence it was forcibly divorced, pushed to the surface animals and plants.[7] Again, Heraclitus's vital fire "feeds on vapors which rise from the damp."[8] All this comes to mind as we read Bacon's essay and his other discussions of his theory, and doubtless he is indebted to it to some extent; but it does not account satisfactorily for his doctrine. Bacon speaks of spirits as well as of a spirit, and he traces their origin to the stars. It has been remarked that Paracelsus does likewise,[9] and I believe this observation to be the key to the whole question, provided that we extend it to the alchemists in general. Paracelsus's "smoke-souls,"[10] which coagulate into the things of earth, but would ultimately be resolved into the universal cosmic spirit were they not nourished by the stars, are at most a modification of the spirits described in all Hermetic writings, and I think I can show that it is to these writings that Bacon is chiefly indebted. Indeed, one is irresistibly reminded of the alchemists in reading the essay on Proserpine. Bacon uses their language throughout. Proserpine is surely the "anima mundi" which they again and again represent as a florid and prolific mother.[11]

Let us compare Bacon's utterances in our essay with those of the alchemists. As for his general conception, let us compare it with the following:

> The quickening power of the earth produces all things that grow forth from it, and he who says that the earth has no life makes a statement which is flatly contradicted by the most ordinary facts. For what is dead cannot produce life and growth, seeing that it is devoid of the quickening spirit. This spirit is the life and soul that dwell in the earth, and are nourished by heavenly and sidereal influences. For all herbs, trees, and roots, and all metals and minerals, receive their growth and nutriment from the spirit of the earth, which is the spirit of life. This spirit is itself fed by the stars, and

> is thereby rendered capable of imparting nutriment to all things that grow, and of nursing them as a mother does her child while it is yet in the womb. The minerals are hidden in the womb of the earth and nourished by her with the spirit which she receives from above.
>
> Thus the power of growth that I speak of is not imparted by the earth but by the life-giving spirit that is in it. If the earth were deserted by this spirit, it would be dead, and no longer able to afford nourishment to anything.[12]

The correspondence is not perfect; yet here we have the influence of the stars, the emphasized independence of the earth-spirit from matter, and, a typical Hermetic view, the regarding of minerals as growths. Hardly less noteworthy is this other, from a second alchemist:[13]

> The elements and compounds, in addition to crass matter, are composed of a subtle substance, or intrinsic radical humidity, diffused through the elemental parts, simple and wholly incorruptible, long preserving the things themselves in vigor, and called the Spirit of the World.

As I have said, the correspondence between the passages quoted above and Bacon's utterances is not perfect. In those passages there is discussed a single spirit, which, furthermore, does not prey on matter but is nourished by the stars alone. The first of these discrepancies, however, is merely apparent. Alchemy was largely an application of mysticism, and the doctrine that men share a universal soul but possess individual spirits was paralleled in the case of "material growths"; that is animals, plants, and things.[14] Indeed, a chain of spiritual being was postulated, and the links were regarded as proceeding from each other. Thus a given metal differed from the rest in virtue of a specific spirit; but this was a modification or state of a common "metalline soul" which in its turn, through the principles of which it consisted, was an emanation of the "anima mundi" informing all matter; and the "anima mundi" emanated from the "spirit of the universe" and ultimately from God.[15] It would seem, then, that the theories of the alchemists rather explain than controvert Bacon's. The second discrepancy is a real one, and it may be that the influence of Heraclitus has something to do with the matter; nevertheless I think it probable that in this case also Bacon is chiefly indebted to the Hermetic philosophers, whose doctrine of transmutation includes beliefs concerning the nourishing of spirits which at once recall his. Before examining this question in detail, however, let us hear Bacon himself in the essay on Proserpine.

Bacon interprets the episode of the pomegranate seed—Proserpine's eating the seed, and her consequent detention—as follows:

> Proserpine remains fixed where she is; the reason and manner whereof is accurately and admirably set forth in those two agreements between Jupiter and Ceres. For with regard to the first, most certain it is that there are two ways of confining and restraining spirit in solid and earthly matter; one by constipation and obstruction, which is simple imprisonment and violence; the other by administering some suitable aliment, which is spontaneous and free. For when the imprisoned spirit begins to feed and nourish itself, it is no longer in a hurry to escape, but becomes settled as in its own land.

Despite the quaintness of his language, Bacon makes his meaning quite clear. He wishes to explain how creative energy may be understood to inform matter. Discarding physical occlusion, he postulates a closer identification analogous to the assimilation of food by the body. As we have seen, he conceives of the spirit as becoming in a sense continuous with the enclosing body through the medium of a process of absorption or transmutation. This process Bacon calls feeding; but it is worthy of note, as will presently appear, that he explains it rather as an act of procreation, by which the spirit generates more spirit from surrounding matter:

> . . . every spirit seated among the grosser parts dwells unhappily; and being in such solitude, where it finds nothing like itself, it the more strives to make and create something similar; and to increase its quantity, it works hard to multiply itself, and prey upon the volatile part of the grosser bodies (V, 325).

Evidently, then, Bacon has two ideas more or less confusedly associated in his mind: that spirit feeds on matter, and that it joins with it in an act of procreation. Let us now inquire whether he can have found similar conceptions in the works of the alchemists.

The Hermetic doctrine of transmutation was founded on the belief that the "metalline soul," when not stunted in its development by somewhat indefinite "impurities," was identical with the spirit of gold; and that when released from matter and introduced in its purity into any base metal, it would draw the metalline soul there into its own state of perfection, assimilating from it what was pure and rejecting the extraneous element.[16] We have here, then, something akin to digestion, and in fact the process is very frequently called by that name.[17] Just as frequently, however, it is called generation,[18] and the transmuting agent is likened to sperm. If it is further considered that the pure metalline spirit is often identified with the "anima mundi"[19] (of which, in fact, it is the metalline manifestation), it becomes apparent that the Hermetic doctrine is closely analogous to Bacon's. Equally suggestive of Bacon's theory is that upon which were founded the attempts to make the philosopher's stone. The pure metalline spirit was not conceived of as a simple principle but as a spiritual soul in a spiritual body or medium of contact with matter,[20] the one active and quick to escape, the other passive and semi-material. Furthermore, these two principles were regarded as identical with the spirits of sulphur and of mercury, the spirit of sulphur being usually identified with the active principle, though some alchemists taught the opposite. By pulverizing and distilling in a closed receptacle a mixture of sulphur and mercury, it was thought possible to extract and mingle the respective spirits. The active principle was then supposed to assimiliate the other, and the result, brought to an unexplained materiality by condensation, was the famous stone. Now the union of the two spirits was technically known as "fixation": but inasmuch as it gave rise to the stone it was constantly described as a marriage;[21] and because the stone was regarded as a mineral sperm, and sperm as highly "digested" blood, it was no less frequently referred to as a digesting of the "body" by the "soul" or a nourishing of the "soul" by the "body."

The peculiar ideas I have just described are more or less explicitly expressed in a number of Hermetic works. Bacon may have found several passages of this kind in a book entitled Pretiosa margarita,[22] published by the Aldine Press in 1546, which, besides the treatise from which it takes its title, contains selections from half a dozen others. Thus in the treatise:[23]

> The generation of gold is of quicksilver, and its nutriment (like that of the chicken in the egg) is of the yellow substance, namely sulphur. Hence the stone is generated of the white, i.e., quicksilvers, and the nutriment of the yellow.

Again, in the selection from Michael Scott:[24]

> But as only that sperm which is prepared in the vital liver generates in the case of animals; so only after long and patient digestion are our mineral spirits capable of producing our Stone.

Not infrequently the gastric, sexual, and spiritual conceptions of the union became somewhat confused in the writer's mind. Thus Sir George Ripley, an English alchemist of the second half of the fifteenth century, advises us to

> Put the Soule with the Body and Spirite
> Together in one that they may meete
> In his Damnes belley till he wax great,
> With giving Drinke of his owne sweate:
> For the Milke of a Cow to a Child my brother
> Is not so Sweete as the Milke of his Mother.[25]

The process of "feeding" was applied to the completed "stone" in order to replenish or multiply it;[26] but in the case of "fixation" it was intended to furnish the active principle with a medium through which it might act on matter, and, what is especially to our purpose, to prevent it from escaping. This last fact is frequently emphasized.

> It is the body which retains the soul, and the soul can show its power only when it is united to the body. Therefore, when the Artist sees the white soul arise, he should join it to its body in the very same instant; for no soul can be retained without its body.[27]

Because the "soul" might escape, the vessel in which it was liberated must be kept well shut till fixation was assured:[28]

> When your Ferments[29] to your matters be put,
> Then your Vessell close you must shut.

Let it be noted too, that in these Hermetic prescriptions Bacon may have found a suggestion of something more specifically to his purpose than fixation in general. Says another English alchemist:[30]

> But when these to sublymacyon continuall
> Be laboryd so, with hete both moyst and temporate,
> That all is whyte and purely made spirituall;
> Then Heaven upon Earth must be reiterate,
> Unto the Sowle with the Body be reincorporate:
> That Earth becom all that afore was Hevyn,
> Whych will be done in Sublymacyons sevyn.

This association of alchemistical with cosmic ideas was frequent and natural, for the alchemist imagined himself to be imitating cosmic processes. Paracelsus, for example, asserts this point of view at length, and indeed explains the earth as a fecundated egg, surrounded by its nourishing albumen the atmosphere, almost in the words of the Pretiosa margarita.[31]

So much for Bacon's interpretation of Proserpine's eating the pomegranate seed. Let us now turn a step backward and consider his explanation of her violent abduction. It goes as follows:

> This spirit is represented as having been ravished, that is suddenly and forcibly carried off by the Earth; because there is no holding it in if it have time and leisure to escape, and the only way to confine and fix it is by a sudden pounding and breaking up; just as if you would mix air with water, you can only do it by sudden and rapid agitation: for thus it is that we see these bodies united in foam, the air being as it were ravished by the water (VI, 759).

Having explained to us how cosmic energy may be conceived to combine with matter, Bacon, in this passage, tells us how it may be supposed to mingle with it in such a way as to make combination possible. We are reminded of Anaxagoras and of Empedocles, and it may well be, too, that Bacon was impressed with the phenomenon of foam, which he mentions again elsewhere (V, 323); yet, when all is said, he is describing the making of an emulsion. He talks more like a chemist than a cosmologist, and the alchemists frequently use much the same language. Wishing to combine the "soul" of the metalline spirit with its "body," they mix sulphur and mercury together as thoroughly as possible, pounding and pulverizing the mixture. Thus Arnold de Villa Nova:[32]

> Our earth is not sublimed in its condition as calx, unless it be first subtly incorporated with mercury. Hence you should pound the earth, saturate it with mercury and digest them till they become one body. This must be repeated over and over again, or else the sublimation cannot take place, because the earth will not be properly incorporated with the mercury.

When sublimation occurred, the two principles, the active immeshed in the passive, as it were, and bearing it up, were supposed to rise together and combine.

Bacon tells us that for vital energy to be properly incorporated with matter it must not only be "pounded up" but also "curdled" or torpid at the time of incorporation:

> It is prettily added that Proserpina was carried off while in the act of gathering flowers of Narcissus in the valleys: for Narcissus takes its name from torpor or stupor; and it is only when beginning to curdle, and as it were to gather torpor, that spirit is in the best state to be caught up and carried off by earthly matter (VI, 759).

I will presently show that Bacon was not the first to understand Narcissus as meaning torpor and to allegorize accordingly. The point just now is his idea about creative energy. Paracelsus regarded all matter as the "coagulation" of such energy,[33] and the word is of constant occurrence among the alchemists. The Hermetic philosophers apply the term not only to the actual formation of matter but also to the union in spiritu of its principles, and not infrequently they imply their belief in a preliminary coagulation of the active principle. For example, Raymondus Lullius, describing a certain method of distillation, says:[34]

> By this continual heat the body is subtilized, and the spirit condensed. The gentler the fire, and the slower the distillation, the more perfectly is the process performed.

Again, Arnold de Villa Nova tells us that:[35]

> Unless the bodies become incorporeal, and the spirits corporeal, no progress will be made. The true beginning, then, of our work is the solution of our body, because bodies, when dissolved, become spiritual in their nature, and are yet at the same time more fixed than the spirit, though they are dissolved with it. For the solution of the body means the coagulation of the spirit and vice versa; each gives up something of its own nature: they meet each other half-way, and thus become one inseparable substance, like water mixed with water.

It should be remembered, too, that the process by which the component parts of the stone threw off their grosser selves was constantly referred to and represented as the death of the two substances.[36]

Bacon's conception of the earth-spirit as something imprisoned and ready to escape would naturally lead him to look upon the metals as more retentive of their vitality than the more porous organic bodies. This, in fact, he does:

> For though the spirit which is contained in metals and minerals is prevented from getting out chiefly perhaps by the solidity of the mass, that which is contained in plants and animals dwells in a porous body, from which it could easily escape if it were not by that process of tasting reconciled to remain (VI, 760).

As I have said, this idea may have occurred spontaneously to Bacon; but in so far as it is concerned with metals it was already a familiar one to the alchemists, whose main reason, indeed, for pounding and calcinating the minerals they used was to set free the spirits within,[37] though as we have seen, they also had in mind the mingling of these principles. One of them, for example, declares that:[38]

> The seed of animals and vegetables is something separate, and may be cut out or otherwise separately exhibited; but metallic seed is diffused throughout the metal and contained in all its smallest parts; neither can it be discerned from its body; its extraction is therefore a task which may well tax the ingenuity of the most experienced philosopher.

The notion that the spirit of organic bodies might escape through their pores may have been suggested to Bacon by Lucretius:

> No pain, however, can lightly pierce thus far nor any sharp malady make its way in, without all things being so thoroughly disordered that no room is left for life, and the parts of the soul fly abroad through all the pores of the body (De rer. nat., III, 252–5).

Bacon tells us that Ceres strove in vain to release her imprisoned daughter; and that two heroes, Theseus and Pirithous, descended into Hell to rescue Proserpine, but were themselves detained there. He interprets both episodes as symbolizing the tendency of certain external agencies to cause the escape of the earth-spirit. In the case of Ceres he says as follows:

> The air meanwhile, and the power of the celestial region (which is represented by Ceres) strives with infinite assiduity to win forth and recover this imprisoned spirit again; and that torch which the air carries—the lighted torch in Ceres's hand—means no doubt the Sun, which does the office of a lamp all over the earth, and would do more than anything else for the recovery of Proserpina, were the thing at all possible (VI, 759–60).

Much the same view is expressed in Historia vitæ et mortis:

> With regard to the second desire, namely, that of escaping and resolving itself into air, it is certain that all thin bodies (which are always movable) move willingly to their likes when near at hand. One drop of water moves toward another, and flame to flame; but much more does this appear in the escape of the spirit into the external air, because it is not carried to a particle like itself, but to a very world of connaturals (V, 325).

Once again we are reminded of Empedocles's imprisoned ether drawn back to its native sphere. We are also reminded of Lucretius, where he says: "For whatever ebbs from things, is all borne always into the great sea of air" (De rer. nat., V, 275–7). Finally, we are reminded of Paracelsus. Bacon also speaks of the influence of the sun; but this is not unnatural, for he knows that luminary as the chief source of life and of corruption.[39] As for the interpretation of Ceres's torch, Natalis Comes identifies her chariot with the sun;[40] but in any case, Bacon's interpretation of Proserpine almost involves that of Ceres.

Bacon's interpretation of the episode of Theseus and Pirithous is much more remarkable than the other:

> The meaning is that the subtler spirits which in many bodies descend to the earth often fail to draw out and assimilate and carry away with them the subterranean spirit, but contrariwise are themselves curdled and never reascend again, and so go to increase the number of Proserpina's people and the extent of her empire (VI, 760).

This would seem to mean that extra-terrestrial bodies project into the earth principles which would release the earth-spirit were it not that they themselves become earthly. Now it will be remembered that the alchemists believed the earth-spirit to be replenished by the heavenly bodies. They did not, to my knowledge, regard these bodies as tending to set the spirit free; but they professed two doctrines in connection with their art which may very well have suggested what Bacon says. One was that in the process of sublimation the active principle bore up with it the passive, but was finally held down by it when fixation occurred. The other was that a superabundance of raw material would overpower the spirits and transform them into its own nature.

It will readily be understood that the first of the doctrines explained above is analogous to that set forth by Bacon. Says Bonus of Ferrara:[41]

> The force of the body should prevail over the force of the soul, and instead of the body being carried upward with the soul, the soul remains with the body, the work is crowned with success, and the spirit[42] will abide with the two in indissoluble union forever.

The process during which the "body" was supposed to be "carried upward with the soul" took place in a closed receptacle, the distilled vapors rising to the top and suggesting "heaven," as we have seen, to one author. Evaporation was followed by condensation and then repeated; so that "heaven" came to "earth" a number of times and bore up with it the earthly quintessence, till at last it was "coagulated" and "fixed." As for the second doctrine, it may very well have contributed to Bacon's idea that ethereal emanations are transmuted into more material things. Arnold de Villa Nova has this transmutation in mind when he says that "The ferment must exceed or at least equal in weight its sulphur"; and also, in regard to the proportion between crude sulphur and quintessence, that: "if there be a preponderance of the body it will quickly change the volatile sulphur into a powder of its own color."[43]

In regard to Theseus and Pirithous, Bacon tells us that only those mortals might return from Dis who first provided themselves with a certain gold branch growing like mistletoe on a tree in a deep forest; in short, the branch that Vergil has made us all familiar with. He comments as follows:

> As for the golden branch, it may seem difficult for me to withstand the Alchemists, if they attack me from that side; seeing they promise us by that same stone of theirs not only mountains of gold, but also the restitution of natural bodies, as it were from the gates of the Infernals. Nevertheless for Alchemy and those that are never weary of their wooing of that stone, as I am sure they have no ground in theory, I suspect that they have no very good pledge of success in practice. And therefore putting them aside, here is my opinion as to the meaning of that last part of the parable. From many figurative allusions I am satisfied that the ancients regarded the conservation, and to a certain extent the restoration, of natural bodies as a thing not desperate, but rather as abstruse and out of the way. And this is what I take them in the passage before us to mean, by placing this branch in the midst of the innumerable other branches of a vast and thick wood. They represented it as golden, because gold is the emblem of duration; and grafted, because the effect in question is to be looked for as the result of art, not of any medicine or method which is simple or natural (VI, 760–1).

In the passage quoted above, Bacon implies that the alchemists identified the golden bough with the philosopher's stone, and some of them doubtless did. A. Pernety, in his Dictionnaire Mytho-Hermetique, published at Paris in 1787, says as follows:

> Rameau d'or . . . est le symbole de la matière des sages, suivant que l'explique d'Espagnet. Il est pris d'un arbre semblable à celui ou étoit suspendue la toison d'or. Mais la difficulté est de reconnaître cette branche et ce rameau; car les Philosophes, dit le même Auteur, se sont étudíes plus particulièrement à le cacher que toute autre chose.

I am not familiar with Pernety's authority, and have found no specific mention of the golden bough in the alchemists I have read; but I think it very probable that the symbol was traditional. Lacinius represents the metals as a grove of trees,[44] Bonus of Ferrara calls the stone "the Golden Tree,"[45] Maier describes it as a "Tree of Life" bearing rejuvenating golden apples.[46] It would be natural too, for the alchemists to associate Vergil's golden bough with mistletoe,[47] a plant popularly believed to have the power of revealing the presence of gold.[48]

Bacon symbolizes in the Vergilian grove the difficulty of renovating natural bodies. He implies that his interpretation is original; nevertheless it was probably suggested to him by the alchemists. Says Pernety:

> Ils entendent par le terme de forêt la matière terrestre dans laquelle leur vraie matière prochaine est comme confondue, et d'où ils la tirent comme d'un chaos.

Bacon does not believe in the philosopher's stone. Its reproductive powers, its ability to eliminate "impurities" from natural bodies, the "impurities" themselves, indeed, and the evolution of metals which they are supposed to retard: all these he regards as dreams (II, 448). But when it comes to the ultimate objects which the stone is supposed to achieve, he is at one with the alchemists. He believes it possible not only to rejuvenate living beings but also to transmute metals (449). This, it should be observed, is pretty much the position of Albertus Magnus,[49] one of the philosophers themselves. Indeed, in protesting that the performance of the miracle can be accomplished only by a profoundly scientific "art," he is in accord with many alchemists. The difference between him and them is not that he has a much maturer conception than they do of what such a scientific art should be, or that he is singular in requiring, theoretically, that it should be the result of observation and experiment; but rather that he is not sure of possessing it, whereas most of his fellows in stern criticism are.[50] It is by no means astonishing that he should adapt their symbolism to his use; he unquestionably adapts much more than that. We have seen that his conception of spirits and some of his ideas about them are paralleled in Hermetic works. In view of his somewhat disdainful setting aside of the alchemists, it may be well to trace his indebtedness to them further.

I have said that Bacon believes in the possibility of transmuting metals. One of the passages in which he expresses this belief goes as follows:

> In the meantime, by occasion of handling the axioms touching maturation, we will direct a trial touching the maturing of metals and thereby turning some of them into gold: for we conceive indeed that a perfect good concoction or digestion or maturation of some metals will produce gold (II, 449).

As we presently discover, Bacon means that transmutation follows when the spirit of a metal completely "digests" the substance of it, and that the process is to be regarded as a "maturation" of the metal itself. At first sight the passage seems to speak for itself. However, it is not as literally alchemistical as it appears to be, for in a measure Bacon is using the vocabulary of the alchemist in a new sense, much as he does that of the schoolman. According to the Hermetic philosophers, a metal became gold when the metalline spirit informing it was able to achieve the complete "digestion" or assimilation of its "body" by its "soul." Again, when pure metalline spirit was introduced into a base metal, it "digested" or drew into its own nature the imperfect spirit there by ejecting the "impurities" and thus making possible the complete integration of its parts. Now Bacon's spirits, closely similar to those of the alchemists though they are, do not consist of "souls" and "bodies"; and as applied to them, "digestion" means either the actual transmutation of material "humidity" into energy, or a complete interatomic penetration—a complete enfolding of the atoms—by the spirit. And here it becomes apparent that Bacon has borrowed much more than words. He believes that in all metals except gold this penetration is incomplete, but may be artificially completed by loosening the atomic structure of the substance and thus removing the material obstacles in the spirit's way:

> The second is, that the spirit of the metal be quickened, and the tangible parts opened: for without those two operations, the spirit of the metal wrought upon will not be able to digest the parts (II, 449).

Thus the unobstructed spirit of mercury, let us say, becomes the spirit of gold. Who can doubt that all this is an adaptation of Hermetic doctrine?

Although the alchemists frequently veiled their meaning in mythological allegory, I have not been able to discover that any of them called the earth-spirit Proserpine, and I think it probable that Bacon took a hint from the Mythologiæ. Natalis Comes interprets Proserpine in the conventional way, but begins his interpretation thus:[51]

> Cicero, in the second book of De natura deorum, writes that the vital energy of the earth was attributed to Pluto, who was called Pluto and Dis because all things arise from the earth and sink back into it.

With this compare the opening sentences in Bacon's interpretation of Proserpine:

> The fable relates, as I take it, to Nature; and explains the source of that rich and fruitful supply of active power subsisting in the under world, from which all the growths of our upper world spring, and into which they again return and are resolved.

Bacon doubtless knew his Cicero as well as Comes did; but Comes introduces Pluto as an accessory detail in an essay on Proserpine, thus suggesting precisely the subordination which Bacon brings about. Furthermore, a second and more striking parallel follows. Bacon and Comes draw closely analogous conclusions from the mention of Narcissus in the myth. Says Comes:[52]

> Seed, when it is filled with nourishment, will produce and gather, as it were, other seed; therefore Proserpine is said to have been carried off by Pluto as she was gathering flowers. And what flowers? The flowers of Narcissus especially, which word signifies torpor and sluggishness (torporem et segnitiem). For indeed

> the seed does not sprout immediately, while it is gathering nourishment, but retains this matter within it, and in a year's time gradually brings forth a shoot.

Bacon says almost exactly the same in terms of the "death" of matter in transmutation, which was followed, be it remembered, by the "nourishment of the active principle":

> It is prettily added that Proserpina was carried off while in the act of gathering flowers of Narcissus in the valleys: for Narcissus takes its name from torpor or stupor; and it is only when beginning to curdle, and as it were to gather torpor, that spirit is in the best state to be caught up and carried off by earthy matter.

If I understand the matter rightly, we have now before us the chief sources of Bacon's interpretation of Proserpine. That our author is heavily indebted to them, and not for his symbolism alone, seems to me clear. Of the philosopher, however, so curiously mediæval in much of his thinking, I will speak later. Here I should like to point out that aspect of his mind in which, perhaps, he is as much the artist as the philosopher. In this essay even more than in the others, Bacon elevates and blends his acquired conceptions into a loftier and more beautiful whole, and yet gives that whole a picturesque and striking concreteness. To the alchemist, the earth-spirit was chiefly the prolific mother of metals; Comes conceived of Proserpine as the mother of plants. Bacon unites the two into the majestic mother of all things on earth (VI, 737); and as for grimy Pluto, he relegates him to the background.

II. SYMBOLS OF WORLDLY WISDOM

The Sirens (VI, 762 ff.), Dionysus (VI, 740 ff.), and Nemesis (VI, 737 ff.).

Bacon's views on youth, age, and love, even though they be largely adopted views, are not cheerful. His opinion of pleasure, and indeed of all pursuits and even of life itself, is no less bleak. It is set forth at length in the essays on the Sirens, Dionysus, and Nemesis. For these as for the others it is possible to find sources, but sources elaborated with what seems to me an unmistakable emphasis on the gray side of the picture.

"As for the song of the Sirens," says Bacon, "its fatal effect and various artifice, it is everybody's theme, and therefore needs no interpreter." The song of the Sirens is indeed a hard-worked symbol of the allurements of pleasure; but Bacon by no means stops at the simpler and more general meaning attributed to the myth, which last, therefore, he relates in detail:

> The Sirens were daughters (we are told) of Achelous and of Terpsichore, one of the Muses. Originally they had wings; but being beaten in a contest with the Muses which they had rashly challenged, their wings were plucked off, and turned by the Muses into crowns for themselves, who thenceforward all wore wings on their heads, except only the mother of the Sirens. These Sirens had their dwelling in certain pleasant islands, whence they kept watch for ships; and when they saw any approaching they began to sing; which made the voyagers first stay to listen, then gradually draw near, and at last land; when they took and killed them. Their song was not all in one strain; but they varied their measures according to the nature of the listener, and took each captive with those which best suited him. So destructive the plague was, that the islands of the Sirens were seen afar off white with the bones of unburied carcasses. For this evil two different remedies were found; one by Ulysses, the other by Orpheus. Ulysses caused the ears of his crew to be stopped with wax; and himself (wishing to make trial of the thing without incurring the danger) to be bound to the mast; at the same time forbidding any one at his peril to loose him even at his own request. Orpheus not caring to be bound, raised his voice on high, and singing to his lyre the praises of the Gods, drowned the voiced of the Sirens, and so passed clear of all danger (VI, 762–3).

Bacon's interpretation of the myth of the Sirens is curious and minute. For the most part, however, it is not original, as the following table will, I think, show:

Bacon's Interpretation	Parallels in Other Writers
Pleasures spring from the union of abundance and affluence with hilarity and exultation of mind.	That they (the Sirens) were the companions of Proserpine was feigned, I believe, because by Proserpine was understood the abundance

of Sicily in all things; to which abundance are due rich foods and the libidinous actions often provoked by them (Boccaccio).[53]

And formerly they carried men away at once, as if with wings, by the first view of their charms.

They are called in Greek draggers. . . . One is dragged away by the following three allurements of love. . . . The Sirens are called winged because they penetrate so quickly into the minds of lovers (Fulgentius).[54]

For a mischief so fraught with cunning and violence alike, there are proposed three remedies: two from philosophy, the third from religion. The first method of escape is to resist the beginnings, and sedulously to avoid all occasions which may tempt and solict the mind. This is the waxing up of the ears, and or minds of ordinary and plebeian cast—such as the crew of Ulysses—is the only remedy. But minds of a loftier order, if they fortify themselves with constancy of resolution, can venture into the midst of pleasures; nay and they take delight in thus putting their virtue to a more exquisite proof; besides gaining thereby a more thorough insight—as lookers-on rather than followers—into the foolishness and madness of pleasures. Heroes of this order may therefore stand unshaken

Why, amid the sweet songs of the Sirens, was it necessary either to stop up ones ears or to have oneself tied to the mast? Because when one faces the allurements of illicit pleasure one must either turn a deaf ear to them or submit to the strictest control of one's reason (Natalis Comes).[55]

Those things which his comrades passed by after their ears had been waxed Ulysses, though in truth tied to the mast, passed by anyhow. These Sirens (that is the allurements of pleasure) he heard and saw—knew, in other words, and judged of—but he passed them by just the same (Fulgentius).[56] Others have interpreted the Sirens as the voices of flatterers, the eloquence of whom, being admidst the greatest temptations, and refrain themselves even in the steep-down paths of pleasures; provided only that they follow the example of Ulysses, and forbid the pernicious counsels and flatteries of their own followers, which are of all things most powerful to unsettle and unnerve the mind.

pleasant to the hearer, has caused the Sirens to be called daughters of the Muses. However, such voices drag the hearer down to ruin. (Natalis Comes).[57]

But of the three remedies, far the best in every way is that of Orpheus; who by singing and sounding forth the praises of the gods confounded the voices of the Sirens and put them aside: for meditations upon things divine excel the pleasures of the sense, not in power only, but also in sweetness.

Whoever, then, would avoid calamities and hardships, must either follow the example of Ulysses and close his ears to the dishonest promptings of life or he must listen to the admonitions of Orpheus and other wise men and hear them alone. . . . It is necessary, then, that Orpheus or some other friendly and wise man should drown the voices of the Sirens with sagacious and devoted advice. (Natalis Comes).[58]

Bacon's interpretation of the episode of Orpheus, quoted in the preceding paragraph, seems to be his own, and I do not know of any immediate sources for the symbolism of the passage following that in which the wings of the Sirens are explained:

> But doctrine and instruction have succeeded in teaching the mind, if not to refrain altogether, yet to pause and consider consequences; and so have stripped the Pleasures of their wings. And this redounded greatly to the honour of the Muses —for as soon as it appeared by some examples that Philosophy could induce a contempt of Pleasures, it was at once regarded as a sublime thing, which could so lift the soul from earth, and make the cogitations of man (which live in his head) winged and ethereal.

> Only the mother of the Sirens still goes on foot and has no wings; and by her no doubt are meant those lighter kinds of learning which are invented and applied only for amusement; such as those were which Petronius held in estimation, he who being condemned to die, sought in the very waitingroom of death for matter to amuse him, and when he turned to books among other things for consolation, would read (says Tacitus) none of those which teach constancy of mind, but only light verses. Of this kind is that of Catullus [Eleg. 5]:
>
> Let's live and love, love, while we may;
> And for all the old men say
> Just one penny let us care;
>
> and that other [Ovid, Met., IX, 530],—
>
> Of Rights and Wrongs let old men prate, and learn
> By scrupulous weighing in fine scales of law
> What is allowed to do and what forbid.
>
> For doctrines like these seem to aim at taking the wings away from the Muses' crowns and giving them back to the Sirens (VI, 763).

The application of what Bacon says about the Muses to the Sirens is in a measure original but on the other hand it is closely reminiscent of what Boccaccio has to say in defense of poetry. In the eighteenth chapter of the fourteenth book of De genealogiis deorum Boccaccio, fighting valiantly under the banner of Petrarch, turns upon those who attack poetry in the name of "that most famous and holy man, Boethius." It will be remembered that when Philosophy appears to the imprisoned statesman she at once drives away the Muses who are trying to comfort him:

> Beholding the Muses, the inspirers of song, standing round my bed, and lending words to my grief, she was displeased; and looking upon them with a stern and threatening aspect, "Who gives permission," says she, "to these soul-enervating daughters of the theatre to approach this disconsolate person? So far are they from remedying his woes by any art of theirs, that they nourish them by their soft and enfeebling poisons. It is they

> who teach their votaries to choke and destroy, by the pernicious brambles of the passions, the most abundant and useful crops of reason. . . . Be gone, ye baneful Sirens, with your strains that enchant to destruction! Be gone; leave him to me. It is only my sober muse that can effectuate his cure."[58]

Here indeed is a weapon in the hands of prejudiced austerity; but the fiery and skillful Florentine fairly breaks it in two:

> Behold, oh most sagacious King,[59] to what the crafty arguments of these rascals tend! But the plain truth shall suffice to confound them. I have already shown who the Muses were, and what their honorable titles, and how great the obligations of illustrious men towards them. Still the iniquitous voices raised against them are not silent. Forward, then; I must press on further. It must be evident from what has already been said that there are two classes of poets: the one praiseworthy, venerable, and ever dear to pious men; the other base, shameful, wicked, and indeed deserving, as I have said, not merely of being banished from cities but of being driven from the world. The same may be said of the Muses, which are of one genus but two species—The one kind, which deserve all praise, dwell in groves of bay-trees, near the Castalian spring, and are adorned with garlands, and noted for the sweetness of their song; the others, who are led by the comic poets, dwell in theaters, on the stage, amid garish shows, and bestow their favors for gold on the base multitude. . . . The enemies of poetry have perhaps understood, now, that when Boethius cries that the Muses are courtezans he has reference to that trivial kind of Muses; and in fact he says "theatrical courtezans." This the enemies of the poets would know if they had read what Philosophy says next. She says: "Leave him to be cared for and healed by my Muses." And in order to make it even clearer that he blames only those others, Philosophy repeatedly comforts Boethius with verses and poetic fancies. If Philosophy calls the Muses to the aid of her doctrine, evidently they cannot be dishonest or wicked!

The illustrious men whom Boccaccio names as indebted to poetry are such as Job and Jerome, and he cites Josephus and Origen to the effect that the Book of Job is written in hexameters and the Psalms in various classic meters. In other words he follows Petrarch in proclaiming the poeta theologus and thus giving the early Renaissance a battle-cry which, as we have seen, Bacon echoes when he speaks of "Parables, which are a divine poesy." The later Renaissance, turning from the Bible to Plato and Horace, proclaimed the poeta philosophus—the instrument of moral enlightenment rather than of religious inspiration—and this is the kind of thing Bacon has in mind in the essay on the Sirens. The conception was generally accepted and even the pious Comes stood up for the Muses:[60]

> These goddesses are of great comfort in adversity and of no small encouragement to splendid deeds; even as, on the other hand, they restrain us from indulging in illegitimate pleasures. As Theocritus says in the Cyclops:
>
> > Nicias there is no cure to make one well of love.
> > To abate the torments of its burning fever fire
> > Useless are all things, balms and enchanted potions,
> > Save only one: the pure charms of the Muses.
>
> It was in their gift to inflame the souls of warriors to valor in war; in their gift to console the afflicted; in theirs to immortalize noble deeds: and indeed many men have been inspired to the achievement of virtue by the examples placed before them by the Muses, as appears in Plutarch's little book on music. Homer also judged it undeniable that heroes fired by austere and lofty songs which reminded them of great deeds once accomplished, were presently filled with a new might when they faced the enemy. Indeed, such were the purposes of the ancient poets and singers that they professed themselves to be not only the moderators of the souls of men but masters of conduct. In the Greek cities the rudiments of poetry were taught to the young; nor were the Muses stripped of all sensual attractiveness, but rather they appeared modest and chaste. Thus it was that the musicians who taught the measures of song, of the lyre, and of the pipes were able to call themselves the reformers and masters of morals,

> as did Pythagoras and the Pythagorians after him. It was for this reason that Homer called bards correctors of manners, as when he wrote in the third book of the Odyssey that Agamemnon left a bard as the protector and monitor of Clytemnestra.

It is unnecessary to follow Comes further in his confused and yet explicit defense of the Muses. Enough has been said to show that Bacon's views on poetry were those of his times.

There is a tang of almost mediæval asceticism about Bacon's view of pleasure as something to be held at arm's length. Pleasure is a snare. The necessary ethical complement follows in the essay on Dionysus: all objects of eager pursuit are vanity. It will be recalled that Dionysus was the son of Semele by Jupiter. She having been burned to death by the godhead she demanded to behold in her lover, Jove received their unborn child into his thigh, when it came forth a girl-faced boy destined to conquer the world. Dionysus was educated by Proserpine and himself became an educator as well as a conqueror, teaching men how to cultivate vineyards and make wine:

> . . . whereby becoming famous and illustrious, he subjugated the whole world and advanced to the furthest limits of India. He was borne in a chariot drawn by tigers; about him tripped certain deformed demons called Cobali,—Acratus and others. The Muses also joined his train. He took to wife Ariadne, whome Theseus had abandoned and deserted. His sacred tree was the Ivy. He was accounted likewise the inventor and founder of sacred rites and ceremonies; yet such as were fanatical and full of corruption, and cruel besides. He had power to excite phrensy. At least it was by women excited to phrensy in his orgies that two illustrious persons, Pentheus and Orpheus, are said to have been torn to pieces; the one having climed a tree to see what they were doing; the other in the act of striking his lyre. Moreover, the actions of this god are often confounded with those of Jupiter.

Dionysus, it is said, did indeed reveal his god-like nature by arising from the grave shortly after his burial.

Bacon sees in Dionysus the symbol of all overmastering desires —love, greed of gold, ambition, and the rest—and reads this meaning into the details of the myth with what appears to be inspired felicity. If I am not mistaken, the symbolism of the essay on Dionysus is, in fact, rather an original development of hints than anything approaching a mosaic of appropriations. To such hints Bacon's conception of his subject is abundantly open, for it emphasizes eager desire as mental orgasm to the point of making him say that: "Under the person of Bacchus is described the nature of Desire, or passion and perturbation." Now one of the earliest and most frequently repeated interpretations of the myth of Dionysus is that it stands for drunkenness, as well as for the life-story of the vine. The Greeks themselves worshipped the god as an embodiment of the reproductive forces of nature, and Comes repeats this explanation as well as the others. For the Neo-Platonists Bacchus's mirror was the lure and Bacchus's cup the draught of worldly preoccupations by which the soul was partly chained to earth. For Lactantius, finally, Bacchus was the insolent leader of a dissolute rout. Material, then, was not lacking. Nevertheless it did not furnish Bacon with the details of his symbolism,—that is to say, not directly. When he tells us that human passions, like Dionysus, die only to spring up again, he is, by an independent act of his imagination, transferring Comes' symbolism from the vine to man's impulses.

Bacon interprets the parentage of Dionysus and the circumstances attending his birth as follows:

> Under the person of Bacchus is described the nature of desire or passion and perturbation. For the mother of all desire, even the most noxious, is nothing else than the appetite and aspiration for apparent good: and the conception of it is always in some unlawful wish, rashly granted before it has been understood and weighed. But as the passion warms, its mother (that is the nature of good), not able to endure the heat of it, is destroyed and perishes in the flame (VI, 741).

I think I am safe in asserting that in this passage we have the confirmation of what I have said elsewhere concerning the episode of Mordant and Amavia in Faerie Queene, II. 1. There also those who mistake apparent for real good drink the loss of what they seek in the draught of Bacchus. The cup is Circe's; but in the Philebus it is Bacchus who mingles earthly joy and grief in the bowl of the spirit,[61] and in Macrobius it is Bacchus's cup that destroys in the soul descending earthward to embodiment the knowledge of heavenly things:[62]

> As the soul is drawn down to the body it begins to experience a confusion like the confused murmuring of a forest in the wind. This is what Plato means in the Phædo when he says that the soul is drawn into the body in a state of intoxication. By the strange drink he means us to understand the influx of matter which burdens the soul and drags it down. The visible sign of this mystery is the Cup of Bacchus,—that starry cup situated between Cancer and Leo. The intoxication which comes over the descending soul at this point manifests itself as the confused sound of wind in the forest. And with intoxication comes its companion forgetfulness, already beginning to creep into the mind; for if the souls of men brought with them to their bodies a clear memory of heavenly things as they knew them above, there would be no question as to the divinity of mankind.

The Cup of Bacchus becomes also the Mirror of Bacchus,[63] and dazzles as well as intoxicates with earthly preoccupations. Nor is it merely in heaven, a snare to approaching souls only. It offers still deeper oblivion and still more hopeless exile to the lips of mortals.[64] It is the pool that chains Narcissus flat to earth.[65] Yet only the lower part of the soul may be thus enslaved. Says Plotinos:[66]

> Not the whole soul enters into the body. By her higher part, she ever remains united to the intelligible world; as, by her lower part, she remains united to the sense-world. If this lower part dominates or rather, if it be dominated (by sensation) and troubled, it hinders us from being conscious of what the higher part of the soul contemplates. . . . Every soul has a lower part turned towards the body, and a higher part turned towards divine Intelligence.

Bacon, having given an account of the parentage and conception, so to speak, of passion, speaks of its period of gestation in the soul as follows:

> Itself while still in embryo remains in the human soul (which is its father and represented by Jupiter), es-

> pecially in the lower part of the soul, as in the thigh; where it is both nourished and hidden; and where it causes such prickings, pains, and depressions in the mind, that its resolutions and actions labour and limp with it (VI, 741).

In his conception of the duality of the soul, Bacon was doubtless influenced by Telesio. This passage, however, is concerned not with the related souls of Telesian philosophy but with the parts of the same soul, and I believe that we have here one more indication of Bacon's familiarity with the Neo-Platonists.

Earthly desires are insidious and persistent, Bacon tells us (VI, 742–3). Ivy was rightly consecrated to Bacchus, for "the master passion spreads itself like ivy about all human actions and resolutions, forcing itself in and mixing itself up with them"; and it was aptly said that the god came to life again after death:

> For the passions seem sometimes to be laid asleep and extinguished; but no trust can be placed in them, no, not though they be buried; for give them matter and occasion, they rise up again (VI, 742).

Spenser clearly understood the symbolism of ivy, as the "lascivious armes" of that plant in F. Q. II. 12. 61 convincingly prove; and I do not doubt that Bacon understood it also. It is quite possible, however, that Dickens was not the first to observe "the ivy green," and that the insidious inroads of the Biblical tares in the wheat (or indeed of weeds in the philosopher's own flower-beds) had their influence. In the essay Of Nature in Men it is remarked that:

> A man's nature runs either to herbs or weeds; therefore let him seasonably water the one, and destroy the other (VI, 470).

As for the symbolism of Bacchus's resurrection, it may well be, as I have already suggested, a transposition of the interpretation to be found in the Mythologiæ:[67]

> That Dionysus was torn to pieces and buried, and that he rose from the grave: all this concerns nothing more than the cultivation of the vine. For from shoots cut

> off and partially buried, sound and fertile vines spring up. That he slept three years with Proserpine also refers to the vine which, during its unproductive period, is said to sleep with the goddess; for vines grow largely in their roots.

It should be noticed, however, that Macrobius applies this part of the myth directly to the human soul. Explaining individual souls Neo-Platonically as emanations which come from and return to the One, he symbolizes the seeming breaking up of the cosmic spirit thus:[68]

> Indeed, the Orphics conjectured that Dionysus himself was to be understood as <u>νουν δλιχον</u> who came from the one but divided himself into the many. Therefore in their sacred legends it is related that Dionysus was torn to pieces but rose up whole from his buried fragments; for <u>νους</u>, which we have said to mean the soul, emerging from the one into the many, and returning from plurality to oneness, fulfills its earthly functions and yet does not abandon its mysterious nature.

Bacon raises his voice in warning. To become obsessed with earthly pursuits is to commit oneself to a course of action that is often weak or ridiculous; sometimes cruel; always, from a philosophical point of view, unprofitable and vain:

> Most true also it is that every passion of the more vehement kind is as it were of doubtful sex, for it has at once the force of the man and the weakness of the woman.

And again:

> Tigers also are kept in its stalls and yoked to its chariot; for as soon as Passion ceases to go on foot and comes to ride in its chariot, as in celebration of its victory and triumph over reason, then is it cruel, savage, and pitiless towards everything that stands in its way. Again, there is humour in making those ridiculous demons dance about the chariot: for every passion produces motions in the

> eyes, and indeed in the whole countenance and gesture, which are uncomely, unsettled, skipping, and deformed; insomuch that when a man under the influence of any passion, as anger, scorn, love, or the like seems most grand and imposing in his own eyes, to the lookers-on he appears unseemly and ridiculous (742).

And still more impressively:

> And again that part of the allegory is especially noble which represents Bacchus as lavishing his love upon one whom another man had cast off. For most certain it is that passion ever seeks and aspires after that which experience has rejected. And let all men who in the heat of pursuit and indulgence are ready to give any price for the fruition of their passion, know this—that whatever be the object of their pursuit, be it honour or fortune or love or glory or knowledge, or what it will, they are paying court to things cast off—things which many men in all times have tried, and upon trial rejected with disguest (742–3).

I think it safe to believe that the first two passages quoted above are generalizations of what Comes has to say about drunkenness as symbolized by the myth of Bacchus; and it seems to me at least possible that the third passage is an expansion of a certain tirade of Lactantius's against the god. The Mythologiæ says as follows:[69]

> The god also symbolizes the nature of drunkards of whom some are made bold by wine, others as timid and talkative as women. Therefore the god was believed to be both male and female. . . . He was accompanied by wicked and harmful demons called Cobali, among which Acratus held the principal place; for many are the evil consequences of drunkenness and immoderate drinking: talkativeness, boldness, waste, shamelessness, anger, and many other similar ills; and also clamor and uproar; all of which the ancients called bad spirits. . . . Indeed, because of the ways of drunkards the ancients taught that lynxes, tigers, panthers and leopards followed Dionysus and drew his chariot: for intemperate drinking stamps

> men's souls with the natures of these beasts and makes them furious.

To be intoxicated with an obsession is still to be intoxicated. Drunkenness may well be regarded as the type of all violent disorders of the spirit; and Bacon furthermore regards it as the strongest incentive to all such disorders:

> It is a wise parable, too, that of the invention of the vine; for every passion is ingenious and sagacious in finding out its own stimulants. And there is nothing we know of so potent and effective as wine, in exciting and inflaming perturbations of every kind, being a kind of common fuel to them all.

As for the episode of Ariadne, one seems to see the shake of the head and to hear the grave comment when one reads in Lactantius:[70]

> But this invincible master of India basely yielded to love and lust. Having come to Crete with his half-human companions he met a shameless woman on the shore. Doubtless he played the man with all the self-confidence given him by his victories! Doubtless no sign of weakness was seen in him! Yes indeed! This betrayer of her country, this murderer of her brother, this woman abandoned and rejected by another, he set free, and married, and lifted up to heaven with him!

So much for the myth of Dionysus. The grim tone which distinguishes Bacon's interpretation is not, as we have seen, wholly spontaneous; yet it is far from perfunctory, and it occurs again with even more unmistakable sincerity in the essay on Nemesis. For the ancients, Nemesis was the humbler of arrogance. Natalis Comes probably suggested Bacon's interpretation in the main. He too explains the goddess as mutability, which "can shake not only men but also things,"[71] and he explains her parentage and her wings much as Bacon does. Yet the two pieces are strikingly different in tone. The Italian's Nemesis is much like Dante's Fortune: heaven-appointed to superintend equable distribution, to impose moderation, to enforce law. How different is Bacon's:

> . . . it was the office and function of this goddess to interrupt the felicity of fortunate persons, and let no man be constantly and perpetually happy, but step in like a tribune of the people with her veto; and not to chastise insolence only, but to see also that prosperity however innocent and moderately borne had its turn of adversity; as if no one of human race could be admitted to the banquets of the gods except in derision (VI, 738).

And she is crowned because the malignant envy of the people crowns her when a great man falls; and she rides a stag (a long-lived animal) because whoever does not die young and so elude her, has her, so to speak, on his back. Who can doubt that there is bitterness here? For Comes she is the child of night because men are blind to God's justice; for Bacon because, "the human not agreeing with the divine judgment," men cannot see why good Ripheus should fall.

* * * *

The long and curious emblem-book of Bacon's mythological symbols is now ended; before leaving it, I will pause a moment to draw from it certain general conclusions. The most comprehensive of these, which may be inferred from the popularity of De sapientia veterum, has already been touched upon. Bacon was by no means singular in actually giving credence to such interpretations as those in his book. Sandys's translation of Ovid, equipped with a complete commentary of this kind, appeared between 1621 and 1626; a handsome English translation of Ripa's Iconologia (which on the Continent had gone through seven editions between 1593 and 1630) was published in 1709. About this matter, however, I do not suppose that there has been much doubt. There has been uncertainty, instead—or perhaps, indeed, mistaken confidence—in regard to other questions: the originality of Bacon's symbolism and the sources of his thought. On these points I venture to believe that the present investigation has cast fresh light.

In his preface to De sapientia veterum, Mr. Spedding says:

> The object of the work was probably to obtain a more favourable hearing for certain philosophical doctrines of Bacon's own; for it seems certain that the fables themselves could never have suggested the ideas, however a man to whom the ideas had suggested themselves might find or fancy he found them in the fables (VI, 608).

And again:

> The interpretation of each fable is in fact an "essay or counsel," civil, moral, or philosophical; embodying the results of Bacon's own thoughts and observation upon the nature of men and things, and replete with good sense of the best quality (609).

These views, which have been more or less generally accepted, can no longer be held, I think, as they stand. It is doubtless true that Bacon sought to make his book attractive; but we have little reason to believe that he intended to appeal only to the fancy of the public, and none at all to regard the essays as nothing more than the play of his own fancy upon the myths they explain. The very fact that he conceived of classical mythology as probably allegorical should put us on our guard against such an opinion. It was not by discarding the wisdom of learned divines that men sought to understand the mysteries of the Scriptures. But the evidence accumulated in the preceding pages may dispense, I think, with a priori arguments. If the twenty odd parallels in Spenser's case[72] can hardly be accounted for as a matter of coincidence, the more than forty in Bacon's leave still less room for such an explanation. Here too we have not merely general resemblances but correspondences of detail, quirks of expression; here too Comes and Boccaccio make clear what would otherwise be ambiguous or incomprehensible.

The author of a brilliant work on the Renaissance in Italy utters an often-forgotten truth when he says:

> Au fond, changeant d'école, les humanistes n'ont fait que changer de maître. Leur pensée demeure en tutelle. Leur raison garde des béquilles. Ce n'est pas du jour au lendemain que l'esprit peut devenir adulte et se risquer à marcher seul. Les anciens ont remplacé les Pères de l'Eglise; le laurier du poète a supplanté le bonnet du docteur; Cicéron a détroné saint Thomas; mais c'est tout.[73]

This is said about the fifteenth century. By the sixteenth Machiavelli was placing considerable faith in his own experience; and yet he spoke in the name of antiquity and was very much more indebted to Livy, Cicero, Aristotle, Polybius, and others besides than is popularly supposed. In the seventeenth century came Galileo; but let us remember that Galileo was crushed by the defenders of authority. Bacon's England had no inquisition to fear, however little her Puritans lacked the good will; but Bacon himself testifies that it was almost dangerous there to meddle with authority, and the Anatomy of Melancholy is a monument built of ancient opinions and hoary beliefs. Bacon's intuitions were in advance of all this, but his habits of mind were not. He had flung off not only St. Thomas but also Aristotle; yet his ideas were heavily indebted to Empedocles, Plato, Cicero. He had formulated inductive logic; yet his desire to induce from the facts was more than equaled by his impluse to deduce from authority. He had a vision of scientific reform; but the germ of it was in the Italian reformers, in the alchemists, in Tully. He proposes to "hold firm to the works of God, and to the sense," and to conduct a rigidly experimental investigation:

> wherein it will be like that labour of Hercules in purging the stables of Augeas, to separate from superstitious and magical arts and observations, anything that is clean and pure natural, and not to be either contemned or condemned (II, 641).

Aye, but what do we presently find in his notes? This, for example:

> It is an ancient tradition that blear-eyes infect sound eyes; and that a menstruous woman looking upon a glass, doth rust it: nay, they have an opinion that seemeth fabulous; that menstruous women going over a field or garden, do corn and herbs good by killing the worms (II, 648).

If we regard as contrary to fact and probability the originality of Bacon's symbolism, we shall the more readily understand the sources and nature of his philosophical thought. In the essay on Cœlum, in that on Pan, and in others besides, we have seen Bacon appropriate from Comes not only symbolical externals but doctrines too. We have noted his indebtedness to Empedocles also, and to Plato, to Lucretius, to Scripture, probably to the Neo-Platonists. Under the circumstances, it is certainly rash to make much of his indebtedness to Democritus and Telesio. The Renaissance was philosophically eclectic,—or perhaps I should say eclectically tentative. Spenser, in the episodes of the Garden of Adonis and of the Judgment of Nature, is at least hospitable to the views of Plato,

Pythagoras, Aristotle, Lucretius, and Alanus de Insulis. Telesius doubtless did exert some influence on Bacon's conception of the soul; but, in my opinion, so did the Neo-Platonists. He probably did contribute to Bacon's theory of "spirits," and the early Greeks did too; but the fact remains that Bacon persistently uses the language of the alchemists and obviously has them in mind almost as often as he talks of experimental science. Indeed his indebtedness to the Hermetic philosophers is characteristic. Renaissance England did not change ab ovo; but Bacon's mental habits were rooted exceptionally deep in the past. One is tempted to call him a mediæval philosopher haunted by a modern dream.

The dream never ceased to beckon; but what about real life? If Bacon is not a misanthrope, neither, assuredly, is he an optimist. Often he breaks with his usual sources in putting a pessimistic construction upon his myths. For Comes the satyrs are the shepherds of God's forest-bound sheep, and Nemesis is the minister of His justice. For Virgil it is the good (not the as yet untempted) that die young;[74] and Erasmus associates the poet's words with Memnon by setting them over against the myth of Tithonus.[75] Lactantius, too, would perhaps have been startled by what appears to be Bacon's comment on his words. He would not have been puzzled, however. Surely he would have nodded a "Res ita est ut dixit: omnia vanitas!" Would he have done so rightly? Is Bacon's pessimism mediæval? Not more so, I think, than the stern ethics of his mother. Bacon may have been a Lord Chancellor, but he was curiously unlike a lord and still less like an aristocrat. His meticulous piety, his shocked dislike of the nobility, his disapproval of Pygmalion: these are the solid virtues of the middle class. His animadversions on the multitude are no argument against me: Charles II would never have spoken of the good people of England as Bacon did. Bacon's natural bent was not that of the monk but of the scholar, and indeed I think the fact explains much. English scholarship was sedate enough, and Bacon's copious allusions to Cicero and Seneca do not reflect his own predilections alone. I question whether the austerity of his views is not more stoic than ascetic; whether, indeed, it is not, though unintentionally, more academic than sincere. In a measure it is neither religious nor philosophical, but personal and bitter. If Bacon was a precursor he was also a misfit, nursing an uncomprehended dream. He wore the robes of a Lord Chancellor; but the face that looks out at us from his portrait is the anxious face of the servant of the king.

I have said that Bacon was not singular in his times for his belief in mythological symbolism; but he certainly was so for the astonishingly copious use which he made of it in his prose works. As I have shown elsewhere, the only one who approaches him as a symbolist is a poet, Spenser. The fact is not without significance. Much has been said about Bacon's indifference to literature as such, and his own utterances on the subject might seem decisive. So might those of Petrarch on the subject of his Italian poetry. I have said that Bacon's symbolism is not original. But what is mere lath and plaster in the Mythologiæ is a thing of life in the Wisdom of The Ancients. Surely it is not difficult to recognize the hand of an artist in this transformation. The interpretation is touched up, completed, fitted nicely to the myth, which acquires a new vividness as form and content blend in vital unity. The whole conception is made loftier, more spacious, more beautiful; and the simple beauty of word and cadence harmonizes with it perfectly. An artist is at work here; an artist who at times might be compared with Spenser. How extraordinary it would be if this man had possessed the unimaginative accuracy of the scientist. Photography is the negation of good painting. Spenser had a vision of moral law which uninspired persons have tried to reduce to a treatise on ethics; Bacon had a vision of scientific enlightenment. The beginner in painting is told to look through half-closed eyes, that he may grasp values and ignore commonplace details. The born painter is naturally unconscious of such details, to the exasperation of others and sometimes to the ruin of himself. I do not mean to define Bacon as solely a man of letters; a certain duality of nature urged him on in the path which his father had traced for him. Yet, though a painstaking counselor, he made his mark as an orator. And one senses the brilliant artist rather than the shrewd pleader in Jonson's famous tribute. It may be doubted whether Choate, for instance, would have felt elated if the jury he addressed had become absorbed in his eloquence.

Spenser is frequently declared to stand on the threshold of the Renaissance: looking forward, yet half-turning to listen to the voice of the mediæval past. Bacon stands beside him, and one reason for his wealth of picturesque symbolism is that he also has his ear turned to the past. At most he is a short step in advance. His symbolism is self-explanatory, while Spenser's is mediævally cryptic. His, concerns itself with the welfare of men; Spenser's, more exclusively with the welfare of souls. His, theorizes about experimentation; Spenser's, is purely speculative. There, however, I think the difference ends. Beside the picturesque confusion of mediæval romance you may see the perverse ingeniousness of scholastic classification; beside mysticism, mysticism; beside deep piety, deep piety; beside a vision, a vision. Such is the backward-looking aspect which the minds of both men have in common. The other aspect shows Bacon and Spenser to us as equally children of the sixteenth century. Not for them the cool precision of a Copernicus, a Kepler, a Galileo. Bacon stands in a little group of theorists and dreamers, with Telesio, Campanella, Giordano Bruno. The poet and the essayist both breathe the spirit of a great enthusiasm; both speak a gorgeous language, rich with images and melodies, that the age of disenchantment was not to know. _The Wisdom of the Ancients_ is not the _Faerie Queene_, but we shall not understand it if we think of it as something very different.

NOTES

1 Cf. _De natura deorum_, I. 15; and Julian's essay _To The Cynic Heracleios_, 222. D. Since this monograph was written, Professor D. Bush has furnished me with another _a priori_ argument. Cf. his excellent _Mythology and the Renaissance Tradition in English_ Poetry (London, 1932), 241.

2 Spedding, _Francis Bacon and His Times_, I. 641.

3 Natalis Comes, _Mythologiæ sive Explicationis Fabularum_, V. 6; IV. 6; VI. 23. I have used the 1581 Venice edition.

4 Boccaccio, _De genealogiis deorum_, I, sub. _De Pane_; IV, sub _De Prometheo_; VI, sub _De Paride_. I have used the 1511 Venice edition.

5 Op. cit., II, sub. _De Minerva_.

6 _De nat. deor._, II. 26.

7 Gomperz, _Greek Thinkers_ (London, 1912), I. 237.

8 Ibid., 65.

9 II, 94, where, also, it is recalled that the idea of a vital spirit permeating animals and plants "seems to be coeval with the first origin of speculative physiology," and it is stated that Bacon "was one of those by whom this idea was extended from organised to inorganic bodies." I believe this last statement to be without solid foundation.

10 Philosophiæ ad Athenienses, III. 3, III. 6.

11 H. S. Redgrove, Alchemy Ancient and Modern (London, 1911), 26; M. Maier, Scrutinium chymicum (Oppenheim, 1618).

12 Basil Velentine, The Twelve Keys; in Redgrove, op. cit., 25.

13 Benedictus Figulus, A Golden and Blessed Casket of Nature's Marvels, pp. 71 and 72 in A. E. Waite's English trans.

14 Redgrove, 15.

15 Redgrove, 15 and note; Janus Lacinius, The New Pearl of Great Price, A. E. Waite's Eng. trans. 262; Benedictus Figulus, A Golden and Blessed Casket of Nature's Marvels, Waite's Eng. trans., 60. French, Distill., V. 107, with which compare Vincent of Beauvais, Spec. Majus, VIII. 60.

16 Bonus of Ferrara, in The New Pearl of Great Price, 295.

17 Ibid., 215 et seq.

18 Michael Scott, same work, 420; Bonus of Ferrara, 283 et seq.

19 Redgrove, 31.

20 Bonus of Ferrara, 257 et seq.

21 Redgrove, 31.

22 This is the book translated by A. E. Waite under the title of The New Pearl of Great Price.

23 The New Pearl of Great Price, 290.

24 Op. cit., 425.

25 A Short Worke (in E. Ashmole's Theatrum Chemicum Britannicum [London, 1652]).

26 Norton's Ordinall, "The Eleventh Gate" (in Theat. Chem. Brit.)

27 The New Pearl of Great Price, 256.

28 Theat. Chem. Brit., sub Anonymi, chap. IV.

29 The active principle.

30 Sir George Ripley, The Compound of Alchymie, "Eighth Gate" (in Theat. Chem. Brit.)

31 De natura verum, IV.

32 The New Pearl of Great Price, 331. See also 412.

33 Phil. ad Athen. III. 3.

34 The New Pearl of Great Price, 356.

35 Ibid., 316.

36 Redgrove, 32; The New Pearl of Great Price, 38–45.

37 Redgrove, 32.

38 Eirenheus Philalethes, The Metamorphoses of Metals; see Redgrove, 80.

39 Aristotle, De gener. et corruptione, II. 10.

40 Mythologiæ, V. 14.

41 The New Pearl of Great Price, 262.

42 A link between "body" and "soul" sometimes postulated.

43 The New Pearl of Great Price, 334.

44 The New Pearl of Great Price, 30–6.

45 Ibid., 238.

46 Scrutinium chymicum, emblem 9 and epigram 26.

47 It will be recalled that Vergil compares the bough with mistletoe, with which, indeed, he probably identified it. Cf. Æn., VI. 205 et seq.

48 J. G. Frazer, Balder the Beautiful, The Golden Bough (London, 1911), II. 284, et seq.

49 Cf. L. Thorndike, A History of Magic and Experimental Science (London, 1923), II. 568.

50 See for example Paracelsus in his De alchimia. In theory he is as much an experimentalist as Bacon; but he believes himself to have made all the experiments necessary, and is dogmatical about them.

51 III. 16. 166.

52 III. 16. Bacon does not forget Proserpine the plant-spirit. See VI, 760.

53 De gen. deor. VII.

54 Mythologicon, II, 11.

55 IX. 1. 622.

56 Mythologicon, II, 11.

57 VII. 13. 501.

58 De consolatione philosophiæ, I, prose 1.

59 Hugo IV of Cyprus to whom the book is dedicated.

60 VII. 15. 507.

61 Dialogues of Plato, tr. B. Jowett (Oxford, 1924), IV, 637.

62 Comm. in somn. Scip. I. 12.

63 J. A. Stewart, The Myths of Plato (New York, 1905), 239; Plotinos, Fourth Ennead, Book 3, Section 12.

64 Plotinos, Enneads, I. 6. 8; Porphyry, De Ant. Nymph, cap. 34.

65 Plotinos, loc. cit.; Ficino, In Plat. Sympos., cap. 17; Stewart, 240.

66 Enneads, IV. 8. 8.

67 V. 13. 234.

68 Comm. in somn. Scip., I. 12. 12.

69 V. 13. 333.

70 Div. Institutionum, I. 10.

71 IX. 19.

72 Cf. Lemmi, "The Symbolism of The Classical Episodes in The Faerie Queene," P.Q. VIII, 1929.

73 P. Monnier, Le Quattrocento (Paris, 1912), I. 260.

74 Georgics, III. 65 seq.

75 Adagiorum, III. 9. 43.

BACON AND THE DEFENCE OF LEARNING

Geoffrey Bullough

The accession of James I in 1603 gave Bacon, like many other courtiers, an anxious time, for him all the more anxious because of the part he had played against Essex. In vain he appealed to his friends, to Cecil; his hopes of a speedy rise were disappointed, and in July he renounced politics: "My ambition now I shall only put upon my pen, whereby I shall be able to maintain memory and merit of the times succeeding" (to Cecil). The work he contemplated was The Proficiency and Advancement of Learning. If he could not gain the King's attention by indirect influence, obsequiousness, or legal prowess, perhaps his philosophy might stand him in good stead with the British Solomon. The limits of the latter's wisdom were not yet obvious. Hence the First Book of The Advancement, composed before the spring of 1604, was an appeal to James as well as a glorification of humanism written by one defender of the faith to another.

How characteristic of Bacon that he was led to write the first formal presentation of his great scheme by motives more worldly than disinterested! So long as personal ambition was not concerned he had thrown out a few indecisive sketches, a few aphorisms (the Essays of 1597); it needed some hope of office to bring him to a "Method." Though this First Book was printed off before the Second, it is unlikely that he ever intended to publish it separately. More probably he hoped to write the whole rapidly—in time to catch the ear of the King before all the plums were picked—but was prevented during 1604 by parliamentary business, and maybe too by some difficulty in developing his theme. Certainly the Second Book, written during 1605, leaves an impression of inadequate fulfilment, which may be due partly to haste in writing, partly to a certain immaturity of ideas. The matter of the First Book was familiar; that of the Second was novel, even to the author.

Reprinted from Seventeenth Century Studies presented to Sir Herbert Grierson (Oxford, 1938), pp. 1–20, by permission of the author and The Clarendon Press, Oxford.

This novelty has naturally led critics to give more attention to the later half of The Advancement than to the earlier. Philosophically it is the first important clue to his thought. So the philosophers have taken Book I for granted, while literary critics have usually passed over it with a few comments on its wealth of style, or have considered it as little more than a conventional introduction to Bacon's real subject. Thus P. Villey, whose Montaigne et F. Bacon (Paris, 1913) was an important contribution to Bacon studies, describes most of the arguments in Book I as conventional, and considers that Bacon

> a fait trop de place aux argumentations rebattues. Malgré des observations intéressantes et des analyses précises, la dissertation de Bacon rappelle toute cette tradition, elle s'y rattache étroitement. Elle a conservé beaucoup de sa frivolité.

It is worth while inquiring how far indeed "cette introduction . . . reste un morceau d'apparat autant qu'une profession de foi sincère." Is this how Bacon, the King, and other readers would regard a section of the work which, although only a small part of the whole, was carefully denoted in the title of the enlarged De Dignitate et Augmentis Scientiarum of 1623?

Bacon was a man of the world, a courtier, not a professional philosopher. In The Advancement he was writing a popular exposition for men of the world, and against most professional philosophers of the day. His appeal throughout was to lovers of action rather than of metaphysics; he attacked those who spun webs of words and ideas. Of what use would a merely conventional discussion of the validity of learning be to the cause he had at heart? Quite apart from the vigour of his style, suggesting the apostle rather than the re-arranger of platitudes, the whole tenor of Bacon's discourse and our knowledge of his character imply that he took the First Book as seriously as the Second.

Moreover we have his own word, written about 1603, that he feared a collapse of learning. And we have a mass of contemporary witness from writers with many of whom Bacon was personally acquainted that the objections he met were frequently raised in all sincerity. It is my purpose in this essay to examine the nature of some contemporary attacks on and defences of learning so as to sketch in something of the background of Bacon's book.

But first, Bacon's own words. Summarizing, in the *De Interpretatione Naturae Proemium*, his ideals, his qualifications, and the difficulties confronting him, he noted several menaces to learning:

> Nor am I discouraged from it because I see in the present time some kind of impending decline and fall of the knowledge and erudition now in use.
>
> Not that I apprehend any more barbarian invasions . . . ; but from the civil wars which may be expected I think . . . to spread through many countries, from the malignity of religious sects, and from those compendious artifices and devices which have crept into the place of solid erudition I have augured a storm not less fatal for literature and science. . . . And doubtless these hostile influences are destined to overwhelm that fair-weather learning, which needs the nursing of luxurious leisure and the sunshine of reward and praise, and which can neither withstand the shock of adverse opinion nor escape the imposture of quackery . . . (III, 519).

The new science was to be the means of saving knowledge from strife without and disintegrators within.

In *The Advancement* itself he defended learning against four forces: "the zeal and jealousy of divines," "the disgraces which learning receiveth from politiques," "that third sort of discredit . . . that groweth unto learning from learned men themselves," and another springing out of this, "the errors and vanities which have intervened among the studies themselves of the learned." Were these merely academic or really topical questions in England in Bacon's time? Who before him put, or met, the several objections which he faces?

Long before Bacon began to write, the first flush of humanist enthusiasm was over, and while the denunciatory vigour of the early anti-humanists had waned, the praise of learning was for the most part no longer lyrical, although at times, as in Marlowe's *Faustus*, the rhapsodic note of the early Renaissance was recaptured. In the nineties it was widely felt that since neither Renaissance nor Reformation had brought the millennium, nothing remained but to accept the natural man for what he was and not to deify him by magnifying his gifts of body, mind, or spirit. The economic and religious troubles, the political intrigues, of the last ten years of the Queen's life brought a disillusion which widened to include all human activities. If often morbid in its symptoms and results, this disillusion was a salutary corrective to the overweening aspirations of the previous generation —Bacon's work was one result of it which could scarcely have appeared in a time of mystical humanism—yet all the old arguments against learning were particularly rife during this decade or so of bewilderment and discontent. Of these we may well take the religious objections first.

The tradition of scholarship in the early Church associated with such names as Justin, Clement, and Origen had been crossed by another strain, that of devout ignorance, preached by Tertullian, which was carried over through the Catholic Church into Protestantism and fostered by the teaching of Luther and Calvin (themselves no foes to learning) about the essentially intuitive nature of our knowledge of God. Mystical doctors insisting on salvation by Grace tended often to despise earthly knowledge, and, in avoiding the errors of the Romish schools, preached a docta ignorantia very different from that of Nicholas of Cusa. Their objections were: that curiosity after knowledge brought the Fall; that such curiosity was still the fruit of pride; that speculation, even about the Word of God, produced heresy; and that the literature of the Revival of Learning was pagan and immoral. The attack on poetry, drama, translation was often related to a general suspicion of learning, in accordance with the belief (which endured)

> That knowledge without Grace is worse than ignorance.[1]

Even courtiers renowned for their patronage of scholars shared this belief. Thus we find one of Bacon's friends, Fulke Greville, spurning bookish knowledge for religious as well as metaphysical reasons. Because he seeks

> Eternall Truth, almighty, infinite,
> Onely exiled from man's fleshly heart,[2]

he reflects that

> The greatest pride of humane kind is Wit,
> Which all Art out, and unto Methode draws,[3]

cries

> Man, dreame no more, of curious mysteries,
> As what was here before the world was made,
> The first Mans life, the state of Paradise,
> Where heauen is, or hells eternall shade,
> For Gods works are like him, all infinite;
> And curious search, but craftie sinnes delight;[4]

and even refuses to delight his mind with books because they are

> False Antidotes for vitious ignorance,
> Whose causes are within, and so their cure.[5]

Greville was not uncompromisingly hostile, for his Treatie of Humane Learning, apparently a reply to The Advancement, while reiterating the pietist arguments, admits the value of practical knowledge in the work of the world. The dualism was characteristic of him.[6] But the Puritan opposition persisted. It made Milton, in Paradise Regain'd, Book IV, turn against the classical learning of his youth in favour of a purely Hebraic culture. Milton's argument, however, was an old one; and we find it clearly expressed in De Mornay's De la Vérité de la Chrétienne Religion (1581) which Philip Sidney began to translate and Arthur Golding completed in 1587.[7]

De Mornay's book was written against infidels and atheists. Nothing at the end of the century served so much to excite hostility to learning as the growth of religious speculation.[8] The word "atheist" covered most forms of heterodoxy, from political heresy to blasphemy, pantheism, the denial of immortality, or ultimate disbelief. Nashe, in Christ's Teares over Jerusalem (1593), distinguishes from the "inward Atheist" who "deuoures widowes houses under pretence of long prayers," the "outwarde Atheist" who

> establisheth reason as his God, and will not be persuaded that God (the true God) is, except he make him priuie to al the secrecies of his beginning and gouernment.[9]

Learning had no doughtier champion than Thomas Nashe, but he reveals a fear of too-ambitious rationalism which was almost universal in his day. There is no reason to believe that Bacon was less sincere when he used the notion of "double truth" as at once a fortress and a ne plus ultra.

The limits of the natural exercised Lyly when he introduced into *Campaspe* (1580) a scene of discussion between philosophers:

> *Cleanthes (to Plato).* I am of this minde, that a first mouer, which you tearme God, is the instrument of all the mouinge, which we attribute to nature. The earth which is masse, swimmeth on the sea, seasons deuided in themselues, the maiestie of the skie, the whole firmament of the world, and whatsoeuer else appeareth miraculous, what man almost of meane capacitie but can proue it naturall?
> *Anaxagoras.* These causes shal be debated at our Philosophers feast, in which controuersie I will take parte with Aristotle, that there is *Natura naturans* and yet no God.
> *Crates.* And I with Plato, that there is *Deus optimus maximus*, and not Nature. (Act I. iii.)

Lyly also used the matter of this scene in a dialogue, *Euphues and Atheos*, in which the dangers of naturalism were proved theologically. But Lyly, like Nashe, although aware of the perils of humanism, did not therefore claim that all knowledge was folly. Apart from the Puritans, most Elizabethans showed quite as much ingenuity as their medieval ancestors in keeping the borders of reason and faith vague and fluctuating, and apologists allowed the use of secular learning as a handmaid to the faith. Thus Thomas Morton, in a dialogue between a doubter and his monitor, gives a place to the sciences, and after showing how the astronomer, the physician, and the observer of "the lowest flower" or "the silliest worme" know the wonders of God, concludes:

> For the which purpose the studie of naturall Philosophie is to bee accounted, as pleasant so also very profitable, and worthy to be followed by Christians, as their gifts and calings do permit; for without question, they that go downe into the depth of it, see the wonderfull wisedome of God.[10]

—a comment quite in keeping with Bacon's own remarks on atheism.

Similarly Nashe urged all teachers to study hard to overcome the witty atheists:

> No one Arte is there that hath not some dependance upon another, or to whose toppe or perfection we may climbe without steppes, or degrees of the other. . . . No knowledge but is of God. Vnworthy are wee of heauenly knowledge, if we keepe from her any one of her handmayds. Logique, Rethorique, History, Phylosophy, Musique, Poetry, all are the handmaides of Diuinitie. Shee can neuer be curiously drest or exquisitely accomplisht, if any one of these be wanting (op. cit.).

The apologist must meet argument with argument, scholarship with scholarship. In this field De Mornay's book and *L'Académie française* of La Primaudaye (translated 1586) were cardinal works which popularized much elementary knowledge of psychology and theology. To their influence we owe the didactic poems of Sir John Davies and his imitator, John Davies of Hereford. Both of these latter writers knew Bacon—Sir John Davies so well that in 1603 Bacon appealed to him for help in his pursuit of office—but he can hardly have approved of their literary works. Sir John's *Nosce Teipsum* (1599), although it begins by depreciating human knowledge as so marred by the Fall as to be untrustworthy, then proceeds to argue about the nature of the soul and its immortality in a strain of derivative self-assurance. Similarly his verbose namesake's *Mirum in Modum* (1602)—on the soul—and *Summa Totalis* (1607)—on the attributes of God—ventured into speculations with which Bacon had no sympathy. The latter confined himself to the large domain of intelligence which he saw as free from the rule of religious dogma, for he was primarily interested in the means of advancing man's control over the world of this present life. Hence he was at pains to defend his conception of learning against both those who denied its validity on religious grounds and those who wished to use secular knowledge *merely* as an incentive to piety.

157807

The "disgraces which learning receiveth from politiques" include the following: that learning unfits men for arms or action; that it makes them love retirement; that it makes them disputatious and rebellious. The learned man has always been either unduly reverenced or (more frequently) suspected and despised as a bookworm, a parasite, one who lives at secondhand, incapable alike of leading and of following the lead of others. In the Renaissance, when the ideal of *virtù* clashed with that of humanism, controversy on the topic was long—and inconclusive. We see it in such discussions as that between Lodovico da Canossa and Bembo in Castiglione's Il Cortegiano (Bk. I. xlii–xlvi.) whether the courtier should love letters and whether arms or learning were the more worthy pursuit; it occurs in Guazzo's Dialoghi Piacevoli ("Del Paragone dell' Arme e delle Lettere"); it is mentioned by Sidney in his Apologie; while N. Breton gave both sides of the question in his Discourse of a Scholler and a Souldiour (1599). The arguments became commonplaces by repetition, but they were commonplaces which never went stale, because they represented real beliefs and recurrent prejudices. As we shall see, debate on Action as against Contemplation was particularly live during the rivalry of Essex and Raleigh.

Opponents of learning who declared the learned unfit for civil life had plenty of evidence in the person of pedants and eccentrics of all kinds who might be able to "settle Hoti's business," but certainly no other. Elizabethan comedy had its fair share of such figures. But armed with the maxim Experientia docet, the enemy went farther. Since life is an empirical business, what need of study and theory? This common self-justification of "Barbarisme" Ascham had met in The Scholemaster (1570) when he regretted that out of sheer boorishness "some yong Ientlemen of ours count it their shame to be counted learned" while

> Some other, hauing better nature, but lesse witte . . . do not utterly despise learning, but they saie, that without learning, common experience, knowledge of all facions, and haunting all companies, shall worke in yougthe both wisdome and habilitie, to execute anie weightie affaires. Surelie long experience doth proffet moch, but moste, and almost onelie to him . . . that is diligentlie before instructed with preceptes of well doinge. . . . Learning teacheth more in one yeare than experience in twentie: And learning teacheth safelie, when experience maketh mo miserable then wise.

Few would go as far as Ascham in substituting secondary for primary experience. Certainly Nashe did not when in his Anatomie of Absurditie (1589) he declared: "Endeuour to adde vnto Arte Experience: experience is more profitable voide of arte then arte which hath not experience." Ascham, however, was no apostle of pedantry, but a lover of Castiglione and the man developed on all sides of his nature, who, joining "learning with comelie exercises," was the courtly ideal of the day. And where, against those who held that a learned prince must be an ineffectual prince Castiglione (like Bacon) pointed to many historical examples proving the contrary, Ascham (also like Bacon) pointed to a living example not to be denied, the English monarch. In this part of his argument Bacon closely followed the "courtly" tradition, which disposed likewise of the allegation that learned men were disposed to "privateness" or disaffection.

Other objections brought by "practical" people and classed by Bacon as "discredits from learned men themselves" were that scholars are usually poor men and are forced to earn their living in mean employments (e.g. as teachers), that they are too rigid in their idealism and too impersonal in their disinterestedness, that they sometimes behave oddly or indiscreetly.

The abnormal behaviour of scholars had of course long been food for comedy. Their poverty, however, received special attention in literature, just before The Advancement was written. Graduate unemployment is no new phenomenon; it was rife at the end of the sixteenth century; and the plight of those who obtained employment was little better. A graduate of little means had normally two courses open to him. He could enter the Church and seek a curacy or chaplaincy; or he could become a teacher in a school or a family. In either event his income and his social position would probably be wretched. Simony was rampant in the Church, and a tutor's position was little better than menial.

> Can Commonweales florish where learning decaies? [wrote Nashe in 1589] Shall not felicitie haue a fall when as knowledge failes? yea, peace must needes perrish from amongst us when as we rather seeke to choke then cherrish, to famish then feede, the Nurses of it.

He was not alone in complaining that "Learning nowadaies gets no liuing if it come empty handed." Joseph Hall supported the poor scholars in Virgidemiarum (1597), contrasting the spendour of the colleges with the poverty of their inhabitants, but defending learning against the worldly fool who desires no part in Solon, Parmenides, or Heraclitus:

> We scorn that welth should be the finall end,
> Whereto the heauenly Muse her course doth bend,

> And rather had be pale with learned cares,
> Then paunched with thy choyce of changed fares. (Bk. ii, 2)

Yet in two stinging satires he showed that he knew what miseries ensued. One is in the form of an advertisement issued by a country squire requiring a tutor for his children:

> A Gentle Squire would gladly entertaine
> Into his house, some trencher-Chaplaine:
> Some willing man that might instruct his sons,
> And that would stand to good conditions:
> First, that He lie upon the Truckle-bed,
> Whiles his young Maister lieth ore his head.
> Secondly, that he do, in no default,
> Euer presume to sit aboue the salt.
> Third, that he neuer change his trencher twise.
> Fourth, that he vse all comely curtesies:
> Sit bare at meales, and one halfe rise and wait.
> Last, that he neuer his yong master beat,
> But he must aske his mother to define,
> How many ierkes she would his breech should line.
> All these obseru'd, he could contented bee,
> To giue fiue markes, and winter-liuerye. (Bk. ii, 6)

The other might well be the advertisement of a would-be vicar, with the author's comment. I cite only part:

> Who wants a Churchman, that can seruice say,
> Read fast, and faire his monthly Homiley?
> And wed, and bury, and make Christen-Soules?. . .
> Thou seruile Foole: why could'st thou not repaire
> To buy a Benefice at Steeple-Faire?
> Stake three yeares Stipend: no man asketh more:
> Go take possession of the Church-porch-doore:
> And ring thy bels: lucke stroken in thy fist:
> The Parsonage is thine, or ere thou wist.

Such complaints continued from the seventeenth century down to our own day. We think of John Oldham's Satyr addressed to a Frend that is about to leave the University, of Johnson's bitter "pause awhile from letters, to be wise," of a long line of wretched ushers and clerics in the novel from Fielding to Joyce. Space allows only the mere mention of the three Parnassus plays written and performed in Cambridge between 1598 and 1602, in which the disillusionment of students during and after their university courses was treated in detail.[11]

Most of these objections Bacon met by justifying the learned or by refusing to condemn them for occasional abuses. He praised the teaching profession, the disinterested attitude to life, and attacked the fashion of fulsome dedications (this after his own address to James!). But he had little to say "concerning want," except to mention the estimation of poverty in ancient Rome, declaring slyly: "it were good to leave the common place in commendation of poverty to some Friar to handle," and preferring to cite Machiavelli, who praised it for no religious reasons. Clearly the fortune-hunter in Bacon was not at ease on this topic. Nor did he mention here the compensations of the learned—the pleasures of the search for Truth, the hope of lasting fame. These he left for his later summary of the positive benefits of learning.

The social and economic objections had, however, been recently raised and answered very forcefully by Samuel Daniel in Musophilus (1599). This verse-dialogue, dedicated to Fulke Greville, provides not only a defence of poetry but "A generall Defence of all Learning" which burns with the ardour and idealism of the earlier Renaissance. When Philocosmus urges Musophilus to leave his "ungainefull Arte" and follow "this profit-seeking age," Musophilus replies that he loves his art and hopes for fame. This hope Philocosmus mocks by showing how easily reputations may be destroyed by "some viperous Criticke," or by the prevalent contempt for arts. He should try "to fit the times"; otherwise he will bury his deserts "In the obscure graue of Singularitie." Musophilus then attacks the vulgar herd and points out that the monuments of the worldly perish while virtuous learning survives, witness Chaucer, whose immortality proves the possibility of lasting fame:

> O Blessed Letters, that combine in one,
> All Ages past, and make one liue with all:
> By you, we doe conferre with who are gone,
> And, the dead-liuing vnto Councell call:
> By you, th'vnborne shall haue communion
> Of what we feele, and what doth vs befall.

> Soule of the world, Knowledge, without thee,
> What hath the Earth, that truly glorious is?

His opponent retorts that fame is at best local and ephemeral:

> How many thousands neuer heard the name
> Of Sidney, or of Spencer, or their Bookes?

The spread of "Schooles, Artes, Professions" is a disease marked by wrangling and competition. Scholars are retiring and unpractical:

> The worlds affaires require in managing,
> More Artes then those wherein you Clerkes proceede:
> Whilst timorous Knowledge stands considering,
> Audacious Ignorance hath done the deede.

He goes on to attack the flowery eloquence of scholars in a manner of which Bacon might partly approve:

> A manly stile, fitted to manly eares
> Best grees with wit. . . .

Answering these points, Musophilus admits that Fame is local, but says that the real reason for his following the Muses is to fulfil himself:

> This is the thing that I was borne to doo,
> This is my Scene, this part must I fulfil.

Learning needs no ambition; enough for it to explore the world and mankind. Its present state of disrepute is due to the overthrow of the "bound That parted learning and the laiety." The learned fall into strife and competition only through being robbed of their proper rewards,

> For if that learnings roomes to learned men
> Were as their heritage distributed,

they would be content, the universities would revive, and get on with their real work, which is to

> . . . set their bolde Plus Ultra farre without
> The pillers of those Axioms Age propounds:
> Discou'ring daily more and more about,
> In that immense and boundlesse Ocean
> Of Natures riches; neuer yet found out,
> Nor fore-clos'd, with the wit of any man.

The weapons of the mind are "States best strengths," for though some "unlettred practique" may occasionally succeed in politics, in times of difficulty "letred armes and armed letters" will come into their own.

> No state stands sure, but on the grounds of Right,
> Of Vertue, Knowledge, Iudgement to preserue,
> And all the powres of Learning requisite.

He ends by celebrating the power of words—with a special tribute to the genius of the English language.

In its warmth and sincerity, in its vindication of "privateness" on the one hand and of "letred armes" on the other, in its insistence that "the monuments of wit and learning are more durable than the monuments of power or of the hands," above all, in its view of the learned man as an explorer of Nature's riches, Musophilus worthily anticipates The Advancement of Learning. It surveys, however, only part of our field of inquiry, saying little about either the religious objections or the intellectual objections to which we must now turn.

Many of these "errors . . . which have intervened amongst the studies themselves of the Learned" belong strictly to philosophy, and have been frequently treated, so they need no attention in a study which deals only with the less formal and more literary anticipations of the problems raised. In approaching these questions Bacon was not so much defending learning against its traducers as admitting faults which he wished to see eliminated, and anticipating generally some of the more particular remarks of the Second Book.

His attack on "delicate learning"—on Ciceronianism, copia, "when men study words and not matter," has recently been related by American scholars to a contemporary Senecan fashion and to a cult of "Attic" style; the evidence brought by M. Croll[12] and G. Williamson[13] places Bacon well in the vanguard of a most important movement in English prose, yet proves him no isolated forerunner. Similarly his attack on "vain matter" as illustrated in the Schoolmen, and on imposture and credulity as exemplified in "Alchemy, Natural Magic and Astrology" and the inordinate respect for Aristotle, had been anticipated by others. But though he met half-way such common objections as these, Bacon did not consider in this part of his book the frontal assault made upon learning by contemporary sceptics who denied the intellectual validity of human knowledge. This assault was made by men at court with whom Bacon was well acquainted; his answer is implicit.

The revival of philosophic scepticism in the sixteenth century owed much to Cornelius Agrippa's De Vanitate et Incertitudine Scientiarum atque Excellentia Verbi Dei Declamatio (1530), which attacked those who idolized Aristotle, Boethius, and Aquinas in 102 chapters of stinging mockery, some in the manner of Erasmus's Praise of Folly, some serious in their logic, some in a strong religious vein. Surveying all the sciences and arts, Agrippa argued from the limitations of the human body and mind as instruments of science, from the diversity of opinions in all matters of inquiry, and from the evils connected with all human activities, that knowledge is defective and futile, and concluded by urging his readers to seek only the Word of God. The treatise, translated into English in 1569, was widely read, and had much more influence on Bacon's predecessors than Sanchez's Quod Nihil Scitur (1581) and Montaigne's Essais. Hence Nashe in Pierce Pennilesse His Supplication to the Divell (1592) took it as the type of foolish attack on learning, calling it

> a Treatise that I haue seene in dispraise of learning, where he saith, it is a corrupter of the simple, the schoolemaster of sin, the storehouse of treacherie . . . how studie doth effeminate a man, dim his sight, weaken his braine, and ingender a thousand diseases. Small learning would serue to confute so manifest a scandale, and I imagine all men like my selfe so vnmouablie resolued of the excellencie thereof, that I will not by the vnderpropping of confutation seeme to giue the idle witted aduersarie so much encouragement as hee should surmize his superficiall arguments had shaken the foundation of it: against which hee could neuer haue lifted his penne, if her selfe had not helpt him to hurte her selfe.

Nashe mentioned only the moral and social objections, ignoring in contemptuous silence the arguments Agrippa took from Sextus Empiricus and earlier sceptics. But these were current at court as Raleigh's treatise The Sceptic shows, in which, beginning with the idea that the sense-impressions of animals and men differ according to bodily structure, he suggests that reason and other mental activities may be no more absolute. The train of thought might lead to complete scepticism. Solipsism, however, was not the leading motif of Raleigh's creed, for although he was an "atheist" according to Nashe's definition and in popular fancy, he was passionately devoted to learning, a leader in "The School of Night," and an intimate of Harriot the mathematician. While he always remembered the frailty of man, his final belief was in "double truth": "We have sense and feeling of corporal things, and of eternal grace but by revelation"; but he gave reason a much wider field than Bacon, until it is difficult to see where he thought the work of reason should end and reliance on faith begin. He seems to have had no coherent philosophy, and it is difficult to take The Sceptic very seriously. That Bacon had similar arguments of the "Pironicks" in mind, however, is proved by his several references to the "deceits" of the senses, which he considered "very sufficient to certify and report truth, though not always immediately," and to "the weakness of the intellectual powers and . . . manner of collecting and concluding upon the reports of the senses," which weakness it was his hope to rectify by his Method.

Recent work on "The School of Night" makes it unnecessary to do more than mention the passion for learning which burned in Raleigh's friends.[14] Chapman was of all Elizabethan poets the most truculent and persistent in his attacks on "Barbarism," as witness not only his preface to The Shadow of Night (1594), but his poem To M. Harriots (1598), and the long proof, in The Teares of Peace (1609), that learning makes man in God's Image by teaching man

> To give the soul her empire, and so reach
> The rule of all the body's mutinous realm.

The knowledge which Chapman sought was ethical and esoteric. If Raleigh saw the limitations of the mind, yet worshipped reason, Chapman preached the validity of "inspiration," of an intuitive contemplation above reason by which man might escape from the night of the world's confusion to the "mystical night" of union with God.

Into such spheres Bacon could not follow Chapman. He had just a little more in common with Northumberland. The Wizard

Earl was a lover of the arts, himself an experimentalist, and patron of Harriot from 1597 to 1619. An essay cited by Miss F. A. Yates shows him setting the pursuit of learning even above the ties of love, seeing in it

> Myndes quiet, sowles felicitie, resolution of future state, wonderinge at nothinge, Inseeinge into all, iudiciall aboue ordenary, . . . good deedes in abundance, honored of the most, embracing goodnes for goodnes sake.[15]

Bacon knew Percy, though not intimately, in 1603, for he appealed for his help at Court when the Queen was dying, chiefly on the ground

> that your great capacity and love towards studies and contemplations of an higher and worthier nature than popular . . . is to me a great and chief motive to draw my affection and admiration to you (X, 58).

Later, in 1608, when Percy and Raleigh, in the Tower, were turning their prison into a research laboratory, Bacon thought of them as potential investigators for his Instauratio Magna; a jotting in his Commentarius Solutus suggests "the setting on w(ork) my l(ord) of North(umberland), and Ralegh, and therefore Haryott, themselves being already incline to experiments."

But it is clear that he thought of them only as experimenters, not as thinkers. In his ideas he was at once more and less daring than they; less daring in his expressed attitude to religion, more daring in his proposals for a general reorientation of all science. Percy and Raleigh were dilettanti of talent; he was a systematic philosopher. With the transcendental aspirations of their school he had nothing in common; and in The Advancement he showed his disapproval of the alchemy and the hermetic notions in which they dabbled.

It must also be remembered that from 1589 until the abortive rising, Bacon was a member of the Essex faction. His attitude to learning from first to last was much closer to that of other members of his group than to that of " The School of Night," as can quite briefly be shown. Essex himself, though "the fittest instrument to do good to the state," well read, generous to intelligence in others, was no speculative dabbler, but a man of moods and gestures who delighted to think of himself as a soldier, a statesman, or a religious solitary. When he sought retirement it was to sulk and pine, not to philosophize. Two contradictory ideals seem to have influenced him and his friends, "Magnificence" and renunciatory Puritanism. Neither of these led to a passion for learning as an end in itself, and it is a striking fact that of the two of his friends who wrote formal treatises on learning, one, Fulke Greville, took a Puritan view, while both Greville and Bacon emphasized its practical aims. According to Miss Yates, other members of the circle took up a more strictly "villanist" attitude during the rivalry with Raleigh, while Shakespeare's Love's Labour's Lost must be regarded as a move in the controversy.

"Shakespeare's interest was in the general theme of active versus contemplative living" (Bradbrook). Hence we find Berowne declaring:

> Small have continual plodders ever won
> Save base authority from others' books.
> These earthly godfathers of heaven's lights
> That give a name to every fixed star,
> Have no more profit of their shining lights
> Than those that walk, and wot not what they are.
> Too much to know, is to know naught but fame;
> And every godfather can give a name.[16]

To which attack on bookishness and astronomy the king replies, like Nashe to Agrippa: "How well he's read, to reason against reading!"

Berowne, however, is no barbarian. His contempt is for the fanaticism of learning, the academic blindness which leads men to take means for ends, and to abandon the world, love, responsibility, in a selfish pursuit of barren ideas.

> Learning is but an adjunct to ourself

he says, and sets knowledge of life above knowledge of books. This is not to flout learning altogether, but to set it in its place as a servant of humanity. So Shakespeare mocks the intellectual arrogance, the pretended asceticism, the transcendentalism of "The School of Night." I incline to believe that Bacon did the same.

The speeches of the six counsellors in Gesta Grayorum (1594–5) were almost certainly written by Bacon. The first urges the

Prince of Purpoole to war, the second to study the secrets of nature, the third to build himself great monuments, the fourth to study statecraft, the fifth to seek virtue, and the sixth to indulge in pastimes and sports. Each speech is a little study in special pleading, but though the second is remarkable for the practical proposals—a library, a botanical and zoological garden, a museum of machines, and a chemical laboratory—the sixth, as befitted the occasion, gained the day. The whole conception was playful, and I do not see in any part of the relationship between _Gesta Grayorum_ and _Love's Labour's Lost_ "a reflection of some friendly crossing of swords between the two greatest wits of the age, Shakespeare and Bacon" (Yates). Bacon's _Device on the Queen's Day_ in November 1595 suggests that if they drew swords at all it was in the same cause.

In this entertainment a Knight, played by Essex, was tempted by "an old Hermit, a Secretary of State, a brave Soldier," all messengers of Self-love, to leave the love of his mistress (the Queen) for the activities they represented. The Hermit preached Contemplation:

> Let thy master, Squire, offer his services to the Muses. It is long since they received any to their Court. . . . The gardens of love wherein he now playeth himself are fresh today and fading tomorrow, as the sun comforts them or is turned from them. But the gardens of the Muses keep the privilege of the Golden Age: they ever flourish and are in league with time. The monuments of wit survive the monuments of power; the verses of a poet endure without a syllable lost, while states and empires pass many periods . . . that hill of the Muses is above tempests, always clear and calm; a hill of the goodliest discovery that Man can have, being a prospect upon all the errors and wanderings of the present and former times. . . . So that if he will indeed lead _vitam vitalem_, a life that unites safety and dignity, pleasure and merit; if he will win admiration without envy; if he will be in the feast and not in the throng, in the light and not in the heat; let him embrace the life of study and contemplation (VIII, 378–80).

As Abbott saw, "Contrasted with the first passionate _Praise of Knowledge_ written in 1592, the _Praise of Contemplation_ in 1595 seems cold indeed." It is cold, too, as compared with the spirited fancy of Gesta Grayorum. I think the reason for this was probably that Bacon was writing on a different theme in this Device, and with more than a touch of satire. The object of knowledge as praised in 1592 was "the sovereignty of man"; in Gesta Grayorum, "the conquest of the works of nature." Here it was the "contemplation," the selfish enjoyment, of the dilettante School of Night. The Hermit spoke in a style reminiscent of Northumberland's essay; in rejecting his counsel Essex was made to reject the ideals of Raleigh and Percy, and with a trace of scepticism not unlike Raleigh's in The Sceptic:

> You, Father, that pretend to truth and knowledge, how are you assured that you adore not vain chimeras and imaginations? that in your high prospect, when you think men wander up and down, that they stand not indeed still in their places, and it is some smoke or cloud between you and them which moveth, or else the dazzling of your own eyes? Have not many which take themselves to be inward counsellors with Nature, proved but idle believers, that told us tales which were no such matter?

That the Device was believed by spectators to be a skit on members of the court is proved by the letter in which Rowland White described it to Sir Robert Sidney:

> The world makes many untrue constructions of these speeches, comparing the Hermit and the Secretary to two of the Lords, and the Soldier to Sir Roger Williams. . . .[17]

Were all the "constructions" untrue? Was the Hermit Northumberland? We cannot tell; but it is clear that in refusing to abandon love for illusions the Knight (Essex) was not rejecting learning as Bacon conceived it. The truths which the New Method was to discover were to have a sounder basis than "heavenly meditation." They would be practical in their scope and serve the good of humanity. On this he continually insisted, and it is interesting to note that in summarizing the value of moral philosophy in The Advancement he said first that

> it decideth the question touching the preferment of the Contemplative or active life, and decideth it against

> Aristotle. For all the reasons which he bringeth for the Contemplative are private, and respecting the pleasure and dignity of a man's self. . . . But men must know, that in this Theatre of Man's life it is reserved only for God and Angels to be lookers on. . . . But for contemplation which should be finished in itself, without casting beams upon society, assuredly Divinity knoweth it not (III, 421).

In its estimation of the social needs of ordinary human nature The Advancement carried on the ideals of the Essex group. It may indeed be regarded as in some measure an aftermath of the debate on life and learning in which the two factions at court took part. But it is so much more—as even our brief inquiry into the background of its preliminary ideas shows—that we might with more justice call that controversy a preparation for The Advancement. For here, taking the current arguments and prejudices against the study which was the better part of his life, and answering them in his strain of inspired common sense, Bacon built a rampart for true learning against which the little forces of later opponents—Greville in his Treatie, Denham in his Progress of Learning, Rochester in his Satyr against Mankind—broke in vain.

NOTES

1 Edward Wollay, A Plaine Pathway to Perfect Rest.

2 Cælica, 97.

3 Ibid., 63.

4 Cælica, 88.

5 Ibid., 66.

6 I have dealt with this important work, which gives an almost complete summary of the various objections to learning, in my edition of Greville (2 vols., 1939).

7 Cf. ch. 24, p. 514.

8 Cf. J. M. Robertson, A Short History of Free Thought, 3rd ed., 1915.

9 Works, ed. McKerrow, ii. 114 f.

10 A Treatise of the Nature of God, 1599, p. 111.

11 Cf. F. S. Boas, University Drama in the Tudor Age, 1914, ch. xiii.

12 Cf. Studies in Philology, xviii; Schelling Anniversary Papers, 1923; P.M.L.A. xxxix; Studies in English Philology, 1929 [now collected under the title Style, Rhetoric, Rhythm, ed. J. M. Patrick, et.al. (Princeton, 1966)–Ed.].

13 Cf. "Senecan Style in the Seventeenth Century," Philological Quarterly, xv, Oct. 1936 [and The Senecan Amble (London, 1951)–Ed.].

14 Cf. F. A. Yates, A Study of Love's Labour's Lost, Camb. 1936; M. C. Bradbrook, The School of Night, Camb. 1936. Two very stimulating books. [See also Hiram Haydn, The Counter-Renaissance (New York, 1950) and E. A. Strathmann, Sir Walter Raleigh: A Study in Elizabethan Skepticism (New York, 1951)—Ed.].

15 A Study of Love's Labour's Lost, chap. vii and appendix iii.

16 Love's Labour's Lost, I. i. 92 ff.

17 Sidney Papers, i. 362.

FRANCIS BACON'S PHILOSOPHY OF SCIENCE

Mary Hesse

Bacon wrote widely on matters of history, law, politics, and morals, but it is his design for a new science which is best known and has remained most influential, especially as it is contained in his *Advancement of Learning* of 1605 (reissued in an enlarged Latin version, the *De Augmentis Scientiarum*, in 1623) and his *Novum Organum* of 1620. Much of equal philosophical interest is, however, to be found in the shorter, and in some cases fragmentary, works.

The principal philosophical works, in probable chronological order, are as follows:

1603	*Valerius Terminus* (published 1734).
1605	*The Advancement of Learning.*
1608 (?)	*Inquisitio Legitima de Motu* (published 1653).
(?)	*Cogitationes de Natura Rerum.*
1609	*De Sapientia Veterum.*
1612	*Descriptio Globi Intellectus*, and *Thema Coeli* (published 1653).
before 1620	*De Principiis atque Originibus* (published 1653).
1620	*Novum Organum*, and *Parasceve.*
1622	*Historia Naturalis et Experimentalis*, to include:
	Historia Ventorum.
	Abecedarium Naturae (fragment published 1679).
	Historia Densi et Rari (published 1658).
	Historia Sulphuris, Mercurii, et Salis (preface only).
	Historia Vitae et Mortis (published 1623).
1623	*De Augmentis Scientiarum.*
	Sylva Sylvarum (published 1627).

Reprinted from *A Critical History of Western Philosophy*, ed. D. J. O'Connor (Macmillan and Co., New York, 1964), pp. 141–52, by permission of the author and the publisher.

FRANCIS BACON'S PHILOSOPHY OF SCIENCE

His projected life-work was the Great Instauration, which was to lay the foundations of the sciences entirely anew, sweeping away all received notions, returning to a fresh examination of particulars and proceeding from them by an infallible method to axioms of greater and greater generality, and then descending by deduction to new particulars and useful operations upon matter. The work was to correct on the one hand the excessive rationalism of the ancient philosophers, who leaped straight from particulars to ill-founded general axioms and then reasoned only by the syllogism, and on the other hand it was to correct the unregulated empiricism of the alchemists and natural magicians, who wasted their time in unfruitful experimenting, and lit upon true discoveries only by accident. Bacon, by his method of inducing general axioms, intends to establish "a true and lawful marriage between the empirical and the rational faculty" (IV, 19, 25, 81, 92, 96, 321, 413; VI, 710).

This statement of his aim, occurring as it does near the beginning of the Novum Organum, should put us on guard against a frequent misinterpretation of Bacon as a mere fact-collector. The impression that this is the case can be derived from a hasty glance at his works, for a large proportion of these is devoted to unordered accounts of experiments and observations of all kinds and all degrees of reliability. But Bacon did not intend that these should be more than the materials on which his method was to work. The Instauration was to consist of six parts, of which the collection of "Phenomena of the Universe or a Natural and Experimental History" was only one, and of which three were hardly begun by Bacon at all. We may conjecture, however, that even had Bacon lived ten years longer, been less encumbered by affairs of state, and received more enthusiastic cooperation in his projects, we should not know much more of the way his method was intended to work than can now be gathered from his anticipatory examples.

The six parts of the Instauration were to be:

1. The Classification of the Sciences.
2. Directions concerning the Interpretation of Nature, that is, the new inductive logic.
3. The Phenomena of the Universe, or natural history.
4. The Ladder of the Intellect, that is, examples of the application of the method in climbing from phenomena up the ladder of axioms to the "summary law of nature."

5. Anticipations of the New Philosophy, that is, tentative generalizations which Bacon considers of sufficient interest and importance to justify him in leaping ahead of the inductive method.
And,
6. The New Philosophy or Active Science, which will exhibit the whole result of induction in an ordered system of axioms. If men will apply themselves to his method, Bacon thinks that this system will be the result of only a few years' work, but for himself he confesses "the completion of this last part is a thing both above my strength and beyond my hopes" (IV, 22, 32, 102, 252).

Classification of the Sciences: De Augmentis

The Plan of the Instauration and its second part, the Novum Organum, were published in 1620, and for its first part, Bacon made do with a revised version of his Advancement of Learning put into Latin and published in 1623. The book contains much that relates to other parts of the Instauration, but all that need concern us at this point are Bacon's views on the proper scope of natural philosophy (IV, 336).

The Third Book of De Augmentis opens with the familiar distinction between knowledge inspired by divine revelation and knowledge arising from the senses. The latter constitutes philosophy, which is again divided into that concerning God (natural theology), that concerning Nature, and that concerning Man, and common to all these is the Philosophia Prima to which belong general logical axioms such as "things which are equal to the same thing are equal to one another."

Natural theology is only a rudimentary knowledge of God derived from his creatures. It is sufficient to establish his existence, providence, goodness, and some other properties, but not the mysteries of faith, which are obtained from revelation alone. Nature, however, Bacon says elsewhere, bears the signatures of God, and it is these, the true forms of things, which are the goal of natural philosophy, and not the false images imposed on things by man's mind (IV, 33, 51, 110, 341).

Natural philosophy is divided into the speculative and the operative. Here appears one of Bacon's major themes: that the object of natural philosophy is not mere speculative argument but also production of useful works to restore to man that dominion over nature which he lost at the Fall. However, just as due balance must be preserved between the rational and the empirical in developing the inductive method, so here there must be balance between "light" and "fruit." Without "experiments of light" to enable true axioms to be induced, the deductive descent to new works will be limited and imperfect, and without the intention to produce "experiments of fruit" the axioms will not be true reflections of things (IV, 17, 32, 47, 71, 95, 421).

There are two branches of speculative philosophy, the physical and the metaphysical, and two corresponding branches of the operative philosophy, namely the applications of these, which Bacon calls mechanics and magic. He makes the distinction between physics and metaphysics in the language of the Aristotelian causes: physics handles the material and efficient, and metaphysics the formal and final causes; but these terms are not to be understood in their Aristotelian senses, for Bacon regards these as superficial and unprofitable. Matter, for Bacon, is not mere potentiality and formlessness, but has its own existence and primary nature (V, 466), and his material and efficient causes are connected with the natural history of processes rather than with their philosophy, that is, with the accidental ways in which things come into being or are brought about, rather than with their fundamental nature.[1] Form, again, is not to be understood either in the Platonic sense of an ultimately unknowable idea abstracted from matter, nor in the Aristotelian sense of a species which is often merely apparent and has been hastily distinguished from other phenomena. A form is rather a "true specific difference, or nature-engendering nature, or source of its emanation," the discovery of which for all phenomena is the chief end of knowledge (IV, 66, 75, 119, 360; III, 238). We shall discuss Bacon's forms in more detail at a later stage. Final causes, although included in metaphysics in this classification, are in fact not part of Bacon's natural philosophy but of his natural theology. This is because to assign purposes to phenomena is comparatively easy, but it is anthropocentric and distracts the mind from the search for physical causes, which is the true end of natural philosophy. For physical causes enable us to discover a system of axioms from which new works can be derived, and final causes produce no works: "the research into Final Causes, like a virgin dedicated to God, is barren and produces nothing." But the virgin is dedicated to God, that is to say, Bacon does not reject all research into final causes, for he holds that by reflection upon them some of the attributes of God may be discovered. But his elimination of final causes from natural philosophy marks a stage in the transformation of the idea of causal explanation in science: true explanation is not henceforward to be an answer to the question "What for?" however satisfying to the mind such an answer may be, but is rather to be given in terms of consequences of antecedent physical events or conditions (IV, 57, 363, 365).

The real distinction between physics and metaphysics for Bacon is the distinction between the lower and higher axioms of the inductive ladder. Physics stands between phenomena and the primary forms, that is, between natural history and metaphysics, and is concerned with causes which are more closely tied to particular phenomena and therefore more specific and more variable. It therefore deals with the "common and ordinary course of nature," while metaphysics deals with "her eternal and fundamental laws" (IV, 126, 347).

Finally in Bacon's classification come the sciences of man. Here only two points can be noticed as particularly relevant to his philosophy of nature. The first is his doctrine of the dual nature of the human soul, which he divides into the rational and the irrational or sensible. The distinction clearly stems from Aristotle, but for Bacon the division between higher and lower parts of the soul is more radical, for the rational soul is understood in theological terms as that breathed into man by God, knowledge of which is part of revealed theology, while the sensible soul or spirit which man shares with the beasts is a corporeal substance, a "breath," which is the instrument of the rational soul and the physical cause of the motion of the human body.[2] How far this commits Bacon to a mechanical theory of the "animal spirits" similar to that of Descartes, we shall consider when we come to Bacon's views on the primary virtues of matter. The second point about the sciences of man which should be noticed is that Bacon explicitly intends his inductive method to apply to them as well as to the sciences of nature: "I form a history and tables of discovery for anger, fear, shame, and the like; for matters political; and again for the mental operations of memory, composition and division, judgment and the rest; not less than for heat and cold, or light, or vegetation, or the like" (IV, 112). He fulfils his promise to some extent in regard to the history of these things, but, not surprisingly, not in regard to their inductive theory.

The Interpretation of Nature: Novum Organum

We now come to what Bacon himself regarded as the key to the whole project—the new method of induction. He claims that his method will lead to indubitable conclusions "as if by machinery," and believes that the unfallen human mind would naturally work in this way if it were not corrupted by "Idols" or false images which cause men to see everything in relation to themselves instead of in true perspective in relation to the universe. The intellect is to be purged by the practice of true induction,* but the idols should also be pointed out explicitly, "for the doctrine of Idols is to the Interpretation of Nature what the doctrine of the refutation of Sophisms is to common Logic" (IV, 40, 54).

The idols are of four kinds. Idols of the tribe are those arising from the nature of human understanding itself, which is prone to impress its own ideas of order, reality, and importance, and its own preferences, upon nature, and to look rather for confirmations than possible refutations of its opinions. Further, the understanding is hindered by deficiencies of the senses, which take more account of what appears striking, and cannot detect the subtler changes of nature: "For the sense by itself is a thing infirm and erring; neither can instruments for enlarging or sharpening the senses do much; but all the truer kind of interpretation of nature is effected by instances and experiments fit and apposite; wherein the sense judges the experiment only, and the experiment the nature and thing itself" (IV, 58). Secondly, the idols of the cave are those which are peculiar to each man, and arise from his particular interests and preoccupations. Aristotle, for example, saw everything as subsidiary to his logic, and Gilbert to his investigations of the magnet. Thirdly, the idols of the market-place are those imposed by the deceptions of words, so that abstract names are reified, and equivocations are allowed to mislead. Finally,

---

* With regard to the sins of the intellect, Bacon is a Pelagian: the intellect is fallen, but by the exercise of Bacon's method it can recover itself, and Bacon himself performs for the senses "the office of a true priest" (IV, 20, 26). "For man by the fall fell at the same time from his state of innocency and from his dominion over creation. Both of these losses, however, can even in this life be in some part repaired; the former by religion and faith, the latter by arts and sciences" (IV, 247).

the idols of the theatre are those imposed by the received philosophical systems, which are based on common notions or superficial experiments or superstition. All this, says Bacon, must be purged and swept away. The mind is to be made into, what Locke was later to say it is naturally, a "tabula abrasa" (IV, 27; cf. IV, 103).

Thus, some of the idols which obstruct clear ideas of nature are due, not to wilful prejudice, but to the inevitable disabilities of human perception, and in order to overcome these and prepare an adequate natural history of phenomena, the senses must be helped. Again, the natural history when collected must be so ordered that the understanding can deal with it. But Bacon postpones discussion of these "ministrations" to the senses and the reason until he has expounded the method of induction itself (IV, 127). There follow the best-known passages of the Novum Organum, where Bacon illustrates his tables of presence, absence in proximity, and comparison by an investigation of the form of heat. The method of drawing up these tables depends on Bacon's view of forms: "The Form of a nature is such, that given the Form the nature infallibly follows. Therefore it is always present when the nature is present . . . absent when the nature is absent" (IV, 121). One must therefore first draw up a table of instances of presence of the nature under investigation, for example, heat. The natural and previously universal mistake at this point has been to make an induction by simple enumeration and jump immediately to the conclusion that the form of the nature is some other feature obviously present in all these instances, and henceforth to notice only such instances as confirm their co-presence, while overlooking instances in which the alleged form is present without the nature:

> And therefore it was a good answer that was made by one who when they showed him hanging in a temple a picture of those who had paid their vows as having escaped shipwreck, and would have him say whether he did not now acknowledge the power of the gods,— "Aye," asked he again, "but where are they painted that were drowned after their vows?" And such is the way of all superstition, whether in astrology, dreams, omens, divine judgments, or the like (IV, 56, 432).

It is essential therefore that the instances in the table of presence be otherwise as unlike each other as possible, so as to eliminate the largest possible number of natures which are not co-present, and also that one should deliberately look for negative as well as affirmative instances, that is, those in which the nature in question is absent. Since there is an endless number of these, the most important should be collected, and these are the ones which are most akin to the several instances of presence in all respects except the nature in question. In this way all those features which are present in both tables will be eliminated as possible forms of the nature. Bacon illustrates by comparing pairs of instances of presence and absence of heat, among which he lists:

Presence	Absence
Rays of the sun.	Rays of the moon and stars.
Flame.	Phosphorescence, electric sparks.
Boiling liquids.	Liquids in their natural state.

This method of pairing of instances suggests further investigations and experiments when the negative instances are not immediately obvious: thus, experiments would not be made at random, but in accordance with the requirements of the tables. Finally, one may draw up a table of comparison of degrees of heat: "For since the Form of a thing is the very thing itself . . . it necessarily follows that no nature can be taken as the true form, unless it always decrease when the nature in question decreases, and in like manner always increase when the nature in question increases" (IV, 137).

The drawing up of the three tables is, however, only the beginning of the method: "After the rejection and exclusion has been duly made, there will remain at the bottom, all light opinions vanishing into smoke, a Form affirmative, solid and true and well defined. This is quickly said; but the way to come at it is winding and intricate. I will endeavour however not to overlook any of the points which may help us towards it" (IV, 146).

The first of these points is the "First Vintage" or first attempt at the interpretation of nature drawn from the tables. A brief survey of the tables for heat, for example, suggests as the form of heat "a motion, expansive, restrained and acting in its strife upon the smaller parts of bodies" (IV, 154). Bacon does not, however, make clear how this first vintage is to affect the subsequent steps of the enquiry. On the one hand, his whole position rests on a rejection of "anticipations" drawn too hastily from the data without due regard to the method of exclusions. On the other hand, he does intend to devote the fifth part of the Instauration to "The Forerunners; or Anticipations of the new philosophy," and in his unfinished investigations into "Winds," "Life and Death," and "Dense and Rare," he commits himself to some "provisional canons" or "imperfect axioms" which may be "useful, if not altogether true" (V, 136, 196, 320, 398). More surprisingly, in De Augmentis (IV, 423), after quoting Plato's "whosoever seeks a thing, knows that which he seeks for in a general notion; else how shall he know it when he has found it?" Bacon adds "and therefore the fuller and more certain our anticipation is, the more direct and compendious is our search."* But he nowhere gives any indication in practice that he realized how far anticipation or hypothesis must be allowed to guide further enquiry. This is the most notable difference between his method and the practice of his seventeenth-century successors such as Boyle and Hooke who, while paying their respects to him, nevertheless use hypotheses with considerable freedom.

The second step in the interpretation of the tables is consideration of "prerogative instances" (IV, 155), that is, those instances which are to be enquired into first as the most likely to hasten the process of induction. They include experiments to aid the senses in discerning subtle and hidden processes, aids to the intellect in making definite and speedy exclusions, and aids to practical operations. Among them occur the celebrated Instantiae Crucis (Instances of the Finger-Post) (IV, 180), which separate two natures otherwise found together with the nature in question, and which therefore decide which of the two is its form and which is separable from it. Thus, the prerogative instances, and other aids to the process of induction which Bacon mentions but does not expound, give suggestions for drawing up the tables in the most economical way. They allow the great mass of natural data to be reduced to a "Designed History": "Let them but remember this and they will find out for themselves the method in which the history should be composed. For the end rules the method," and "we can command our questions

---

* But it is significant that although Bacon allows this sentence from The Advancement of Learning to stand, he has inserted the words "and more certain" (cf. III, 391). He seems to become more and not less doubtful of the value of anticipation as his work proceeds.

though we cannot command the natures of things" (IV, 254, 427; V, 135, 136, 210). Bacon gives a place to the exercise of judgment at least in shortening the work, but it is to be judgment directed by the requirements of his method, not judgment which relies on inspired guesses at hypotheses. Once the method is learned, therefore, men's wits are leveled; anyone can do science (IV, 109).

Bacon's faith in the infallibility of the method seems to rest on four assumptions:

1. It presupposes that nature is in some sense finite. Bacon remarks that whereas the number of particulars in the universe is very large and perhaps infinite, the number of species or abstract natures or forms of things is few. The same point is made by means of illustration in *Novum Organum* when gold is regarded as "a troop or collection of simple natures." It is yellow, has a certain weight, is malleable, not volatile, not inflammable, "and so on for the other natures which meet in gold." Hence, if anyone knows the forms of these natures and methods for inducing them in some body, that body will be transformed into gold. "For if a man can make a metal that hath all these properties, let men dispute whether it be gold or no" (IV, 122, 126, 361; V, 209, 426, 512).
2. If it be granted that the number of "simple natures" involved in any body or process is finite, it is necessary, in order to draw conclusive inductions from the tables, that all the simple natures should be enumerated. If there appear to be, for example, several natures in common in the instances of presence of heat, any of which may be its form, the method of exclusions by negative instances presupposes that this list of common natures is exhaustive.
3. The method also presupposes that it is possible to eliminate all natures not involved in the form either by finding appropriate negative instances existing naturally, or by constructing experiments to demonstrate them. Hence Bacon insists on the importance of artificial experiment: nature must usually be put to the question, not allowed to run her ordinary course

(IV, 29, 263). But even so there can be no guarantee that the appropriate experiment will always be practically possible.

4. Bacon also assumes a one-to-one correspondence between the form and the nature under investigation: "the Form of a thing is the very thing itself, and the thing differs from the form no otherwise than as the apparent differs from the real or the external from the internal, or the thing in reference to man from the thing in reference to the universe." The form is convertible with the thing; hence when Bacon draws from his tables for heat the "form or true definition of heat," that "Heat is a motion, expansive, restrained, and acting in its strife upon the smaller parts of bodies," he means "not that heat generates motion or that motion generates heat . . . but that Heat itself, or the *quid ipsum* of Heat, is Motion and nothing else" (IV, 121, 137, 150, 154; III, 236).

If these four conditions are fulfilled, then what Bacon is describing is a purely deductive argument, based on experimental rejection of the consequents of all but one of a limited number of possibilities. Bacon claims originality for this part of the method only in the sense that no one had previously recommended or practiced the systematic investigation of negative instances, although Plato had remarked on its logical form (IV, 98, 164).

Forms and the Ladder of Axioms

Before considering what may have led Bacon to assume with very little argument that the conditions presupposed by his method are satisfied in nature, it is necessary to look more closely at what he means by "Forms." We have seen that the word is not used in the Platonic or Aristotelian senses; indeed, Bacon apologizes for using it at all: "a name which I the rather adopt because it has grown into use and become familiar." His most explicit definition is as follows: "The true Form is such that it deduces the given nature from some source of being which is inherent in more natures, and prior in the natural order of things . . . to the Form itself. For a true and perfect axiom of knowledge then the direction and precept will be that another nature be discovered which is convertible with the given *nature, and yet is a limitation of a prior nature, as of a true and real genus*" (IV, 120, 121).

Bacon's clearest example of this process is the problem of finding the form of whiteness. This occurs in an early work, *Valerius Terminus*, but the result there arrived at is ratified in *Novum Organum* and *De Augmentis* (IV, 157, 361; III, 236). In *Valerius Terminus* the stress is on the operations required to produce whiteness rather than upon the discovery of forms, and the terminology used is correspondingly different. Nevertheless, when Bacon speaks of the "freeing of direction," that is, finding a recipe for whiteness which is independent of particular initial materials or means, he is clearly foreshadowing the search for forms as defined in the passage just quoted. From the observation of instances in which air and water mixed together produce whiteness (foam and snow), Bacon rises to greater generality by discarding at each step the particular accompaniments of air and water, such as colorlessness and transparency, and finally reaches, in the "sixth direction" (which he admits he has not fully proved by induction), the statement that "all bodies or parts of bodies which are unequal equally, that is in a simple proportion, do represent whiteness." He adds the further axioms that "absolute equality produceth transparence, inequality in simple order or proportion produceth all other colours, and absolute or orderless inequality produceth blackness" (III, 237).

We may represent this ladder of axioms symbolically as follows. The most general nature from which the rest can be derived is the property of a body of having its small parts in a certain ratio of size. Let this property be represented by $\underline{A}$. It is then asserted that $\underline{A}$ is the form of color (including transparency). Instances of $\underline{A}$ can be further specified in four ways: as having their small parts equal ($\underline{Aa_1}$), in simple proportion ($\underline{Aa_2}$), in complex proportion ($\underline{Aa_3}$), and of random sizes ($\underline{Aa_4}$). Then we have:

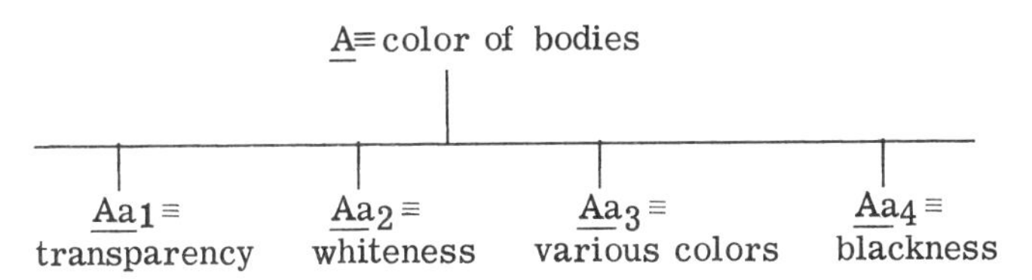

From $\underline{Aa_2}$ it is possible to descend the scale of axioms again to the original instances of whiteness by adding more specific determinations to Aa_2, until the particular recipe of mixing air and water is reached, and it is also possible to predict that any as yet unobserved instance which is a further specification of Aa_2 will also exhibit whiteness. Another way in which predictions may be made is by deduction from the relations between the four forms given. For example, it is clear that a mixture of two bodies which are separately instances of Aa_1, will fall under Aa_2, and hence will be white. Again, some instances of Aa_3 will approach Aa_1, since two numbers which are nearly equal are in complex proportion, but instances of Aa_2 and Aa_4 will never approach Aa_1, and hence Bacon concludes that of all colors, "whiteness and blackness are most incompatible with transparence." The ladder of axioms set out in this way therefore satisfies Bacon's demand that

> In establishing axioms by this kind of induction, we must also examine and try whether the axiom so established be framed to the measure of those particulars only from which it is derived, or whether it be larger and wider. And if it be larger and wider, we must observe whether by indicating to us new particulars it confirm that wideness and largeness as by a collateral security; that we may not either stick fast in things already known, or loosely grasp at shadows and abstract forms; not at things solid and realized in matter (IV, 98).

The ladder of axioms therefore appears to be constructed as follows: at each rung there is a convertible proposition which states that the form of a given nature is identical with a certain specification of a more general nature, and each of these propositions has been obtained by means of the inductive tables. We shall now consider some characteristics of the forms in more detail.

1. A form is not a cause in the sense of another nature merely found in constant conjunction with the given nature. Thus, Bacon's aim in using his inductive method is quite different from that of Mill, although Mill's methods of agreement and difference are based on the principles of Bacon's tables. But if Mill discovers from his methods that *A* causes *B*, for example that a certain fertilizer causes a good crop, this result is compatible with *A* having effects other than *B*, and with *B* being caused by something other than *A* in different circumstances. But if *A* is the *form* of *B*, then it *is B* under all circum-

stances and its effects are simply B's effects and no others (IV, 146).

2. A form is not an abstract conception, but a physical property or "nature." This follows from the fact that the form has come up the ladder of axioms by appearing in tables of presence with the nature under investigation and not appearing in its tables of absence. A question arises here about "hidden" or practically unobservable forms, for example, subtle atomic processes. How are they to be elicited from tables of presence and absence? Bacon is fully aware that detailed knowledge of nature will involve hidden and subtle processes (IV, 124, 204; II, 380; V, 419, 492) and partly aware of the problem they present, for some of his prerogative instances direct attention to the need for "aids to the senses" such as microscopes and telescopes, and he also admits a certain amount of reasoning from observed to unobserved natures, as for example when the motion which is the form of heat is said to be motion of small (not directly observable) particles. The arguments by which he arrives at this specification of the form of heat are not inductive after his own recipe, but hypothetical and analogical; but it must be remembered that they are only arguments leading to the first vintage, and elsewhere Bacon warns against injudicious use of the method of analogy for eliciting "things not directly perceptible" (IV, 164, 192, 202). It cannot be said that he deals adequately with the difficulty inherent in explanations in terms of hidden natures, but given the presuppositions of his method it is impossible to see how he could have done better, for hidden natures demand hypothetical arguments.

3. A form is not a mere mathematical description of the phenomenal nature in question but must get behind this to its real cause. There are two outstanding examples of Bacon's application of this principle, in his discussions of astronomy and of optics. In criticizing both Ptolemy and Copernicus he remarks, "I am attempting a far greater work: for it is not merely calculations or predictions that I aim at, but philosophy: such a philosophy I mean as may inform the human understanding, not only of the motion of the heavenly bodies and the period of that motion, but likewise of their substance, various qualities, powers, and influences . . . what is found in nature herself, and is actually and really true" (V, 511; cf. V, 556). And again with regard to the form of light: "Neither in perspective nor otherwise has any inquiry been made about Light which is of any value. The radiations of it are handled, not the origins. But it is the placing of perspective among the mathematics that has caused

this defect . . . for thus a premature departure has been made from Physics" (IV, 403). In other words, Bacon would be satisfied with a wave or corpuscular theory of light, but not with mere geometrical optics.

His attitude to mathematics is not always so negative, but he considers that its proper place is not among the lower axioms, which should be concerned with concretes; it is, rather, an essential constituent of higher axioms which deal with generalities, for "of all natural forms . . . Quantity is the most abstracted and separable from matter." And the nearer an investigation approaches to simple natures "the easier and plainer will everything become. . . . And inquiries into nature have the best result, when they begin with physics and end in mathematics" (IV, 93, 126, 206, 369). How quantity might enter the ladder of axioms and facilitate a descent to new particulars is indicated in the example of whiteness, but Bacon gives no further such examples of the use of mathematics in his later works.

4. The form of a given nature is not only to be a specification of a nature which is more general in the sense of being exhibited in more particulars; it is also to be prior, that is, to reflect the nature of things in relation to the universe and not in relation to man. In Bacon's comments on the direction for whiteness he sees this as a condition ensuring that the directions will actually enable the nature in question to be produced by operations: "To make a stone bright or to make it smooth it is a good direction to say, make it even; but to make a stone even it is no good direction to say, make it bright or make it smooth; for . . . evenness is the disposition of the stone in itself, but smooth is to the hand and bright to the eye" (III, 240).

This is one of Bacon's clearest statements of a distinction between primary and secondary qualities, and of the view that forms must be found among the primary qualities. But his notion of a primary quality is here confused with that of a quality which can most easily be induced in a body by man. The two notions are certainly not identical, for it might be easier, for example, to heat a body by bringing it in contact with another hot body rather than by directly putting its small parts into motion, and in Novum Organum Bacon makes this distinction between the form of heat and the method of inducing heat. He does not, however, enlarge on his early distinction between primary and secondary qualities, and it must be assumed that he thought that they could only be identified as a result of the application of his method, and not as its starting point. It does at least follow from the requirements of the method that primary qualities have the property of relative independence of the accidental circumstances under which they are perceived. This is only a special case of the rule that the form of a given nature is to refer to another nature more general than that under investigation. Thus, Bacon distinguishes sensible heat from heat itself; the same tepid water may feel hot to the cold hand and cold to the hot hand, but these two instances do not appear in the tables of presence and absence of heat respectively, but in the table of degrees of heat. The form is elicited independently of them, and then used to explain them: they are due to "the effect of heat on the animal spirits" (IV, 144, 150, 155). Whatever else Bacon means by the primary qualities which are candidates for forms, they must at least be among the qualities of which the senses give most consistent reports. His robust realism is untroubled by doubts about the status of even these qualities.

5. The character of Bacon's realism is further indicated by his references to forms as laws. It is not that forms or species have some existence apart from, or even embodied in, individuals, but that those individuals really act according to fixed laws: "For though in nature nothing really exists beside individual bodies, performing pure individual acts according to a fixed law, yet in philosophy this very law, and the investigation, discovery and explanation of it, is the foundation as well of knowledge as of operation. And it is this law, with its clauses, that I mean when I speak of Forms" (IV, 120; cf. IV, 58, 146). The word "law" does not here connote a "correlation" of phenomena, for, as we have seen, mere correlations do not express forms; it has rather the older association with order imposed by the civil power: "the first congregations of matter; which like a general assembly of estates, doth give law to all bodies." In regard to these laws, Bacon is a moderate determinist: "If a man knew the conditions, affections, and processes of matter, he would certainly comprehend the sum and general issue (for I do not say that his knowledge would extend to the parts and singularities) of all things, past, present, and to come." Two conceptions of the source of this order seem to be involved. If we could comprehend the configurations of matter clearly and truly, as they really are in nature, their laws of action would become apparent to us, but the resulting order is also (as we know by faith) due to divine power. Bacon sees no incompatibility between seeing things as reflections

of divine purpose and seeking their natural causes, and leaves it an open question whether matter, once created with its original force, would in course of time have shaped itself into the existing configurations of things, even without specific design.[3]

6. One further feature of forms which Bacon assumes, at least in his discussion of whiteness, appears to lead to a serious inconsistency between the demands of the inductive method and the construction of a ladder of axioms by means of forms. The notion of the ladder requires that a form be understood as relative to the state of development of the ladder at any given moment. Bacon remarks, for example, that the "direction for whiteness" which he gives in terms of relative sizes of particles, is not yet completely "free," since it is tied to bodies, whereas a more general direction would refer to the medium through which whiteness is conveyed to the eye and to the act of sense itself. In other words, he conceives of extending the ladder of axioms upward to account for all sensible appearances of whiteness by including a wider range of particulars relating to the medium and the conditions of sensation. Thus, there seems to be nothing to prevent unfinished portions of a ladder being incorporated in a more general structure, until we reach Bacon's ideal of the "summary law of nature," the "cone and vertical point," which "produces all the variety of nature" (IV, 362; V, 463; VI, 730).

It therefore seems to be a reasonable interpretation of Bacon's intentions, and is indeed compatible with the subsequent development of science, that the forms identified with specific natures should change with every extension of the ladder of axioms based on instances of those natures. For if the ladder of axioms for color illustrated above were incorporated in a more general scale of which the summary form were B (where B might be wave-motion in the ether), then each axiom of the new ladder would show A identified with a certain specification of B, say Bb_1, and so the form of whiteness would now be Bb_1a_2. But remember how Bacon considers that the axiom "$Aa_2 \equiv$ whiteness" has been obtained. It is supposed to be derived deductively from the tables of discovery and this presupposes that Aa_2 is a simple nature, whereas it has now been found to be further analyzable as a specification of B. It seems that either the claim that induction is based on exhaustive enumeration of simple natures must be given up, and hence the claim to certainty of inductive conclusions, or no form can be discovered until the whole scheme of axioms is complete. To make matters worse, Bacon doubts whether the summary law of nature can ever be reached, and if this is so, the conditions of the method can never be fulfilled (Bacon admits that "no one can divide things truly who has not a full knowledge of their nature" (V, 210).) The only way out of the dilemma would appear to be some kind of classification of natures into grades or types appropriate to each rung of the ladder of axioms, so that at each stage an exhaustive enumeration could be given. Bacon makes some mention of primary, secondary, tertiary, etc. qualities, and of "Forms of the first class" (IV, 67, 361; V, 135), but it is not clear whether, or how, he meant to develop this classification, or even that he was aware of the dilemma to which it might have provided a solution in logic, although hardly in practice.

The notion of a ladder of axioms does not, however, depend on Bacon's untenable assumptions about his inductive method nor on his particular view of forms, and it is unfortunate that the greatest stress has been laid on these, and not on his vision of the deductive structure of the new science, in respect of which events have been kinder to him. In comparing his ladder of axioms with the subsequent hypothetico-deductive structure of theories, two points of similarity may be noticed. The first is the possibility of deducing new particulars, which depends, as we have seen, partly on logical or mathematical relations between the various forms. Bacon does not, however, develop this in detail, and he certainly underestimated the part that pure mathematical deduction would play in it. He is concerned not with the machinery of deduction, but with the identification of the forms with particular phenomena, and this is the second point of similarity with later theories. For, whatever may be the case more recently, it was certainly a requirement in the earlier stages of physics that theoretical explanations should be given in terms of models, initially mechanical models, and this involves identifying the properties of phenomena, for example heat, light, and sound, with a limited set of more general mechanical properties. Bacon's tables provide a systematic way of setting out the analogies which suggest the identification of heat with mechanical motion, and his "Consents and Dissents of Visibles and Audibles" suggest the comparison of the modes of transmission of light and of sound (II, 429). Where the tables proved scientifically useful, as in these two investigations, it was in virtue not of infallible inductions but of hypotheses suggested by the analogies they exhibited. It was a favorite pastime in the nineteenth century to criticize Bacon for not being a Galileo or a Newton, but this is somewhat beside the point, for neither Galileo nor Newton, in his Principia, was dealing with explanations of "secondary" phenomena in terms of mechanical models, and it is here if anywhere that Bacon's contribution lies.

Primary Matter and Its Qualities

The method of induction as Bacon presents it depends entirely on the possibility of identifying all the simple natures in a given instance: "Exclusion is evidently the rejection of simple natures: and if we do not yet possess sound and true notions of simple natures, how can the process of Exclusion be made accurate?" He promises to provide these sound and true notions by means of his aids to the understanding, but the prerogative instances are the first and only ones of these to be treated, and presumably Bacon intended to treat the important matter of simple natures later under the heading "*Limits of Investigation* or a Synopsis of all Natures in the Universe" (IV, 149, 155).

There is no doubt that Bacon remained uncertain what simple natures should go into this list. He attacks the superficial division of things into species of animals, plants, and minerals, and also the theory of four elements and the Aristotelian classification of change. He gives several lists of qualities, variously described as cardinal and universal virtues, elementary qualities, and configurations of matter, which almost always begin with "Dense and Rare" (a title which is "so general, that if it were fully drawn out it would anticipate many of the succeeding titles"), and go on through "Heavy and Light," "Hot and Cold," "Tangible and Pneumatic," to such apparently complex natures as organization and animation (IV, 29, 66, 356; V, 354, 425, 510, 555). It is never clear which, if any, of these natures are to be regarded as *simple*, and indeed, the term is in any case a misnomer, since, as we have seen according to the ladder of axioms, there can be only one, or at least only a few, irreducibly simple natures, namely those involved in the summary form of which all other natures are specifications. It is clear that if Bacon's method is to work at all there must be some way other than the method itself for anticipating, at least in general terms, what the simple natures or the summary forms are, since they are presupposed by the method. If the summary form is conceived, for example, in terms of Democritean atomism, the tables of presence and absence may be used to indicate what particular configurations and motions of atoms are co-present and co-absent with the given nature, as Bacon does in the cases of heat, "visibles and audibles," winds, and dense and rare. It is therefore important to consider the non-inductive arguments which led Bacon to anticipate some form of mechanism as the summary law of nature.

Of all the ancient philosophers whose works he considers shallow and hopes to supersede, Bacon speaks most highly of Democritus (IV, 58, 193; V, 419, 461; III, 228). But his views on the adequacy of atomism underwent considerable changes during the period of his philosophical writings; even in the early works he is by no means an orthodox atomist, and later he becomes convinced that atomism is false. It is convenient to take a work which apparently dates from his middle period, certainly before the *Novum Organum*, to indicate the progress of his views, since it is here that the most detailed arguments are to be found. The work is the *De Principiis et Originibus*, a revision of part of the *De Sapientia Veterum* of 1609, where Bacon had adopted the popular device of interpreting the ancient myths of the gods as allegories of cosmological and philosophical theories.

In *De Principiis* he rewrites and expands the fable of Cupid as it appears in the earlier work (V, 461; VI, 729). He takes Cupid to be a representation of the nature and virtues of primary matter. In the myth Cupid is said to be without parents, to be naked, to be an infant, to be blind, and to shoot arrows. Each of these properties Bacon takes as representative of the characteristics of primary matter; first, it and its motions are without natural cause, that is, without parents; secondly, Cupid's nakedness provides Bacon with an allegory in terms of which he comments on five views of the nature and properties of primary matter; and (in *De Sapientia Veterum* only), the other three properties represent respectively the changelessness of matter, the "blind necessity of fate" inherent in the primary motions of matter, and the fact that if atoms are placed in a void they must necessarily act at a distance, or otherwise no motion would take place.

It is to the second property that Bacon devotes most attention (V, 468). In the myth Cupid is said to be a "person" with attributes, and this already contradicts the Aristotelian view of matter as mere potentiality and formlessness. But Cupid is represented as naked rather than clothed, and this Bacon takes as an allegory of atomism, whose adherents make "the principle of things one in substance, and that fixed and invariable; but deduce the diversity of beings from the different magnitudes, configurations, and positions of that same principle." There are other views which, as it were, represent

Cupid as clothed; those of the monists, who assert that there is one principle and all things consist of its variations, of the pluralists, who set up many principles, and of those who set up an infinity of (or at least very many) specific principles and thus have no need for any device to account for the multiplicity of things. Of the monists Bacon mentions Thales, Anaximenes, and Heraclitus, who all attribute to primary matter a form which is "substantially homogeneous with the form of . . . the secondary essences." Bacon attacks this procedure on the following grounds: first, the monists pick out one nature which seems to them most excellent, and say that this is the only one which is what it seems, while all others are really the same as this although they appear to be different. But all natural things should be treated alike. Or if the monists mean to speak of an "ideal" water or air or fire, then they are guilty of equivocation and are no more intelligible than those who speak of abstract matter. Secondly, they do not describe how the variation of their principle occurs and produces "such armies of contraries in the world," for if it is really present in everything it must be received by the senses, and if it does not appear to be present, a reasonable explanation of the appearances must be given, "but you should by no means be required to assent to those things whereof neither the being is manifest by the sense, nor the explanation probable by the reason." Thirdly, if there is only one principle, it ought to have a visible superiority, there ought to be nothing diametrically opposed to it, and it ought both to generate and to dissolve things indifferently. But none of this is the case with the principles suggested by the monists.

Bacon now turns to the pluralists, who, he says, have to be examined one by one, since they seem to have more strength on their side and certainly more prejudice (V, 476). The De Principiis is, however, incomplete, and closes here with a detailed attack on Telesius, who makes the first active entities to be heat and cold, whose textures are respectively rarity and density. In general Bacon has a good opinion of Telesius, whom he calls "the first of the moderns" (V, 495), but in the case of his active principles he is easily refuted by numerous instances of qualities more general than heat and cold and not arising from them, for example, impenetrability, cohesion, and heavy and light.

We may now return to the discussion of atomism. If Cupid's nakedness indicates that no form "homogeneous with the secondary essences" must be ascribed to the atom, and yet that it is not entirely abstract, then what form may be ascribed to it? Bacon's answers to this are not wholly consistent. In De Principiis he commends Democritus, who affirmed that atoms and their virtues "were unlike anything that could fall under the senses; but distinguished them as being of a perfectly dark and hidden nature," but complains that Democritus falls short of his own insight when he ascribes two particular primary motions to the atom: those of descent and of impact (V, 464). (It is unlikely that Democritus ascribed these motions to the atom, although Lucretius—Bacon's source—did so.) In motion as in substance the atom must be other than all larger bodies, and this would be discovered by the method of exclusions. But at this point Bacon realizes that insistence on the "heterogeneity" or otherness of the atom will result in the impossibility of saying anything at all about it, and continues with the remark that it is only in the case of God that "when his nature is inquired after by the sense, exclusions shall not end in affirmations." In the case of the atom something in the end can be affirmed after due use of the method of exclusions: "not only some notion . . . but a distinct and definite notion," and later the atom is said to be "a true being, having matter, form, dimension, place, resistance, appetite, motion and emanations; which . . . amid the destruction of all natural bodies, remains unshaken and eternal" (V, 465, 492). Why these properties are not subject to the same objections he brings against the monists and pluralists, Bacon does not explain.

There are other places, however, where Bacon does not adopt the Democritean view that atoms are "fixed and invariable" and have diverse shapes and sizes. In Cogitationes de Natura Rerum he commends Pythagoras for assuming a smaller number of primary properties of the atom, for he makes the atoms "equal," so that variety can be produced only by their different numbers and configurations. Thus, for Pythagoras "the world consists of numbers." Bacon thinks that Democritus' view that the atoms are diverse can be overthrown, for experiment tends to show that "all things can be made out of all things" (V, 422). It was perhaps such experiments, together with the desire on theoretical grounds to minimize the number of fixed and primary properties of matter, which led Bacon by the time he published Novum Organum effectively to abandon atomism. There, in connection with the doctrine of atoms, we read that the presuppositions of the vacuum and the unchangeableness of matter are false (IV, 126). All that is left of the principle of changelessness is the axiom that the quantity of matter in the universe is invariable. Bacon repeats this throughout his writings, and as far as natural philosophy is concerned, he regards it as an a priori principle of divine revelation, since nothing except God can create or destroy matter, and the activities of God are outside the scope of natural philosophy (IV, 197; V, 320, 339, 398, 426; VI, 726).

A change in his views on void also contributed to the abandonment of atomism. In the earlier writings Bacon is prepared to consider its existence, and even in Novum Organum, in spite of the definite statement quoted above, he still vacillates, but in Historia Densi et Rari "There is no vacuum in nature" is given as a "provisional canon." There seem to be three main reasons for this hardening of view. First, Bacon becomes increasingly impressed with new empirical facts relating to gases which were then coming to light and which indicated the possible existence of subtle matter even in space void of air; secondly, he comes to think that Hero's theory of the interspersed vacuum is not necessary to explain expansion and contraction of bodies; and thirdly, he embraces a quasi-Aristotelian view that matter can "fold and unfold itself in space . . . without interposition of a vacuum," and comes to regard density and rarity as possibly the most fundamental properties of matter.[4]

This brings us to Bacon's views on the primary powers of matter. Here he is never an orthodox atomist, for according to orthodoxy the atoms move each other only when they come into contact, but Bacon never takes impenetrability and impact to be fundamental powers. Indeed, he usually speaks of the powers of matter in terms like "desire," "aversion," "instinct," or "force," as in his first account (IV, 214; VI, 729, 730) of the fable of Cupid, where Love is "the appetite or instinct of primal matter; or to speak more plainly, the natural motion of the atom; which is indeed the original and unique force that constitutes and fashions all things out of matter." This is "the summary law of nature, that impulse of desire impressed by God upon the primary particles of matter which makes them come together."* And when Bacon lists his primary motions it is clear that he is not using the word "motion" in the sense of local motion only, but in the general sense of "change," as in the Aristotelian kinēsis, and of the powers of bodies to produce change. In Novum Organum (IV, 67, 214, 356; V, 510) the "principal kinds

---

* Elsewhere, however, he repudiates sympathies and antipathies (II, 493, and in the references under note 5).

of motion or active virtues" are listed among "Prerogative Instances" as "Instances of Strife and Predominance," and include, as well as such purely local motions as expansion, motion of descent under gravity, and rotation; also such forces or qualities as those of impenetrability, cohesion, and excitation of new powers in a body, as when it is heated or magnetized.* And in his later works, Bacon speaks of bodies having "perceptions" when they are changed in some way in the presence of other bodies, although perception in inanimate bodies must be distinguished from sensation: "For though there are many kinds and varieties of pain in animals . . . it is yet most certain that all of them, as far as the motion is concerned, exist in inanimate substances; for example, in wood or stone, when it is burnt or frozen . . . though they do not enter the senses for want of the animal spirit" (IV, 165, 402; II, 528, 602; V, 432).

On the other hand, it is possible to reconcile this apparent animism with a mechanical view by noticing the pervasive powers which Bacon ascribes to "spirits" or pneumatic bodies. There is no doubt that he regards these as subtle material bodies, and that when he speaks of perceptions and influences passing between gross bodies, he usually conceives these as transmitted by spirits which, like the Stoic pneumata, are responsible for many of the qualities of bodies, and whose action may be in some sense mechanical.[5] This reconciliation of his apparently conflicting views may be correct as far as it goes, but it does not solve the problem of what exactly Bacon conceives these mechanical actions to be. He may not be committed to endowing bodies with all the animistic powers beloved of his sixteenth-century predecessors, but on the other hand, he is certainly not satisfied with atoms acting purely by impact, either in the case of gross bodies or of spirits. His reasons for this dissatisfaction are empirical, and are to be found, for example, in his discussions of cohesion and tenacity, or the "desire for continuity" of bodies, a nature which he thinks "will not easily be found out on enquiry" and which cannot be accounted for by spirits; also in his dis-

---

* In Inquisitio Legitima de Motu and even in De Augmentis the primary motions are listed as if they were simple natures out of which the inductive tables are to be constructed, but in Novum Organum Bacon appears less sure of their fundamental nature, and dismisses them to mere helps in determining the relative strengths of the virtues of bodies (IV, 230).

cussions of impenetrability and resistance to destruction, which he thinks must be accounted an "active virtue" of bodies, not a passive property; and, finally, he considers that certain actions at a distance, as of the magnet, appear to imply virtue "subsisting for a certain time and in a certain space without a body" and this is impossible on the assumption of atomism (IV, 164, 191; II, 429, 436, 644; V, 424, 429, 495).

Bacon is unable to solve the problem which these facts present. The suggestions in his late fragmentary works are inconclusive and inconsistent. In Historia Densi et Rari he seems to be inclining to a continuum theory in which the most fundamental qualities are those of density and rarity; in Historia Sulphuris, Mercurii, et Salis, sulphur, the oily, fatty, inflammable principle, and mercury, the watery, crude non-inflammable principle, are judged to be "the most primeval natures, the most original configurations of matter, and among the forms of the first class almost the principal" (V, 205, 539). The inconclusiveness is of course inevitable, for Bacon only claims to be trying to anticipate the results of induction. Nevertheless, his general conclusion in favor of some kind of mechanism or Pythagorean atomism is sufficient to account for the unshakeable faith in the simplicity of nature which underlies his method and convinces him that natural laws are there to be discovered.

To summarize, many things may be said in criticism of Bacon's method: he made little first-hand contribution to science by means of it, and his successors did not use it; he underestimated the place of hypothesis and of mathematics in scientific theories; he claimed a mechanical certainty for the method which is quite unjustified; and he failed to see the difficulties involved in introducing hidden entities and processes into science. On the other hand, it must be put to his credit that he encouraged detailed and methodical experimentation; he saw clearly the need to look for negative instances or refuting experiments in relation to all positive or confirmatory instances; he visualized a structure of scientific laws which is formally not unlike that of subsequent hypothetical-deductive systems; his tables of discovery constituted a method of systematic analogy which assisted the development of theoretical models; his influence in introducing mechanical hypotheses into seventeenth-century science can be compared with that of Descartes and Gassendi; and yet finally he did not allow the attractions of mechanism to blind him to the difficulties of pure atomism. On this last point some connection has been seen between Bacon's discussions and the basically similar, although more subtle and better informed, attacks upon atomism by Leibniz.[6]

NOTES

Note Where the original is in Latin, references are to the English translations in the Spedding edition (where given). I have made some modifications in quotations from these translations.

1 IV, 122, 346, 362; cf. the distinction between astronomy and philosophy (V, 524, 557).

2 IV, 396. Bacon here follows the De Rerum Natura (1586) of Telesius.

3 V, 491, 512; VI, 726. Cf. Locke: Essay Concerning Human Understanding, Bk IV, Ch. III, 25.

4 On the void and density, IV, 231; V, 339, 398, 497, 518. Compare Bacon's account of Hero's theory in Cogitationes de Natura Rerum (V, 419) with his repudiation of it in Novum Organum (IV, 231). The date of the Cogitationes is uncertain, but is almost certainly later than the 1604 assigned to it by Ellis and Spedding. Its discussion of atomism is in some respects more subtle than that of De Principiis. On gases, V, 321, 349; II, 380.

5 IV, 195, 242; II, 380, 616. Cf. Ellis's Preface (I, 55) on the apparent inconsistency and its resolution.

6 Cf. Ellis's Preface to De Principiis (III, 71–73), and Leibniz: "The Confession of Nature against Atheists" (1669), Philosophical Papers and Letters, ed. Leroy E. Loemker (Chicago, 1956), I, 168–73.

BACON'S MAN OF SCIENCE

Moody E. Prior

The dominating motive of Bacon's intellectual life was the complete reformation of learning, and he labored under the conviction that he was, almost single-handed, promoting a revolution in knowledge to the end that man might win a new empire over things. In those of his writings which he regarded as the parts of his grandiose plan, he gave frequent expression to his new conception of the proper goals of human knowledge and proposed new methods by which they were to be attained. And clearly implicit in this new approach to learning was an alteration in the conception of the learned man. Since the new aim and the method were to make unprecedented demands on the knower, it became necessary for Bacon to conceive a new scientist as well as a new science. This is not immediately apparent because it was to the development of his aims and methods that Bacon gave primary attention in his writings. Incomplete as his system remains, the outlines of his plan are clear and explicit, and portions are developed in detail; but the details of his picture of the new man of science are scattered, and the image has to be pieced together. From the writings of such later men as the early members of the Royal Society, for whom Bacon was a patron saint, the common elements of an image of the new scientist are clearly discernible; but though it was largely from Bacon that they caught the lineaments of the ideal which inspired them, the later portrait appears generalized and simplified when compared to the original. Every detail of the character of Bacon's new scientist is rooted in the goals which he set up and the methods he proposed. All of Bacon's objection to the learning of the past, all his hopes for the future, and all his philosophical aims are reflected in the image which he seems to have clearly visualized of the new scientist who was to be the instrument of the new learning as well as its product.

Reprinted from the Journal of the History of Ideas, Vol. 15 (1954), pp. 348–70, by permission of the author and the publisher.

BACON'S MAN OF SCIENCE

The intellectual, psychological and ethical qualities which Bacon demanded of his new scientist form an organic concept, but it is possible to distinguish certain qualities which are associated very closely with the requirements of the method and certain others which are necessarily bound up with the proper aims of learning and the role which they impose on the scientist. The immediate purpose of Bacon's methodological principles was nothing less than truth and certainty, and the goal he proposed was nothing less than the profound improvement of man's lot. The spirit and tone of his writings is therefore strongly optimistic. But Bacon did not ground his hopes on any extravagant estimate of man's powers. The hard realism of his mind, so clearly manifested in his comments on worldly affairs, is also revealed in his adoption of a very critical attitude toward the limited capacities by means of which man perceives and comes to a knowledge of his universe. Bacon's method, therefore, is founded on a review not only of the errors and defects in learning but of the deficiencies of the knower. If the past was to be swept aside, the mind wiped clear, and a new way charted, the positive program could begin only after all established illusions about man himself had been anatomized and taken into account.

For a rigorous critique of the failings in man which stood in the way of attaining certainty Bacon had not far to seek. The Sceptics of antiquity had systematically analyzed the defects in man's capacity to perceive and judge of reality, and had concluded on the basis of this analysis that nothing can be known. Strengthened by new illustrations and revitalized by literary embellishment, notably in the writings of Montaigne, this ancient school enjoyed a vigorous revival during the sixteenth century. But neither in motives nor conclusions were the ancient Sceptics or the new essentially akin to Bacon. Bacon—like others among the philosophers of the new developments in natural science—found the sceptical critique of man powerfully stimulating; moreover he recognized it as something to be acknowledged and met before a way to truth could be recommended. Bacon's awareness of the force of the sceptical arguments is everywhere apparent, but it is in the famous discussion of the Idols in *Novum Organum* (I, xxxviii–lxviii) that the influence is most direct. Incorporated into a novel analysis and surrounded by many important original extensions can be discovered all of the sceptical "modes." The sceptical deductions and conclusions are, however, missing. Bacon simultaneously accepted scepticism as a critique and rejected it as a philosophy of knowledge:

he represented himself as one who maintained not that nothing can be known, but that nothing can be known except in a certain way.

This way—the new method—was thus to provide correctives for the limitations of the knower. The critique of the Sceptics Bacon acknowledged, but despair in consequence of it he regarded as merely the result of neglecting the aid available: "The doctrine of those who have denied that certainty could be attained at all, has some agreement with my way of proceeding at the first setting out; but they end in being infinitely separated and opposed. For the holders of that doctrine assert simply that nothing can be known; I also assert that not much can be known in nature by the way which is now in use. But then they go on to destroy the authority of the senses and understanding; whereas I proceed to devise and supply helps for the same" (N.O., I, xxxvii; IV, 53). Scepticism becomes therefore not a philosophy of knowledge but a principle of method: "that which I meditate and propound is not _Acatalepsia_ but _Eucatalepsia_; not the denial of the capacity to understand, but provision for understanding truly" (IV, 111–2).

For the defects of the senses Bacon proposed as correctives the use of instruments and, most important of all, experiments. The correction of the defects of the understanding, however, demanded more subtle forms of control. Scepticism as a method called for calmness of spirit equal to the demands of systematic doubt—of unwillingness to assent or deny prematurely. But this was an attitude very different from the _ataraxia_ and _epoche_ of the ancient Sceptics, which it resembles superficially, just as it had little in common with the ultimate triumph over passion of the Stoics.[1] And it was necessarily opposed to the dogmatism of the system-builders and to the agitation encouraged by the disputatious methods of the schools. Bacon described it as an attitude that mediated between the extremes of dogmatism and scepticism, "between the presumption of pronouncing on everything and the despair of comprehending anything" (IV, 39). And its ultimate destination was truth: "Another error is an impatience of doubt, and haste to assertion without due and mature suspension of judgment . . . if a man will begin with certainties, he shall end in doubts; but if he will be content to begin with doubts, he shall end in certainties" (III, 293).

This restraint of the intellect—the chronic doubt and suspension of mind which were the necessary temperamental consequences of scepticism used as method—failed to meet the sceptical argument that certainty was unattainable because life was short and art was long, the depth of nature profound and infinite, and the span of man's life finite and subject to the cycles of time. Bacon understood the discouraging potency of these arguments: "But by far the greatest obstacle to the progress of science and to the undertaking of new tasks and provinces therein, is found in this—that men despair and think things impossible. For wise and serious men are wont in these matters to be altogether distrustful; considering with themselves the obscurity of nature, the shortness of life, the deceitfulness of the senses, the weakness of the judgment, the difficulty of experiment and the like; and so supposing that in the revolution of time and of the ages of the world the sciences have ebbs and flows; that at one season they grow and flourish, at another wither and decay, yet in such sort that when they have reached a certain point and condition they can advance no further" (IV, 90; also III, 227, 231, 265). Bacon's answer to this melancholy wisdom of the ages was to substitute for it a radical, progressive attitude toward truth and knowledge. One error in the old sceptical view lay in approaching the problem of knowledge in terms of the limits of a single life and to despair because the goal was so clearly out of reach. Bacon was indifferent to this despair because he placed certainty as the limit toward which a properly organized search for knowledge continuously moved. "I propose," he wrote in the Preface to Novum Organum, "to establish progressive stages of certainty." The fullness of knowledge lay in the fullness of time, and time was generative in a progressive way: "let great authors have their due, as time which is the author of authors be not deprived of his due, which is further and further to discover truth" (III, 290). For Bacon, "truth is the daughter of time."[2] Truth will therefore appear impossible only when viewed from the conventional perspective as something to be encompassed by individual men through the exercise of their powers of understanding: "touching impossibility, I take those things are to be held possible which may be done by some persons, though not by everyone; and which may be done by many, though not by any one; and which may be done in succession of ages, though not within the hourglass of one man's life; and which may be done by public designation, though not by private endeavour" (III, 328–9, 231). Thus while granting a premise that traditionally led to despair, Bacon's progressive view of knowledge encouraged an optimistic outlook in the scientist, not only because the new method promised accelerating results but because fulfilment was continuous. Bacon sometimes seems naïve in his hopes that through collaborative effort on the right principles a complete history of nature might be a finite task whose end could be foreseen, but it is difficult to determine at times whether the source of his enthusiasm lies there or in the possibility of continuous progress: "There is therefore much ground for hoping that there are still laid up in the womb of nature many secrets of excellent use, having no affinity or parallelism with anything that is now known, but lying entirely out of the beat of the imagination, which have not yet been found. They too no doubt will some time or other, in the course and revolution of many ages, come to light of themselves, just as the others did; only by the method which we are now treating they can be speedily and suddenly and simultaneously presented and anticipated."[3]

In this progressive view of the problem of knowledge and certainty there was, moreover, a further consequence for the character of the Baconian scientist more profound than chronic optimism. For him there could never be the gratification of bringing all truth into a single order through the strength of the intellect. This, Bacon insisted, was an illusion of the dogmatists, who, out of arrogant pride in the operation of his intellect, substituted the patterns of his mind mistakenly for the complexities of the universe (III, 292; also IV, 48, 51, 101). Real confidence and hope lay only in the realization that the true goal was distant and that it required not one man but many, not one lifetime but generations of men working with a common purpose (IV, 102). In the optimism which grew out of a progressive and collective view of knowledge and truth the Baconian scientist buried his pride.

This subduing of the pride of intellect has a direct bearing on Bacon's views concerning the proper end of knowledge. The failure of learning, Bacon maintained, had resulted from "the mistaking or misplacing of the last or furthest end of knowledge" (III, 294, 222), and the hope for the future of learning lay in the realization of its proper goal: "It is not possible to run a course aright when the goal itself has not been rightly placed. Now the true and lawful goal of the sciences is none other than this: that human life be endowed with new discoveries and powers" (IV, 79). If knowledge was to dedicate itself to "the glory of the Creator and the relief of man's estate" (III, 294), it must be directed toward a deep understanding of the behavior of nature and the application of this knowledge of the systematic development and improvement of the arts. The difference between civilization and barbarism, Bacon maintained —replying at the same time to various old and current theories—

"comes not from the soil, not from climate, not from race, but from the arts." And "the empire of man over things depends wholly on the arts and sciences. For we cannot command nature except by obeying her" (IV, 114, 47, 119).

In the light of this aim, many conventional and apparently normal motives to study lose their importance for Bacon and in effect become base or misleading: "For men have entered into a desire of learning and knowledge, sometimes upon a natural curiosity and inquisitive appetite; sometimes to entertain their minds with variety and delight; sometimes for ornament and reputation; and sometimes to enable them to victory of wit and contradiction; and most times for lucre and profession; and seldom sincerely to give a true account of their gift of reason, to the benefit and use of men" (III, 294). Some of these common and traditionally admired motives may be, Bacon conceded, "more worthy than others"; they are nevertheless "all inferior and degenerate" (III, 222). Moreover, their setting aside involves a radical departure from traditional standards for the character and conduct of a learned man. The traditional ideal of contemplation as the perfect activity and final good of rational man is abandoned—and so apparently must be its modern analogue, disinterested curiosity. Bacon's scientist is disinterested only in preferring the common good to private good, and Bacon finds it necessary to reject the Aristotelian and scholastic ideal of the contemplative life: "It [the common good] decides the question touching the preferment of the contemplative or active life and decides it against Aristotle. For all the reasons which he brings for the contemplative respect private good, and the pleasure and dignity of a man's self; in which respects no question the contemplative life has the pre-eminence . . . . But men must know that in this theatre of man's life it is reserved only for God and the Angels to be lookers on" (V, 8; IV, 110). The contemplative ideal, by exalting the "pleasure and dignity of a man's self," perverts the end of learning by depriving it of its power. Only a change in emphasis can restore to learning its true character: "this is that which will indeed dignify and exalt knowledge, if contemplation and action may be more nearly and straitly conjoined and united together than they have been" (III, 294).

The inspiration for true learning was for Bacon not the pleasure of study and the excitement of discovery, but the needs of mankind. Though many assertions made during his divided life by this remarkable man have been looked at with suspicion, it is impossible to question the sincerity of his expressed compassion for the lot of man. In his celebrated letter to Burghley, which contains the first recorded statement of his intellectual ambitions, he concludes: "This, whether it be curiosity, or vain glory, or nature, or (if one take it favourably) *philanthropia*, is so fixed in my mind as it cannot be removed" (VIII, 109). Bacon may have listed the inferior motives because he did not wish to expose his earnestness and sincerity too clearly before the worldly minister, but later expressions of this theme appear with no concessions. The superior ethical motive became inseparable from the intellectually superior end, as though Bacon had realized that no motive other than "philanthropia" could ever guarantee that science would hold to the proper end of learning and consequently employ correct methods. If learning was to become the mastery of nature for the uses of life, it could be guided only by men who were continually inspired by compassion for the lot of man. At the conclusion of the "Prœmium" to the *Magna Instauratio* Bacon thus explains his haste in publishing: "The cause of which haste was not ambition for himself, but solicitude for the work; that in case of his death there might remain some outline and project of that which he had conceived, and some evidence likewise of his honest mind and inclination towards the benefit of the human race. Certain it is that all other ambition whatsoever seemed poor in his eyes compared with the work which he had in hand, seeing that the matter at issue is either nothing, or a thing so great that it may well be content with its own merit, without seeking other recompence" (IV, 8). Even in his most worldly practical discourses, Bacon discredited as inferior the actions that stem from self-love ("Of Wisdom for a Man's Self"), and proclaimed "philanthropia" as the noblest of man's capacities ("Of Goodness and Goodness of Nature"). Philanthropia was the seed from which the new science must grow, and so the new man of learning must of necessity be touched by the needs of others. How deeply Bacon's own feelings ran can be seen by the following lines from the Preface to *The Great Instauration*:

> Wherefore, seeing that these things do not depend upon myself, at the outset of the work I most humbly and fervently pray to God the Father, God the Son, and God the Holy Ghost, that remembering the sorrows of mankind and the pilgrimage of this our life wherein we wear out our days few and evil, they will vouchsafe through my hands to endow the human family with new mercies (IV, 20).

Compassion is the invariable mark of Bacon's true scientist. Of the personage who addresses the gathering of learned men in Redargutio Philosophiarum he writes: "aspectus . . . admodum placidi et sereni; nisi quod oris compositio erat tanquam miserantis" (III, 559). And in the description of one of the Fathers of Salomon's House in New Atlantis, almost the first detail has to do with compassion: "The day being come, he made his entry. He was a man of middle stature and age, comely of person, and had an aspect as if he pitied men" (III, 154).[4]

The identification of scientific truth with use and therefore with charity, with power and therefore with pity, is fundamental to Bacon's conception of true learning. There are, however, several puzzling passages in Bacon's writings which seem to contradict this frequently expressed position, as though Bacon had temporarily forgotten, in a moment of personal enthusiasm, his formal rejection of the traditional ideal of contemplation; for instance, the following from the Novum Organum:

> Again, if men have thought so much of some one particular discovery to regard him as more than man who has been able by some benefit to make the whole human race his debtor, how much higher a thing to discover that by means of which all things else shall be discovered with ease! And yet (to speak the whole truth), as the uses of light are infinite, in enabling us to walk, to ply our arts, to read, to recognize one another; and nevertheless the very beholding of the light is itself a more excellent and fairer thing than all the uses of it;—so assuredly the very contemplation of things, as they are, without superstition and imposture, error or confusion, is itself more worthy than all the fruit of inventions (IV, 115).

This statement is particularly surprising in the Novum Organum. The very aim of this work—the discovery of "that by means of which all things else shall be discovered with ease"—appears to have been assigned inferior status to the pure contemplation of truth which Bacon elsewhere so clearly rejects. It is true that in the same work (I, cxxiv; IV, 110) Bacon raises this very question: "Again it will be thought, no doubt, that the goal and mark of knowledge, which I myself set up . . . is not the true or the best; for that the contemplation of truth is a thing worthier and loftier than all utility and magnitude of works." In resolving the problem Bacon distinguishes between true knowledge and fanciful philosophical systems, and concludes: "Truth therefore and utility are here the very same things: and works themselves are of greater value as pledges of truth than as contributing to the comforts of life." The difficulty cannot be completely explained in this way, particularly as there are other instances in Bacon of apparent discrepancies of the same sort. For example, the extended analysis of the defects of learning in The Advancement of Learning is followed by a briefer section extolling the virtues of learning, and the theme of this section is announced by examples of the attributes and acts of God and the angels, concluding: "So in the distribution of days, we see the day wherein God did rest and contemplate his own works, was blessed above all the days wherein he did effect and accomplish them" (III, 296). This may be construed as a hyperbole symbolic of the beauty of truth, since contemplation is proper to God and the angels; but such an explanation does not account for the curious interpretation of the Cain and Abel story which shortly follows: ". . . in the two simplest and most primitive trades of life, that of the shepherd (who by reason of his leisure, rest in a place, and living in view of heaven, is a lively image of a contemplative life,) and that of a husbandman, where we see again the favour and election of God went to the shepherd and not to the tiller of the ground" (III, 297). The Essay "Of Truth" seems in some respects to be a development of these themes: ". . . truth, which only doth judge itself, teacheth that the inquiry of truth, which is the love-making or wooing of it, the knowledge of truth, which is the presence of it, and the belief of truth, which is the enjoying of it, is the sovereign good of human nature." This portion of the essay is climaxed by a translation of Lucretius' eulogy of the pleasures of truth, which concludes, along with Bacon's parenthetical insertion, "but no pleasure is comparable to the standing upon the vantage ground of Truth (a hill not to be commanded and where the air is always clear and serene) and to see the errors, and wanderings, and mists, and tempests in the vale below" (VI, 378; also III, 318).

In their context, however, most of these expressions of the pure delight in knowledge are undercut by qualifications which diminish their emphasis and by rhetorical overtones which weaken their force. In reading Bacon's comments on the story of Abel's sacrifice, for instance, it is difficult to erase the effect of the extended analysis of the "peccant humours" of learning which precedes it and which concludes only a few paragraphs before on a strong note of utility. "The end ought to be . . . to preserve and augment whatsoever is solid and fruitful; that knowledge may not be as a curtesan, for pleasure and vanity only, or as a bond-woman, to acquire and gain to her master's use, but as a spouse, for generation, fruit, and comfort" (III, 295). The Advancement of Learning is in some respects a rebuttal of the contemporary attacks on learning,[5] and from this perspective the gloss on Abel's sacrifice makes the distinction, common to Bacon, between the life devoted to learning and the life of public affairs. Bacon had noted immediately before this Biblical example that in the hierarchy of the angels, "the angels of knowledge and illumination are placed before the angels of office and domination"; but what is perhaps more significant is that Bacon assigns to contemplation a second place even among angels: "the first place or degree is given to the angels of love, which are termed Seraphim, the second to the angels of light, which are termed Cherubim, and the third and so following places to thrones, principalities, and the rest, which are all angels of power and ministry" (III, 296). First comes charity. And this is the resolution of the essay "Of Truth." The preoccupation with truth is there pronounced "the sovereign good of human nature" and God's pure love of truth is expressed through the symbolism of the initial creation of light; but when Bacon concludes his quotation from Lucretius, which climaxes this exaltation of pure contemplation, he adds: "so always that this prospect be with pity and not with swelling or pride. Certainly it is heaven upon earth to have a man's mind move in charity, rest in providence, and turn upon the poles of truth" (VI, 378). Learning can be freed from the distortions of pride only through charity, which projects itself through pity for the lot of men, in which case learning cannot properly be detached from use.

Bacon never lost the sense of excitement and the feeling of superiority which accompany the pursuits and discoveries of the mind He recognized, moreover, that the pursuit of any enterprise for its own sake is a characteristic chiefly of learned men: ". . . only learned men love business as an action according to nature, as agreeable to health of mind as exercise is to health of body, taking pleasure in the action itself, and not in the purchase: so that of all men they are the most indefatigable" (III, 272). Moreover, although he defined the proper end and final product of learning as the improvement of life through the improvement of the arts, he realized that this great end was, paradoxically, more likely to be advanced by the contemplative type of mind rather than the mechanical and inventive: "For the mechanic, not troubling himself with the investigation of truth, confines his attention to those things which bear upon his particular works, and will not either raise his mind or stretch out his hand for anything else. But then only will there be good ground of hope for the further advance of knowledge, when there shall be received and gathered together into natural history a variety of experiments, which are of no use in themselves, but simply serve to discover causes and axioms; which I call "*Experimenta lucifera*," experiments of *light*, to distinguish them from those which I call "*fructifera*," experiments of *fruit*" (IV, 95). Light, in fact, is one of Bacon's favorite symbols, associated at its highest with the attributes of God in the first act of the creation. But though Bacon realized that it is natural to the learned man to rest in the delight of the pursuit and contemplation of knowledge, and though his own enthusiasm emerges at times in expressions of this delight, he recognized it as a serious danger having the power to corrupt the man whom it seduces. If the prime need and sole hope of mankind lay in gaining empire over things, contemplation could not be held up as the perfect human activity: truth could not be a final end in itself, nor mere curiosity the chief motive to learning. Contemplation, Bacon said, is proper as an end only to God, expressing thereby at once the nobility and grandeur of the activity and its inappropriateness to mere man. Among mortals, only Adam was privileged to savor this delight in an inferior form:

> After the creation was finished, it is set down unto us that man was placed in the garden to work therein; which work so appointed to him could be no other than work of contemplation; that is, when the end of work is but for exercise and experiment, not for necessity; for there being then no reluctation of creature nor sweat of the brow, man's employment must of consequence have been matter of delight in the experiment, and not matter of labour for the use (III, 296–9).

But this was the pre-lapsarian Adam, who had no need to gain empire over things.

The story of the Fall exercised a strong fascination for Bacon and he alludes to it frequently, particularly in relation to the problem of knowledge and man's welfare. He nowhere questions its literal validity; nevertheless, he approaches it in much the same spirit as inspired his extraordinary interpretations of classical myths as symbols or "emblems" prefiguring truths which, when expounded properly, invariably show remarkable parallels to Bacon's favorite notions.[6] Biblical myths he found useful in the same way. In putting the Cain-Abel story to the service of his preference for contemplative activity over the life of practical affairs he says parenthetically, "the Scriptures have infinite mysteries, not violating at all the truth of the story or letter" (III, 297). He might with equal appropriateness have asserted this principle in connection with his numerous allusions to and glosses on the myth of the Fall.

Bacon had almost inescapably to take cognizance of this Biblical episode, if only because it had come to mean that men can know too much and that God had set limits to man's restless Faustian search for knowledge. Early in The Advancement of Learning he challenges the popular notion that "the aspiring to overmuch knowledge was the original temptation whereupon ensued the fall of man." Bacon's interpretation of the Fall imposes no limits on the pursuit of natural knowledge: "it was not the pure knowledge of nature and universality, a knowledge by the light whereof man did give names unto other creatures in Paradise, as they were brought before him, according unto their properties, which gave the occasion to the Fall; but it was the proud knowledge of good and evil, with an intent in man to give law unto himself and to depend no more upon God's commandments, which was the form of the temptation" (III, 264–5). The danger was not in the quantity: "it is merely the quality of knowledge, which be it in quantity more or less, if it be taken without the true corrective thereof, hath in it some nature of venom or malignity, and some effects of that venom, which is ventosity or swelling" (III, 266).

Thus understood, the story of the Fall became a support of Bacon's aims and hopes. But the myth carried further traditional implications at odds with these, for it represented man, as well as nature, ruinously changed in consequence of the first transgression and thus incapable of improving his lot by a dependence on his own powers. For the new scientist, however, optimism concerning man's ability to gain empire over things and command nature was required as an act of faith. Bacon accordingly endowed the Biblical story with new implications which inspired incentive to effort in this direction. Paradise could be regained. Bacon speaks of the true end of learning as "a restitution and reinvesting (in great part) of man to sovereignty and power (for whensoever he shall be able to call the creatures by their true names he shall again command them) which he had in the first state of creation" (III, 222). Bacon did not minimize the several ruinous consequences presumed to have been produced by the Fall, but he insisted that man was not without resources: "For man by the Fall fell at the same time from his state of innocency and from his dominion over nature. Both of these losses, however, can even in this life be in some part repaired; the former by religion and faith, the latter by the arts and sciences" (IV, 247–8). To these Bacon added a third resource: in De Augmentis Scientiarum Bacon considered poetry as a means of compensating for some absent beauty and order in the world.

> For if the matter be attentively considered, a sound argument may be drawn from Poesy, to show that there is agreeable to the spirit of man a more ample greatness, a more perfect order, and a more beautiful variety than it can any where (since the Fall) find in nature . . . . Whence it [poesy] may be fairly thought to partake some what of a divine nature; because it raises the mind and carries it aloft, accommodating the show of things to the desires of the mind, not (like reason and history) buckling and bowing down the mind to the nature of things (IV, 316).

The original paradise was not to be restored in its pristine entirety or through any singly directed effort, but was to be achieved in parts; religion, poetry, science was each in its own way responsible for a particular alleviation of man's post-lapsarian deficiencies. Whether Bacon thought the Biblical paradise historically real or merely symbolic, the important element in his preoccupations with it is his conviction that it was within man's powers to make great amends in this life for the deficiencies which oppressed mankind. He accepted the Christian religion as the instrument through which man can come by a knowledge of God's will and law. He found in the continuing accomplishments of poetry adequate means to satisfy man's thirst for ideal beauty and order.[7] The overwhelming lack in the conditions for man's earthly felicity was in the area of science and the arts. Bacon tells us in the Prooemium to Instauratio Magna that "he thought all trial should be made, whether that commerce between the mind of man and the nature of things, which is more precious than anything on earth, or at least than anything that is of the earth, might by any means be restored to its perfect and original condition, or if that may not be, yet reduced to a better condition than that in which it now is" (IV, 7). This restitution was not beyond the powers of man, though the inadequacy of former and prevailing means and aims stood in the way: "For creation was not by the curse made altogether and forever a rebel, but in virtue of that charter 'In the sweat of thy face shalt thou eat bread,' it is now by various labours (not certainly by disputations or idle magical ceremonies, but by various labours) at length and in some measure subdued to the supplying of man with bread; that is, to the uses of human life" (IV, 248). Milton's "paradise within" was not enough for Bacon. He seemed too acutely aware of "the miseries of the human race and this pilgrimage of our life in which we wear out our evil days and few." The scientist had a role equal to that of the poet or the servant of God—in fact, Bacon came to think of him as though he were a servant of God and a dedicated soul.

It is everywhere apparent in Bacon that the virtues of the man of science are not wholly intellectual, any more than are his possible shortcomings. In Bacon's conception of the scientist there is a pronounced ethical element. The world of science has its sinners as well as its elect. Bacon attacks on practical methodological grounds the reliance on the pure intellect, because reason sets aside reality and imposes schemes created out of its own inner order upon the complex world of nature; but to this methodological error he regularly assigns the moral taint of pride. In a curious passage in the *Natural and Experimental History* he describes this prevailing evil of the learned world as the consequence of a kind of second Fall of man:

> For we copy the sin of our first parents while we suffer for it. They wished to be like God, but their posterity wish to be even greater. For we create worlds, we direct and domineer over nature, we will have it that all things *are* as in our folly we think they should be, not as seems fittest to the Divine wisdom, or as they are found to be in fact; and I know not whether we more distort the facts of nature or our own wits; but we clearly impress the stamp of our own image on the creatures and works of God, instead of carefully examining and recognising in them the stamp of the Creator himself. Wherefore our dominion over creatures is a second time forfeited, not undeserv-

> edly; and whereas after the fall of man some power over the resistance of creatures was still left to him —the power of subduing and managing them by true and solid arts—yet this too through our insolence, and because we desire to be like God and to follow the dictates of our own reason, we in great part lose (V, 132).

If the fatal sin against the canons of true science is pride, the all-embracing virtue is charity. In the exercise of this virtue man might wish to be like God without error: "In aspiring to the throne of power the angels transgressed and fell, in presuming to come within the oracle of knowledge man transgressed and fell; but in pursuit towards the similitude of God's goodness or love (which is one thing, for love is nothing else but goodness put in motion or applied) neither man or spirit ever hath transgressed, or shall transgress" (III, 217).

There is an obvious similarity between Bacon's notions about the deadly sin and cardinal virtue in science and the moral ideals of man in the Christian tradition. But the distinction between the ethical virtues and vices of a scientist is not insisted upon in Bacon because it is essentially religious and Christian. Christianity may be the source, but it is not the sanction. The grounds of Bacon's analysis are naturalistic and humanistic, and he derives them out of the aims of true learning and the demands of good method. It is a question of success and failure in the discovery of useful knowledge. The scientist must cultivate charity and shun pride not in consequence of being a Christian but in consequence of being a scientist. Bacon, it is true, represents his scientist as a religious man. To some extent he does so to defend the new learning against the charge that it leads to atheism. Bacon concedes that "a little natural philosophy inclineth the mind to atheism, but a further proceeding bringeth the mind back to religion" (III, 221, 267–8). Bacon claims also that learning does a service to religion, since the deep investigation into God's works inspires admiration for His glory, and leads to "meditation of the omnipotency of God" (III, 301). Bacon may have written thus in all sincerity. But these considerations play a relatively minor role in his preoccupation with science and his apologetics for the new learning: compare, for instance, the trifling and inconspicuous place which the argument from design occupies in Bacon's thought with its ubiquity and extensive development among the English scientists of the next generation. Bacon separated completely the realms of religion and of natural knowledge in the interest of establishing a science free of superstition and presumably a religion free of sophistry. The basis of religion was for him the knowledge of God's will and law, matters which lay beyond man and hence were knowable only through divine revelation. Bacon urged therefore "that we do not presume by the contemplation of nature to attain to the mysteries of God" (III, 266), that the pursuit of natural knowledge be kept clear of religion, and that men "do not unwisely mingle or confound these learnings together" (III, 268). Religion in scientific matters was recommended largely indirectly as a corrective: against the fear that through science unknown power may be granted without adequate restraints, he advised "that all knowledge is to be limited by religion and is to be referred to use and action" (III, 218, 266), and against the danger of "the debasement of arts and sciences to purposes of wickedness, luxury, and the like," he expressed the pious hope that "the exercise thereof will be governed by sound reason and true religion" (IV, 115). But when viewed from the center of Bacon's thought, this strain seems like conventional embroidery. In the pursuit of the true end of learning with the proper methods, Bacon's man of science had to possess and exercise qualities which by their nature rendered such admonitions superfluous. As long as he functioned as a good scientist he had of necessity to be incorruptible and a good man. Bacon often leaves the impression that the career of science is something of a religion in its selflessness and sense of dedication, and he at times spoke of the future scientists as though they were a priesthood. And always he speaks of the pursuit of natural knowledge as though it were the noblest of human activities.

This idealization of the seeker of truth in the pursuit of the secrets of nature may be set in relief by comparing it with Bacon's analysis of other sorts of notable activity, especially as these are presented in the Essays. This is not to imply the conventional view of the Essays as largely cynical and worldly commentaries on success in the great world of affairs. The Essays are of a piece with everything Bacon wrote. He recognizes in them certain capacities and inclinations in man which endow human actions with nobility and dignity. One is the inclination to knowledge, and he terms the pursuit and contemplation of truth as "the sovereign good of human nature" ("Of Truth"). The other is "philanthropia," "the affecting of the weal of man," which he believes is "implanted deeply in the nature of man," and which "of all virtues and dignities of the mind is the greatest."

("Of Goodness and Goodness of Nature.") These are the poles between which human activity is measured. Their relation to the prime virtues essential to Bacon's scientist is at once apparent. Since the essays deal largely with the actions and ornaments of men in public life, "philanthropia" is the measure directly or tacitly applied for the most part. Thus, selfishness is despised: "it is a poor centre of a man's actions, himself," "it is a depraved thing" ("Of Wisdom for a Man's Self"). In public life, "merit is the end of man's motion" and "power to do good is the true and lawful end of aspiring" ("Of Great Place"). Riches "are for spending, and spending for honour a and good actions" ("Of Riches"). Thus, activities or passions which are inimical with the proper aims of life and their realization, Bacon treats with suspicion or contempt ("Of Love," "Of Revenge"). Where they are indifferent to these ends, Bacon tends to analyze without resolving the issues ("Of Marriage"). Where they may be an aid, he treats them with respect ("Of Friendship"). The worldly and at times cynical tone of the Essays arises from the fact that when Bacon concerns himself with the operational aspects of public life—as always realistically and dispassionately, in the spirit of Machiavelli, whom he admired for treating of men as they are and not as they ought to be—he finds himself in an area where man's conduct becomes less than noble. However lofty one's aims, when it is a question of gaining power or of knowing what to do "if you would work any man" in the exercise of it, there is no escaping the ruthless and grimy world of "Of Negotiating." In the best hands the instruments of power have an evil aspect. The rising to great place is "sometimes base, and by indignities men come to dignities." Power can corrupt because the means are corrupting. But the seeking of power over nature is not corrupting because the ends and means which make for success are of necessity corrective of the defects of men and require the exercise of his noblest inclinations. Bacon's expressed preference is always for the life of true learning against the life of power; in the traditions of ancient times, he notes, lawgivers and statesmen have been honored by titles of worthies and demigods, but inventors of new arts have been consecrated among the gods themselves (III, 301–2; IV, 113–5); God preferred Abel's sacrifice to that of Cain (III, 297); the angels of power and ministry rank below those of knowledge and illumination (III, 296, 316–9). Bacon could never have had any grave doubts on this matter during a life of divided purpose between the ambitions of the great scholar and the great man. "The commandment of knowledge," he wrote, "is yet higher than the commandment over the will" (III, 316). At the collapse of his fortunes he knew that he had betrayed his calling as one of the elect and had misspent that one talent which is death to hide. This sense of tragic futility he summed up in a prayer which he composed after his indictment: "Besides my innumerable sins, I confess before thee, that I am debtor to thee for the gracious talent of thy gifts and graces, which I have neither put into a napkin, nor put it (as I ought) to exchangers, where it might have made best profit; but misspent it in things for which I was least fit; so that I may truly say, my soul hath been a stranger in the course of my pilgrimage" (XIV, 230–1).

When viewed as a whole, Bacon's ideal of the scientist establishes a new ideal of man, different from the ideal of the patriot, the saint, the gentleman courtier and prince of the Renaissance, and even the citizen of the perfect state. The good man is one who possesses or is capable of exercising the intellectual and ethical virtues demanded by the aims and methods requisite for the discovery of truth in the study of nature, and the good life is the dedication to the improvement through this means of man's lot on earth.

For this man, Bacon envisioned a new role in society and a society vastly improved by his dominant role in it. The character with which Bacon endowed him rendered him superior to others, and hence Bacon saw him as occupying a superior position in society. His scientist would be a member of an élite class, though not by virtue of birth, or political status, or the possession of an aloof intellectual supremacy. Bacon found it necessary to combat certain conventional notions of social superiority in order that members of the gentry and aristocracy might not be deterred from devoting themselves to such studies under the mistaken notion that certain activities were base. Science required experiments, and therefore the work of artisans and craftsmen was to be cultivated. Moreover, Bacon was impressed by the fact that in the mechanical arts important inventions and discoveries were followed by progressive improvements, whereas in pure learning impressive achievements seemed to end in themselves (III, 347; IV, 14–5, 99–100). He came to respect the qualities which were associated with the mechanical arts, and made a point of calling attention to his own activities in this direction with pride: "For myself, most excellent king, I may truly say that both this present work, and in those I intend to publish hereafter, I often advisedly and deliberately throw aside the dignity of my name and wit (if any such thing be) in my endeavour to advance human interests; and being one that should properly perhaps be an architect in philosophy and the sciences, I turn common labourer, hodman, anything that is wanted; taking upon myself the burden and execution of many things which must needs be done, and which others through an inborn pride shrink from and decline" (V, 4). These views accord with both the humility and the realism which Bacon required of his scientist, but they do not imply that he required of his scientist the psychology of a glorified menial humbly content with his useful drudgery. Though he despised the arrogance which he associated with older ideals of the learned man, when he came to present the picture of the scientist in New Atlantis in an imagined perfect setting, he pictured him surrounded by the pomp and reverence usually associated with kings and prelates. The visit of one of the Fathers of Salomon's House is preceded by awesome heraldings of his arrival, and he comes handsomely accoutered, and impressively carried about "in a rich chariot without wheels litter-wise; with two horses at either end, richly trapped in blue velvet embroidered; and two footmen on each side in the like attire" (III, 154). His impressive train is reported, nevertheless, to lack some of the accompaniments of purely regal processions, out of a desire "to avoid all tumult and trouble" (155). His behavior suggests the high priest: "He held up his bare hand as he went, as blessing the people, but in silence" (155). The mariners in the story recount among the remarkable features of Bensalem the courteous refusal of the local dignitaries to accept the usual marks of obeisance, yet Bacon's narrator reports of their visit to the Father of Salomon's House: "When we came in, as we were taught, we bowed low at our first entrance; and when we were come near his chair, he stood up, holding forth his hand ungloved and in a posture of blessing; and we everyone of us stooped down, and kissed the hem of his tippet" (156). In Bensalem the scientists are a consecrated priesthood, and it seems less correct to say of them that they were religious men than that they constituted a religious cult in themselves: "We have certain hymns and services, which we say daily, of laud and thanks to God for his marvellous works: and forms of prayers, imploring his aid and blessing for the illumination of our labours, and the turning of them into good and holy uses" (166).

The loyalties of such men would not be bound by conventional standards. They could have no compelling class affiliations, since useful information could come from the most humble sources. What is more important, such scientists would not be confined by national boundaries. This point is effectively presented in New Atlantis. The citizens of Bensalem are forbidden by royal decree from travel outside their kingdom but this restraint does not apply to certain fellows of Salomon's House, who are termed Merchants of Light (164). At regular intervals they are sent out to all parts of the globe to gather information on the advances in the arts and sciences: "But thus you see we maintain a trade, not for gold, silver, or jewels; nor for silks; nor for spices; nor any other commodities of matter; but only for God's first creature, which was Light; to have light (I say) of the growth of all parts of the world" (146–7). One must not minimize the importance of this theme because of the utopian setting. Bacon's utopia, at least with reference to Salomon's House, comes much closer to being a picture of what the author believed to be possible—as distinct from what he believed to be ideally desirable—than is the case with most ideal commonwealths. In a more straight-forward context he had made his views on this point quite clear: "Further, it will not be amiss to distinguish the three kinds and as it were grades of ambition in mankind. The first is of those who desire to extend their own power in their native country; which kind is vulgar and degenerate. The second is of those who labour to extend the power of their country and its dominion among men. This certainly has more dignity, though not less covetousness. But if a man endeavour to establish and extend the power and dominion of the human race over the universe, his ambition (if ambition it can be called) is without doubt a more wholesome thing and more noble than the other two" (IV, 114). The humanitarian impulse of the scientist could not be confined to local loyalties and limits, and true knowledge, by its nature, transcended time and space: ". . . if the invention of the ship was thought so noble, which carrieth riches and commodities from place to place, and consociateth the most remote regions in participation of their fruits, how much more are letters to be magnified, which as ships pass through the vast seas of time, and make ages so distant to participate of the wisdom, illuminations, and inventions, the one of the other?" (III, 318). The scientist was of no country, as scientist; he was a member of an international freemasonry.

That there were dangers in the extension of man's dominion over nature, Bacon was aware. Had his scientist no responsibility to these? Bacon's answer to this question was usually evasive. Certainly it was possible that the new learning might be put to base uses, but are not all good things perverted by evil and foolish men from their proper ends, and is that sufficient reason for discouraging the good things themselves (IV, 115)? It was also true that the new knowledge might "open a fountain, such as it is not easy to discern where the issues thereof will take and fall," and that it would make available vast resources to all men; Bacon consoled himself in the hope that the new knowledge and power would be beneficently employed by the exercise of right reason and religion.[8] But Bacon knew too well the psychology of power to feel greatly comforted by his own casual reassurances. All men were not scientists. Bacon's failure to confront this important question with his customary resoluteness and realism suggests the real measure of his fear. It was only in the utopian setting of New Atlantis that he faced the issue squarely and carried the implications of his fears to their logical conclusion: "And this we do also. We have consultations, which of the inventions and experiences which we have discovered shall be published, and which not: and take all an oath of secrecy, for the concealing of those which we think fit to keep secret: though some of those we do reveal sometimes to the state and some not" (III, 165). This brief passage says in effect that just as in the interest of mankind scientists must constitute themselves an international free-masonry or priesthood, in the same interest they must set themselves above the state. To appreciate how remarkable is the appearance of this idea in Bacon, it is only necessary to recall that in defense of the royal prerogative he had opposed Coke in the theory of common law, and that in the essay "Of Judicature" he had described the judges as lions, but as lions under the throne. Bacon had stated with unmistakable clarity his conviction that science—though not necessarily the scientist—must in his own day be separated from religion. The brief passage from New Atlantis indicates that Bacon had more than a premonition of the necessity for separating science from politics in future times when the character of scientific discovery and the vital role of the scientist in a technological civilization would place in strong relief the foolish and vicious possibilities in the use of the new knowledge by society and its exploitation by political power.

This fact is illustrative of the direct way in which Bacon's conception of the new man of science reflects in detail every facet of his thought—his criticism of knowledge, his plans for its reform, his hopes for the human race. Herein lies its richness and complexity. Among the seventeenth-century writers on science whom Bacon most directly influenced, the portrait of the man of science has already undergone some simplification. They call attention to the scientist's slowness to assent, to his freedom from contention, and to his devotion to truth rather than victory, and they emphasize, to a much greater degree than Bacon, the Christian piety to which the scientist is disposed by virtue of his science. But even when some eloquent apologist presents the scientists as a new race of Olympians,[9] certain of Bacon's more interesting and impressive overtones are lacking. In more modern times the ideal of the scientist has become almost exclusively identified with the exact and disinterested pursuit of scientific truth independent of all other considerations. And there have been hopes that on the demonstration through science that man is capable of this virtue, a new ethics for a modern society might be constructed.[10] It is only in very recent times that this latest ideal has been brought into question through unusual developments in science itself and through new developments in political theory.

Comparisons with Bacon suggest themselves, but it is at the moment hazardous to indulge in them.[11] The changing conception of the scientist is one of the unwritten pages in the history of science. When it is written, the chief irony in it may be that Bacon, who has been described as a cynic and a Machiavellian and who has been condemned for having destroyed the connection between science and religion and thus deprived science of its ethical foundations, should have created in the first clearly realized image of the scientist a figure more impressive in some respects than its successors and possibly too flattering to human nature.

NOTES

1 On Bacon's attitude toward the ancient philosophic sects see F. H. Anderson, The Philosophy of Francis Bacon (Chicago, 1948), especially chapters X, XI, XII.

2 Novum Organum, I, lxxxiv (IV, 82). Bacon said of his own contributions to knowledge, "I am wont for my own part to regard this work as a child of time rather than of wit." (Magna Instauratio (IV, 11). See also Novum Organum, I, lxxviii (IV, 77).

3 Novum Organum, I, cix (IV, 100); see also cxxix (113–5). This progressive aspect of Bacon's view of knowledge seems particularly to have fascinated the English writers on science of a later generation. Their enthusiasm seems often to arise not

so much from expectation, also voiced by Bacon, that the new science would bring in a speedy harvest, as that it gave promise of infinite progress in the effective exploration of an infinite complexity. Glanvill wrote in Plus ultra (1668), 7: "They [the Royal Society] believe, there is an inexhaustible variety of treasure which Providence hath lodged in things, that to the world's end will afford fresh discoveries, and suffice to reward the ingenious industry and researches of those that look into the works of God, and go down to see his wonders in the deep."

4 "He detested self-revelations, but whenever he painted the portrait of his ideal philosopher, pity for mankind is the dominant trait." (Benjamin Farrington, Francis Bacon, Philosopher of Industrial Science [New York, 1949], 70.)

5 See Geoffrey Bullough, "Bacon and the Defense of Learning," and Rudolf Metz, " Bacon's Part in the Intellectual Movements of His Time," in Seventeenth Century Studies in Honor of Sir Herbert Grierson (Oxford, 1938).

6 Bacon's most ambitious collection of interpretations of classical myths is De Sapientia Veterum. This aspect of his thought and art is discussed at length by Charles Lemmi, The Classic Deities in Bacon (Baltimore, 1933). Lemmi does not treat the problem of Bacon's analogous use of Biblical stories.

7 "I can report no other deficiency in Poesy; for being as a plant which comes from the lust of the earth without a formal seed, it has sprung up and spread abroad more than any other kind of learning" (IV, 318).

8 IV, 115, also III, 218, 266. See Robert P. Adams, "The Social Responsibilities of Science in Utopia, New Atlantis and After," Journal of the History of Ideas, X (1949), 374–98.

9 The following example is from Glanvill's Scepsis scientifica (London, 1665), 176–7: "Reflecting upon which great persons [the members of the Royal Society] me thinks I could easily believe, that men may differ from one another, as much as Angels do from unbodyed souls . . . . Such as these, being in good part freed from the intanglements of sense and body, are imployed like the spirits above; in contemplating the divine artifice and wisdom in the works of nature; a kind of anticipation of the aetherial happiness and imployment."

10 For instance, Karl Pearson, "Science and Citizenship," in The Grammar of Science (Everyman's), 11–12. For more recent and more popular examples, see Walter Lippmann, A Preface to Morals (New York, 1929), 235–41, and Anatol Rapoport, Science and the Goals of Man (New York, 1950).

11 A full account requires also comparisons with Bacon's contemporaries and predecessors. Such a study would show, what is already generally conceded about many other aspects of Bacon's thought, that parallels can be found for many details in the writings of Bacon's era. A good historical perspective for this purpose can be gained through Hiram Haydn's The Counter-Renaissance (New York, 1950), in particular the section specially devoted to Bacon, 251–76. It does not appear, however, that such parallels establish an equally clear perception on the part of writers other than Bacon of the necessity for remaking the model of the learned man along scientific lines, and in any event the composite picture which emerges from Bacon is his own and is, moreover, the one which fired the imagination of the next generation of scientists and popularizers of science, especially in England.

II. Bacon on Law, Politics and History

FRANCIS BACON ON THE SCIENCE OF JURISPRUDENCE

Paul H. Kocher

The world sometimes forgets that Francis Bacon was a great jurist as well as a great philosopher of natural science. All his life he fought for basic reforms in both fields, and, in both, his proposals have the same unready, unaccomplished grandeur. In the physical sciences he expected to carry the world well past Aristotle. In law by his concept of the legal maxim he hoped to stand higher than Coke in the eyes of posterity and by his digests of case and statute law to emulate on English soil the innovations of Justinian. Moreover, of prime importance to his total philosophy, he believed his inductive method as valid in the one field as in the other. About these large matters I shall make such remarks as the scope of a single essay allows.

I

As Bacon's schemes for renovation in the natural sciences grew out of a general climate of discontent with Aristotelian science in the late sixteenth century, so his plans for law reform seem to have sprung from a widespread Renaissance dissatisfaction with the state of the law inherited from the Middle Ages. Maitland points out that particularly in the second quarter of the sixteenth century there occurred in England and throughout Europe a humanist, Protestant revolt away from the barbarism, medievalism and Catholicism of the common law, with its bad Latin and worse French, its disorganization and lack of code, and towards the Roman Civil Law.[1] The latter's greater elegance and order made it a natural model for those Englishmen who sought some remedy for what seemed the growing chaos of their country's laws. Also, the authoritarian bias of the Civil Law suited the Tudor monarchy. At the height of this move-

Reprinted from the Journal of the History of Ideas, Vol. 18 (1957), pp. 3–26, by permission of the author and the publisher.

ment Henry VIII established chairs of Civil Law at Oxford and Cambridge, whence were to emanate some of the highest royalist doctrines of the Stuart period. In the event, the common law proved much too strong to be displaced, but by the end of the century some leading lawyers and statesmen were inclining to the view that a restatement of it was necessary. The Lord Keeper Puckering in his opening speech to the Parliament of 1593 urged an abridgement of the multitude of old laws rather than the passage of new, and repeated the same theme in the Parliament of 1597.[2]

Just how early in his life Bacon began thinking about legal reform seems impossible to say, but probably very early indeed. Bacon scholarship has tended to overlook the significant fact that Bacon's father, the Lord Keeper Sir Nicholas Bacon, himself favored the new movement in Henry VIII's time and "upon the dissolution of the monasteries in 1539 he drew up an excellent scheme, though never executed, for a seminary of ministers of state, by the foundation of a college for the study of the civil law, and the purity of the Latin and French tongues, in which young men of the most eminent parts being educated should some of them be sent with ambassadors abroad, and train'd up in the knowledge of foreign affairs . . . ."[3] It would be strange if young Francis Bacon brought up by such a father and sent in 1576 at the age of fifteen on diplomatic service to France, a country governed by Civil Law, on purpose to absorb a knowledge of foreign affairs, did not speedily turn his thoughts to some comparison of that law with the English common law, and thence to possible ways of improving the latter. The more so, because we know from Rawley's biography that Bacon while at Cambridge from 1573 to 1575 had already conceived ideas of reform in natural science (I, 4). Inevitably his ideas in the two fields would tend to inseminate one another, though relative temporal priorities cannot be established.[4]

The Lord Keeper's speech to the Parliament of 1593 gave Bacon, then a member, his first politically opportune moment to bring forward in a speech suggestions which he had apparently long been meditating. The laws of England were now too voluminous, he said, to be recast by any one Parliament, "being so many in number that neither common people can half practise them, nor the lawyer sufficiently understand them . . . ."[5] He therefore proposed that a commission be appointed to undertake a thorough revision after the example of the Romans under Justinian, the Athenians under Pericles, and the French under Louis XI. Citation of these precedents, especially that of Justinian's Civil Law, suggests a drive in Bacon's mind towards some kind of codification, as yet undefined. And in his masque, Gesta Grayorum (1594), written in the following year, he makes the Fifth Counsellor advise the Prince in general terms to "purge out multiplicity of laws, clear the incertainty of them, repeal those that are snaring, and press the execution of those that are wholesome and necessary; define the jurisdiction of your courts. . . ." (VIII, 339). Prescriptions like these aimed at moulding the law into a clearer and more coherent system permitting greater certainty of prediction by client, lawyer and judge in new cases—in short, at bringing law closer to a science of prediction.[6]

By the time the Lord Keeper's speech to the Parliament of 1597 gave Bacon another chance for a public hearing, he was ready to attack the problem of law reform on a different, more philosophical, front. With immense diligence he had compiled three hundred legal maxims, twenty-five of which he submitted to Queen Elizabeth in manuscript with a dedication and a preface explaining their use (VII, 313 f.). Only these twenty-five survive today, the remainder being apparently irretrievably lost. Even so, their sheer bulk and the compactness of their legal scholarship suggests that if the lost two hundred and seventy-five are like them Bacon may well have been at work on the total number since earliest manhood. The extant twenty-five did not see print until 1630, after Bacon's death, under the title Maxims of the Law. But as his first treatise on juridical theory and first presentation of his concept of the legal maxim which was to be central ever afterwards to his inductive method in law they will repay careful study.

His major aim in collecting these maxims, Bacon explains in the Preface, is to help remedy "the uncertainty of law, which is the principal and most just challenge that is made to the laws of our nation at this time . . . ." For that purpose he will "visit and strengthen the roots and foundations of the science itself . . . by collecting the rules and grounds dispersed throughout the body of the same laws. . . ." But how will a knowledge of these rules make the laws more certain? He replies,

> hereby no small light will be given, in new cases and such wherein there is no direct authority, to sound into the true conceit of law by depth of reason; in cases wherein the authorities do square and vary, to confirm the law, and to make it received one way; and in cases

> wherein the law is cleared by authority, yet nevertheless to see more profoundly into the reason of such judgments and ruled cases, and thereby to make more use of them for the decision of other cases more doubtful (VII, 319).

Here, then, as in his recommendations of the preceding years, Bacon's intent is to reform the law by making it more full, harmonious, and predictable, and in these senses scientific. But precisely what is his concept of the legal maxims which are to accomplish so much? Bacon makes it quite clear, here and in all subsequent discussions, that a maxim "points at the law but does not settle it" (V, 106). That is, a maxim is not itself law. Only actual decisions of courts or statutes passed by a legislature have the status of law. A legal maxim, on the other hand, is a generalization reached by reason from a number of such court cases or statutes. Some such maxims, the Preface continues, are already commonly known, but others have to be "gathered and extracted out of the harmony and congruity of cases, and are such as the wisest and deepest sort of lawyers have in judgment and use, though they be not able many times to express and set them down" (VII, 320). Or as Bacon was later to put it in De Augmentis Scientiarum (1623), they are "gathered from the harmony of laws and decided cases . . . and are in fact the general dictates of reason, which run through the different matters of law, and act as its ballast" (V, 105).

Since maxims thus "run through the different matters of law," they should be taken not merely from any one legal field, like torts or contracts, but from several fields at once. For example, Bacon elicits Regula I of Maxims of the Law, "In jure non remota causa, sed proxima spectatur," from cases of annuities, leases, trusts, and conveyancing of real property, and might manifestly have drawn also upon other legal areas.[7] Yet although maxims are thus generalized from the less general, they are still not legal rules of the very highest class of generality, such as, for instance, the principle that justice gives to every man his own. Rather, they seem to be generalizations or axioms of that middle order which Bacon throughout his philosophical writings describes as most fruitful for works (III, 245; IV, 50). In natural science the utility of the middle axiom is to state a rule applicable to new physical situations. In jurisprudence the utility of the maxim is similarly to provide the premises by which new cases can be decided, contradictions in existing cases erased, and analogies more safely followed out. Because of this regulative function, maxims are legum leges, "laws of laws," as Bacon several times describes them (VII, 320; V, 89).

But this is not the only significant resemblance between the legal maxim and the middle axiom of natural science. Both are arrived at by induction from accumulations of individual cases and then, once formulated, are applied back to determine new particulars. It is of the utmost importance for both, consequently, that the materials from which they are taken should be complete and accurate. Hence Bacon's well-known insistence on world-wide collections of natural history, Sylva Sylvarum, as grist for the physical and biological sciences (e.g., IV, 251–63). Hence, also, his lifelong and finally successful struggle for full, regular, painstaking reporting of law cases.[8] Furthermore, he prefers that both the legal maxim and the scientific axiom be stated aphoristically rather than hierarchically and methodically. So much is clear for natural science in the aphorisms of the Novum Organum (1620), while for law it appears in the loose unsystematic ordering of the maxims, justified thus by Bacon in the Preface to Maxims of the Law:

> Thirdly, whereas I could have digested these rules into a certain method or order . . . yet I have avoided to do so, because this delivering of knowledge in distinct and disjoined aphorisms doth leave the wit or man more free to turn and toss, and to make use of that which is delivered to more several purposes and applications. For we see all the ancient wisdom and science was wont to be delivered in that form, . . . but chiefly the precedent of the civil law, which hath taken the same course with their rules, did confirm me in my opinion (VII, 321).

Since Maxims of the Law is, I believe, the earliest of all Bacon's known writings to champion the aphorism and certainly the earliest to display it in active use, we must reckon seriously with the possibility that he was much influenced towards it by his legal studies, and specifically by his study of the Civil Law.

As is well known, Bacon considered it essential to his inductive method that it should proceed through negative instances and exclusions to every affirmative propostion (III, 387; IV, 25, 129 ff.). He applied this requirement to legal argument in his Reading on the Statute of Uses in 1600, saying: "The nature of an use is best discerned by considering first, what it is not; and then what it is: for it is the nature of all human science and knowledge to proceed most safely by negative and exclusion, to what is affirmative and inclusive" (VII, 398). And twenty years later in the Novum Organum he was merely broadening the same idea in declaring that his method, with all its features, was not restricted to natural science but embraced all fields of learning:

> It may also be asked . . . whether I speak of natural philosophy only, or whether I mean that the other sciences, logic, ethics, and politics, should be carried on by this method. Now I certainly mean what I have said to be understood of them all . . . . (IV, 112).

In the usual Baconian classification, politics includes the law.

We should therefore expect to find exclusions operating in the induction of his legal maxims. And such indeed seems to be the case, even so early as 1597. To be sure, Bacon does not take us behind the scenes to demonstrate just how he comes to each of the twenty-five specimen generalizations of his Maxims of the Law. He presents them fully formed, each followed by a number of specific cases to show where it does or does not apply. Nevertheless, we know from the Preface that each maxim derives by induction from "the harmony and congruity of cases," presumably the very cases cited under it. Presumably also, then, the cited cases to which Bacon says the maxim does not apply are in fact the negative instances he considered in formulating the maxim itself. Thus, for example, after stating the third maxim "Verba fortius accipiuntur contra preferentem" (a man's deeds and his words shall be taken strongliest against himself), Bacon writes, "But this rule, as all others which are very general, is but a sound in the air . . . except it be duly conceived in point of difference, where it taketh place, and where not" (VII, 333). He then carefully distinguishes instances of its applicability and non-applicability in the fields of grants and pleadings. These negative instances are about as numerous and emphatic as the affirmative ones. It is hard to suppose that Bacon did not mean the former to play an active role in shaping the maxim, as well as in limiting its scope after it had been shaped.[9]

To decide just how original Bacon was in this concept of the maxim would be an immense and delicate task involving a virtual history of English and continental legal philosophy. Details must remain outside our present scope. Suffice it to say generally that maxims were certainly a commonplace of legal thinking long before Bacon, as in Plowden, "A maxime is the foundation of Law, and the conclusion of reason,"[10] and in Sir John Fortescue's fifteenth-century treatise, A learned commendation of the politique lawes of England: ". . . they are certein uniuersall propositions, which thei that be learned in the Lawes of Englande, & likewise the Mathematicals do terme Maximes . . . and the Ciuilians terme them rules of law."[11] Fortescue adds that "they are knowen by induction by the waye of sense and memorye." Civil lawyers seem to have been particularly interested in the maxim or regula. Sir John Doderidge, Bacon's contemporary, quotes this definition from them in The English Lawyer (1631): "Regula juris est multorum specialium per generalem conclusionem brevis comprehensio" (p. 153). This pretty well tallies with Bacon's view. In truth, the guess is not very rash that in this, as in so many of his other attempts to systematize the law, he drew heavily upon Civil Law theory.[12]

Nevertheless it would appear that Bacon stressed the maxim's inductive aspects much more strongly than did the Civilians. And he himself considered as especially new and useful, indeed as a distinctive new departure, his practise of tying each maxim down to particulars by citing under it the concrete legal situations from which it was induced. His maxims, he remarks in the Preface to Maxims,

> be not set down alone, like short dark oracles . . . but I have attended them (a matter not practised, no not in the civil law to any purpose, and for want whereof, indeed, the rules are but as proverbs, and many times plain fallacies), with a clear and perspicuous exposition; breaking them into cases, and opening their sense and use and limiting them with distinctions; and sometimes showing the reasons above whereupon they depend, and the affinity they have with other rules (VII, 323).

This claim of innovation through keeping close to particulars in law is of course the same that Bacon made over and over in the natural sciences. It may serve to remind us once more that his aims and methods in both provinces of knowledge were much the same.

But the culmination of Bacon's concept of the maxim is yet to come. It is not merely a "law of laws," that is, a generalization from specific man-made laws, but a statement of an important precept of a higher law of reason or universal justice. We have noted the repeated assertions in *Maxims of the Law*, echoed later in Book 8 of *De Augmentis Scientiarum*, that maxims are "general dictates of reason" or "conclusions of reason." We may now add Bacon's even earlier definition in the Bridewell case (c. 1587) that "The Maxims are the foundations of the Law, and the full and perfect conclusions of reason" (VII, 509). "Common law is common reason," he affirmed in his *Reading on the Statute of Uses* (VII, 415). But maxims, in being reasonable, are also "rules which are inherent in the very form of justice; and whereby it comes that for the most part nearly the same rules are found in the civil laws of different states; except perhaps that they may sometimes vary with reference to the forms of constitutions" (*De Augmentis*, Bk. 8, Aph. 83; V, 106). Here enters the idea that since all men possess essentially the same reason, which perceives the same "form" of universal justice, the resulting laws, and maxims educed from them, will be essentially the same in the various societies of mankind. So it is not surprising that Bacon should recognize with satisfaction in the Preface to *Maxims of the Law* close similarities between English common law and Roman Civil Law, both being "dictated verbatim by the same reason" though they may vary in detail in the course of "accommodating the law to the different considerations of estate . . ." (VII, 321).

It develops, further, from *The Advancement of Learning* (1605) that this basic likeness is founded in "nature":

> there are in nature certain fountains of justice, whence all civil laws are derived but as streams; and like as waters do take tinctures and tastes from the soils through which they run, so do civil laws vary according to the regions and governments where they are planted, though they proceed from the same fountains (III, 475).

These ideas of "reason," "justice," and "nature" are drawn still nearer together by Bacon's statement in *De Augmentis* that laws derive from "natural equity" and by his proposal "to exhibit a character and idea of justice, in general comparison with which the laws of particular states and kingdoms may be tested and amended" (V, 88). His *Post-Nati* (1608) argument likewise expounds at length the view that English law in particular "is grounded upon the law of nature" (VII, 663). And the circle is closed by *An Advertisement Touching An Holy War* (1622), where the "laws of nature and nations" are said to be fixed by "Natural Reason" (VII, 30).

We shall deal presently with some of the problems raised by Bacon's thus introducing norms of universal justice into his inductive science of law. For the moment, however, suffice it to notice that a broad conspectus of his works shows him in effect equating the Law of Reason with the Law of Nature governing man's ethical and political behavior. This is a sufficiently ordinary identification, prevailing indeed in Greek, Roman, medieval and Renaissance philosophy.[13] Less orthodox, perhaps, is Bacon's making both laws practically synonymous with the Law of Nations or jus gentium, though for this also he would have the authority of Civil Law.[14] At all events, the maxims we have been studying as inductive "conclusions of reason" turn out to be at the same time principles of the "law of nature and nations." Bacon is thus voicing a conviction that the content of this law can be known by induction from existing positive laws.

Now on the surface the maxims which Bacon offers to the world in Maxims of the Law have little in common with the principles which he elsewhere, particularly in the Post-Nati case, announces as constituting the law of nature. The latter are statements of the broadest human rights such as "life, liberty, and dower" and the universal membership of all human beings in a world citizenship. On the other hand, the maxims deal with such matters as the role of intent in criminal and civil cases (Regula VII), acts done under duress (Regula V), proximate as against remote cause (Regula I), and the like. Nevertheless, unless we are to distinguish "universal justice" from the "law of nature" in a way that would have been inconceivable to Bacon, the two types of matter must be essentially the same. And they are so in fact. Some of the maxims are simply legal presumptions, rules of evidence, canons of interpretation, etc., designed to effectuate and protect the broad human rights when they reach the stage of litigation. They establish practical ties between basic human rights and the ordinary court-room scene without which the former would remain mere uninstrumented airy platitudes. Others of the maxims are themselves lesser substantive components leading up to the more broadly generalized statements of the rights. So we must visualize some dimensional thickness within Bacon's concept of the law of nature to allow for different degrees of generality and instrumentation.

In brief, then, a maxim is for Bacon a precept of the law of nature or universal justice, resembling a middle axiom in natural science. It is obtained by induction from congruous lines of cases running through several different fields of law and, when applied back to those fields, serves to promote consistency within and between them. It is thus a prime means for reforming the completeness, coherence, predictability, certainty of the law. It is, in short, the heart of a Baconian legal philosophy militantly designed to secure exactly that kind of reform.

II

During the remainder of Elizabeth's reign the cause of English legal reform made no progress. And after 1603, when James VI of Scotland became also James I of England, it became entangled in the political struggle over union of the laws of the two kingdoms. For men like Bacon who wanted something more than a merely nominal union under the person of the king the problem was to reduce the legal systems of the two countries to a genuine working unity without abolishing the cherished national differences of either (e.g. VII, 663–4). As a first step he proposed in Articles Touching the Union of the Kingdoms (1604) that "there must be made by the lawyers of either nation a digest, under titles, of their several laws and customs, as well common law as statutes; that they may be collated and compared, and that the diversities may appear and be discerned of" (X, 230). The task, if conservatism could be overcome, should not be too hard technically, he thought, because "their laws and customs have the like grounds that our have, with a little more mixture of the civil law and French customs" (X, 336). It is clear that for reconciling two national systems of law thus "dictated by the same reason" the formulation of maxims common to both would be a great help. And this seems to have been what Bacon had in mind in two rather cryptic items entered in his private journal, Commentarius Solutus, on July 31, 1608, under the heading of "Services on Foote": "The Equalling the Lawes of ye 2 Kingdomes" and "For equalling lawes to proceed wth my Methode and to shew ye K. title of prerogative as it is doon."[15] His "Methode" would appear to mean the compiling of related groups of legal maxims by induction from English and Scottish law and their use to guide subsequent legislation into harmony in the two countries. But the political difficulties proved too great to be overcome, and in 1607 Bacon found himself in the melancholy position of having to oppose as premature, in the absence of his proposed digests, a motion in Parliament for immediate union of laws (X, 336).

As the rift between James and his successive Parliaments widened, the Parliamentary party, led largely by common lawyers, came more and more to regard the common law as the one great bulwark of English liberties, and any change in it as unthinkable. Already in 1604 Coke had prefaced Part 4 of his Reports with some strong warnings about the schemes of law reform then current, among them meaning no doubt Bacon's:

> for any fundamental point of the ancient common laws and customs of the realm, it is a maxim in policy, and a trial by experience, that the alteration of them is most dangerous; for that which hath been refined and perfected by all the wisest men in former succession of ages, and proved and approved by continual experience to be good and profitable for the common wealth, cannot without great hazard and danger be altered and changed.[16]

Coke agreed to repeal of penal statutes that "remain but as snares to entangle the subjects withal" (Bacon's own favorite phrase) and to reorganization of the others into "one plain and perspicuous law divided into articles." But the sacred common law must not be so tampered with:

> For bringing of the common laws into a better method, I doubt much of the fruit of that labour. This I know, that abridgements in many professions have greatly profited the authors themselves: but as they are used, have brought no small prejudice to others: for the advised and orderly reading over of the books at large . . . I absolutely determine to be the right way to enduring and perfect knowledge; and to use abridgments as tables, and to trust only to the books at large . . . .[17]

Bacon might have replied quite truly that he agreed with every one of the points thus made, that he sought no subtle undermining of any basic tenet of the common laws but only the dropping of obsolete and repetitive laws, the resolution of contradictions and the like. Yet who could tell whether even these apparently harmless changes might not go to the very substance of the law and redound to the advantage of King or Parliament, depending on the ways in which they were made and the party allegiance of the men who made them?

Under such conditions of mutual mistrust any law reform whatever was rapidly becoming unattainable.

Bacon, however, was nothing if not persistent. In 1611, 1613, and 1614 he alluded again to his proposals, and in 1616, as Attorney General, drew up A Proposition Touching the Compiling and Amendment of the Laws of England, which expanded them further.[18] His plan for a thorough reworking of the penal statutes was evidently beginning to take some concrete shape. Bacon had been appointed by the King as head of a distinguished group of lawyers whose labors were already "of a great bulk" but nowhere near ready for final submission. It would be preferable in fact, Bacon urged, that the work be taken over by a commission named by the two houses of Parliament, since the results would eventually have to be approved by Parliament anyway.

On the more critical and touchy question of common law reform Bacon suggests, first, compilation of a book De antiquitatibus juris consisting of cases before Edward I, summarized chronologically, to serve as "reverend precedents, but not as authorities"; and, second, a digest of cases also chronological, since Edward I, omitting all cases now on the books which are obsolete, repetitive, or "idle," compressing those which are prolix and submitting to the courts for new decisions those which are contradictory (XIII, 67). These two digests are to be the body of the law itself. As auxiliaries to its study Bacon proposes an improved law dictionary, a well organized, brief summary of the whole law like Justinian's Institutes, and a book of maxims De regulis juris like his own Maxims of the Law.

On the latter he places special emphasis. "I hold it," he says, "of all other things the most important to the health (as I may term it) and good institutions of any laws." He repeats the old warning that maxims must be presented not nakedly but with "good differences, ampliations, and limitations, warranted by good authorities." He adds that in the collection of such maxims he had himself labored "at the first more cursorily, since with more diligence," and that he is "in good hope that when Sir Edward Coke's Reports, and my rules and decisions shall come to posterity, there will be (whatsoever is now thought) question, who was the greater lawyer?" (XIII, 70). So although in Bacon's view the book of maxims cannot be more than an auxiliary to the case digests which are themselves the law, it is an auxiliary of such importance that he is willing to rest on it his chief prospects for professional fame.

Also vitally significant in A Proposition is Bacon's refusal to go all the way towards the codification of case law. Although mentioning Justinian by name and obviously taking many ideas for the case compilations from the Roman Digest,[19] when Bacon comes to the crucial point he balks at rewriting English common law under orderly heads and titles in the manner of the Civil Law. Bacon's case digests are always to be chronological, preserving the sequence of the Year Books. Some may argue, he admits, that "Labour were better bestowed in bringing the common laws of England to a text law, as the statutes are, and setting both of them down in method and by titles." But he replies,

> It is too long a business to debate whether lex scripta aut non scripta, a text law or customs well registred, with received and approved grounds and maxims, and acts and resolutions judicial from time to time duly entered and reported, be the better form of declaring and authorizing laws . . . Customs are laws written in living tables; and some traditions the Church doth not disauthorize. In all sciences, they are the soundest that keep close to particulars: and sure I am there are more doubts that rise upon our statutes, which are a text law, than upon the common law, which is no text law. But howsoever that question be determined, I dare not advise to cast the law into a new mould. The work which I propound tendeth to proyning and grafting the law, and not to ploughing up and planting it again; for such a remove I should hold indeed for a perilous innovation.[20]

In taking this stand Bacon no doubt had one eye on the political impossibility of radically recasting the common law at that time. But it also represents, as the reference to keeping "close to particulars" shows, a deep personal conviction extending all through his world outlook. For him a system of case law which, though streamlined into as much clarity and consistency as possible, yet retained its basically historical pattern was far preferable to a neatly finished code from which all subsequent law had to be deduced. He liked the greater flexibility of a series of case decisions, chronologically arranged, from which new inductive generalizations might constantly be made.

Nothing tangible came of A Proposition or even of the labors of Bacon's group on the penal statutes. They evaporated exasperatingly into the political miasmas of the period. Even after his fall in 1621 Bacon again offered to prepare a digest of English case law along the lines indicated in A Proposition, provided that the King would appoint the necessary legal assistants.[21] But if Bacon wanted to be an English Trebonianus, James would not or could not be an English Justinian. Bacon's last word on the subject in Book 8 of De Augmentis (V, 88–109), therefore, is addressed not to an English but to a world audience and discusses means of attaining certainty not in the laws of England specifically but in any legal system whatever. It presupposes neither code nor case law, neither monarchy, aristocracy, nor democracy. Assuming only that there are both courts and legislatures, it is a discourse on the methods of legal science in so far as they pertain to making laws as clear, harmonious and exhaustive as humanly possible. True, Bacon's ideas of the problems which beset the search for legal predictability are colored by his own experience with English law and politics. And the aphorisms in which he frames them are visibly scarred with the struggles of his past career—to protect Chancery against the encroachment of the common law courts (Aph. 45), to defend such instruments of monarchical centralism as the Court of Star Chamber (Aph. 32ff.), to assert the King's prerogative over the laws in some respects (Aph. 58), to repeal snaring penal laws (Aphs. 13 & 53), to secure proper reporting of cases (Aph. 73), and so on. In fact, many of the proposals which he makes here are brought over bodily from his earlier recommendations for systematizing English law, especially from A Proposition. But since those recommendations were themselves very broadly conceived from the first and incorporated many ideas from Roman, Athenian and French reforms, the universality of the product is not seriously impaired.

Now if there is to be any "certainty" in law, there must exist in each field legal generalizations under which every new case that comes up will clearly fall. In a system of case law these generalizations must be attainable easily by induction from a line of settled authorities. Bacon therefore begins his treatment in De Augmentis with a series of aphorisms considering the problem situations in which no such settled line can be found, but there are cases similar, though not exactly in point (Aphs. 11–20), or, if a few cases in point, not enough of them to be authoritative (Aphs. 21–31). Especially interesting here are Bacon's repeated warnings (Aphs. 15, 23–4) that the historical circumstances under which any given case was decided must be taken into account in using it as a precedent for modern cases, since "the times also when they passed give light to a wise judge" (Aph. 76). For this suggests that Bacon recognizes some social and historical limitations to rigid induction in law. Also troublesome in a similar way are situations in which different courts, competing for jurisdiction over the same class of cases, hand down contradictory judgments (Aphs. 94–7), or where statutes are obscure by reason of ambiguity, verbosity, or overconciseness (Aphs. 65–71).

Granting, now, that clear and consistent legal generalizations obtain in a given field, yet the application of them by deduction to some specific case where the circumstances are out of the ordinary may result in obvious injustice. This, the problem of equity, is raised by Bacon in an important group of aphorisms (32–46). The growing resort to equity in the sixteenth century for relief against the strictness of the common law in England had led to more and more friction between Chancery and common law courts like the Court of Common Pleas, finally necessitating the King's intervention in 1616 to define and establish equity jurisdiction.[22] As the son of a Chancery judge and as Chancellor himself from 1618 to 1621, Bacon was bound to advocate that equity be kept separate from law (Aph. 45). And as a jurist with a strong penchant for making law as scientific as possible he was also bound to be keenly aware that if too many cases were left, as some must be, to "the judgment and discretion of a conscientious man" no definite science of law would remain: "the judge would pass into the legislator, and everything would be at discretion" (Aph. 44). He therefore stipulates that exceptions to legal generalizations reached either by case law or by statute must be restricted to "monstrous and extraordinary cases" (Aph. 36). They must not become so numerous as to destroy the generalizations themselves. Law must remain a science, not a chaos of individual judicial temperaments.

If, finally, the legal generalizations in force in any one country become, by gradual historical accretion, so obsolete, confused, and contradictory as to cease to provide a valid basis for prediction, they should be completely overhauled by the preparation of new digests of both case law and statute law (Aphs. 59–64). This is "a heroic work," says Bacon (Aph. 59), and by using the term "instauration" (Aph. 64) he palpably suggests a comparison with his Instauratio Magna for the natural sciences. The references to Justinian and Trebonianus (Aphs. 60. 61), together with the specific program for abolishing the obsolete, resolving the contradictory, compressing the prolix, and so forth, repeated largely from A Proposition, leave little doubt that Bacon had in mind here the example of Justinian's reforms. Nevertheless here, as before, he stops short of recommending codification of case law by writing a new text organized under topics. The new case digest is still to be "in chronological order, and not by method and titles" (Aph. 76). He sees no objection, however, to a thorough topical reorganization and rewriting of statute law, provided that the wording of the old statutes is retained so far as possible (Aph. 62). In this, as we have noted, even Coke concurred, at least so far as penal statutes were concerned.

How does the legal maxim fit into the De Augmentis aphorisms? From Aphorism 6 it would appear that Bacon at first thought of including in De Augmentis a series of maxims like those in his early Maxims of the Law, in fact making it his chief example of "Universal Justice":

> I will therefore set down according to the best of my judgment, what may be called certain "laws of laws," whereby we may derive information as to the good or ill set down and determined in every law.

We know from his own statement in A Proposition that since those early days he had been working "more diligently" on their compilation and expected to challenge comparison with Coke through them. Yet quite abruptly in Aphorism 7 he changes his tack in order to discuss "the virtues and dignities of laws in general." Whereupon we get not the promised maxims but a treatise on the certainty of laws as described above.

The probable explanation is that at the last moment Bacon decided that his new maxims were not yet ready for publication. And small wonder. To make them real examples of "Universal Justice" he would have had to extract them not solely from English law but also from all other national laws according to his own principles of induction. This titanic task was obviously out of the question for a man now old and sick, still harboring untold designs for natural science, and hurrying as much of his work as possible into the press. He therefore substituted for it his aphorisms on legal certainty, which required only generalizations from his long struggle for English law reform.

Yet even there he managed to reserve an honored place, as in A Proposition, for the suggestion that a book of maxims be prepared as an aid to all practitioners of the law: "A good and careful treatise on the different rules of law conduces as much as anything to the certainty thereof; and it deserves to be entrusted to the ablest and wisest lawyers" (Aph. 82). In the three following aphorisms Bacon then went on to expound its theory and utility in the same terms as when he first broached the subject twenty-six years before in Maxims of the Law. Although, therefore, neither he nor anyone else in his day consummated what Bacon thought was the greatest legal work of all, and though his own efforts in it after 1597 have quite disappeared, he never abandoned faith in the book of maxims as a cornerstone of legal philosophy. He felt to the end that only by its aid could legal generalizations within each field be harmonized with one another and with the law as a totality. Only so could the law realize its full character as a rational science.

III

Bacon's bribe-taking as Chancellor to the contrary notwithstanding, he was interested in making the law not merely more scientific but more just, more in conformity with an absolute standard of "nature" or "reason" subsisting eternally outside and above it. Indeed in his own mind the whole point of his long struggle to make the law more certain was thereby to make it more just. Opening the aphorisms of De Augmentis, Book 8, he wrote: "Certainty is so essential to law, that law cannot even be just without it" (Aph. 8). And to him legal maxims, which are a prime philosophical device for procuring maximum certainty, are likewise a means for procuring justice. They are "general dictates of reason" which "are inherent in the very form of justice" (Aphs. 82, 83). As such they help to ensure that the laws within particular legal fields to which they apply will be kept healthily sound, for "particular and positive learnings of laws do easily decline from a good temper of justice, if they be not rectified and governed by such rules" (VII, 320). Bacon shows that he uses them for this purpose by stating in the Preface to Maxims of the Law that in their formulation "in some few cases, I did intend expressly to weigh down the authorities by evidence of reason, and therein rather to correct the law, than either to soothe a received error, or by unprofitable subtlety, which corrupteth the sense of the law, to reconcile contrarieties" (VII, 322).

But this requirement of justice poses a fundamental problem for Bacon's inductive method. For if the cases from which a maxim is drawn should happen to be unjust, the maxim itself will infallibly be unjust also. Yet a maxim by very definition is a "conclusion or dictate of reason" and therefore cannot be unjust. Bacon nowhere discusses this dilemma explicitly in good set terms, but the line of his answer is clear enough. It is, quite simply, that the great majority of cases and statutes in the great majority of legal systems are just. Of English laws in general, for example, he said in A Proposition: "Certainly they are wise, they are just and moderate laws; they give to God, they give to Caesar, they give to subjects, that which appertaineth" (XIII, 63). That was why he could maintain that his Maxims corrected existing laws only "in some few cases," and also why he could honestly believe that a thorough clarification was a sufficient program for English legal reform. Furthermore he was convinced that the same conditions obtained in most laws of most foreign states, because in fact the laws of the several states were essentially alike, as indicated in Aphorism 83 of Book 8 of De Augmentis: ". . . for the most part nearly the same rules are found in the civil laws of different states; except perhaps that they may sometimes vary with reference to the forms of constitutions" (V, 106). Without this faith that the vast majority of man-made laws are just, Bacon could not have believed in both induction and justice.

Now Bacon was not so fatuous or so callous a watcher of the hardships of the law as to hold that whatever is is right. One of his earliest complaints (in Gesta Grayorum, 1594) was against "snaring" penal statutes and one of his latest the bitter observation (in De Augmentis, Bk. 8, Aph. 6) that "there is a strange and extreme difference in laws; some being excellent, some moderately good, and others entirely vicious." But this viciousness of some laws would not make Bacon's inductive method irreconcilable with justice, provided that the induction were broad enough to rest on the good majority rather than the evil minority. True, a whole line of authorities might in some rare instances go wrong. The remedy then was to broaden the area of observed cases to other fields of law within the same national system, or to the same fields in other national systems. From this extended base a true maxim could then be induced, and by its touchstone the line of erring cases condemned. This was in fact what Bacon was about in his final, abortive attempt to discover from the laws of all nations "certain 'laws of laws' whereby we may derive information as to the good or ill set down and determined in every law" (Aph. 6).

But beyond lingers still unsatisfied the ultimate problem of how the majority of laws, or indeed any individual law whatever, comes to be just. In the last analysis, surely not by induction merely, for induction of itself is only a process of logic which has no necessary connection with external norms of justice but builds its coherent and predictable systems out of all materials at hand, just and unjust alike. Any such system might conceivably be perfectly symmetrical and at the same time perfectly evil. Following Renaissance custom, Bacon therefore links induction to justice by two other sources of legal knowledge, divine revelation and Natural Reason, but with rather more emphasis on the latter.

This Natural Reason is clearly something other than the rational process of induction which Bacon also calls "reason." It is a kind of intuitive apprehension, native to the human mind, which enables it to read accurately the law of universal justice or nature written in the heart of every man. Christopher St. Germain's influential little Dialoges (1569) describes it typically:

> And thys lawe is alwaye good and righteous, styryng and enclyning a manne to good . . . And it is wrytten in the hart of euerye man teachynge him what is to be done and what is to be fled . . . And therefore againste this lawe, prescription, statute, nor custome maye not preuaile . . . .[23]

This was one of the many senses of the term "reason" customarily accepted among common lawyers as well as Renaissance political, ethical, and religious thinkers.[24] But everyone agreed that the danger to any unassisted use of such reason lay in passion or prejudice, which might blind it into reading justice awry.

Precisely how Natural Reason and logical induction worked together in the development of law is a problem that Bacon did not dissect in detail. He was too much interested in exploring the empirical, inductive side of the process. But he seems to have thought of the rationally intuitive (if the term is permissible) as operating mainly at the beginning of a new legal system or a new train of cases within an old one. Thus for him the inception of any great new corpus of laws by a king such as Justinian or Edward I or his own King Solamona in New Atlantis has in it something transcendent (III, 144: "a divine instrument, though a mortal man"). The lawgiver is God's instrument, whose perception reaches out more aptly to the law of nature or justice than does that of ordinary mortals. Thereafter every case, every statute, for which there is no firm precedent requires the same kind of insight. Law is grounded on a series of such insights. For "time, according to the ancient saying, is the wisest of all things, and daily creates and invents new cases" (De Augmentis, Bk. 8, Aph. 32). In this way the "particulars" from which induction seeks to generalize its systematic rules of law are impregnated from the first with the individual judge's or legislator's estimate of what is just.

Yet Natural Reason may become idiosyncratic, and law cannot survive simply as a series of unrelated individual judgments. The scientist in Bacon feels a special horror of the kind of judge-made law where "everything would be at discretion" (Aph. 44), as we have noted before. After the initial statutes have been passed and cases decided, therefore, induction looks broadly about for majority points of view, elicits from them its principles or maxims, and by these helps to render the future uniform with the past.

Even this description of the primary functions of the two forms of "reason," inductive and intuitive, in Bacon's jurisprudence is something of an oversimplification, however. For he knows that there is never any clear-cut beginning where intuition operates alone; there are always prior laws or analogies which induction will offer as precedents.[25] Similarly, there are never, in the complexities of human lot, any two legal cases so exactly alike but that a jurist, while consulting the authority of principles induced from the past, will not consult also his own sense of fair play in reaching a decision. This is the very essence of equity, which Bacon is always most anxious to preserve. Consequently, though one form of "reason" may be uppermost at one time and the other at another, both are constantly present and in active interplay.

Bacon's chief concern here is to insist that the two kinds of "reason" do not conflict. If they seem to do so in any given case it is because either the induction is not broadly enough based or the intuition is not sufficiently free from passion and prejudice. An induction that looks to the whole of the pertinent man-made law and an intuition that lucidly apprehends the engraved law of nature will always reach the same result, for, despite the Fall, the first sort of law is a valid expression in human terms of the second sort. Reason as intuitive apprehension therefore does not destroy or make impossible a science of law. It merely assures that this science shall keep always in close touch with justice.

So, in this respect, Bacon recognizes a world of difference between jurisprudence and, let us say, the science of physics or biology. A law of physics only states what is; but the "law of nature" which is the subject of jurisprudence states what ought to be. For the former, induction is a sufficient, indeed the only, method. For the latter, it must be coupled with rational intuition. More, it must sometimes be coupled also with divine revelation, as will now appear.

Bacon usually keeps the question of religion well out of his legal thought, though it haunts the background indistinctly in some of his references to universal justice. When, however, he confronts the legal institutions of certain states which strike him as totally bad or barbarous he frequently appeals explicitly to divine revelation as well as to the rationally known law of nature in order to condemn them. Thus he describes Irish laws, which are founded on "blood, incontinency and theft" as violating both "religion reformed" and the laws of all civilized communities (X, 48, 51). They merit only complete extirpation and replacement by English law. Similarly, Papal attempts to murder English sovereigns are "not only against all Christianity and religion, but against nature, the law of nations . . . ," so that there should be directed against the Papal state "some holy war or league among all Christian princes of either religion for the extirpating and rasing of this opinion and the authors thereof from the face of the earth . . ." (VIII, 275, 306; and XII, 157). In both these cases Bacon arrives at a concept of the law of nature, by which to condemn the offending system, both through divinely revealed Scripture and through induction from the accepted legal practices in most countries of western Europe. The one method supplements and reaches the same conclusion as, the other.

Bacon's clearest and most far-reaching use of this dual approach is in his late, unfinished dialogue, An Advertisement Touching a Holy War (1622), on the question whether a Christian crusade against the Turks is justifiable. The debate is intended to display the views of six speakers, a soldier, a statesman, a courtier, and three clergymen of different persuasions, but unhappily Bacon completed only the opening argument by Zebedaeus, described as "a Romish Catholic Zelant." The latter's thesis is that the basic institutions of the Turks are damned "both by the laws of nature and nations, and by the law divine, which is the perfection of the other two" (VII, 28 ff.). All these laws have been ordained by God, the original donor of government, who requires that men should found their societies in His image. Therefore any state deeply and openly flouting them becomes an outlaw justly subject to suppression by the community of civilized nations. As parallel instances Zebedaeus cites such other unnatural states as that of the pirates of Algiers, the naked Peruvians of the New World who sacrifice and eat each other, the Amazons where women rule men, the Anabaptists of Munster who depend merely on inspirations of the spirit, the Mamelukes where slaves govern the free, and so on. Any war against such an outlaw is a holy war.

We need not suppose that Bacon, who was neither "zelant" nor Roman Catholic, would necessarily have taken quite such high religious ground as Zebedaeus or thrown quite so wide a net of condemnation. Nevertheless the latter was doing substantially what Bacon himself did in the cases of the Papacy and Ireland. He was proceeding by induction from the legal mores of civilized mankind to a law of nature or nations (here substantially identified), and at the same time deducing the provisions of this law from Scripture. The results of the two methods do not clash in any way. Reason and revelation are equally capable of disclosing the law of nature, and what they disclose turns out to be the same. As before, Bacon's underlying assumption is that civilized laws in the large are accurate rendering of this higher law. And it is all too clear that for him the laws of western Europe, chiefly the English common law and the Roman Civil Law with its more recent manifestations, constitute civilization. But we really should not expect of Bacon and his contemporaries the relativistic tolerance of the modern cultural anthropologist.

In one case only did Bacon ever admit that the consensus of civilized national laws might fail to express the law of nature as revealed by religion. This was in his Post-Nati argument in favor of the English citizenship of all children born in Scotland after James's ascent to the English throne in 1603. There Bacon appealed to the Bible and to the Christian dogma of creation as establishing a world citizenship for every human being by the law of nature, despite a unanimity of national laws to the contrary:

> For, my lords, by the law of nature all men in the world are naturalized one towards another; they were all made of one lump of earth, of one breath of God; they had the same common parents; nay, at the first they were, as the Scripture sheweth, unius labii, of one language, until the curse. . . . It was civil and national laws that brought

> in these words, and differences, of civis and exterus, alien and native.[26]

Obviously this was a highly exceptional case, in which the fault lay not so much with the laws as with the very existence of separate national states. Yet it shows that where a conflict did arise between revelation and inductive reason Bacon was prepared to abandon the latter, for nations may be wrong sometimes but Scripture never.

In Bacon's view, therefore, the relation between Scripture and human knowledge is radically different in jurisprudence from what it is in the natural sciences. In the natural sciences Bacon insists strongly that the Bible makes no attempt whatever to reveal scientific truth (e.g., III, 486). The only road to such truth is through induction. But the Bible may say something very important indeed about law, politics, ethics, and the like. When it does, its word is paramount. Yet this word, consisting of the most general precepts, does not diverge significantly in normal cases from what human laws, in their more specific ways, provide. For, after all, these laws are initially grounded upon, and continually refreshed by, recourse to the same law of nature which it is the business of Scripture to reveal. Only in the rarest instances does all mankind go utterly astray. This normal rightness of human laws is what makes possible a science of law which is inductive and at the same time just and religious. "The knowledge of man," Bacon wrote in The Advancement of Learning, "is as the waters, some descending from above, and some springing from beneath; the one informed by the light of nature, the other inspired by divine revelation" (III, 346). He would never have dreamed of admitting that in law, as in all other fields of human science, the two streams did not run together in the end. Consequently, for him both approaches to the law of nature, the rational (inductive or intuitive) and the revelational, retain their propriety. This is indeed the only possible solution for a philosopher whose metaphysics forces him to believe in a dualism of God and matter, revelation and rational induction.

The religious element in Bacon's thought is, I think, deep and permanent. Yet his personal preference in most subjects, law among them, is for the waters "springing from beneath." One token of this is the notable absence of specifically religious ideas anywhere in either Maxims of the Law or the legal aphorisms of De Augmentis. We hear much of reason and justice and nature, but nothing of God.

No doubt if asked, or if special occasion offered, he would have been the first to admit that God was the source of all these, therein aligning himself with such other English thinkers as Richard Hooker, Christopher St. Germain, and Sir John Fortescue. This had been the medieval attitude, and it was still that of most Renaissance philosophers, especially in England.[27] But when not specially compelled by the argument, he felt more at home in rising to generals through particulars, in framing his maxims out of a "harmony of cases," in seeking justice through certitude by polishing the internal coherence of the law. In this preference we may well see the seeds of that increasing separation of the concept of the law of nature from Christian religion which was to proceed through philosophers like Grotius, Pufendorf, and Locke to a culmination in the Enlightenment.

Finally, a word about the place of law in Bacon's over-all philosophy. Side by side with law in the Baconian classification of Human Philosophy lie the kindred sciences of ethics and politics. We have Bacon's word for it in the _Novum Organum_ and elsewhere that their methods characteristically resemble those of law in being both inductive and normative. Farther off, but still closely related to all three, lie the natural sciences, which are simpler because solely inductive. All these groups of sciences contribute their respective axioms or maxims by induction to a still more inclusive mother of all sciences called by Bacon _Philosophia Prima_ (III, 346 ff.; IV, 336 ff.). Here are mingled, related, and distilled to a higher quintessence the most general principles of law, physics, politics, mathematics and the other contributory fields. And still farther above these, if man could only see it, hovers mysteriously the "summary law of nature," a kind of super-Einsteinian formula, neither wholly humanistic nor wholly naturalistic, by which God governs the created universe (III, 265; VI, 730).

It follows that none of the individual sciences can really be understood or perfected except in relation to all the others. This is Bacon's often repeated principle of the unity and interdependence of the sciences. Thus he believed that anyone developing a system of law within a given nation must take into account not merely other national systems, as we have noted, but also, obviously, the principles of psychology, ethics, and politics, and, less obviously, those of biology, chemistry, physics, and the rest. So, in dedicating his _Arguments of Law_ (c. 1616) to his colleagues in Gray's Inn, Bacon was able to claim

> these arguments which I have set forth (most of them) are upon subjects not vulgar, and therewithal, in regard of the commixture that the course of my life hath made of law with other studies, they may have the more variety, and perhaps the more depth of reason: for the reasons of municipal laws severed from the grounds of nature, manners, and policy are like wall flowers, which, though they grow high upon the crests of states, yet they have no deep roots (VII, 524, 529; and X, 328).

He means here not just that a court of law should know something about geology and engineering in a mining case, for example. He means that the more a barrister or judge knows about the principles of other sciences the better he will be able to generalize from them by induction to the yet broader principles of Philosophia Prima, and the better able then to apply the latter to the individual case before him by deduction. Philosophia Prima is to law in general what the legal maxim is to particular laws.[28] It is both a harmony of all the sciences and a standard by which each, or any part thereof, should be tested. It is a means of assuring that law will advance in consort with other fields of knowledge. Induction within the law itself is not enough. Law must seek the broadest possible base for its empirical processes, and ideally this base cannot be anything less than the whole of human experience.

NOTES

1 Frederic W. Maitland, "English Law and the Renaissance," in Select Essays in Anglo-American Legal History (Cambridge University, 1907), I, 168–207. Cf. W. S. Holdsworth, A History of English Law (London, 1922–), IV, 276–8, 288; Paul Vinogradoff, "Reason and Conscience in Sixteenth-Century Jurisprudence," Law Quarterly Review, XXIV (1908), 373–84.

2 Holdsworth, V, 486. See Works, VIII, 209, and IX, 77.

3 Thomas Birch, Memoirs of the Reign of Queen Elizabeth (London, 1754), I, 10, citing Burnet, History of the Reformation, 2nd ed., I, 269.

4 Holdsworth, V, 239, emphasizes the influence of Bacon's legal studies, especially under a case law system, upon his general philosophic thought.

5 VIII, 214. See p. 130 of the same volume for a Device presented by Bacon in 1592 before Queen Elizabeth praising her for "a course taken by her own direction for the repealing of all heavy and snared laws, if it had not been crossed by those to whom the benefit should have redounded."

6 Good general essays on law as a science are Frederick Pollock's "The Science of Case Law," Essays in Jurisprudence and Ethics (London, 1882), 237–60, and James Bryce's "The Methods of Legal Science" in Studies in History and Jurisprudence (Oxford, 1901), II, 174f. Cf. Holdsworth, IV, 288.

7 Spedding, VII, 327. Other typical maxims: Regula X: "Verba generalia restringuntur ad habilitatem rei vel personae" (all words . . . if they be general and not express and precise, shall be restrained unto the fitness of the matter and the person); Regula XI: "Jura sanguinis nullo jure civili dirimi possunt" (rights conferred by blood relationship cannot be taken away by any civil law); Regula XII: "Receditur a placitis juris potium quam injuriae et delicta maneant impunita" (law will dispense with its own positive rules rather than leave crimes and wrongs unpunished).

8 In 1614 Bacon as Attorney General prepared A Memorial Touching the Review of Penal Laws and the Amendment of the Common Law, in which he urged that "his Majesty may be pleased to restore the ancient use of Reporters," a request soon afterwards put into effect by the appointment of two official court reporters (XII, 86). Bacon later devoted to the question four aphorisms (73–6) of De Augmentis, Bk. 8 (V, 104).

9 Cf. Bacon's language in the Preface to Maxims of the Law, describing his manner of limiting maxims already proverbially known: ". . . I have reduced them to a true application, limiting and defining their bounds. . . . For as, both in the law and other sciences, the handling of questions by commonplace, without aim or application, is the weakest; so yet nevertheless many common principles and generalities are not to be contemned, if they be well derived and deduced into particulars, and their limits and exclusions duly assigned" (VII, 320).

10 Quoted by Sir John Doderidge, The English Lawyer (London, 1631), 152. Interestingly enough, Doderidge, 149–258, makes

a long proposal on the extraction and use of legal maxims, which seems an imitation of Bacon's much earlier work.

11 Fol. 21[v].

12 The facts that he calls his maxims regulae, that he fetches his description of them as "laws of laws" from an unnamed "great civilian," that he says he follows Civil Law precedent in presenting them aphoristically, and that he sometimes, as in Regula XI, adopts the very wording of Civil Law maxims for his own all point in that direction. On the latter item see Bacon's statements in Maxims of the Law, VII, 321 and 357.

13 Sir Frederick Pollock, "The History of the Law of Nature," Journal of the Society of Comparative Legislation, N.S., II (1900), 418–33; Charles G. Haines, The Revival of Natural Law Concepts (Harvard University, 1930), 39–44.

14 The Civil Law, ed. S. P. Scott (Cincinnati, 1932), editor's Preface to I, 19; James Bryce, "The Law of Nature," Studies in History and Jurisprudence, 135ff.

15 XI, 94. Six days earlier, on July 25, he had listed among his compositions a book, "Regulae Juris cum limitationibus et casibus," presumably a later version of the Maxims. Ibid., 60.

16 Sir Edward Coke, The Reports, ed. J. Thomas & J. Frazer (London, 1826), II, pt. 4, p. v.

17 Ibid., x. Coke is careful to add that the same caution applies also to important statutes "woven into the common law."

18 For the 1611 and 1613 allusions see XI, 242, 372. For A Proposition see XIII, 61ff. A Memorial Touching the Review of Penal Laws and the Amendment of the Common Law (1614), XII, 84–6, contained in germ the ideas developed in A Proposition.

19 Compare Bacon's detailed proposals for removing Homonymiae (repetitions) and Antinomiae (contradictions) with Justinian's prefaces to Code and Digest, especially in the latter his instructions to the commission headed by Tribonian: "If you find in the old books anything that is not suitably arranged, superfluous, or incomplete, you must remove all superfluities, supply what is lacking, and present the entire work in regular form. . . .

Therefore, in no part of the aforesaid treatise, shall there be any place for antinomia [this was derived by antiquity from a Greek word], but there must be such conformity and consistency therein that there will be no opportunity for contradiction . . . We desire . . . that all repetition shall also be banished from this compilation." Civil Code, ed. Scott, II, 180–1; XII, 3, 6ff.

20 XIII, 67. In the Memorial of 1614 Bacon likewise emphasized that "the Common Law of England . . . is no Text law" and recommended the same kind of chronological case digests purged of superfluities and contradictions (XII, 85).

21 An Offer of a Digest, XIV, 358ff. This document is much like A Proposition but less specific in details of the plan and longer as to the reasons why it should be undertaken. See also Bacon's notes in preparation for an interview with the King in March, 1622: XIV, 351.

22 Holdsworth, IV, 275ff.; Bacon, XII, 383, 385ff.; Vinogradoff, 378–9.

23 Fol. 4r. Bacon uses the expression "Natural Reason" specifically in An Advertisement Touching a Holy War (VII, 30), and it is evident that many of his previously cited references to the rationality of the legal maxim are purposely ambiguous, containing this meaning as well as the inductive one.

24 Pollock, "The History of the Law of Nature," 432. Richard Hooker, Laws of Ecclesiastical Polity, is of course the best known English exponent of the doctrine.

25 Bacon often says, for instance, that English laws, though put on a firmer foundation by Edward I, go back to Saxon, Danish, and Roman antiquities; and he was well aware that Justinian merely codified more ancient Roman laws.

26 VII, 664. The doctrine has Stoic overtones. See Cicero, De Legibus (Loeb), I, x; Bryce, "The Law of Nature," 139.

27 Bryce, "The Law of Nature," 157ff.; Haines, 21–7.

28 Valerius Terminus, III, 229: ". . . sciences distinguished have a dependence upon universal knowledge to be augmented and rectified by the superior light thereof, as well as the parts and members of a science have upon the Maxims of the same science, and the mutual light and consent which one part receiveth of another."

DISCUSSION IN PARLIAMENT AND FRANCIS BACON

Karl R. Wallace

Students of rhetoric who concentrate on the English Renaissance have had much to say about the principles, practice, and teaching of speech-making in the days of Elizabeth and James, 1558–1625. They have had almost nothing to tell us about another form of oral communication, discussion and conference. Doubtless they have ignored the form because the writings of the Renaissance have little to say about the processes of arriving at group decisions through systematic colloquy. The men of Elizabeth spoke eloquently and they talked much about eloquence, little of discussion as such. The principal reason for this state of affairs was that parliamentary debate had by no means stabilized and regularized its forms and procedures in Elizabeth's reign, 1558–1603. These years were the late adolescent age of parliamentary debate. The reign of James I, 1603–1625, saw parliamentary discussion take on a sort of green, rather than ripe, maturity. Discussion was stimulated principally because the struggle between divine kingship and popular, representative government came to a focus, although not to a climax, under James. The chief sign of emerging parliamentary maturity is probably seen in the growth and stability of the committee, for it is in committee procedures that discussion rather than speechmaking controls decisions.

Francis Bacon seems to stand unique among the men of our period. He was the only great personality to combine the interests and activities of cyclopedist and theorist on communication and rhetoric with the practical experience of political speaker and participant in conference. In the Advancement of Learning and its expanded Latin translation, De Augmentis Scientiarum, he took all knowledge as his intellectual province and presented a systematic, consistent chart of the fields of learning, in which he found a significant and essential place for the arts and sciences of language

Reprinted from The Quarterly Journal of Speech, Vol. 43 (1957), pp. 12–21, by permission of the author and the publisher.

in general, and for grammar, rhetoric, and logic in particular. His experience in nine parliaments of Elizabeth and James embraced 36 years, 1584–1621, from his entry as ordinary citizen to his emergence and fall as Lord Chancellor, Viscount St. Alban. If we may judge from the respect and confidence he enjoyed in the House of Commons as orator from the floor, as reporter of their business and their King's, and as participant in scores of committee sessions, he was extremely active and effective in political deliberation. Out of that experience, as a man of theory and a man of action, Bacon distilled some observations on group discussion which, so far as I can discover, are unique to his day.

How much influence, if any, Bacon exerted on parliamentary customs it is hard to say. Conversely, one cannot say confidently how much impact his experience in parliament made upon his thought and writings. Nevertheless, his observations assume depth when viewed in the context of his experience. Our abstractions, T. S. Eliot once wrote, are likely to have their objective correlatives.

Most of Bacon's observations, practical in nature, appear in the essays, "Of Discourse," "Of Dispatch," and "Of Counsel." A few remarks, largely theoretical, occur in the *Advancement of Learning*. To me it is significant that the essay on discourse, together with those on faction and negotiation (three of the ten essays in the first edition, 1597) were probably shaped during Bacon's early parliamentary years.[1] Although not published until 1607, the *Advancement* was undergoing final composition during the last two of Elizabeth's parliaments and the first two of James's, when parliament was more active than it ever had been. The essays on dispatch and counsel first appeared in the 1612 edition of the essays. When he wrote to Henry, Prince of Wales, about them, Bacon was aware of their chief inspiration. The essays are, he said, "of a nature, whereof a man shall find much in experience, litle in bookes; so they are neither repeticons nor fansies."[2] In 1607 Bacon became Solicitor General, and the duties of that office may have gradually shifted his primary allegiance from the Commons to the Crown.[3]

One does not fully grasp Bacon's pronouncements on political discussion and conference except in the context of parliamentary activity.[4] We shall turn now to the chief features of parliamentary discussion as exemplified by the committees of the House of Commons. With some knowledge of committee activity as a frame of reference, we can then present Bacon's observations on group discussion.

DISCUSSION IN PARLIAMENT AND FRANCIS BACON

I

During Bacon's time, the committees of the House of Commons took over the chief burden of discussion and deliberation. By about the 1620's, motions, bills, and petitions received their fullest discussion in committee rather than on the floor of the House. In the reigns of Elizabeth and James, a bill normally went through three readings, and at the second reading, a good deal of informed debate could—and sometimes did—take place.[5] In 1607, if we may accept the observation of the House Clerk, Bowyer, "important" matters were discussed at the second reading: ". . . by the Custome of the House, Matters of Importance are to be discussed openly in the House before the same be committed; and so was this Bill [re draining of the Fenns] argued in the open House, and Ordered That Councell was for the Bill as against it shall be heard in the House on Wednesday next, and in the meane tyme it was not committed."[6] The tendency to curtail House debate seems to have disturbed Bacon as early as 1600! "We have turned out divers Bills without Disputation: and for a House of Wisdom and gravity as this is, to bandy Bills like Balls, and to be silent as if no Body were of counsel with the Common-Wealth is unfitting."[7]

Nevertheless, at the second stage most bills were referred to committee. Referral was partly for the purpose of amendment, partly for the purpose of securing fuller debate than the House as a whole could manage efficiently. One observer in 1621 remarked that "few matters are debated in the House, but are referred to a committee and there debated." The same observer saw clearly that the growing amount and diversity of legislation made impossible any return to "the old course of debating matters" at second reading.[8] Scobell reports that there were at least five Standing Committees in the early 17th century, to which were referred matters of religion, privileges and elections, grievances, conduct of the courts of justice, and trade and commerce.[9] Bowyer reports that in James's parliament of 1605, the House employed at least thirty-three committees, most of them in the "select" or special category.[10]

Doubtless the gradual transfer of debate to committee was prompted by forces other than the increasing number and complexity of bills. A member could speak in the House but once to a bill or a substantive amendment.[11] In the House committee he could participate as freely as he liked.[12] Free participation encouraged frequent question and answer, the brief exchange, and the short "speech."

Participants occasionally speak of the "short arguments" in committee. Apparently the long speech had little place, for in one meeting in 1601 when Sir Walter Raleigh had obviously started off on an eloquent speech, a Mr. Wiseman broke in: "Let us draw to some head and leave our orations and speeches. We are to consider all what is fit to be gained. . . . I will be bold enough to deliver my opinion first because someone must break the Ice."[13] One is reminded, of course, of Bacon's observation that eloquent speechmakers aren't necessarily effective in group discussion. "Long and curious speeches," Bacon wrote, are about as useful in discussion "as a robe or mantle with a long train" is in a race. One is reminded, also, of Bacon's desire to see the art of discussion and conversation given "better inquiry" and study than it had received. And as an art to be investigated systematically it could be fostered either as a branch of rhetoric or of political science ("policy").

The committees of this period, like committees today, collected information and applied their knowledge in argument. One of the standard modes of obtaining information, then as now, was the hearing of witnesses and their lawyers, especially when private bills were being considered. Probably Bacon had the hearing in mind when in his Essay "Of Counsel" he remarks that "let such as are to inform counsel out of their particular professions (as lawyers, seaman, and the like . . .) be first heard before committees . . . and let them not come in multitudes or in a tribunitious manner; for that is to clamour counsels, not to inform them" (VI, 427). Although he does not comment pointedly, Bacon was also doubtless aware of the problem of evaluating evidence. The lobby, the logographer, the bribe, the statement prepared by the expert and read by the witness—these and other tactics—were well known to Elizabethan committees. At least one sharp member of a committee in 1585 knew well that he preferred original, direct testimony to that offered by a lawyer and perhaps prepared by someone other than the speaker. He phrased his preference thus:

> "He that spake first . . . his tale deserves the less credit, because I can show it him in writing, for he hath it from the searchers . . . I prefer the clothier before the searcher, and the truth before them both."[14]

The scope and activity of the committee can only be hinted at here. Roughly classifying its business as public and private bills, the committee might consider problems such as the transportation of beer or the current evils of the monopoly on wine (held at one time by Sir Walter Raleigh); it was concerned about a husband for Elizabeth and the price James paid to farmers for his food stuffs (purveyance); it paid heed to attempts to silence dissenting ministers and to its own privileges of freedom of utterance and freedom from arrest.

At least three committee customs provide further insight into the character of discussion and debate. First, any member of the House had the privilege of attending any committee session. Furthermore, like any member of a committee, he could speak as often as he wished. The result was that a committee by the end of James's reign could consist of 60 to 150 persons, a considerable increase from the average of eight persons in Henry VIII's reign. The size suggests strongly that members were interested rather than uninterested in legislation. And a sizable number of participants, of course, can mean a thorough canvass of all points of view, as well as wide dissemination of information. The second custom probably encouraged respect for relevance and point, and perhaps promoted some taste for logical rather than emotional thought. The custom was inherent in two of the requirements which were met by a committee report to the House proper. By about the middle of James's reign, the House stipulated that reports from its committees must always contain reasons for their recommendations as well as the substance of the recommendation itself.[15] The third custom was the preparation by the committee or one of its members of a written brief or epitome of amendments or other changes in a bill. The speaker of the House habitually used the brief in indicating the substance of the bill prior to its reading by the Clerk. It would seem that these two characteristics of the committee report afforded practical and workable goals of discussion. Bacon's only specific comment on reporting relates to the selection of the reporter himself: "In choice of instruments, it is better to choose men of a plainer sort that will like to do that that is committed to them, and to report back again faithfully the success, than those who are cunning to contrive out of other men's business somewhat to grace themselves, and will help the matter in report for satisfaction sake" (VI, 493).

A third requirement of committees probably also helped to give direction and order to discussion; at least it served to keep committees from rendering independent and final decisions in the name of the House and of failing to report upon their deliberations. As early as 1573, John Vowell (sometimes called John Hooker) wrote that "When any Bil is committed, the committees have not authoritie to conclude: but onely to order reforme, examin, and amend the thing committed unto them and of their dooings they must give reporte to the house again, by whome the Bill is to be considered."[16] Such a regulation was well understood by the end of Elizabeth's reign and closely adhered to, although Vowell's testimony suggests that during the early part of her reign the point needed making.

II

Another kind of committee with which Bacon accumulated considerable experience during his parliamentary career was the joint or conference committee of the Lords and Commons. This device for adjusting conflicting legislation of the two houses came of age during Bacon's time. It reached maturity considerably later—perhaps 50 years later—than the House committee did. The members of either house could meet among themselves upon fairly even terms, socially and educationally. But a joint meeting brought together social strata as different as lords, bishops, and judges on the one hand, and knights, burgesses, and ordinary citizens on the other. Since Bacon took part directly in the development of the conference committee, we should understand what was going on.

The term "conference" was employed during the period to designate certain features of regularized discussion between Lords and Commons. The features: (1) each house selected a few of its members, the Commons, in James's reign, having the right to name two members to the Lords' one: (2) under well-defined circumstances, members sought and gave information, argued back and forth, and where possible came to agreement through compromise; and (3) any decisions arrived at had to be reported to both houses for final action.

Legislators during the period were self-consciously aware of what a conference entailed. It was not a "meeting"! In 1623, Sir Edwyn Sandys was pricked to criticism when a messenger from the Lords requested a "meeting." "If we give them a Meeting," he said, "we give them an Audience, and no Conference."[17] In 1626, the Commons asked the Lords for a "conference," but the Lords thought a conference inappropriate and requested a meeting. In his Precedents and Proceedings in the House of Commons, Hatsell is probably right in saying that "conference" always meant that both parties took part in discussion (Ibid., note). In 1606, when the House was disturbed by the over-zealous suppression of non-conformist ministers, Bacon himself made a procedural proposal which touched off an exchange that Bowyer records thus:

> SIR FRA[NCIS] BACON moved touching the Conference to be had on Thursday with the Lords That the Committees maie first meete and conferre, Allso for asmuch as in his opinion the conference is not to rest meerely upon proposicions of the Lords but the Committees appointed to conferre do likewise propose to their Lordships: their[fore] he wished that some might be sent to their Lordships to signifie so much and to desier that their Committees maie come authorised accordinglie: and that this howse would be pleased to authorise the Committees for the conference to propose as well as to heare, and to direct them what and how to propose, for said he otherwise if they shall only heare what the Lords will saie this is not conference:[18]

The Speaker was prompted to remark: ". . . it will not be amisse that unto certaine selected persons be appointed what they every one handle and speake unto, not restraining anie other of the Committees." Whereupon a Doctor Perkins observed: ". . . that wee ought allso to propound otherwise it weare no conference but a reference" (Ibid., p. 25). The exchange recorded here implicitly reveals the scope of participation in the conference committee. Prior to the last years of Elizabeth the conference was either a "hearing" of one side by the other, or an exchange of formal speeches by persons appointed and instructed by each house.[19] By the middle of James's reign, the conference, although still organized, permitted anyone to speak.

The customary occasion for a conference committee appeared when one house amended a bill that the other house had passed, the house of origin refusing to accept the amendment without adjustment. The first mention by D'Ewes of a joint committee (whether "conference" or "meeting" is not indicated) is March 3, 1558.[20] The Lords had sent a bill back to Commons with some "provisos" attached. Commons wanted to eliminate one proviso, and so asked for, and was granted, a conference. In the same year the Act of Supremacy received full debate in each house and in a series of joint conferences (Ibid. pp. 28–9). The chief object of the conference, then, was to adjust conflicting legislation. In fact, the Commons could insist upon the point, as is evident in Bowyer's report of a House altercation in 1606, when someone suggested a joint committee with the Lords to prepare a bill: "It was affirmed to be contrary to the custome and usage of this howse to ioine in drawing anie bill but that every bill ought to be drawen and passed in one of the howses and sent to the other."[21] Another member even disavowed a possible precedent! Especially on bills of revenue and supply, the Commons were loath to hold preliminary conferences with the Lords. We learn from the Parliamentary History, 1593, that the Lords suggested an exploratory meeting, Commons sent the suggestion to committee, the committee reported favorably, but the whole House, despite the influence of Robert Cecil and Bacon, rejected its committee's recommendation, 128–217.[22]

Time and circumstances, however, brought occasions when the joint conference was used to test temper and attitude, to pool information, and to secure preliminary agreement on crucial points. In March, 1605, the Commons were hard at work on a bill designed to redress some of the evils springing from the Crown's practice of obtaining foodstuffs and other living supplies directly from the farmer and producer. Both houses were worried about two issues: Could they question the King's right to the practice without appearing to question his prerogatives? Should they object only to the confiscatory prices set by his agents? Confronted with such tender matters, the Lords suggested a conference. The Commons agreed, and ceased work on their bill.[23] Eventually Commons sent a committee to confer with the Lords on the issue of prices. The Parliamentary History reports a similar situation, also in 1605. Again the Commons stopped their deliberations, accepted the Lords' proposal for conference, with the result that "several Meetings of the Committees of both Houses were had about it; the Result of all was, the passing of two new acts."[24] In trying to speed up discussion of the Union of Scotland and England, Bacon himself remarked in Commons:

> Whether it be to be carried severally in the houses, or by conference? I incline to the latter: because it is a matter of state, a matter of future providence, and not of present feeling. Our state is good now,

> and therefore to see what it may be, let us take help of those who sitting on higher ground by such advantage have the further prospect to see more. . . .
> If then Conference, the question is where to begin. Dies diem docet. Imitate yourselves in the last great bill of Recusants (provided always it be not so long). That was to make one Church, this to make one Nation. Then we made a selected Committee to prepare: so did the Lords: and our labours fell all out with that consent, that when the King's letter came from Royston, it made a unison; and therefore I wish this should have the like course (X, 304).

In December, 1661, the two houses appointed a joint committee to examine, during Parliament's recess, any designs "to disturb the union and peace of the kingdom." This seems to set up an investigating group. Hatsell thinks that the device was invented to secure common evidence and testimony and thus prevent misunderstanding which might arise if each house investigated separately.[25]

In preparing his essay, "Of Counsel," for the 1612 edition of the essays, Bacon took occasion to look back on his experience with committees. He commends the labors of the committee which dealt with the Union, and permits himself a general observation:

> The counsels at this day in most places are but familiar meetings, where matters are rather talked on than debated. It were better that in causes of weight, the matters were propounded one day and not spoken to till the next day. . . . So it was done in the Commission of Union between England and Scotland; which was a grave and orderly assembly (VI, 426).

In conference with the Lords, the Commons seem to have held their own. They might appear at a disadvantage in some ways, it is true. The Lords could set the time and place of the conference. The Commons members had to stand, and the Lords could sit. Sometimes the Commons delegation had to stand around a long time before the Lords arrived, and the legs of older persons might give way. Occasionally the Lords would try to dominate discussion, and doubtless succeeded. About one case, at least, Fuller complained pretty caustically on the floor of the House that "The Lords both conferr, and set as Moderators, for when they please, the Kings Counsell and Iudges overrule us with their Censure, and when we desire the Opinion of the Iudges it is denyed." In referring again to the judges, some of whom traditionally sat as legal counsellors in the Lords, Fuller alluded to their proper role: "at Conferences, they sitt as Assistants, not as Iudges."[26]

But the Commons had their advantage also. By the early years of James's reign, almost all bills—and certainly the important ones, such as the money and subsidy bills—originated in the Commons. The Lords often waited for work to do, and if they changed a bill, they had to lead in asking for a conference and theirs was the burden of proof. The Commons were free to refuse a conference, and they often did. If they granted a conference, they were superior numerically; for by late in James's reign, they outnumbered the Lords, two to one, on the joint committee. Moreover, Commons members learne a delaying tactic to offset the surprise situation in which the Lords had superior information and preparation. In effect they would say politely: We understood only that the general matter would be discussed, not the specific points. Or, we expected only to listen and report, not to dispute. In such cases, they would excuse themselves, go back to the House for instructions and information, and resume the conference later. In one case when the conference was upon the naturalization of the Scots, at the time of the Union, Commons members returned to the House for instructions. As debate started, the House proposed to instruct its conference members, for the reason which Sir Herbert Croft advanced on the floor:

> I thinck That before Conference, it will be convenient that among our Selves wee consider of the Matter of Convenience, and this to be in the House, not by Committees; For as I doe confesse that in Committees by short Arguments many times truth is beaten out, yet I have observed, That in Committees when every man may reply, some special Persons of Place by Speaking often, and [by] countenance doe prevaile more then by their reasons.[27]

Furthermore, in instances of significant legislation, the Commons could hold out for the compromise they wanted. One example makes this convincingly clear. The joint conference was over one of many bills in James's times directed at the non-conformists, principally the Catholics. The Lords, more tolerant than the Commons, wished to give persons plenty of time to meet the communion requirements in the Established Church, but the Commons bill called for a short time and stringent penalties. In a letter to the Earl of Mar, the Earl of Salisbury cites the reasons the Lords had used in debate to maintain their position, and concludes: "Neverthelesse because the bill had many other excellent parts, which wee were loath to overthrowe, wee consented in the end to appoint a punishment upon the non-Communicant."[28]

III

Thus we have before us the objective correlative of Bacon's views on political discussion. We can now turn to his observations on conference and counsel, the working of committees, and, broadly speaking, the management of talk in small groups. Bacon did not employ such modern terms as "group discussion" or "group dynamics," but he had their processes in mind.

Out of his experience in political discussion, Bacon concluded that oratory and discussion in some respects involve different skills. A speaker, he said, should be able to mould and fit his "proof and persuasions" in keeping with his auditors. Such application, says Bacon in an echo from Plato's Phaedrus, ought ideally "to extend so far, that if a man should speak of the same thing to several persons, he should speak to them all respectively and several ways" (IV, 457–8). This ability the greatest orators often lack, for they have been ensnared by "their well-graced forms of speech." In offering this observation, Bacon is talking about rhetoric. Yet what we think of as discussion and conversation clearly intrigues him, for he turns aside and names this readiness and skill in speaking appropriately to persons, the "politic part of eloquence in private speech" (III, 411). He wants it to receive "better inquiry" and study than it had hitherto enjoyed. And within his scheme of the arts, although he is willing to see it a part of either rhetoric or political science ("policy"), I believe he preferred to see discussion keep company with politics. After all, "discretion of speech is more than eloquence; and to speak agreeably to him with whom we deal, is more than to speak in good words or in good order."[29]

Most of Bacon's observations are more practical than theoretical. Sometimes he is concerned with the method and plan of conference and discussion; more often he is interested in general advice and specific precept for the participant.

As for plan, method, and order in discussion, these contribute more to efficiency of discourse than anything else: "order, distribution, and singling out of parts, is the life of dispatch." Furthermore, in the public discussion of any problem, there are always "three parts of business: the preparation, the debate or examination, and the perfection." Preparation is best undertaken by relatively few persons. Debate over proposals and policies is appropriate to many persons. The shaping of details, the final touches, are also "the work of few."

The fundamental advice to the participant is to seek out what is true, to cultivate judgment and discernment about "what should be thought" on the problem at hand. It is better to contribute a sound and true argument than it is to assemble an armory of all possible arguments with which to make ready show of one's intelligence and "wit." In expressing this opinion, Bacon is clearly saying that the Elizabethan schoolboy practice of commonplacing and thememaking is no more useful to discussion than to speechmaking. "Some have certain common places and themes wherein they are good, and want variety; which kind of poverty is for the most part tedious, and when it is once perceived, ridiculous." "The honourablest part of talk," Bacon reminds us, is to keep in accord with the occasion, to respect the reasonable limits of the point at hand and then "to pass on to somewhat else; for [thus] a man leads the dance."

Such observations on the politic part of eloquence are general in nature, in keeping with Bacon's ranging, inclusive mind. But he does not entirely overlook the specific precept. To encourage dispatch, he remarks, there is nothing like keeping the issue in the open: "there is no such gain of time as to iterate often the state of the question." Frequent iteration of this kind not only supplies appropriate emphasis to the issue; it also discourages "long and curious speeches." Furthermore, keeping attention on the issue puts a damper on elaborate devices of introducing an argument, of managing artful transitions, and of addressing complimentary references "to the person."

To give final flavor to Bacon's precepts on discussion I shall be content with the following, for the most part expressed in the Lord Chancellor's own language. "He that questioneth much, shall learn much, and content much; but especially if he apply his questions to the skill of the persons whom he asketh; for he shall give them occasion to please themselves in speaking, and himself shall continually gather knowledge." But let him not, however, ask questions that are "troublesome"; for he may only seem like a professional examiner. "And let him be sure to leave other men their turns to speak." There is no place in discussion for the bluffer, if for no other reason than that he is almost bound to be caught by his own bluff: "If you dissemble sometimes your knowledge of that you are thought to know, you shall be thought another time to know that you know not." Nor is there place in discussion for the egotistical creature, who, by direct or indirect means, must serve his own vanity. "Speech of a man's self ought to be seldom, and well chosen." The sharp retort, the sarcastic and satirical thrust are personal matters, not material. "Speech of touch towards others should be sparingly used; for discourse ought to be as a field, without coming home to any man." Our last example of Bacon's precepts is perhaps directed to some harassed chairman: "If there be any that would reign and take up all the time, let him find means to take him off."

In the essay, "Of Counsel," although Bacon is primarily interested in advising King James, he is not unmindful of general implications. Indeed, in this essay, he is occasionally drawing upon his parliamentary experience. He feels, for example, that counsels (i.e., small deliberative groups) have become too familiar and informal; there is too much mere talk and not enough debate. Decisions are taken and carried out much too rapidly. He is concerned too, about the choice of persons who comprise committees. His main concern he voices thus: "In choice of committees for ripening business for the counsel, it is better to choose indifferent persons, than to make an indifferency by putting in those that are strong on both sides."

Possibly Bacon's willingness to place discussion, as an art, within the orbit of politics was influenced by his long service on committees and counsels. Out of the same experience, also, probably emerged his practical observations and advice on the conduct and management of group discussion when persons combine to undertake a political task. He distilled his experience into aphorisms for the more efficient conduct of the public business.

NOTES

1 How long before publication Bacon had been formulating his "conceits" is impossible to determine precisely. In the dedi-

catory epistle to his brother, he says merely that "they passed long agoe from my pen . . . ." (VI, 523).

2 Richard Whately, Bacon's Essays With Annotations (Boston and New York, 1875), pp. xxxvii–xxxviii.

3 On Bacon's activities in the Parliamentary session of 1606–1607, Willson remarks: "Bacon's position was a rather anomalous one. On most points he stood for the Crown and spoke in the House with the purpose of gaining favor at Court. Yet at the same time he enjoyed the confidence and regard of the Commons in a high degree and was constantly employed by them upon committees and in conferences. He was therefore not a leader but a mediator, forever seeking a compromise between King and Commons." The Parliamentary Diary of Robert Bowyer, 1606–1607 (Minneapolis and London, 1931), p. xxi.

4 For knowledge of parliamentary customs, especially of committee procedures and deliberations, we have to depend upon such records as the 24-volume "Parliamentary or Constitutional History of England" extending from the earliest times to 1660, the Journals of the House of Commons from 1547 onward, Sir Simonds D'Ewes and Hayward Townshend's collections of the journals of Queen Elizabeth's parliaments. Especially valuable, when extant, are the records of the clerks of the House of Commons. The most complete such record I have encountered is The Parliamentary Diary of Robert Bowyer, 1606–1607 (Minneapolis and London, 1931), ed. David H. Willson. Professor Wallace Notestein's work as editor of the journals of the Stuart parliaments is of course well known. Sometimes one turns up first-hand reports from such manuscript collections as the Lansdowne, Stowe, and Cotton. From the labors of scholars, one finds other original materials, along with some interpretation and comment. J. E. Neale's The Elizabethan House of Commons (London, 1949) is invaluable; so also is the earliest of contemporary accounts I have found, John Vowell's The Order and Usage of the Keeping of a Parliament . . . , probably published in 1575. The study by William Wallace, Sir Edwin Sandys and the First Parliament of James I (Philadelphia, 1940), and John Hatsell's four-volume work, Precedents and Proceedings in the House of Commons (London, 1796), are often helpful in understanding committee customs. Of the many other general sources which have been of assistance, I shall mention but four here: William

Hakewill, Modus tenendi Parliamentum (London, 1660), Edward Porritt's The Unreformed House of Commons, 2 vols. (Cambridge, 1909), Joseph Redlich's three-volume history called The Procedure of the House of Commons (London, 1907), and Henry Scobell, Memorials of the Method and Manner of Proceedings in Parliament in Passing Bills (London, 1670).

5 Consult Neale for the stages of reading, pp. 369–73. Cf. Sir Thomas Smith's sketch of procedure as presented by G. M. F. Campion, An Introduction to the Procedure of the House of Commons (London, 1929), p. 17.

6 Bowyer's Diary, p. 254.

7 Parl. Hist., IV, 437.

8 See Neale, p. 378.

9 Campion, p. 22.

10 Bowyer's Diary, p. xi.

11 Just how firm was the rule and to what it applied is not always clear. Vowell, sitting in Parliament, 13th Elizabeth, 1571, declares: ". . . but having once spoken to any Bil: he may speak no more for that time." (Vowell, p. 32.) In 1604, Bacon, having spoken twice, was not allowed to speak a third time. (Hatsell, II, 96.)

12 In commenting on House rules against a member's speaking too often, Hatsell observes: "It is to allow more ample and frequent discussion than this order will admit, that a Committee is instituted, where every member may speak as often as he pleases. . . ." (Hatsell, II, 99–100.)

13 Parl. Hist., IV, 439.

14 Neale, p. 387.

15 Bowyer's Diary, pp. 291, 378. The importance of the oral report to centuries of parliamentary deliberation can hardly be overvalued. Bacon was often selected as reporter and seems to have met high standards of accuracy, conciseness, and clarity. On one occasion, May 15, 1606, when Bacon reported back to the Commons what he had said in introducing their grievances to King James, his account was apparently the full text of what he said: "And so repeated his owne Speech used to the King be-

fore he did reade the Grievance, which was an Eloquent Speech, which was not long, yet impossible for me, or any man to take in such sorte as he delivered the Same." (Ibid., p. 165.) On another occasion when Bacon reported to the House on a conference with the Lords, Bowyer fared better. (Ibid., pp. 323–4.)

16 Vowell, facing p. 34.

17 Hatsell, IV, 26.

18 Bowyer's Diary, p. 24.

19 See Wallace, especially pp. 29–31.

20 Journals of All the Parliaments during the Reign of Queen Elizabeth; both of the . . . Lords and . . . Commons, collected by Sir Simonds d'Ewes . . . revised and published by Paul Bowes (London, 1682), p. 21.

21 Bowyer's Diary, p. 57.

22 Parl. Hist., IV, 381 seq.

23 Bowyer's Diary, pp. 57–8.

24 Parl. Hist., V, 145–6.

25 Hatsell, III, 34.

26 Bowyer's Diary, p. 158.

27 Ibid., p. 246.

28 Ibid., p. 161n.

29 Unless otherwise noted, all quotations below are from the essays "Of Counsel," Works, VI, 423–7; "Of Dispatch," ibid., 434–5; "Of Discourse," ibid., 455–7; "Of Negociating," ibid., 492–4.

SIR FRANCIS BACON'S THEORY OF CIVIL HISTORY-WRITING

Leonard F. Dean

Criticism of Bacon has quite naturally and properly been centered upon his activity as a philosopher, scientist, and essayist. Yet if the recent effort to re-evaluate his worth as a thinker and writer is to be complete, some consideration must be given to a minor but neglected subject, his theory of history-writing. Although he never elaborated his theory in an independent essay, his scattered pronouncements deserve to be studied both for their intrinsic importance and for the light they shed on his relation with his intellectual milieu. During the Renaissance the *ars historica* came to be a popular and well-defined critical genre; consequently additional insight into the character and relative novelty of Bacon's thought may be gained by comparing his theory of history-writing with others of his age. Furthermore, a knowledge of Bacon's ideas about the proper nature, function, and composition of history should enable a modern reader to interpret and judge *The History of Henry VII* more accurately. Finally, a person's conception of the way the past should be described and its utility for the present is necessarily an important part of his general philosophy.

Bacon divides Civil History into ecclesiastical, literary or intellectual, and civil or political (IV, 300 ff.). This article is concerned with civil or political history, the only division about which Bacon theorized at any length. Today such a limitation would be artificial. Modern historiography and historical theory are distinguished for their breadth of scope; all human activities are legitimate subjects for the historian, and in interpreting the past he utilizes many diverse learnings and emphasizes the inter-relations of intellectual, religious, political, social, economic, or physical activities. In Bacon's time this was significantly not so. Purely political history was then held in greatest repute and the *artes historicae*

Reprinted from *English Literary History*, Vol. 8 (1941), pp. 161–83, by permission of the author and The Johns Hopkins Press.

deal mainly with it. For that reason, our limitation of subject is not arbitrary as it would be today.

Bacon's most general statement about history occurs in his classification of human learning according to the three mental faculties. "History has reference to the Memory, poesy to the Imagination, and philosophy to the Reason" (IV, 292; III, 329; V, 503). If this is to be regarded as anything more than a convenient encyclopedic classification, two important questions are suggested by Bacon's reference of history to the memory. First, did he mean to imply that history should be the exclusive product of memory, a mere record to be judged solely on its factual accuracy and inclusiveness? Secondly, did Bacon mean to rank the products of the mental faculties according to the conventional hierarchy of the faculties themselves, in which reason stood at the top? Specifically, did he regard history as inferior to philosophy, if not to poetry, and what limitations did he see in it?

The first step in answering these questions is to examine the explanations which Bacon added in the Descriptio Globi Intellectualis (1612) and the De Augmentis (1622–3) to his bare statement which had appeared in The Advancement of Learning (1605). These two explanations have in common a description of the process of cognition. Discrete sense impressions are recorded by the memory.

> These the human mind proceeds to review and ruminate; and thereupon either simply rehearses them, or makes fanciful imitations of them, or analyzes and classifies them. Wherefore from these three fountains, Memory, Imagination, and Reason, flow these three emanations, History, Poesy, and Philosophy; and there can be no others. For I consider history and experience to be the same thing, as also philosophy and the sciences (IV, 293; V, 503–4).

Here history is clearly defined as the bare rehearsal of mentally recorded sense impressions, and hence the exclusive product of the memory. It is distinguished from poetry by being true rather than feigned, and from philosophy by being composed of unanalyzed sensations rather than general notions.

Is there any evidence that this was not Bacon's final and considered opinion? First, it should be noticed that he was not wholly satisfied with the conventional faculty psychology upon which the foregoing conception of history is based. In The Advancement of Learning he observed that ". . . that part of inquiry is most necessary, which considereth the seats and domiciles which the several faculties of the mind do take and occupate in the organs of the body; which knowledge hath been attempted, and is controverted, and deserveth to be much better enquired" (III, 369). Eighteen years later he added significantly in the De Augmentis: "Neither again is that arrangement of the intellectual faculties (imagination, reason, and memory) according to the respective ventricles of the brain, destitute of error"; for "the origins of these faculties ought to be handled, and that physically. . . . In which part nothing of much value . . . has as yet been discovered. . ." (IV, 378, 398–9).[1] More important is a statement by Bacon proving that by 1623 he was favorably disposed towards the theory of cognition held by Telesius and his followers in which the three faculties are not separated but rather unified to form the Thinking Faculty.

> . . . one of the moderns has ingeniously referred all the powers of the soul to motion, and remarked on the conceit and precipitancy of some of the ancients, who in too eagerly fixing their eyes and thoughts on the memory, imagination, and reason, have neglected the Thinking Faculty, which holds the first place. For he who remembers or recollects, thinks; he who imagines, thinks; he who reasons, thinks; and in a word the spirit of man, whether prompted by sense or left to itself, whether in the functions of the intellect, or of the will and affections, dances to the tune of the thoughts . . . (IV, 325).[2]

It is fairly clear, then, that by 1623 at the latest, Bacon had become dissatisfied with the mechanical and oversimplified faculty psychology and that he was looking for an explanation that took into account the unity and complexity of the process of cognition. Consequently, not much confidence can be placed in his statement that history is the exclusive product of the memory, nor in his implication that the historian is a mere recorder. Perhaps the chief source of confusion is Bacon's use of the word history to denote both the collection of evidence with which the historian should work, and the final synthesis of those materials. It will become clear as we proceed that Bacon was careful to distinguish the historian from the recorder, and to characterize his work as the product of the whole mind rather than of one faculty. It is significant that Bacon saw no need to explain carefully his assignment of history to the memory. Today such an act would identify one with a definite party, those who assert that the historian can properly do little more than accumulate factual evidence. In Bacon's time the lines were not so sharply drawn; the problem did not exist in its modern form.

The second question raised by Bacon's classification of learning according to the three faculties is whether he intended thereby to rank history, the product of memory, below science or philosophy, the products of the preëminent faculty, reason. Did Bacon believe that the histórian could employ the inductive, experimental method and consequently achieve the certain and beneficial results of the natural scientist? We know that Bacon wished to break down the walls between the departments of knowlege. He believed that "moral and political philosophy" would "altogether lack profoundness, . . . unless natural philosophy be carried on and applied to particular sciences and particular sciences be carried back again to natural philosophy" (IV, 79). More particularly, he asserted that the inductive method is applicable to some of the subject-matter of civil as well as natural history.

> It may also be asked . . . whether I speak of natural philosophy only, or whether I mean that the other sciences, logic, ethics, and politics, should be carried on by this method. Now I certainly mean what I have said to be understood of them all; and as the common logic, which governs by the syllogism, extends not only to natural but to all sciences; so does mine also, which proceeds by induction, embrace everything. For I form a history and tables of discovery for anger, fear, shame, and the like; for matters political; and again for the mental operations of memory, composition and division, judgment and the rest; not less than for heat and cold . . . or the like (IV, 112).

At the same time, Bacon often admitted that "Civil Knowledge is conversant about a subject which of all others is most immersed in matter, and hardliest reduced to axiom" (III, 445; cf. III, 406; IV, 452; V, 32). He seems generally to have felt that scientific exactness in the treatment of civil affairs is impossible. Being so "immersed in matter," they are not open to the kind of investigation required in the discovery of "forms" for the benefit of mankind.

It may be concluded that Bacon was more interested in extending the scope of the application of the inductive method, than in attacking the problem of whether civil history can be "scientific." His statements that it can be, sound like the indirect product of enthusiasm for his program of the natural sciences. His doubt concerning the reliability of history will be further considered when we discuss his criticism of the function and value of historical examples.

Bacon's attitude toward the problem of attaining historical truthfulness may be approached more directly by examining his explicit statements on that subject and his relation with the work being done in his day to improve the resources and methods of the historical scholar. Protestations that history should be truthful are valueless without accompanying explanation. From classical times truthfulness had been acclaimed as the "first law of history," but by writers with such diverse basic philosophies that they virtually contradict each other. Truth to a mediaeval Christian chronicler meant theoretically something higher than adherence to fact. For simple annalists the statement that history should first of all be truthful was often no more than a naïve incantation to ward off error and adverse criticism. During the Renaissance the meaning of historical truthfulness was progressively particularized. Not only were religious and secular "truth" separated, but there were formulated, following the classics, increasingly explicit directions for the achievement of secular historical truthfulness.

Bacon belongs to this movement. The separations of religious and secular knowledge is, of course, fundamental to his whole philosophy. He is openly scornful of the incredibility of much ecclesiastical history.[3] He objects to universal histories, typical of the Middle Ages and still being composed in his own day, because ". . . the laws of regular history are so strict, that they can scarce be observed in such a wide field of matter. . . . For the writer who has such a variety of things on all sides to attend to, will become gradually less scrupulous on the point of information . . . ; he will take up with ruinous and popular reports. . . ." It is far better to "choose a manageable and definite argument, whereof a perfect knowledge and certainty and full information may be had. . . ."[4] Bacon seems also to have been distrustful of histories which cover a vast sweep of time because he saw with unusual clearness for his day the difficulty and necessity of attaining perspective in the writing of history.

> For to carry the mind in writing back into the past, and bring it into sympathy with antiquity; diligently to examine, freely and faithfully to report, and by the light of words to place as it were before the eyes, the revolutions of times, the characters of persons, the fluctuations of counsels, the courses and currents of actions, the bottoms of pretences, and the secrets of governments; is a task of great labour and judgment . . . (IV, 302).

The importance of Bacon's ideas in this quotation is pointed by a comparison with the attitude of a contemporary historian, Sir John Hayward, whose feeling for historical perspective was weakened by a fondness for rhetorical display and a desire to make his examples applicable to the current political situation.[5] When Hayward's Henrie IIII (1599), with its pointed reference to the intrigues of Essex, aroused Elizabeth's anger, Bacon assured her that Hayward was guilty of felony rather than treason, "for he had taken most of the sentences of Cornelius Tacitus and translated them into English and put them into his text" (VII, 133). And Coke, in the course of Hayward's two trials (1601 and 1602), drew from the defendant the statement that it "be lawfull for any historiographer to insert any historie of former tyme into that hystorie he wright albeit no other hystorian of that matter have meued the same. . . ."[6]

Although Bacon recognizes with unusual clarity that to compose a truthful history it is necessary "to carry the mind in writing back into the past, and bring it into sympathy with antiquity," he was not led thereby to take a serious interest in the problems of chronology. This was partly due to his conception of the utility of history, which, as we shall see, did not include a perception of the profit of studying the growth of ideas of institutions. In this respect he is like his Italian counterparts. For Machiavelli whatever is instructive is contemporary, and Patrizzi is concerned only with such details as how to narrate two or more groups of actions which take place at the same time.[7] Bacon had little in common with those who were chiefly interested in chronology in his day, the adherents of the German Reformation; consequently few echoes are to be found in his writings of their long discussions of the Four Monarchies and of their attempts to synchronize secular and biblical systems of reckoning.[8] He argues both for and against a Golden Age in "uttermost antiquity" (III, 123–4, 225; VI, 697). Occasionally he attempts to divide the past into periods of ignorance and enlightenment, and he had a hopeful belief in the greatness of his own age (III, 291, 300; IV, 73, 77, 82, 90; V, 110). But these ideas are not developed or integrated with his theory of history-writing, which, in fact, demanded no careful attention to periodization of time.

The historian's evidence and its proper use, Bacon discusses briefly under the headings of Memorials and Antiquities. The evidence is composed of "Commentaries" (bare narratives "of actions and events without the causes and pretexts, . . . the counsels and orations"), "Registers" ("titles of things and persons in order of time, . . . or collections of public acts, such as edicts of princes, decrees of councils, judicial proceedings, public speeches, letters of state"), and "Antiquities" ("genealogies, annals, titles, monuments, coins, proper names and styles, etymologies of words, proverbs, traditions, archives and instruments as well public as private, fragments of histories scattered about in books not historical") (IV, 303). Compared to the fullness of this list, Bacon's instructions in the use of evidence are scanty. It is in this respect, of course, that Bacon and others of his age are farthest from such present-day writers on history as Bernheim or Langlois and Seignobos, who are chiefly interested in the handling of documents. Bacon contents himself with remarking that by the use of the kind of evidence he has listed it is possible for the historian "to supersede the fabulous accounts of the origins of nations, and . . . fictions of that kind" (IV, 304). It may be observed, incidentally, that Bacon's opposition to historical primitivism is typically humanistic, as is his ironical conclusion that antiquarianism is "entitled however to the less authority, because in things which few people concern themselves about, the few have it their own way" (*Idem*).

The problem of Bacon's relationship to the growing historical antiquarianism of his day is now raised, and it is made more urgent by the recent researches of Professor Marc Friedlaender, who concludes that ". . . by 1625 the historical manuscripts and records of the period between the conquest and the reign of Henry VIII were largely recovered, deposited in a relatively few places of research, and easily available to the student who would use them."[9] Now although Bacon must have been aware of the activities that were leading to this result, and was indeed on intimate terms with antiquarians like Cotton, Camden, and Selden, as well as with Keepers of the Rolls, there is no evidence that he aided them or even fully realized the importance of their work. It is notable that he felt it proper to write his *History of Henry VII* (1621–2) while he was cut off from the most important depositories of documents except Cotton's and forced to rely chiefly on previous literary chronicles, Andrea, Vergil, Hall, Holinshed, Stow, and Speed.

As a matter of fact, Bacon sharply distinguished the labors of the research scholar from those of the historian, observing somewhat petulantly that a great inconvenience in historical composition in his time was the lack of adequate chronicles or catalogues of brute facts on which the historian could exercise his powers of interpretation and synthesis.

> But unto me the disadvantage is great, finding no public memories of any consideration or worth, in sort that the supply must be out of the freshness of memory and tradition, and out of the acts, instruments, and negotiations of state themselves, together with the glances of foreign histories; which though I do acknowledge to be the best originals and instructions out of which to write an history, yet the travel must be much greater than if there had been already digested any tolerable chronicle as a simple narration of the actions themselves, which should only have needed out of the former helps to be enriched with the counsels and speeches and notable particularities (VI, 18–9).

It must be granted that Bacon wished the historian to work with facts, as many as can be accumulated; but in his discussion of history-writing the emphasis is always on the proper treatment of facts rather than on their collection. He creates the impression that, while it would be convenient to have more factual information, the most glaring lack is the skilful interpretation of the facts already available. It is probably this belief that made the writing of _Henry VII_ without extensive preliminary research seem a justifiable undertaking.

There are only two pieces of evidence that cast doubt on the foregoing conclusion. The first is that Bacon chose to write on the reign of Henry VII rather than a more recent one. This may have some significance in view of the fact that it was the last reign for which documentary evidence was readily available, all later reigns depending on State Papers which were closely guarded. Greville and Fletcher, for example, were denied access to the Papers for the reign of Elizabeth, and Camden was allowed to use them only at the order of Burghley.[10] Bacon's choice of subject may be explained in other ways, however; by the fact, for instance, that Henry VII was his own prime minister and therefore furnished plentiful examples in his activities for the discussion of practical politics.

The second piece of contradictory evidence is the statement of John Selden, who was preëminently fitted to judge, that Bacon's history was notable, with Camden's, for being based on documentary evidence. "For, except onely the Annals of Queene Elizabeth, and the life and raigne of King Henry the VII. lately set forth by learned men of most excelling abilities, we have not so much as a publique piece of the Historie of England, that tastes enough either of the Truth or Plenty that may be gained from the Records of this Kingdome."[11] That Bacon's work was superior to many composed in or by his time must be admitted. Selden, indeed, must have been more conscious than we are of the multitude of flimsy epitomes, amorphous chronicles, and second-hand rhetorical histories that were flooding the market.[12] Consequently, the History of Henry VII may have seemed to him by comparison to be more scholarly than it really is. There appears to be no evidence that Bacon should be ranked with Camden in regard to historical research; and certainly he does not point in either theory or practice towards the group of later historians, of whom Selden was one, who made extensive use of the documentary sources then available.

That Bacon was more interested in other aspects of history-writing than research is further substantiated by an examination of his theory of the proper function and subject-matter of history. Bacon believed that the chief functions of history are to provide the materials for a realistic treatment of psychology and ethics, and to give instruction by means of example and analysis in practical politics. It is a commonplace that Bacon belongs with those Renaissance writers who sought to develop a natural science of morality. In recent times Professor M. W. Croll, for example, has discussed this matter in connection with his studies of prose style and its relation to climates of opinion.[13] And in the history of psychology Bacon has long been known as an "early advocate of a general science of man: a laborious collection of evidence about individuals [that] should result in a concept of man formed in a purely empirical fashion and designed to show the actual nature and limits of human capacity. This . . . reflects the influence of that movement toward scientific anthropology which had already begun."[14] Now the important thing for us is that Bacon believed that the "wiser sort of historians" provide the best sort of materials for this new "science of man."

> . . . the best provision and material for this treatise is to be gained from the wiser sort of historians, not only from the commemorations which they commonly add on recording the deaths of illustrious persons, but much more from the entire body of history as often as such a person enters upon the stage; for a character so worked into the narrative gives a better idea of the man, than any formal criticism and review can; such is that of Africanus and Cato the Elder in Livy, of Tiberius, and Claudius, and Nero in Tacitus, of Septimius Severus in Herodian, of Louis XI., King of France, in Philip de Comines, of Ferdinand of Spain, the Caesar Maximilian, and the Popes Leo and Clement, in Francesco Guicciardini. For these writers, having the images of these persons whom they have selected to describe constantly before their eyes, hardly ever make mention of any of their actions without inserting something concerning their nature (V, 21).

Among the "wiser sort of historians," who provided this valuable information about human nature, Bacon ranked highest Machiavelli and Tacitus. "We are much beholden to Machiavelli and others, that write what men do and not what men ought to do" (III, 430); and although "the ethics of Plato and Aristotle are much admired . . . the pages of Tacitus breathe a livelier and truer observation of morals and institutions."[15] This kind of evidence reveals Bacon's sympathy with the reaction against the artifically adjusted and foreshortened biographical examples of virtuous or evil conduct which bulk so large in mediaeval and early Renaissance chronicles.[16] The first step in that reaction had been taken in England by writers like Sir Thomas More and Polydore Vergil, who attempted to organize their materials and make their examples more readily applicable by analyzing the character of a great tyrant as he rose to power and fell.[17] But the *de casibus* example even when handled with More's dramatic skill, is an artificially confining pattern.

What Bacon admired is the still more realistic, detailed, and relatively amoral kind of characterization that is exemplified in the histories of Machiavelli and Guicciardini and described theoretically in the essays of Patrizzi and Aconcio. Patrizzi, for example, argues that the historian should attempt a detailed anatomy of his character's mind. It is important for the historian to know and describe not only his subject's natural inclinations and controlling passion but also his training and experience, for the choices that a man makes are dictated by a customary habit of mind which is the product of natural endowments, early training, and later discipline. The reader receives a greater benefit from such a complete characterization since he cannot acquire another's innate qualities, but only those virtues which are the result of imitable education.[18] Aconcio's discussion of the proper use of historical examples is thoroughly realistic. He is not worried about the possible insidious influence upon the reader of examples of evil conduct;[19] instead he emphasizes that if the reader is to make accurate and instructive comparisons between the present and the past, the historian must provide him with characterizations which are realistic and detailed. Otherwise the reader will "know nothing in the ende, but the discents, genealogies, and petygrees, of noble men, and when such a King or Emperour raigned, & such lyke stuffe. . . ."[20]

Bacon in his treatment of ethics tried, likewise, to distinguish between ideals of conduct and the ways by which we may approach those ideals. The latter and more important aspect had been neglected, he felt, and for the same reason which accounts for the imperfection of all knowledge: men have preferred to dwell on final causes. He desired instead to analyze the psychological sources of our conduct.[21] Previous writers, he observes, have "made good and fair exemplars and copies, carrying the draughts and portraitures of Good, Virtue, Duty, Felicity; propounding them well described as the true objects and scopes of man's will and desires; but how to attain these excellent marks, and how to frame and subdue the will of man to become true and conformable to these pursuits, they pass it over altogether or slightly and unprofitably. . . . The reason of this omission I suppose to be . . . that men have despised to be conversant in ordinary and common matters . . ." (III, 418). And it is the proper function of history to provide the materials for this practical study of ethics.

> . . . the poets and writers of histories are the best doctors of this knowledge; where we may find painted forth with great life, how affections are kindled and incited; and how pacified and restrained; and how again contained from act and further degree; how they disclose themselves, how they work, how they vary, how they gather and fortify, how they are inwrapped one within another, and how they do fight

> and encounter one with another, and other the like particularities: amongst the which this last is of special use in moral and civil matters; how (I say) to set affection against affection, and to master one by another . . . upon which foundation is erected the excellent use of praemium and poena, whereby civil states consist . . . (III, 438).[22]

This approach to the good life through the realistic analysis of human nature by historians and others is concerned not only with the individual, it will be observed, but also with society as a whole. Histories, that is, should contain the kind of instruction in politics that will promote civic happiness. In this respect, also, Bacon is in sympathy with Machiavelli and his classical models—Tacitus, Polybius, and Thucydides—[23] and is like them opposed to the rhetorical and moralistic conception of history-writing. Machiavelli had explicitly stated in the Proemio that his Istorie fiorentine was meant to provide more profitable political instruction than the rhetorical narratives of his predecessors, Bruni and Poggio. "When I examined their writings carefully," he says, "I discovered that although they had indeed been most circumstantial in their account of the foreign wars waged by the Florentines, they had treated the internal political history of Florence so briefly as to afford the reader neither profit nor pleasure." In very nearly the same words, Bacon condemns the rhetorical historian's preoccupation with wars and military show, and calls for a study of policy. "For they be not the great wars and conquests . . . the rehearsal of which maketh the profitable and instructing history; but rather times refined in policies and industries, new and rare variety of accidents and alterations, equal and just encounters of state and state in forces and of prince and prince in sufficiency, that bring upon the stage the best parts for observation" (VI, 19). Similarly, he argues that "it not a little embases the authority of a history to intermingle matters of lighter moment, such as triumphs, ceremonies, spectacles, and the like, with matters of state" (IV, 310).

In Bacon's judgment, that is, the true dignity and worth of history spring not from theatrical subject-matter but from political examples and analysis. It was with this criterion in mind that he selected the period of English history from the Union of the Roses to the Union of the Crowns as the most fit and profitable for study, for it contains a "rare variety of accidents and alterations" in ecclesiastical, legal, political, and military affairs (III, 336; IV, 306; VI, 19). And it was for this reason that he asserted that the historian should summarize the laws of the period he was treating and attempt to interpret them in the light of contemporary conditions.

> . . . it is some defect even in the best writers of history, that they do not often enough summarily deliver and set down the most memorable laws that passed in the times whereof they write, being indeed the principal acts of peace. For though they may be had in original books of law themselves; yet that informeth not the judgment of kings and counsellors and persons of estate so well as to see them described and entered in the table and portrait of the times (VI, 97).[24]

It is clear, then, that Bacon was in agreement with those writers who felt that the historian could increase the utility of his work by presenting a more realistic and detailed exposition of political or ethical problems. It is not clear, however, that his sense of realism led him, like some of those same writers, to question the belief that history actually is instructive. The theory of Historia, magistra vitae rested on the assumption that human nature remains essentially constant and that situations repeat themselves. This assumption was finally being examined. Patrizzi, for example, after predicating that the greatest possible happiness comes from living in a peaceful and well-ordered society, asks whether it is really possible for men to draw lessons from history which will help them to attain this social felicity.[25] Guicciardini, likewise, had doubts, about our ability to really understand the past and about the value of general political principles derived from history. He attacked Machiavelli's Discorsi on the ground that lessons deduced from the political experience of the Romans must be arbitrary and dogmatic.[26] It is a great mistake, he remarks elsewhere,[27] to speak of events generally and absolutely, because by reason of the variety of circumstances almost all have distinctions and exceptions. Hence they deceive themselves who try to make instructive comparisons between the present government and that of Rome; their analogies must always be imperfect because the conditions then and now are not identical.[28]

Bacon's position in regard to this problem is not perfectly clear and consistent. Like Guicciardini, he felt, as we have seen, that because civil affairs are so "immersed in matter" they can scarcely be reduced to axioms. Nevertheless, he believed in the inspiring and instructive force of historical examples.[29] His writings abound in examples from the past, many of them used in a shockingly uncritical and unhistorical fashion. Examples valuable only as illustration are made the basis for extended arguments, with complete disregard for the most elementary rules of logic and historical perspective.[30] While Bacon's comment upon the method of Machiavelli's Discorsi is in some respects more profound than Guicciardini's, it is less severe. He argues that historical examples have supplanted ancient fables for the conveyance of practical wisdom, and that

> therefore the form of writing which of all others is fittest for this variable argument of negotiations and occasions is that which Machiavel chose wisely and aptly for government; namely, discourses upon histories or examples. For knowledge drawn freshly and in our view out of particulars knoweth the best way to particulars again. And it hath much greater life for practice when the discourse attendeth upon the example, than when the example attendeth upon the discourse. . . . For when the example is the ground, being set down in an history at large, it is set down with all circumstances, which may sometimes control the discourse thereupon made and sometimes supply it, as a very pattern for action; whereas the examples alleged for the discourse's sake are cited succinctly and without particularity, and carry a servile aspect toward the discourse which they are brought in to make good (III, 453).

This admirably sound warning against historical rationalizing was as far as Bacon ever went in his criticism of the use of examples from the past. He was unable to go beyond the general opinion of his time and suggest, for instance, that it is more useful to study the origin and development of institutions and beliefs than to try to model one's conduct on historical examples.

To modern minds, one of the most interesting solutions to the difficulty raised by the questioning of the utility of historical examples was that suggested, if not developed, by Jean Bodin. An important purpose of Bodin's Methodus ad facilem historiarum cognitionem (1566)[31] was to discover some method or order in the apparent diversity of human experience which will justify the reading and writing of history. This is apparent in the first chapter of the Methodus, where Bodin divides history into four kinds: divine, mathematical, natural, and human. Of these different kinds only human history is wholly confused and mutable; the others are unchanging and certain. The student of human history, therefore, needs to orient himself in the midst of diversity by finding fixed points of reference. Bodin essays to discover these fixed points by determining the relation of human with divine history through a study of religions, and with natural history through a study of geography and climates. In short, Bodin tries to explain human institutions and man, and to find some uniformity in the welter of events by examining the inter-relations of the human will with divine and natural forces.

This solution, however, does not seem to have made much of an impression upon Bacon or other Renaissance historians and theorists. Dependence upon the belief in the certainty of divine providence had already, as we have observerd, been largely abandoned as impracticable; and there are few echoes of Bodin's theory of the influence of climate. Instead, it is generally decided that situations really do repeat themselves and that a study of history can be truly useful if causes and circumstances are presented in sufficient detail to permit accurate comparisons to be made between the present and the past. Thus, essays like Patrizzi's Della historia are largely composed of patterns for the guidance of historians in constructing narratives that will be fuller and therefore more instructive than the usual bare chronicle of events. Be careful to observe and include this and this, says Patrizzi, for they are the things which are essentially constant and instructive when described in accurate detail. It was this kind of material which Blundeville thought expedient to translate rather than Patrizzi's neoplatonic philosophizing and academic arguments. Likewise, those classical historians who placed the greatest stress upon the interpretation of causes and circumstances became more popular during the later Renaissance. Camden, for example, follows Polybius in stating that

> Circumstances I have not in the least omitted, that not only the Events of Affairs, but also the Reasons and Causes thereof, might be understood. That of Polybius pleases me mightily. Take away from History, Why, How, and To what end, things have been done, and Whether the thing done has

> succeeded according to Reason; and all that remains will rather be an idle Sport and Foolery, than a profitable Instruction: and tho' for the present it may delight, for the future it cannot profit.[32]

With these ideas Bacon is in complete agreement. He finds the full, consecutive narrative of Tacitus more persuasive than the disconnected biographical examples of Suetonius.

> For as when I read in Tacitus the actions of Nero or Claudius, with circumstances, inducements, and occasions, I find them not so strange; but when I read them in Suetonius Tranquillus gathered into titles and bundles, and not in order of time, they seem more monstrous and incredible . . . (III, 366–7).

"Above all things," insists Bacon "(for this is the ornament and life of Civil History), I wish events to be coupled with their causes . . ."(IV, 301). Because they lack this quality, Bacon condemns epitomes, so popular in his day, as the "corruptions and moths of histories, . . . base and unprofitable dregs" (IV, 304). Similarly, commentaries are history unfinished since they merely "set down a bare continuance and tissue of actions without the causes and pretexts, the commencements and occasions, the counsels and orations . . ." (IV, 303). Of a like nature, but more penetrating, is Bacon's criticism of chroniclers and annalists on the ground that they attribute to their subject-matter an unhistorical dignity and fail to paint a realistic and useful picture because they consider it inelegant to look for hidden or commonplace motives. This kind of composition, he says,

> . . . represents the magnitude of public actions, and the public faces and deportments of persons, but omits and covers up in silence the smaller passages and motions of men and matters. But such being the workmanship of God, that he hangs the greatest weights upon the smallest wires, it comes commonly to pass that such a history, pursuing the greater things alone, rather sets forth the pomp and solemnity of business than the true and inward springs and resorts thereof. Moreover, when it does add and insert the counsels and motives,

> yet from its love of grandeur it introduces into human actions more gravity and prudence than they really have; so that a truer picture of human life may be found in a satire than in some histories of this kind (IV, 304–5).

Equally searching for his time is Bacon's estimate of the value of histories which are more than national in scope. Although he was skeptical, as we have seen, of a writer's ability to maintain strict truthfulness in a universal history, he recognized that "the affairs of men are not so far separated by the divisions of empires or countries, but they have a connexion in many things; and therefore it is certainly of use to have the fates, acts, and destinies of one age described and contained as it were on one tablet" (IV, 308–9).[33]

It scarcely needs to be said of Bacon, considering the direction of his whole philosophy, that his conception of causation is human rather than supernatural. The possibility of divine control is not denied but is effectually ignored by being relegated to a separate historical category, the History of Providence and of Prophecies and their accomplishments.[34] There is little profit in this kind of narrative except, perhaps, to frighten a few wicked persons. The utility of history springs rather from a realistic analysis of human actions and motives.

Bacon's analysis of causes was realistic, however, in only a narrow sense. It has been remarked before[35] that in the History of Henry VII Bacon explains events almost wholly by an interpretation of personal motives, and neglects social and economic causes. It may be said of him as of his model Machiavelli, that he "was lacking in the discernment of hidden causes . . . the development of practical interests—of trade and commerce, mechanics and agriculture—and the way in which those new interests and the new social stratification which they represented had grown strong enough to take an essential part in determining the politics of modern times, —all this escaped him, dominated as he was by his formal conception of politics as a play of intrigue and a struggle for power."[36]

Neither did Bacon perceive that emphasis on the interpretation of hidden causes and motives opens the way to the introduction of fiction, no matter how plausible, into ostensibly factual histories. Such a perception was rare in Bacon's time. Sidney's refreshingly caustic criticism, for example, springs from his special bias as a defender of poetry against the conventional eulogy of history.

"Manie times he [the historian] must tell events whereof he can yeeld no cause, and if he do, it must be poetically."[37] It was enough for Bacon and other theorists if the causes and motives adduced were probable; and probability, it was felt, could be secured most surely through practical experience rather than through research. "It is not . . . closet penmen that we are to look for guidance in such a case; . . . [but] those who have handled the helm of government, and been acquainted with the difficulties and mysteries of state business" (VI, 305).

The aspects of history-writing that have been discussed in the foregoing paragraphs were the only ones with which Bacon concerned himself. He was clearly one of the most important English advocates of what may be called the Polybian or Florentine theory of history-writing. The adherents of this theory held certain beliefs in common which set them off more or less distinctly from the chroniclers, the rhetoricians, and the antiquarians. They denounced rhetorical excesses and advocated a more realistic and analytical treatment of the past. They believed that the utility of historical narratives should be increased by more penetrating political and psycholog[ical] analyses rather than by the methods of the dramatist or the cloistere[d] scholar. They associated history-writing with political theory rather than with oratory or research, and they studied the past not so much to find examples with which to enforce conventional morality as to learn what is politically expedient. History, to them, was a form of didactic literature concerned with the difficult art of political administration.

NOTES

1 Compare Huarte's puzzlement caused by an anatomy of the brain which revealed no difference in substance or appearance in the three ventricles. Examen de Ingenios, Cap. 8 (Biblioteca de Autores Españolas, Madrid, 1913, 65. 434), or in the Renaissance English translation which Bacon may have known, although he nowhere mentions Huarte, The Examination of Mens Wits (London, 1594), pp. 54–5.

2 "One of the moderns" is said by Bacon's editors to be A. Donius. He was a follower of Telesius, the only Renaissance encyclopedist whom Bacon respected. (Cf. I, 51 ff.; V, 495); and Virgil K. Whitaker, Bacon and the Renaissance Encyclopedists, Stan-

ford University doctoral dissertation, 1933, p. 27). Telesius likewise objected to the faculty psychology and advocated in its place a theory of cognition based on memory and motion. The sense of the difficult Latin seems to be this. Sensations excite a kind of mental activity which can later be revived because it forms a pattern. When any fragmentary part presents itself to us, the totality is recalled by filling out the pattern that has been established in our mind as a sort of habit. The intelligence, then, is really memory rather than pure reason. (De rerum natura, a cura de Vincenzo Spampanato, Modena, 1910, 3. 89–90.) On the similarity of the psychological theories of Telesius and Bacon, see G. S. Brett, A History of Psychology (London, 1921) 2. 148.

3 III, 288: ". . . ecclesiastical history; which hath so easily received and registered reports and narrations of miracles . . . ; which though they had a passage for a time . . . ; yet . . . when the mists began to clear up, they grew to be esteemed as old wive's fables. . . ." Cf. III, 219; IV, 66, 296.

Bacon's scorn was, of course, not novel. The case against the factual accuracy of ecclesiastical history had been stated even more pointedly by Vives, for example, a century before. Cf. De disciplinis, tr. Foster Watson, Vives: On Education (Cambridge, 1913), pp. 248–9.

4 IV, 309, 305. Bacon's criticism of universal history may well be original, but it is very like the opinion of Thomas Hobbes that Thucydides is superior to Dionysius of Halicarnassus because he took an argument that was "within his power well to handle. . . ." [The English Works of Thomas Hobbes, ed. Sir William Molesworth (London, 1843), 8. xxiii.] This similarity suggests the possibility that Bacon may have been influenced by Hobbes to include in the De Augmentis the discussion of the relative merits of universal and particular histories which is lacking in The Advancement of Learning. Hobbes' statement appears in the preface to his translation of Thucydides, which was published in 1629 but composed much earlier. ["it lay long by me," English Works 8.ix.] Aubrey seems to be the only source of our information about Hobbes' relation with Bacon: ". . . presumably between the chancellor's fall and his death (1621–1626), he [Hobbes] had been known to Bacon. Hobbes, according to Aubrey, wrote from

Bacon's dictation, . . . and helped in turning some of his essays into Latin." [DNB, s.v. Hobbes.] At the same time it must be admitted that Aubrey's account is not perfectly clear in regard to dates, since he believed that Bacon and Hobbes were together at a time which was really two years after the former's death. [Brief Lives, ed. Andrew Clark (Oxford, 1898), 1. 331.]

Another parallel is to be found in Francesco Patrizzi's Della historia, diece dialoghi, Venetia, 1560. In his sixth dialogue, "Dell'Historia Universale" (especially p. 31b), Patrizzi observes that universal history is more difficult to compose accurately than particular history because the historians whose works must be used as sources are almost infinite in number, and because most of them are ignorant, biased, and lazy. This opinion was not in the part of the Della historia translated by Thomas Blundeville in 1574 as The true order and Methode of wryting and reading Hystories. There is, as a matter of fact, no explicit evidence that Bacon had read either the Della historia or Blundeville's partial version of it, although he did make use of some of Patrizzi's philosophical writings [cf. I, 564; III, 39, 147, 85, 722, 753; IV, 359; V, 538] and there are other important parallels, which will be pointed out later, between his and Patrizzi's theories of history-writing.

5 Hayward's conception of the political utility of history was based on a belief in what may be called political patterns. That this was a rather commonplace conception is indicated by Professor Lily Bess Campbell in "The Use of Historical Patterns in the Reign of Elizabeth," The Huntington Library Quarterly, 1 (1937–8), 135–68.

6 It was convenient for Hayward to say this, but there is no reason to think that he disbelieved it, since he continued the practice in later works. Coke, of course, was trying to get Hayward to confess that he had inserted and invented material in order to make his history point more directly at contemporary politics. Hayward defended himself by arguing that, on the contrary, he was simply following an accepted practice.

Coke's notes on the trial, including Hayward's answers are preserved in State Papers Domestic, Elizabeth, vols. 274–5; the quotation has been taken from the summary by Margaret Dowling, "Sir John Hayward's Troubles over his Life of Henry IV," The Library, 11 (1930), 212–24.

7 Della historia (Venetia, 1560), pp. 61–3.

8 Rather perfunctory references to Daniel's prophecy, the ages of the world, and the Four Monarchies are to be found in III, 221; IV, 92, 311, 395; V, 87–8; V, 257.

9 Growth in the Resources for Studies in Earlier English History, 1534–1625, University of Chicago doctoral dissertation, 1938, p. 228.

10 The evidence for these statements is fully presented by Professor Friedlaender, op. cit., pp. 189–93.

11 Prefatory letter to Augustine Vincent's A Discoverie of Errours In the first Edition of the Catalogue of Nobility, Published by Ralphe Brooke, Yorke Herald, 1619 . . . (London, 1622), fol. a, verso; quoted by Professor Friedlaender, op. cit., pp. 188–9.

12 For a survey of these kinds of histories, see Dr. Louis B. Wright, "The Elizabethan Middle-class Taste for History," JMH, 3 (1931), 175–97; reprinted with slight changes in Middle-class Culture in Elizabethan England, University of North Carolina Press, 1935.

13 See especially "Attic Prose: Lipsius, Montaigne, Bacon," Schelling Anniversary Papers (New York, 1923), pp. 117–50, and "Marc-Antoine Muret and Attic Prose," PMLA, 39 (1924) 254–309.

14 G. S. Brett, op. cit., 2. 182.

15 Temporis Partus Masculus, III, 538 [here the translation by Benjamin Farrington in The Philosophy of Francis Bacon (Liverpool, 1964) has been used. —Ed.] Compare Montaigne's commendation of Tacitus and Plutarch and his opinion that histories should be studied for their picture of human nature. "To some kind of men, it [history] is a meere gramaticall studie, but to others a perfect anatomie of Philosophie; by meanes whereof, the secretest part of our nature is searched-into." Plutarch is profitable because he imprints "not so much in his schollers mind the date of the ruine of Carthage, as the manners of Hanniball and Scipio, nor so much where Marcellus died, as because he was unworthy of his devoire he died there. . . ." [Essays, 1. xxv, Florio's translation.] "I know no author [than Tacitus], that in a publike register entermixeth so many considerations of

manners, and particular inclinations . . . he had a more powerfull and attractive matter, to discourse and relate, then if hee had beene to speake or treat of battels and universal agitations. . . . It is a seminary of morall, and a magazine of pollitique discourses, for the provision and ornament of those, that possesse someplace in the managing of the world" [3. viii].

16 Examples of this kind persisted, of course, in the popular Renaissance epitomes and civic annals, and continued to receive theoretical defense in essays like Richard Braithwait's The Schollers Medley (1614), revised and enlarged as A Survey of History (1638) Braithwait's purpose was to discuss the art of writing history and to show the middle-class reader how to improve his business, manners, and conversation by studying histories. In the long run, the treatise on history-writing is swamped in a sea of examples and moralizing.

17 In Polydore Vergil's English History may be seen side by side three stages in the development of the biographical example. Early in the History, when Polydore is perforce following his mediaeval sources rather closely, there appears the story of Alfreda, the light dame with an eye for the main chance. She is portrayed as an unprincipled schemer who, after murdering her stepson Edward in order to further her own ambitions, suddenly repents, scourges herself, founds nunneries, and dies. The abrupt and (from a secular point of view) insufficiently motivated transformation in her character is typical of the mediaeval Christian method. This is an illustration, in Bacon's words, of what men ought to do rather than what they really do. A second stage is exemplified by Polydore's account of Gloucester's overthrow. Although Henry and Margaret are described to a certain extent as stock types, thereby suggesting that their characters were not completely historical but rather partly invented to provide a motivation for the subsequent action and a basis for the moral lesson, it must be granted that the characterization is more realistic and convincing than that of Alfreda. The more fully conceived portrait of Richard III is an example of a third stage. [Cf. English History, ed. Sir Henry Ellis, Camden Series, 29 (London, 1844), 70–3, 174–225; 36 (London, 1846), 248.]

18 Della historia, pp. 47–8b, and for the English translation, Blundeville, op. cit., pp. 22–3.

Cf. Bacon, V, 22–3, where it is argued that "not only should the characters of dispositions which are impressed by nature be received . . . , but also those which are imposed on the mind" by external conditions.

19 This was a much-debated problem among the early humanists. Probably the most widely read discussion of it was Simon Grynaeus' De utilitate legendae historiae (Basle, 1531), which was reprinted in the Artis historique penus (1574), and frequently prefixed to historical works, such as Lodge's Josephus (1603) and Wilkin's Justin (1606).

20 The True order and Methode of wryting and reading Hystories (London, 1574), pp. 59–60.

21 Cf. Harald Höffding, A History of Modern Philosophy, tr. B. E. Meyer (London, 1900), 1. 206.

22 The ideas in this statement were not altogether novel. They are reminiscent, for example, of Juan Vives' opinion that the most profitable histories are those which clearly reveal "what the human passions are: how they are aroused, how quelled"; because when that is known, rulers possess an instrument with which they can sway their subjects and carry out their plans, and citizens have the key to rational happiness. De disciplinis, op. cit., pp. 231–3.

23 It is significant that only in Bacon's time were these classical historians receiving the attention that had earlier been given to writers, like Valerius Maximus and Sallust, who emphasized the moral and theatrical in their histories.

24 Bacon felt, however, that "many laws were of a more private and vulgar nature than ought to detain the reader of history" (VI, 159). Even so he was more liberal than Hayward, who argued that it is "improper for a true carry'd History" to contain a report of any Parliamentary acts except those which "occasion Tumults or Divisions, or some remarkable Alteration in State . . . albeit a noble Writer in our time [undoubtedly Bacon] esteems it to be a maxim in History that the Acts of Parliament should not be recited. . . ." [Edward the Sixt, in White Kennet's Complete History of England (London, 1706), 2. 290.]

25 Della historia, pp. 49–51, 53–4.

26 In *Considerazioni intorno ai Discorsi Machiavelli sopra la prima deca di Tito Livio*.

27 *Ricordi*, serie seconda, 110, 111, 114, in *Scritti politici e ricordi*, a cura di Roberto Palmarocchi (Bari, 1933), pp. 308–9.

28 The value of history was also questioned, of course, by the early Renaissance skeptics, who foreshadowed the contemptuous attitude of the Enlightenment; but their criticisms took the form of a general disbelief in the possibility of historical truthfulness. Cornelius Agrippa, for instance, denies that histories are valuable by way of example, since they are nothing but lies. [*De incertitudine et vanitate scientiarum declamatio* (1530), Cap. V.] For references to Charles de la Rulle (*Succintz adversaries contre l'histoire et professeurs d'icelle*, Poitier, 1573) and others, see Dr. John L. Brown, *The Methodus ad Facilem Historiarum Cognitionem: A Critical Study* (Washington, D.C., 1939), pp. 162–8.

29 See statements to this effect in *Works* III, 270–1; VI, 25; VII, 11, 100.

30 The most notorious instances of the misuse of historical examples are to be found in the first book of *The Advancement of Learning*. Cf. III, 269–73, 302–14.

31 The *Methodus* was fairly well known in England. Thomas Heywood translated the fourth book as a preface to his English version of Sallust's *Catiline* (1608), and it was used or referred to by such writers as William Harrison (1587), John Stow (1580), Sir Philip Sidney (1580), Thomas Nashe (1596), Edmund Bolton (c. 1618), and Degory Whear (1623). Bacon, consequently, probably knew the *Methodus*, but he never mentions Bodin by name and gives no sign of appreciating the novelty and relative profundity of some of Bodin's ideas.

See the present writer's article, "Bodin's *Methodus* in England before 1625," *Studies in Philology*, 39 (1942), pp. 160–6.

32 Preface to the *Annals of the Reign of Elizabeth* (1613), in White Kennett, *op. cit.*, 2. 362.

33 The absence of patriotic bias in Bacon's theory of history-writing is notable. Although it was generally admitted that such a bias was the cause of much untruthfulness in historical composition, writers from Grafton to Bolton continued to ask for a more

glorious and exclusive history of England. The chauvinistic attack on Polydore Vergil and others who questioned national legends has often been noticed. Cf. Edwin Greenlaw, "The Battle of the Books," Studies in Spenser's Historical Allegory, Johns Hopkins University Press, 1932.

34 IV, 312–3. Bacon likewise, attributes little power to Fortune; cf. III, 433–4, 455, 461, 466, 473; IV, 61; V, 64–5, 71–2; VII, 246.

35 "Bacon as a Historian," TLS (April 8, 1926), p. 254.

36 Höffding, op. cit., 1. 24.

37 The Defense of Poesie, The Works of Sir Philip Sidney, ed. Albert Feuillerat (Cambridge, 1923), 3. 12.

HISTORY AS PSYCHOLOGY IN FRANCIS BACON'S THEORY OF HISTORY

George H. Nadel

The identification of Bacon's historical theory as psychological or as anything else must be preceded by the uncomfortable question whether Bacon had any theory of history at all. Since he set out to encompass all knowledge by his new, scientific vision, he necessarily included history among the subjects he wanted to remodel. But were his sketchy recommendations coherent and meaningful or were they merely programmatic grandiloquence expressing positivist aspirations In what follows, I shall not attempt to identify Bacon's theory of histor until I have assembled the evidence that might settle this question, namely, Bacon's stated historical principles and specific recommenda tions, and the relationship between them.

I

To begin with the obvious. Bacon's division of historical study into the study of Natural History and of Civil History means that each is to be pursued in terms of the purpose and method which are commo to both.

It is the purpose of the writer of natural history—the historian of science and of scientific phenomena—to obtain knowledge either of particular things or of the primary materials of ultimate knowledge. In the former case, the study will be fruitful, yielding short-term utility, and possibly pleasure; in the latter, it will be enlightening, establishing causes in general and leading to the formation of "axioms" (of which all knowledge consists). Only the latter purpose is legitimate for the advancement of knowledge, and the way to achieve it is to compile fundamental data, the so-called "histories" or "tables of discovery." The criterion governing compilation is to ignore im-

Reprinted from History and Theory, Vol. 5, No. 3 (1966), pp. 275–87, by permission of the author and Wesleyan University Press.

mediate effects or appearances, indeed the workability of the investigation on hand, and instead to "seek out and gather together such a store and variety of things as may suffice for the formation of true axioms" (Parasceve, IV, 254; N.O., IV, 95; Desc. Globi Int., V, 507–8).* As is well known, Bacon's recommended method for the formation of axioms from primary materials was his logic of induction. Axioms were to be induced from primary materials through propositions ascending from the data in order of increasing generality, a procedure whose details Bacon discussed in various philosophical and scientific contexts. Suffice to say here that he thought conventional syllogistic logic commanded assent to words rather than things because it rested on improper induction, that is, on oversimplified or hasty abstraction from facts: "Our only hope therefore lies in a true induction" (Aphorisms xi–xiv, N.O., IV, 48–9). That induction had to be "true"—both in respect to the facts reported and in the manner of abstracting from them—was the criterion governing the logical method to be applied to compilation.

What holds for the writer of natural history, holds necessarily for the writer of civil (or human) history. There is no difference in principle between enquiry into "the deeds and works of nature" and into "those of men." Bacon admits that one may well ask in what manner the procedures of natural science apply, say, to the study of politics. The answer is that his new logic, like common syllogistic logic, applies to all disciplines alike; its prerequisite is merely the compilation of the appropriate histories, be the data physical or political in content. But the next step—the establish-

---

* Abbreviations used are: De Aug. (De Dignitate et Augmentis Scientiarum, 1623), N.O. (Novum Organum, 1620). Desc. Globi Int. (Descriptio Globi Intellectualis, 1612). Where the Spedding edition has an English translation, volume and page numbers quoted refer to it, not to the Latin text. I have generally not cited from The Advancement of Learning (1605), since its later Latin version, De Augmentis, supersedes most of it. Also, I have not used his historical work, the History of the Reign of King Henry VII (1622), for whatever relationship between it and his theory of history exists is of biographical and not of critical significance. Bacon's historical work, like that of most philosophers, was not written to throw light on philosophical theories nor, in the opinion of recent students of the subject, does it do so.

ment of increasingly general propositions and thence axioms—which in common logic is a set of prescribed mental operations, is, in his own system, to be modified by "such rules and guidance that it may in every case apply itself aptly to the nature of things" (N.O., IV, 112). What Bacon calls the doctrine of interpretation would offer guiding precepts adapting the application of the natural science model to different subjects of enquiry. He himself left no such doctrine to the historian. Overtly, there is only occasional advice; for example, how it is possible, in principle at any rate, to achieve law-like statements of social and political behavior, which is ostensibly "most immersed in matter and with most difficulty reduced to axiom" (De Aug., V, 32). But there is some implied guidance to a scientific approach to history—enough at any rate to permit the conclusion that Bacon wanted the practice of history to be joined to theory. What he offers is less concerned with logical method than with substance. Going beyond the Aristotelian position that different sciences require different modes of reasoning, he lays down what scientifically studied history requires the historian to do: specifically, what kinds of facts he should compile and what kinds of behavior are described by the historian's generalizations. (The second and third sections of this paper will deal, respectively, with these two recommendations.)

The historian of the deeds of nature and the historian of the deeds of man should have in common adherence not only to the new logic, but also to the same method of study. To supply the data needed for ultimate knowledge obliges each to begin with certain prescribed compilations. For the natural historian, there is a catalog of 130 subjects or "particular histories" on which information is to be compiled (Parasceve ad Historiam Naturalem et Experimentalem, IV, 265–71). For the civil historian, Bacon suggests and classifies 23 branches and sub-branches of political and other history. For both, the enumeration of the subjects is conceived in a systematic, not random, manner; for the express aim is to uncover the gaps which have impeded the accumulation of "the stuff and subject matter of true induction" and hence have blocked the road to knowledge. It hardly needs adding that this entire procedure of compilation and inductive method is the ground plan of Bacon's Instauratio Magna as such. What the historian has to do for history is merely a specific version of what Bacon himself sketched for all knowledge: The Advancement of Learning provided the compiler with a guide from knowledge to gaps in knowledge; the Novum Organum provided the method.

II

Bacon's catalog of subjects for the study of civil history is extensively annotated (*De Aug.*, IV, 300–14). In outline form, it can be condensed into not much more than two dozen lines. It is articulated according to the traditional scheme of dividing a subject as a tree is divided into branches: each branch has subdivisions, and each subdivision has further divisions, which may themselves be subdivided again. The following is a condensation of the complete catalog:

> All history, as we already know, is either natural history or civil history. Civil history has three branches: *history of learning; ecclesiastical history*, which is subdivided into that of church, prophecies, and providence; and, most importantly, *civil history of actions*, roughly synonymous with political history, the term "actions" distinguishing it from yet a fourth species of the genus civil history, namely, the *civil history of words* (the study of speeches, letters, and apophthegms), which Bacon added as an afterthought. Two of the three subdivisions of political history are made in terms of sources (imperfect histories): *memorials*, which contain chronicles not assigning causes to events, and registers, divided into documents of state and chronological records; *antiquities*, which are archaeological or literary fragments. The third subdivision, *perfect history*—a conventional term for history which is not fragmentary or antiquarian—has itself three subdivisions: *history of periods* ("times"), whether universal or particular, consisting of annals and journals; *lives*, which, being confined to describing a single person, are more detailed and therefore more reliable than history of periods; and *narrations*, histories of particular topics (like the Peloponnesian War), also preferable to history of periods "because they may choose a manageable and definite argument whereof a perfect knowledge and certainty and full information may be had; whereas the story of a time . . . is sure to meet with many gaps in the records . . . which must be filled up . . . by conjecture" (*ibid.*, 305). Finally, civil history can also be divided in terms of presentation. Perfect history is continuous *pure history*; nar-

ratives on political or cosmographic subjects not woven into a continuous history constitute mixed history.

These divisions or classifications are not very startling. They are for the most part oriented to obvious differences in subject matter and are quite conventional. Bacon's predecessors, contemporaries, and near-contemporaries presented similar catalogs, sometimes even in diagrammatic form with divisions and subdivisions fanning out across the page by means of braces. Several of them, of whose work Bacon almost certainly had no firsthand knowledge or no knowledge at all, integrated their divisions with philosophic concerns or reasoned for and against specific divisions; Bacon does neither to any significant extent.[1]

Nevertheless, there are items in the catalog which recall the scheme to its specific Baconian objective, to the collection of materials for true induction. The most obvious is preoccupation with the ascertaining of facts and restricting them to what is true and certain. For example, ecclesiastical (religious) history, to which Bacon in an earlier version gave equal status with natural and civil history, is demoted, in the final version, to a branch of civil history. This is not what Bacon's predecessors had done, who often accepted it either as being beyond profane truth or as politic lies—or who, save for mere mention of the category, kept quiet about ecclesiastical history altogether. Nor is there a lapse in Bacon's orthodoxy from the earlier to the final version; on the contrary, the latter suppressed hints about clerical dishonesty which the former had contained (The Advancement of Learning, III, 288). Bacon merely aimed at bringing one branch of ecclesiastical history, the history of the church, within the ambit of civil history in order to lay it open to common investigation, to the ascertaining of accurate facts about it.

Similarly, he did not, like many other writers on historical method—among whom Bodin and Vossius were perhaps the most famous—confine himself to perfect history and leave imperfect (antiquarian) history alone. He at least sanctioned the idea of reconstructing data from archaeological and other fragmentary remains; but, worried about their verifiability, he declared the antiquary engaged in this pursuit to be "entitled however to the less authority" than the historian working in more generally and numerously accessible fields (De Aug., IV, 304). Both in his Essays and in his philosophical work, Bacon seems singularly free from flippant bias against pedantes and others commonly accused of pursuing otiose or antiquarian knowledge (De Aug., I, 438–9); he disliked their vanity, but not the genre of their learning, occasional outbursts against the use of "antiquities and citations or testimonies" notwithstanding (Parasceve, IV, 254). His lack of outright prejudice against recondite historical knowledge arose from his respect for facts and was underwritten by his general defense of the utility of learning.

Bacon's belief that properly abstracted facts could serve the intended purpose shows in his treatment of the conventional topoi of the historical theorizing of his day. About causes Bacon wrote: "Above all things (for this is the ornament and life of Civil History), I wish events to be coupled with their causes" (De Aug., IV, 301). Here he echoed the well-known classical desideratum, eloquently stated by Polybius, who had written that mere facts may be of interest but adding their causes makes them fruitful. But to Bacon —alone, perhaps, among the humanists writing about the study of history—this was no mere professional injunction but a philosophically meaningful requirement. The addition of causes made information not only more enlightening and intelligent; it helped to turn it into potential raw material for axioms by providing guidelines for generalizations. As Bacon's chaplain, who claimed to have known Bacon's intentions particularly well, reminded posterity: his lordship deliberately made "some gloss of the causes" in his own writings to help others proceed from the vast wood of experience to the eventual formation of axioms (Sylva Sylvarum, pref., II, 336). At the level of compilation itself, there should be no—or at best only a minimum of—philosophizing. A cause should be narrated "simply" and "historically." It can be any of several antecedent or accompanying facts of the phenomenon recorded. It is important, therefore, to establish what kinds of fact the historian must not fail to record, lest he fail to report a cause.

What kinds of fact to record was a long-lived problem in historical theorizing, from Lucius and Longinus to Descartes and Voltaire. It revolved chiefly around the question whether confining history to what was memorable, and omitting what was trivial, was the correct thing to do. Bacon's answer was as expected. God "hangs the greatest weights upon the smallest wires"; those writing large-scale histories necessarily concentrate on the greater things alone; thus what is trifling, small, and private eludes them, yet it is those things which tend to be "the true and inward springs and resorts" of events (De Aug., IV, 304). Concentration on the large, the elevated, the pompous, the grave, and the prudent deceives. Writing of natural history, Bacon declared: "it often comes to pass that mean and small things discover great better than great can discover small" (*ibid.*, 297). In civil history, the biographer, if he is careful, is the most reliable historian, for he will relate necessarily things trifling as well as important. The worst historians are those who omit most details, the producers of epitomes ("the corruptions and moths of histories"). Even biographers can obscure credibility and create uncertainty if they present them as part of moralized biographical collections instead of in their context. "Certainly when I read in Tacitus of the actions of Nero and Claudius," Bacon explained, "invested with all the circumstances of times, persons, and occasions, I see nothing in them very improbable; but when I read the same in Suetonius Tranquillus, gathered into titles and common places, and not presented in order of time, they seem something prodigious and quite incredible" (*ibid.*, 366–7).

That Bacon applied his emphasis on the credibility of facts to biography was no accident. The study of lives was for him, as for sixteenth- and seventeenth-century scholars generally, an obviously useful branch of history. His contemporaries would not merely have drawn up the same list of subjects for civil history which Bacon recommended: "the revolution of times, the characters of persons, the fluctuation of counsels, the courses and currents of actions, the bottoms of pretences, and the secrets of governments." They would also have agreed that "the characters of persons" was morally the most instructive subject. For Bacon, a biographer himself, it had especial significance, but not, as we might expect, in relation to biographies as a genre of historical writing; those books he praised for usefulness in teaching certain kinds of conduct but thought such conduct could be better learned from letters of famous men (*De Aug.*, V, 56–7).[2] It was rather that the subject of biography, "the characters of persons," was to him both object and validation of history studied as a science. The conventional position, accepted by everyone, that we improve ourselves morally by drawing the appropriate lessons from reading about the lives of others was too vague for Bacon, however much he agreed with its sentiment. And the procedure sometimes proposed, that we note down actions under headings good and evil in commonplace books to better learn morality, could not have struck him as a method evidencing a scientific approach.

What was needed was a number of basic reconsiderations to see if civil history in its preoccupation with human action could issue in something like a scientific corpus of behavioral knowledge. The field of behavioral knowledge was of course already inhabited, as becomes clear if we give it its less anachronistic title: it was moral philosophy, in its widest sense. If there was to be substance to Bacon's theory of history, propositions guiding us in the application of scientifically undertaken historical study, it was moral philosophy which had to be reconsidered.

III

Bacon's theories about mental and moral phenomena show a profound commitment to psychology. By observations, judgments, hints, and aphorisms, his interest in the functioning of the mind is evident in almost all those writings for which he is most widely known, like the Essays and the discourse on the sources of fallacies (the "idols"). What he has to say explicitly about psychology he says in criticism of the errors of philosophy and in praise of history.

This critique can best be understood as part of a general shift in sixteenth-century philosophical thought from the traditional metaphysical and moral philosophies, operating deductively from "precepts," to history as the teacher of prudential morality induced from "examples." Bacon and Machiavelli have long been recognized as the principal exponents of the proposal to reorient the study of moral philosophy towards an empirical or historical study of behavior; what I shall attempt to do here is to identify Bacon's theory of history in terms of that proposal.[3]

Bacon's starting point was Aristotelian faculty psychology. This, as is well known, imputed to man a rational soul, which was divine; and an irrational or material soul, common to man and animal, which Bacon believed to be corporeal (situated in the head and running along the nerves). He had no quarrel with the notion of intellectual and sensitive faculties with which each soul was said to be endowed, and believed that faculties such as "understanding, reason, imagination, memory, appetite, will" make up "all with which the logical and ethical sciences deal" (De Aug., IV, 399). He found some fault with existing identifications of the physical locations of the faculties in the body, in particular with Plato's (ibid., 378). He agreed with an unnamed materialist critic of faculty psychology—Donius—that the ancients had overdone the distinction of the three faculties of the rational soul, memory, imagination, and reason. None of these is self-contained, but each shares in the property of the rational soul, namely, thinking; whether drawing on memory, imagining, or reasoning, we always think (De Aug., IV, 325). History, the branch of learning which Bacon derived from memory, was thus not purely mnemonic; cognitive operations came into it as well. But these criticisms did not impair Bacon's belief in faculty psychology as such. They made little difference to his justification of history and other learning in terms of it, a justification that may be summarized as follows:

(1) We form images or impressions of the data ("individuals") which our senses have received. (2) These impressions are stored unaltered in the memory. (3) We call them up subsequently in three possible ways: in their original form, or fancifully, or analyzed and classified. (4) This tripartite operation is the product, respectively, of our faculties of memory, of imagination, and of reason, which give rise in their turn to three branches of human learning: history, poetry, philosophy. (5) There are no other sources, and therefore there can be no other branches, of human learning—at least none which is not reducible to these three. Experience, for example, is the same as history; science the same as philosophy (De Aug., IV, 292–3; Desc. Globi Int., V, 504).

The crucial distinction was not really tripartite. It was between history and poetry on the one hand, and philosophy on the other. The former two deal with individuals circumscribed by time and place; history with real, poetry with imaginary, individuals. Even natural history deals with individuals, its frequent generalizations being merely a shorthand, justifiable by resemblances among natural objects ("insomuch if you know one you know all, it would be a superfluous and endless labour to speak of them severally," Desc. Globi Int., V, 505). Philosophy, however, is interested neither in individuals nor in the actual impressions received from them. It deals with abstract notions derived from the impressions, and reason guides the philosopher to make his notions accord with the laws of nature. Finally, thinking, as we have seen, attaches to the mnemonic and imaginative faculties just as much as it does to the reasoning faculty; thus they too apply some notions of reasoning ("pre-notions") to the ordering of the individuals with which they deal. History and poetry, therefore, provide an alternative to philosophy: they are self-sufficient and valid branches of knowledge, concerned with individuals and, so far as history is concerned, identical with real-life experience.

If that were all there was to Bacon's view of historical knowledge, there would be little further to say. Some neat formal derivations from Aristotelian psychology and corresponding epistemological criteria of differentiation would hardly entitle us to say that Bacon had a meaningful theory of history or, if he did, that it was psychological in any except the traditional sense. But Bacon's main point about history was not its derivation from memory. True, this was in line with his empiricist philosophy of knowledge, provided formal support for his conviction that history mirrored reality, and even —at least according to some introductory remarks to an early essay —explained why historians wrote more objectively than philosophers and poets (The History of the reign of K. Henry the Eighth, VI, 17–8). But it is not possible to derive his theory of history from it. For that, what matters is not Bacon's version of "ancient" learning, but his "modern" insistence that the subject matter of history is individual and social psychology.[4]

The argument that history is the source of psychological insight begins with an indictment of philosophy. Philosophy has failed to deal, or has incorrectly dealt with, the real problems of moral philosophy. It has totally neglected the culture of the mind—that is, learning how to be virtuous. The full indictment need not be summarized; it is not one of Bacon's best efforts. Apart from the accusation that philosophers recite merely formal precepts, the reasons he gives for their failure to discuss moral training are petty. (Earlier he had made the contradictory claim that philosophers have in fact handled moral, but not intellectual training [A Letter and Discourse to Sir Henry Savill, Touching Help for the Intellectual Powers, VII, 97]. As far as I can see, the only thing the two claims have in common, apart from being false, is that they serve to justify Bacon's reopening of the subject.) What follows the indictment is his discussion of how to fill the gap (De Aug., Book VII). It is there that he explains what history has to offer.

The theory of moral culture demands that we study three things, the different types of dispositions, the emotions, and the remedies. These aids to the cultivation of mental or moral health correspond in medicine—so Bacon maintains in one of his frequent analogies between mental and physical sickness—to constitution, disease, and cure. How do we learn about dispositions? The best source of information is the wiser sort of historians, like Livy, Herodian, Commines, and Guicciardini. They describe personality ("character") as part of the historical situation, actor and actions together, and "a character so worked into the narrative gives a better idea of the man than any formal criticism or review can" (De Aug., V, 21). We should not try to learn anything directly from these historical portraits, but should abstract the basic features of which all human dispositions are an arrangement and thus arrive at scientific and accurate rules "for the treatment of the mind." This procedure refers not only to constitutional but also to acquired characteristics, to the influence of place, station in life, adversity, prosperity, and so on. We learn from Tacitus, for example, that honors and prosperity tend to make dispositions worse not better, and how rare the exceptions to that rule are. Next come the emotions, which Bacon characterized as an invariable source of dissatisfaction, unrest, and sedition. He thought of emotions in these terms because he was concerned throughout with showing that the rules for moral behavior are also the rules for political behavior (ethics being private, and politics being public, morality). Aristotle and the Stoics had some few interesting things to say about the emotions—

> But to speak the real truth, the poets and writers of history are the best doctors of this knowledge, where we may find . . . how affectations are kindled and excited, and how pacified and restrained . . . how they disclose themselves though repressed and concealed . . . (ibid., 23).

We learn how emotions are at war with one another, and how one can be set upon the other to master it, equally in the government of states and in the internal government of the mind. The third and last type of phenomena for study—the remedies which induce virtuous behavior—is distinguished from the first two by being rational, or at any rate voluntary, components of the moral regimen. Bacon lists a variety of factors capable of influencing the mind to control will and appetite—custom, habit, imitation, study, praise and blame, and the like. But these and the rules for their application are not of direct relevance here.

So far discussion has been confined to individual morality, with its effects on private or public (or political) conduct. Next, Bacon takes up "external" or social morality, an area of conduct to which traditional moral philosophy is inappropriate and which has to be governed by what he calls civil knowledge. ("Civil Knowledge, which is commonly ranked as part of Ethic," he announced, "I have already emancipated and erected into an entire doctrine by itself—the doctrine concerning man congregate . . ." [De Aug., IV, 405].) Again, Bacon's analysis of this knowledge and its division into three branches—conversation, negotiation, government—need not concern us here for its own sake. But his discussion of it illustrates the inductive method in history, the study of behavior by "examples." This illustration is rather roundabout. A sixty-page discourse on rules for the best responses in given social situations takes the form of a lengthy exegesis of Solomon's Proverbs. These rules are confirmed in the writings of Tacitus and Machiavelli; but Solomon remains the principal source.[5] Now the point of the preceding arguments had been to show that history, because it is true to life, is the source of knowledge of behavior. Consequently, the reliance on the Proverbs has to be explained away, and the function of real-life case histories or historical examples has to be emphasized. Bacon does both, explaining that proverbs, parables or fables

> were formerly substitutes and supplements of examples, but now that the times abound with history, the aim is more true and active when the mark is alive. And therefore the form of writing [which is fittest to deal with various branches of civil knowledge] is that which Machiavelli most wisely and aptly chose for government; namely, Observations or Discourses upon Histories and Examples (V, 56).[6]

Examples must precede the discourse; not the discourse the example. That, we are told, is not merely a point of order, in the sense that to obtain knowledge of particulars, one must begin with induction from particulars and then ascend to the general statements from which particular applications are deduced. It is also a point of substance. Examples, if stated first and in full detail, determine and correct what the subsequent discourse is to explain; examples merely illustrating the prior discourse do not supply full or independent knowledge (ibid.).

This admonition on the use of historical examples shows once again a distinctly Baconian twist given to a conventional topic. The usual function imputed to historical examples was, so to speak, that of the poor man's philosophy: easily and instinctively apprehended sources of practical wisdom, contrasted to the formal precepts of the learned, of the *pedantes*, of the schools. But Bacon, though he condemned those precepts he regarded as empty philosophical and rhetorical abstractions, did not condemn precepts as such. He thought it possible to have precepts properly induced from, and controlled by, examples. This involved him in a defense both of the value of examples and of pedantic (pedagogic) learning, to which he devoted the beginning of The Advancement of Learning. Similarly, the point of the discourse on Solomon's Proverbs was to show how precepts can be drawn from examples—specifically the precepts (general propositions) governing various branches of the doctrine of civil knowledge. There is no reason to fear "that the matter of this knowledge should be so variable that it falls not under precept; for it is much less infinite than that science of government, which notwithstanding we see excellently laboured and reduced" (ibid., 36–7).

All this is a consequence of his desire to create a "great concurrence between learning and practical wisdom." As occasion warranted it, he would defend either the dependence of learning on experience ("everything is subject to chance and error which is not supported by example and experience") or the dependence of experience on learning ("learned men with but little experience would far excel men of long experience without learning"). In Bacon's theory that history functions as behavioral science, we can trace the inspiration that lay behind the belief in the "great concurrence." True, his ideas on history are disconcertingly scattered throughout his discourse on the mind and are not gathered into a neat, articulated theory explaining in detail the operation of the function that he assigns to history. Nevertheless, there are persistent and consistent themes, which even the summary I have attempted here will have made clear. There is the position that moral philosophy should not be formal but lifelike, that is, in accord with the "actual nature of things"; that historians possess the power to reveal the seen and unseen springs of human behavior, which provide us with a true knowledge of the functioning of the mind; and that, therefore, history, its insights psychological, its method inductive, must replace conventional moral philosophy in the instauration of learning. That learning should be "true to life" is the overarching inspiration behind all Baconian thought. The application of this insight to mental and moral processes established a preference for history over philosophy in the study of man; a preference which formal considerations of faculty psychology served to confirm. A simple sentence sums it up: "Aristotle's and Plato's moral doctrines are admired by many; but Tacitus utters observations on morals that are much truer to life" (Temporis Partus Masculus, III, 538).[7]

NOTES

1 For example, in Jean Bodin's Methodus (1566) the human-natural-divine divisions correspond to the respective virtues, prudence, knowledge, and faith; to the modes of appearance, probability, certainty, holiness; and to the degrees of probability, uncertain, certain, most certain. In Reiner Reineccius' Methodus (1583), topography and genealogy are established as major divisions, and, incidentally, so-called pragmatic history subdivided into the same divisions as Bacon's civil history. (Hence the tempting notion that Bacon's proposal for a history of learning, for example, was novel is wrong.) Bartholomaeus Keckermannus' Commentarius (1610) attacked all his predecessors' divisions, observing that man is inseparably the subject of both natural and human history; that divine history confuses theology with its history; and that natural history confuses natural science with its history (as it did with Bacon, who, however, was not mentioned, The Advancement of Learning having not yet been translated into Latin.) Keckermannus' opponent Gerard Vossius, who knew Bacon's work, offered a more formal set of classifications, an elaborate diagram serving as the synopsis of his Ars historica (1625), in which they were discussed and documented in great detail; Peter Heylin's ΜΙΚΡΟΚΟΣΜΟΣ (1625) borrowed much from Bacon but came up with a more comprehensive scheme, with comments written into the diagram that represented it.

2 It should be remembered that biography as a genre, as Bacon knew it, referred to the writings of the ancients, notably Plutarch and Suetonius. Incidental character portraits or accounts of the actions of individuals were another matter, which Bacon knew not only from the ancients but from the (only) four modern historians he mentions: Machiavelli, Guicciardini, Commines, De Thou. The first major historical biography in the English language was Bacon's own Henry VII. So far as I know, it was preceded only—if we except the inevitable minor, moralized lives of Richard III—by Sir John Hayward's Henry IIII (1599), which has remained virtually unknown and certainly unread. Bacon's own view of Henry IIII—delivered in response to Queen Elizabeth's enquiry whether the book involved treason—

was that Hayward "had stolen many of his sentences and conceits out of Cornelius Tacitus" and thus was guilty of felony only (Apophthegms, New and Old, VII, 133).

3 The most stimulating discussion of Bacon and the shift from moral philosophy to history is still Leo Strauss's The Political Philosophy of Hobbes (Chicago, 1952), 86–94. Equally perceptive, but primarily devoted to placing Bacon into the school of Renaissance historiography concerned with "a realistic treatment of psychology and ethics," is Leonard Dean's "Sir Francis Bacon's Theory of Civil-History Writing," English Literary History, VIII (1941), 161–83. The present paper, like other studies of Bacon, owes much to the inspiration provided by that pioneering essay.

4 In one of his rare but complete lapses from scholarship, R. G. Collingwood writes as if derivation of history from memory were Bacon's sole contribution to historical theory. This would explain why Collingwood imputes to Bacon the position—the opposite of which is true—that history is an interest in the past for its own sake. The Idea of History (Oxford, 1946), 58.

5 The ubiquity of Solomon in Bacon's writings generally, according to Miss Frances Yates, a foremost scholar of Renaissance symbolism, remains a mystery.

6 If the original Latin has been correctly transcribed, the conjunction "Histories and Examples" ("Discursus . . . super Historiam et Exempla" in De Aug., I, 769) differs from the earlier rendering in the Advancement of Learning, where it is "discourse upon histories or examples" (III, 453). The meaning differs accordingly.

7 "Aristotelis et Platonis moralia plerique mirantur, sed Tacitus magis vivas morum observationes spirat." In the first complete English translation of Temporis Partus Masculus, which has appeared only recently, the rendering is freer: "The ethics of Plato and Aristotle are much admired; but the pages of Tacitus breathe a livelier and truer observation of morals and institutions." Benjamin Farrington, The Philosophy of Francis Bacon (Liverpool, 1964), 71–2.

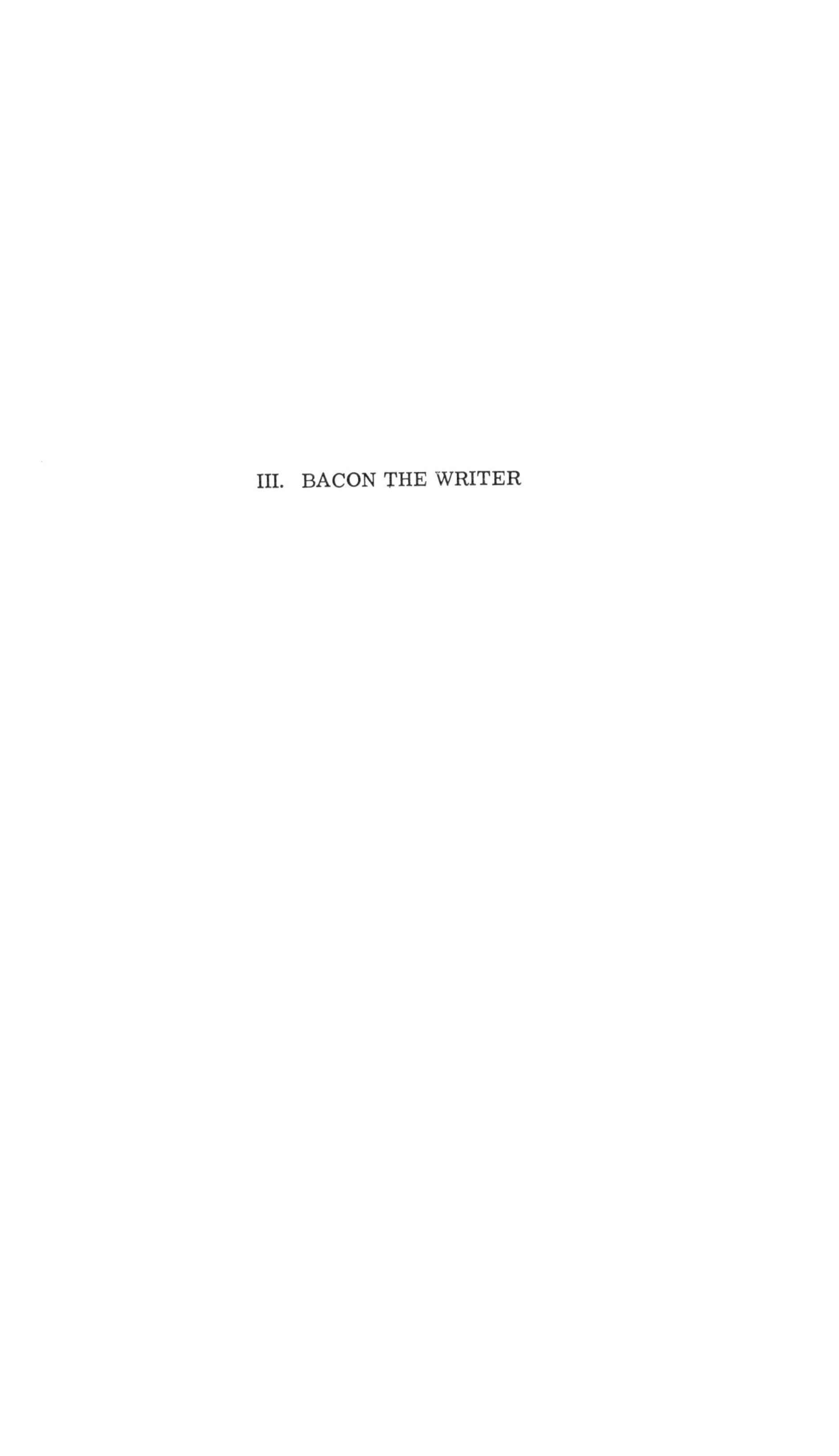

III. BACON THE WRITER

BACON'S VIEW OF RHETORIC, POETRY, AND THE IMAGINATION

John L. Harrison

Much of the writing on Bacon in recent decades has depended from an a posteriori view of his influence on the seventeenth century. A true estimate of his idea of poetry has been prevented by too exclusive attention to his role in the advancement of scientific learning.[1] The following statements are representative: "At any rate Bacon seems to have given the coup de grace to allegory in England." "The science which is placed at the service of humanity has as its final aim technical mastery, which now in Bacon's estimation supplants artistic culture." C. M. Dowlin appears to believe that Bacon excluded elegies, odes, etc., from poetry. L. C. Knights and K. R. Wallace both seem to underestimate the role Bacon assigned to poetry in satisfying the needs of human nature, Wallace going so far as to report cryptically: "But poesy, because it is a part of learning that is 'extremely licensed' and obeys no rational laws, is later eliminated from serious investigation." Bundy claimed that Bacon had made no original contribution to the theory of poetry. Originality is always a difficult question. But Bacon was surely original in foreseeing the fabulous extension of the area of science and the consequent proportional diminishing of the area of poetry—which had once been "all knowledge." And secondly, in order to save poetry from complete dismissal Bacon resolutely determined its area as that of morality and touching on divinity, and its genesis as in the imagination.

The evidence provided by Bacon's writings, that is, can be redisposed to reveal a view of poetry and rhetoric consonant with what was continuous in the Medieval-Renaissance tradition, a view which tended to value poetry as a branch of learning in its own right and of an order different in kind from science. Bacon stood at the cross-

Reprinted from The Huntington Library Quarterly, Vol. 20 (1957), pp. 107–25, by permission of the publisher.

roads of the then bedrid general soul of the medieval world,[2] and the "all subdued" and "open laid" world of Newton.[3] That his view of poetry did not become the later seventeenth-century view is manifest; it should be recognized, nevertheless, that without Bacon the new philosophy might well have diminished poetry further than it did.

The main points of this paper are three: (a) Bacon's interest in allegory and myth tended to preserve through a bleak silver age the golden thread of imagination whereby poetry could still bind, by an idealistic verisimilitude, images of things into that "unity of effect" which he recognized as the persuading heart of poetry; (b) his linking of divine illumination and poetry, and separation of poetry and "philosophical" knowledge, gave poetry credit different in kind, and not merely in degree, from the scientific registers of information; and (c) his acknowledgment of the large role Imagination played in both poetry and rhetoric, authorized its importance in matters political and ethical, segregate and congregate, no matter what the vehicle.

I

Bacon's theory of poetry is based on the traditional dualism of rational and moral faculties,[4] and on the relation between their functions of logical examination or "probation" leading to "Truth," and the "procuring of the affections" leading to good action (IV, 455–9). The Janus-faced Imagination acts as a nuncius between the judicial and ministerial parts of the mind, is a faculty of the appetitive rather than the intellectual soul (with qualifications to be seen later) although it serves both, and is the principal mental agent of both poetry and rhetoric (IV, 405–6, 455; III, 382). The Imagination receives images directly from the senses; reason then judges these images and leaves its final selection with the Imagination in order that by this means it may incite the will to action. Rhetoric is studied under the Art of Transmitting, one of the four arts of logic, and is "subservient to the Imagination." Poetry is completely under the aegis of Imagination and less hampered by rational restrictions than rhetoric.

Bacon's system of knowledge is correspondingly based on a three-fold division into memory, imagination, and reason, and on a parallel division of the branches of human learning into history, poetry, and philosophy. The tripartite distribution had been anticipated by both Cardanus and Campanella, and was to persist throughout the seventeenth century and later as the trinity of wit, judgment, and memory. History and poetry are disposed of in the second book of the De Augmentis, and the remainder of the treatise deals with philosophy in the following (simplified) manner:

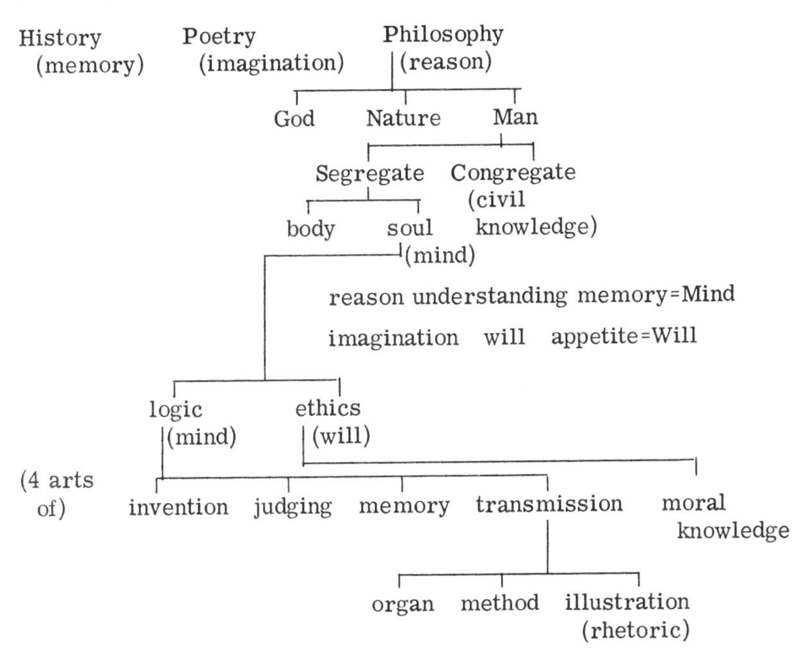

We have just been told that Imagination is one of the faculties referred to under the term "will" and is therefore a part of Ethic, not Logic. Now we see that one of its chief arts, rhetoric, is subsumed under Logic. K. R. Wallace provides an admirable summary of the relations intended by Bacon between logic and rhetoric:

> To summarize, then, rhetoric relates to logic, first, as a part does to the whole; second, as a science which may utilize the logical methodology of scientific discovery, thereby adding to extant rhetorical theory, and as a practical art which may adapt a scientific method of inquiry to the finding of probable facts unknown to the speaker;

third, rhetoric as a practical art employs the topics of ordinary logic; and finally, as a practical activity rhetoric will utilize the precepts of everyday logic for the criticism of the inference that appears in discourse.[5]

But in addition, the Ramist (for one) reformation was stressing a simplified logic which by incorporating the major parts of traditional rhetoric served both to simplify rhetoric and to emphasize its prognostic logical basis and its dialectical (although open) palm. Bacon acknowledged the shift in emphasis when he reiterated that rhetoric applies reason to the imagination. Obviously, one of the ways to "save" Imagination was to insist that its activity formed part of what was to become increasingly the commended way of "judgment."

Then, too, Bacon has willingly sacrificed neat division in order to outline the dual proctorial duties of the Imagination. The seeming blurring of edges in defining Imagination was traditional and persisted through the century in the writings of Richard Carew, Burton, Hobbes, and Dryden, to name a few. It had the important advantage, however, of preserving the image of man from the butcherings of mechanistic faculty psychologists which finally occurred during the later eighteenth century. It was owing to this refusal to oversimplify (there is a major difference between oversimplification and purposely avoiding suspect distinctions) that Bacon, as this paper will show, was able to preserve poetry at all from—and for—his seventeenth-century disciples.

But Imagination is assigned not only to both logic and ethic but also to poetry which properly derives from its activity. Bacon is aware of the apparent anomaly, for he reviews the triple duty of the Imagination and decides not to redispose it under philosophy since it "hardly produces sciences" (IV, 406). It remains, then, as the begettor of poetry and also as the servant of both reason and the will in their own sciences. It has a great power in oratory and can lead the mind where it will, even against reason (ibid.); rightly employed it serves as a free-lance artisan providing images which lure to civil concord and individual morality, and raise the mind to behold ideal patterns.

Further, the Imagination is an instrument of "illumination," especially through poetry. Purity of illumination was lost at the Fall together with perfect freedom of will, but Bacon believed (conventionally) in partial reillumination both through the sciences, which include rhetoric, and poetry (IV, 405–6). "In matters of faith and religion," the Imagination by means of poetry draws men by "similitudes, types, parables, visions, dreams." Religion is based on faith in revelation and "a more perfect interpretation of the moral law" (V, 113). Moral laws are "beyond the light of nature," yet they sometimes "flash upon the spirit of man by an inward instinct."

> And in this latter sense chiefly does the soul partake of some light to behold and discern the perfection of the moral law, a light however not altogether clear, but such as suffices rather to reprove the vice in some measure, than to give full information of the duty.

In a similar flashing upon the inward eye, Bacon adds:

> . . . The divine grace uses the motions of the imagination as an instrument of illumination, just as it uses the motions of the will as an instrument of virtue (IV, 406).

It follows that religion uses poetry, although care must be taken that it does not contract the grandeur of the mysteries to the narrowness of the mind (V, 114; IV, 317). Most previous commentators have appeared to undervalue Bacon's allowance to poetry on this score of illumination, where the soul "Shuns the sweet leaves and blossoms green" to express "The greater Heaven in an Heaven less."

It follows, therefore, that the "duty and office" of rhetoric—"to apply and recommend the dictates of reason to imagination, in order to excite the appetite and will" (IV, 535)—is related to that of poetry. The duty of poetry or "feigned history" is assigned in three parts according to the three main kinds of poetry: epic-narrative, dramatic, and allegorical. Owing to the fact that the sensible world appears to be ill-proportioned and unsuited to the "dignity" of the human spirit, poetry in all these kinds satisfies the mind of man by depicting a more ample greatness and variety and a more perfect order than is to be found in nature (IV, 315–6). That an ideal moral order is meant here is apparent from the earlier version in the Advancement of Learning (1605), where instead of the phrase "a more perfect order" stands "a more exact goodness." Bacon makes it clear that man because of the Fall cannot find in nature the order he desires, and that poetry represents an ideal pattern by which he is stimulated to strive for knowledge and virtue.[6] The Imagination, further, when governed by reason, is especially persuasive as a moral director since it already stands with one foot in the kingdom of ethics. And when Bacon does admonish men for reading a non-existent order into nature—the followers of Paracelsus, Galen, and the alchemists, for example—he is not speaking of poetry but of the Idols which deter the discovery of sciences (IV, 432, 63–4). The function of the Imagination in poetry, then, is "truly noble" and seems "to satisfy the mind with the shadows of things when the substance cannot be obtained" (IV, 315).

Bacon commends poetry, that is, (a) for supplying the shadows at least, when the substance is not to be found; and (b) for satisfying the mind with these shadows, not as a soporific but as a stimulant toward good works.[7] Poetry provides an ethical interpretation of the world which shows truth and virtue and the aesthetics of order to be the fit end of animal risibile. History (fact) denies this pattern to the soul of man; and, Bacon adds, one can even argue in the reverse direction, that the presence of such pattern, such variety and noble order in poetry, is evidence of man's inherent capacity for and orientation toward such things.[8] Poetry "commonly exaggerates things beyond probability" because "the sensible world is inferior in dignity to the rational soul" and the high moral and aesthetic demands of the soul must be met.[9] The idea of order appears throughout Bacon's writings, e.g., in his contention that the "government of the world" is harmonious, although appearing "harsh and untunable" to human ignorance (IV, 326). It is this harmony which poets must, like Orpheus, teach delightfully. And like Pan's only wife Echo (in another of Bacon's exegeses of myth), the poet must echo "most faithfully the voices of the world itself." Bacon adds that Pan loves only two, either Echo, or Syringa if the "discourse" (reasoning) desired "be of the more exact and delicate kind . . . whether poetical or oratorical"; but Pan favors Echo (IV, 326–7).

Having observed a degree of idealistic verisimilitude in poetry, Bacon went on to say that the poet is obliged to exaggerate in order to fulfill the traditional function of "delight." This concept was the seventeenth-century measure of aesthetics, but it was more than that. Of the same order as rhetoric's pleasurable seduction of the Imagination from the passions to good actions, the poet achieves delightful persuasion by reciting "things unexpected and various and full of vicissitudes" (IV, 316). The Scriptures also are applauded for comprehending "the vicissitudes of all ages" (V, 117), a striking link in the intimate relation between poetry and religion which has already been touched on. The mind of man, we hear in another place where the hindrances to learning are being discussed, is "delighted in beholding the variety of things and vicissitudes of times" (III, 265).

Likewise, the theory of poetic justice serves the same ends of delight and ideal verisimilitude. In order to imitate an ideal pattern, actions must be displayed with both "sufficient grandeur" and impeccable morality. Poetic justice gives meaning to the moral order depicted or intimated by the poet. It is not in its comfortable reward in this life of virtue that its ratio lies, but in its symbolic representation of the possibilities of perfection. Bacon nowhere offers any criticism of poetry as such for its lack of "realism," and simply says here that historical and poetical events differ in character and outcome. He was too wise to claim that the historical and apparent must be the real, and too religious to believe that it could be so.

The result of this ideal patterning of events in poetry, then, is to conduce not only to delight but also to "magnanimity and morality" (IV, 316), the chief "cause" of poetry throughout the seventeenth century in England, although becoming more limited in application as time passed. It is in this sense of moral improvement as well as the more obvious one, that poetry can be said to raise the mind, "accommodating the shows of things to the desires of the mind" (ibid.) instead of buckling it down to the "nature of things." Bacon's point is not that poetry violates the order of nature (he merely says that it does not represent the "sensible world") but that it provides an ideal or universal picture of things which is of a kind with, but not the same as, the picture of perfect order in nature known by man before the Fall. Sidney had asked the central question of the controversy: if poetry were realistic, "then how will you discerne what to followe but by your owne discretion, which you had without reading?"[10]

But when all this has been said, it will be argued that poetry is given only one short chapter and three or four other passing references in a lifetime of writings. The obvious answer, and one that has been notoriously ignored, is that Bacon was professedly dealing with deficient arts (IV, 284). Even though he saw the deficiency of dramatic art to be considerable, yet it comprised moral defection, not technical lack, while apart from the study of ancient fables there was no deficiency in the study of poetry (IV, 318). Similarly, Bacon cuts short his exposition of poetry as an art of speech because it is not deficient: "With this, therefore, we need not trouble ourselves" (IV, 444).

In the Descriptio Globi Intellectualis (V, 503), however, Bacon sets down an estimate of poetry which, some might claim, is with difficulty explained except in terms of a wilful desire to diminish poetry. Poetry, it is claimed, is the "sport" of the mind because it is not bound to things; and since all knowledge is the "exercise and work" of the mind, poetry is treated as no longer even a branch of knowledge. But in the first place, it is quite likely that Bacon would have agreed with the then familiar comment of Aquinas on Proverbs viii.30: ". . . because of the leisure that goes with contemplation the divine wisdom itself is always at play, playing throughout the whole world." Secondly, it is certain that he recognized, with Sidney, and thus was allowing for, the fact that poetry should be for the reader's "owne use and learning," not for his "well knowing."[11] Further, Bacon was giving here a highly cursory account of knowledge prefatory to a work which otherwise deals solely with astronomy. Again, that he purposely set out to neglect poetry in order to augment what he called "interpretative" learning has nowhere been denied. Lastly, to describe poetry as sport is to say nothing less than is true, even if it does not say enough. Even imperfect interpretative sciences are called "sports of nature" and of little use "for getting insight into nature" (IV, 166–7). Therefore the reference to poetry as sport does not dissociate it entirely from rational activity, any more than the use of the word "play" for mimic action.

In another place we are told that the Imagination "hardly produces sciences" (IV, 406). But Bacon time and again insists that his reformation of learning is not intended to upset the arts already established, but merely to improve them as well as to invent new ones (IV, 41–2, 52); the imaginative arts of poetry and rhetoric are not to be contemned simply because the Imagination produces no sciences. Further, Bacon admits that the Imagination can "strengthen and establish" reason (IV, 455), and that poetry can "raise itself above our reason . . . as an instrument of illumination" (IV, 406). Once raised, poetry has a power of communication equal to the "persuasions . . . wrought by eloquence" of rhetoric.

Nor is there any reason to think that Bacon commonly expected of Imagination either a vicious inflammation of the passions or the setting of reason at naught. It is true that rhetoric irked him in its liability to error "by reason of the use of the opinion ['untruth in nature'] in similitudes and ornaments of speech" (IV, 295). It irked in this respect George Herbert, seven years University Orator. It was, in fact, a conventional Renaissance caution, an objection that found a perverted apotheosis at the end of the century in Locke's vigorous and repeated dismissals of rhetoric almost altogether. But on the whole Bacon thought very highly of it,

> . . . a science certainly both excellent in itself, and excellently well laboured. Truly valued indeed, eloquence is doubtless inferior to wisdom. . . . Yet in profit and popular estimation wisdom yields to eloquence . . . (IV, 454–5).

He took pains to order and commend the art at great length both in the Advancement of Learning (III, 382–4, 409–17) and the De Augmentis (VI), and sternly wrote that "It was a great injustice in Plato . . . to place rhetoric among arts voluptuary . . ." (IV, 456).

Bacon's apparent lack of interest in poetry must be admitted, but only provided one does not read into such a statement more than evidence of his far greater interest in the "logical" as opposed to the "ethical" sciences. Poetry was not deficient; the art of rhetoric, however, received more attention than any of the four logical arts with the exception of invention.[12] The traditional caution, mentioned above, when speaking of rhetoric was observed, as in the Parasceve (IV, 254), where he warns that "all that concerns ornaments of speech, similitudes, treasury of eloquence, and such like emptinesses" are to be utterly dismissed.[13] But this is written in view of an experimental history and does not cancel out Bacon's high rating of rhetoric as an art to "convey the conceit of one man's mind into the mind of another without loss or mistaking" (III, 248).

The high opinion of works of the Imagination is indubitable if we consider Bacon's use of the word "raise" in contexts that have already been referred to. It occurs in the Advancement of Learning in a setting which admirably illustrates its weight. Bacon has been speaking of the Fall, which came to pass not through the "pure knowledge of nature and universality," but through "proud knowledge of good and evil." Man, he continues, cannot have a surfeit of the former, since God

> hath framed the mind of man as a mirror or glass capable of the image of the universal world, and joyful to receive

> the impression thereof, as the eye joyeth to receive light; and not only delighted in beholding the variety of things and vicissitude of times, but raised also to find out and discern the ordinances and decrees which throughout all those changes are infallibly observed (III, 265).

It is true that Bacon has his eye here as much on inductive experimental philosophy as on poetry. But despite their seemingly opposite workings, the one composing and dividing mental impressions "according to the pleasure of the mind" rather than "according to the nature of things as it exists in fact,"[14] certainly the "ordinances and decrees" referred to include the "law of providence," the "more perfect order," and the something "divine" of which poetry partakes (IV, 316). Milton's intention for poetry was the same, expressed in the opening invocation of Paradise Lost (I. 22–6):

> What in me is dark
> Illumin, what is low raise and support;
> That to the highth of this great Argument
> I may assert Eternal Providence,
> And justifie the wayes of God to men.

Central to Bacon's view of the role of poetry in any New Atlantis is his awareness that the crux of the problem lies in the feigning of a greater uniformity in nature than really is. "Feigning" is Bacon's word, and since it is by feigning "a more perfect order" that poetry raises the mind, the opening of the seventeenth-century onslaught on the idealistic mimesis of the poet may be said to begin here. Bacon contended that there was a great disharmony between the spirit of man and the spirit of nature, and that therefore man cannot in his imperfect state be regarded as the mirror of nature (IV, 432–3). In addition, man's mind "distorts and discolours the nature of things by mingling its own nature with it" (IV, 54); and the unregenerate appetites as well as erroneous sytems of logic, etc., cloud and pollute the mind (IV, 405). Therefore it follows, first, that man is not likely ever to know the world's order (not a new discovery, of course, but used more forcefully than ever before in favor of the mechanical sciences); and second, that since poetry mingles the desires of the mind with the shows of things, the poet cannot be trusted as a mirror. Similarly, man "knows" only so much as he observes in fact or thought of nature (IV, 47); but poetry turns from nature: therefore poetry provides no knowledge.

Bacon is not denying a universal order, however, but merely stating that man is unable to envisage and comprehend order in observable nature owing to a multitude of "unique" and "dissimilar" particulars. This seems to be more of a criticism of science than of poetry. In fact, in regarding poetry as more of "a pleasure or play of wit" than a science, Bacon had obviated the direct application of such criticism to it, much as nearer to our own time the doctrine of "art for art's sake" has been used to justify the social irresponsibility of art. For although the poet bends nature to the mind, his action is obviously not, even from the point of view of the most extreme Baconian, as pernicious as the natural philosopher's if the latter should do the same thing. This is so for three reasons: (a) no one looks to poetry for an exact mirroring of the specifics of the world of nature; (b) poetry is justified by its poetic justice, since it conduces to morality and human dignity; and (c) poetry is referred to the Imagination, which men know to be free to make unlawful matches and divorces of things (IV, 315).

If taken as a picture of observable nature, however, poetry can be pernicious, like the false imaginings of the inhabitants of Plato's cave which retarded the progress of true philosophy (IV, 433, 27, 55). This view is in fact part of Bacon's cherished doctrine of the necessity of induction and experiment in all science, without which the uneven mirror of the mind would eventually so misrepresent the nature of things that finally, one must assume, even the doctrinal and exemplary virtues of poetry would be of little avail to men. But once remove fallacious judgment according to "natural human reason" and

> there may spring helps to man, and a line and race of inventions that may in some degree subdue and overcome the necessities and miseries of humanity (IV, 27).

The prosaic-minded Bacon was personally little interested in

> Annihilating all that's made
> To a green Thought in a green Shade.[15]

And for the single reason that poetry was not a science, was not bound to the nature of things, Bacon, although fully appreciating its value, was prepared to leave it pretty much alone even though its face might be turned heavenward.

Thus, if not in a flash—because the structure had begun to sway ominously some time before—yet "at a trumpet crash" Bacon, shaking the pillars of animistic faiths until they crumbled, brought down finally, although many averted their eyes, the Medieval-Renaissance multi-analogical conception of the micro-macrocosm, and with it the view of poetry as its handmaid. If man is incapable of the true "image of the universal world," then he can no longer be regarded as a microcosm any more than nature can be proved a macrocosm, and the poet cannot mirror this fractured world; it is not his function to deal with irreconcilables. Bacon's answer was definite and final: he cannot. Therefore discard the pretense that the poet is a mirror of nature, cry aloud that he is not and never can be the world's philosopher (in the Baconian sense), and define his task anew in terms of fashioning for the delectation and profit of man "a more ample greatness, a more exact goodness, and a more absolute variety, than can be found in the nature of things" (III, 343). The poet can no longer pretend to mirror the scientists' world-as-it-is; accept the dualism and save poetry as a mirror of reality-as-moral/aesthetic pattern. Alas that the misinterpretation of doctrine should have resulted in the parochialisms of Davenant's epics of manners.

II

Bacon's high regard for poetry can be seen most clearly in his evaluation of dramatic and parabolical poetry, particularly the latter. Nothing new is added concerning dramatic poetry. Its function is that of "educating men's minds to virtue," its advantage over the epic lying in the greater susceptibility of men's minds to persuasion when they are gathered together (IV, 316). There is nothing here not to be found in Jonson and hosts of other Renaissance critics and theorists, although a great deal more could be found in most. The fact that Bacon finds nothing to say of Shakespeare let alone Marlowe, Jonson, Fletcher, and the rest would appear surprising only if such were not the common reception of the drama of his day. "And though in modern states play-acting is esteemed but as a toy,"[16] was the accepted opinion of most liberally educated men.

Bacon's remarks on the "Idols of the Theatre" reveal another aspect of his views on drama. In the glancing quibble of "playbooks of philosophical systems," he intends to characterize the element common to both drama and the Idol: the raising of an opinion of the world other than it is. This becomes quite clear as he continues:

> . . . in the plays of this philosophical theatre you may observe the same thing which is found in the theatre of the poets, that stories invented for the stage are more compact and elegant, and more as one would wish them to be, than true stories out of history (IV, 63).

The dramatist is allied with the poet and against the deductive philosopher who is not permitted, as the former are, to create "a more perfect order." "Superstitious" philosophy is called "fanciful and tumid and half poetical" (IV, 66). It is clear that Bacon does not confuse the two; while he confesses that one may observe "the same thing" in both drama and philosophical system, yet their methods of arriving at the greater unity and elegance are opposite (roughly, the one commission, the other omission) and only the latter is culpable.

Parabolical poetry is rated highest of the Kinds by Bacon, not unusual for a time which held that Tasso, Ariosto, and Spenser had achieved the heights of poetry with their historia cum typo, quae intellectualis deducit ad sensum, and which had not yet descended to the seventeenth-century evaluation of the epic as merely a narration of manners. Parabolical poetry serves as a means of communication between divinity and humanity, and for both "illustration" and "infoldment" or "retirement." The theory of infoldment is set out most fully in Henry Reynolds's Mythomystes, but was a popular enough item of Renaissance poetic and particularly frequent in prefaces to editions of the mystical poets. Parabolical poetry is most characteristic, Bacon continues, of the poetic genre, i.e., story telling, which is more perspicuous than argument and more apt than historical example.[17] Perhaps more exactly in fable or myth than in any other Kind of poetry are the mere "shows of things" accommodated to the aspiring mind of man, so that from his cave he might behold at least the shadows of the divine pattern of the world.

The infolding species of parabolical poetry provides for the rarer instances when the dignity of things is not inferior to the dignity of the rational soul, and truths are couched in concealing fables and parables (IV, 317). It is related to the method of dispositio labeled by Bacon "Acroamatic or enigmatical," designed for the communication of esoteric knowledge to the élite only; he warns against its misuse in the false ascription of value to pretentious information (IV, 450). Fables represent a rich store of wisdom which Bacon wished to have explored for the advancement of learning, and he personally thought enough of this branch of knowledge to examine at length thirty-one ancient myths in the De Sapientia Veterum (1609). That Bacon should have rightly seen these myths to be supreme manifestations of poetry—the inspired "picturing foorth" of the envisaged harmony of the universe—speaks eloquently for his conception of poetry. For in so far as the poet reveals a universal pattern of things, it can be said that he is dealing with the secret and hidden, or what Bacon called the infolded, and in the representation of which he found the most important function of poetry. It was right, then, that poetry should be feigned history in which the secret of things was incorporated for the erecting of man. So important, in fact, is Bacon's recognition of the myth-heart of poetry that a closer examination of his conception of parabolical poetry is in order.

In the early Advancement of Learning Bacon seems reluctant to commit himself concerning the validity of historical interpretations of classical fables. All he will say there is that parabolical poetry, whether for illustration or retirement of matter, employs fables, and that in the latter case it is sometimes used to obscure mysteries of "religion, policy, or philosophy." In 1605, that is, Bacon only relaxed caution to say that certain fables can be interpreted with "great felicity" although doubtless "in many the like encounters" the fable was first, the exposition devised afterwards (III, 344–5). It is added later in the same work that fables had been employed in ancient times to convey moral observations (453).

In the De Sapientia Bacon is obviously concerned to show that many of the ancient fables were expressly written to body forth for instruction matter previously conceived in the form of prosaic statement. So that in the Preface he now maintains "that beneath no small number of the fables of the ancient poets there lay from the very beginning a mystery and an allegory." But he goes further:

> . . . in some of these fables . . . I find a conformity and connection with the thing signified, so close and so evident, that one cannot help believing such a signification to have been designed and meditated from the first, and purposely shadowed out (VI, 696).

(It is apparent here that Bacon has in mind the persisting and fairly rigorous parallel correspondence of allegory, and not—let us say—the twentieth-century notion of symbol, to be likened in its far less rigid application to the field of gravity, heat and light about a nova or pulsating star.)

The very extravagance of fables, Bacon continues, coaxes belief in an inner meaning, which in most cases can be assigned to a pre-Homeric oral age. Those who "in no case" accept the allegorical meaning are now forthrightly called of "the dull and leaden order." Yet even relinquish the infolding aspect and one must confess that fables are of "prime use to the sciences, and sometimes indispensable" in teaching new and abstruse matters (loc. cit.). This is another major concession to poetry, as well in principle as for the Kind, since once grant that parabolical poetry serves science and the general remarks on poetry as feigned history take on a new significance. The acknowledged desertion of the nature of things nevertheless serves to assist in conveying truths concerning that nature, and poetry is at least partially vindicated from "philosophical" inconsequence.

A similar point is made in the Advancement of Learning (III, 302). Nature, the second of God's books and including all his other works except the Scriptures, and therefore including all but scriptural poetry, illuminates the understandings of men by drawing them into "meditation of the omnipotency of God." This study of nature is likened to the fable of Orpheus. Here the liability of man to domination by appetite is offset by reason so long as he engages in such meditation, and "gives the ear to precepts, to laws, to religion, sweetly touched with eloquence and persuasion of books, of sermons, of harangues. . . ."

Part of the preface to the De Sapientia and three of the fables are included in the De Augmentis (IV, 317–35), where Bacon once again affirms his belief that "a mystery is involved in no small number of them." The reply seems to be fully given to Henry Reynolds, who in Mythomystes accused Bacon of "willing contradictions" in this matter, and of closing up "that discourse of his of Poetry with It is not good to stay too long in the Theater" out of sheer dislike of parabolical poetry.[18]

Bacon faces toward the past rather than toward the future, then, in his view of allegory, as did the majority of Renaissance authors. The definition of Demetrius, representative classical rhetorician, prevailed roughly to Bacon's time: that allegory was an example of sublime language veiled both in order to excite awe and horror and because "what is clear and evident is apt to excite contempt. . . ."[19] Sidney, in denying that the poet lied, commented that he writes "allegorically" and "figuratively." Aesop's allegories teach virtue illustratively and in such a case the poet is a popular philosopher and does not, like the philosopher proper, "teach obscurely." For the poetry of infoldment, Sidney like Bacon maintained that "it pleased the heavenly Deitie, by Hesiod and Homer, under the vayle of fables, to give us all knowledge," many of which fables were written "darkely."[20]

From Bacon's time on a progressive deterioration of the view of poetry as allegory took place, so that (for example) Davenant could reject Spenser's The Faerie Queene for "resembling (methinks) a continuance of extraordinary Dreams,"[21] less natural and therefore less apt for moral instruction than "matter of a more useful kind." Such dismissals meant the death warrant of allegory and the initiation of the non-superstitious, rational, ordered universe of both nature and manners which did not require poetry drawn from divided and distinguished worlds to mirror it. The sense of history was now more acute, and the proprieties of space and time more closely observed, unlike, for example, the world of The Faerie Queene of which Coleridge noted "the marvellous independence and true imaginative absence" of space and time.[22]

The new realism was accompanied by an attenuated and externally applied didactic intent at the price of an implicit morality. The prefatory poems to Gondibert of both Waller and Cowley commend Davenant's depiction of "men and manners" above the romantic fantasies of earlier poetry; their attitude to "monsters" was no longer, like Bacon's, one of interpretation but of dismissal. Cowley elsewhere wrote of fables that "They are all but the Cold-meats of the Antients, new-heated," "confused antiquated Dreams."[23] The mystery unacknowledged, there was little incentive to allegorize. The shows of things were to be no more submitted to the inclusive desires of the mind than was embracing reason submitted to things in totality. A careful selection of things was subjected now to an arrogant, circumscribed reason despite Bacon's warning. The casting out of "superstition" in misinterpretation of his injunctions represented at its worst the violent extremism of an atomistic physical order replacing a complex moral one. Fulke Greville had prophesied it—and ironically, in terms that the reformers themselves used of earlier poetry:

> Nature we drawe to Art, which then forsakes
> To be herselfe, when she with Art combines. . . .[24]

The latter part of the century betrayed Bacon's view of poetry by the rejection of its myth-heart:

> Stripping the truth bare was what that age and generation felt itself to be mainly engaged upon, stripping it bare of mythology and all the accretions of paganism and popery.

Professor Willey adds truly that the reason for this was a conception of nature not as "original and primitive" but as corresponding to the tastes of the "most civil."[25] As Bacon saw, poetry is the product of the Imagination imitating history "at pleasure" (IV, 315)—that is, without being tied to individuals "circumscribed by place and time" (IV, 293) and depicting without restriction a pattern of the world suitable to the dignity of man's mind. The Imagination is then free to form its complexes of images without direct responsibility to a reason dedicated to an external end—an anti-poetic end because not the image complex itself. Thus poetry, although a "dream of learning" (IV, 336), has "some participation of divineness" (III, 343).

NOTES

1 L. C. Knights, "Bacon and the Seventeenth Century Dissociation of Sensibility," Scrutiny, XI (1943), 268–85; C. M. Dowlin, "Plot as an Essential in Poetry," Review of English Studies, XVII (1941), 166–83; K. R. Wallace, Francis Bacon on Communication and Rhetoric (Chapel Hill, 1943); R. Metz, "Bacon's Part in the Intellectual Movement of his Time," Seventeenth Century Studies Presented to Sir H. J. C. Grierson (Oxford, 1938), pp. 21–32; D. L. Clark, Rhetoric and Poetry in the Renaissance (New York, 1922); M. W. Bundy, "Bacon's True Opinion of Poetry," Studies in Philology, XXVII (1930), 244–64. The following quotations are respectively from Clark, p. 156; Metz, p. 30; Wallace, p. 6.

2 The phrase is taken from Henry Reynolds, "Mythomystes" (1632?), in Critical Essays of the Seventeenth Century, ed. J. E. Spingarn (Oxford, 1908), I, 144.

3 J. Thompson, "To the Memory of Sir I. Newton" (1727), line 37.

4 Elsewhere referred to as logic and ethic, the latter inclusive of civil knowledge (IV, 315, 405, 455), or to the division of faculties into intellect and will, or the division of knowledge into judicial and ministerial (III, 382).

5 Op. cit., p. 45.

6 IV, 315–6, 405. It is significant that the second reference to the Fall occurs in the opening paragraph of Bk. V, which outlines the four arts of logic, treats of Imagination, and leads on to a full review of rhetoric. The cross-patterning with the passage on poetry shows how closely the subjects were associated in Bacon's mind. Also see infra, pp. 262 ff.

7 IV, 316; cf. Sidney, Apologie [Arber's ed. of Olney's version] (London, 1868), pp. 31–3.

8 De aug., loc. cit.; cf. Aristotle, Rhetorica, 1355 a 38, 1355 a 15.

9 IV, 315–6. "Probability" is not used by Bacon in Aristotle's sense of "probable and possible order of things" as opposed to historical plot (De Poetica, 1451 a 38–1451 b 1 ff.; 1451 b 30). Aristotle uses the term in Bacon's sense as well, stressing factual fidelity alone (ibid., 1451 a 12, 28, 33; 1451 b 15; etc.).

10 Op. cit., p. 36.

11 Loc. cit.

12 Noted by Wallace, op. cit., p. 25.

13 The conventional warnings are numerous: Margaret Newcastle, The Description of a New World (London, 1668), p. 56; William Chamberlayne, Pharonnida, I.ii.140, 174–6 (but see I.iii.424, for a defense); Bishop Jewel, Oratio Contra Rhetoricam, in J. Atkins, English Literary Criticism: The Renascence (London, 1947), pp. 71–4; Montaigne, Of the Vanity of Words; Lucius Cary, Discourse of Infallibility and The Reply (London, 1651), pp. 183, 224.

14 V, 504; IV, 292. But both are tied to the primary material of knowledge, the impressions or images of "individuals."

15 Marvell, The Garden, 47–8. The whole stanza represents Bacon's view of poetry.

16 Loc. cit. He dismisses masques as "toys" (Of Masques and Triumphs, VI, 467). Also see De aug., IV, 496-7, 317; and Spedding's note, IV, 317. Cf. Henry Peacham, The Compleat Gentleman (1634; first publ. 1622), ch. VI; Donne, "To Sr Henry Wotton," The Poems of John Donne, ed. H. J. C. Grierson (London, 1933), pp. 166, 19–22; also "Elegy XV," 59–62; "Elegy XVI," 35–6.

17 (IV, 317). Whether it be verse or prose does not matter here, since verse is treated under arts of speech and "has nothing to do with the matter" of a poem (IV, 315; cf. Sidney, Apologie, p. 28). This does not mean that satire, elegy, epigram, and ode are relegated to rhetoric—as D. L. Clark, for example, contended (op. cit., p. 86).

18 In Spingarn, op. cit., I, 177.

19 On Style, tr. T. A. Moxon (London, 1941), p. 102.

20 Apologie, pp. 52, 35, 72.

21 "Preface to Gondibert," The Works of Sir William D'avenant, Kt (1673), p. 3.

22 Cit. D. G. James, The Dream of Learning (Oxford, 1951), pp. 105–6.

23 "Preface to Poems" (1659), in Spingarn, op. cit., II, 88, 90.

24 Of Humane Learning, stanza 27. Greville added that Nature can put all the arts to school, and "prove the science monger but a foole."

25 Basil Willey, "The Turn of the Century," Seventeenth Century Studies Presented to Sir H. J. C. Grierson (Oxford, 1938), pp. 379–80. See D. G. James's recognition of the importance of Bacon's elevation of myth in this connection, op. cit., p. 31, n. 1.

THE RELATION OF BACON'S ESSAYS TO HIS PROGRAM FOR THE ADVANCEMENT OF LEARNING

Ronald S. Crane

The prevailing opinion concerning the relation of Bacon's Essays to the great philosophical enterprise of his middle and later life would still seem to be that formulated, nearly a generation ago, by the late Edward Arber. The Essays, he wrote,[1] "formed no essential part" of Bacon's work; "they entered not into his conceptions of the proficiency and advancement of knowledge. Like his History of Henry VII . . . and his intended History of Henry VIII . . . these Counsels are by-works of his life, the labours, as it were, of his left hand; his right being occupied in grasping the Instauration."

In spite of the fact that this view is in apparent harmony with Bacon's own opinion, expressed in 1622 to Bishop Andrewes,[2] it is, I believe, a demonstrably mistaken one. In particular, it fails to take account of the large number of close resemblances, both of substance and of form, between the Essays—especially those first printed in 1612 and 1625—and certain portions of the Advancement of Learning (1605) and of the De Augmentis Scientiarum (1623). Though some of these resemblances have been noted by earlier students of Bacon,[3] their general significance for the interpretation of the Essays has never, to my knowledge, been adequately appreciated. It is the intention of this paper to consider their bearing, first on Bacon's purpose and choice of themes in the Essays, and second on the changes in method and style which distinguished the Essays of 1612 and 1625 from those of 1597.

I

"I will now attempt," Bacon wrote at the beginning of the Second Book of the Advancement of Learning, "to make a general and faith-

Reprinted from The Schelling Anniversary Papers (New York, The Century Co., 1923), pp. 87–105, by permission of Mrs. R. S. Crane and the publisher.

ful perambulation of learning, with an inquiry what parts thereof lie fresh and waste, and not improved and converted by the industry of man; to the end that such a plot made and recorded to memory may both minister light to any public designation, and also serve to excite voluntary endeavours . . . " (III, 328). For the present study, two stages of this "perambulation" are of particular importance—those dealing respectively with "moral" and with "civil" knowledge.[4]

"Moral knowledge" Bacon divided into two parts: "the Exemplar or Platform of Good, and the Regiment or Culture of the Mind; the one describing the nature of good, the other prescribing rules how to subdue, apply, and accommodate the will of man thereunto" (III, 419). In treating the first of these topics he contented himself largely with a somewhat scholastic analysis of the aspects of good—individual good and good of communion, good active and good passive. When he reached the second, however, his attitude became once more that of the pioneer, intent on setting forth "what ground lieth unmanured." "This part therefore," he wrote, "because of the excellency thereof, I cannot but find exceeding strange that it is not reduced to written inquiry. . . . It is reasonable therefore that we propound it in the more particularity, both for the worthiness, and because we may acquit ourselves for reporting it deficient. . . . We will therefore enumerate some heads or points thereof, that it may appear the better what it is, and whether it be extant" (III, 433). And he proceeded to outline at length three principal desiderata: "descriptions of the several characters and tempers of men's natures and dispositions, specially having regard to those differences which are most radical in being the fountains and causes of the rest" (434–7); similar descriptions of the passions or "affections" (437–41); and studies of the most appropriate means of reducing the mind "unto virtue and good estate" (441–3).

Under "civil knowledge" Bacon included three topics: "wisdom of the behaviour," or conversation; "wisdom of business," or negotiation; and "wisdom of state," or government (445). The first of these, as it had already been "elegantly handled" (447), he dismissed in a few words, devoting the greater part of an unusually long section to pointing out, with much illustrative detail, the "omissions and deficiencies" of the other two. The subject of negotiation or business, in its two aspects of rules for the handling of particular situations and of precepts for advancement in life, seemed to him especially in need of cultivation; "it is," he remarked (447), "by learned men for the most part despised, as an inferior to virtue and an enemy to meditation; for wisdom of Government, they acquit themselves well when they are called to it, but that happeneth to few; but for the wisdom of Business, wherein man's life is most conversant, there be no books of it, except some few scattered advertisements, that have no proportion to the magnitude of this subject." As for the "wisdom of government," his first sketch of the subject, in the Advancement (473–6), was brief and somewhat perfunctory. He made up for this, however, in the De Augmentis (I, 792–828) by treating at length two main desiderata—the doctrine "de proferendis finibus imperii" and the doctrine "de justitia universali."

Such, in brief, was the program outlined by Bacon in 1605 and retouched and made more explicit in several particulars in 1623. It was, I believe, in the light of this program and as a partial fulfilment of it that he composed a large number of the essays first published in the editions of 1612 and 1625.

The proof of this assertion lies in the number and closeness of the correspondences between the themes and substance of these essays and the discussions of desiderata in the sections of the Advancement and the De Augmentis which have just been analyzed. Consider, in the first place, the following passage of the Advancement, in which Bacon is urging the value of "sound and true distributions and descriptions of the several characters and tempers of men's natures and dispositions":

> Of much like kind are those impressions of nature, which are imposed upon the mind by the sex, by the age, by the region, by health and sickness, by beauty and deformity, and the like, which are inherent and not extern; and again those which are caused by extern fortune; as sovereignty, nobility, obscure birth, riches, want, magistracy, privateness, prosperity, adversity, constant fortune, variable fortune, rising per saltum, per gradus, and the like. . . . These observations and the like I deny not but are touched a little by Aristotle as in passage in his Rhetorics, and are handled in some scattered discourses; but they were never incorporate into Moral Philosophy, to which they do essentially appertain . . . (III, 436–7).

Is it fanciful to suppose that in writing the essays "Of Youth and Age," "Of Beauty," "Of Deformity," "Of Nobility," "Of Great Place,"

"Of Riches," "Of Adversity," and "Of Fortune"—all except "Of Adversity" (1625) first published in the edition of 1612—Bacon was attempting to supply a want which he himself had pointed out only a few years before? The very number of the parallels lends support to the supposition. Again, it seems to me altogether probable that in composing such essays as "Of Love" (1612), "Of Envy" (1625), and "Of Anger" (1625) he had consciously in mind the lack, noted in the next paragraph of the Advancement, of "active and ample descriptions and observations" concerning the "diseases and infirmities of the mind, which are no other than the perturbations and distempers of the affections" (437). The "best doctors of this knowledge," he remarked, are the poets and historians. In them

> we may find painted forth with great life, how affections are kindled and incited; and how pacified and refrained; and how again contained from act and further degree; how they disclose themselves, how they work, how they vary, how they gather and fortify . . . (438).

Now, not only did Bacon in these particular essays make abundant use of material drawn from poets and historians, but in one of them—"Of Anger"—he dealt explicitly with several of the points on which he thought their testimony of most value:

> We will first speak [he wrote in the first paragraph of this essay] how the natural inclination and habit to be angry may be attempered and calmed. Secondly, how the particular motions of anger may be repressed, or at least refrained from doing mischief. Thirdly, how to raise anger or appease anger in another (VI, 510).

Much the same thing, once more, may be said of the essays "Of Custom and Education" (1612), "Of Praise" (1612), "Of Nature in Men" (1612), "Of Studies" (1597; enlarged in 1612 and 1625), "Of Friendship" (1612; rewritten in 1625), and "Of Fame" (published by Rawley in 1657) (VI, 519): they all treat subjects which Bacon in 1605 had noted as "deficient":

> Now come we to those points which are within our own command, and have force and operation upon the mind to affect the will and appetite and to alter man-

> ners: wherein they ought to have handled custom, exercise, habit, education, example, imitation, emulation, company, friends, praise, reproof, exhortation, fame, laws, books, studies . . . (III, 438).

In the case of one of these essays, the dependence upon the Advancement is particularly close. After the passage just quoted, Bacon introduced, as "an example of the rest," a page of aphorisms or "precepts" on the subject of "Custom and Habit." Now two of these "precepts" are to be found in the essay "Of Nature in Men" (1612) (VI, 571–2), and what is more, nearly the whole of this essay may be reconstructed out of material given here and in an earlier page of the Advancement (III, 415).

So much for the essays which seem directly related to Bacon's program for the advancement of "moral knowledge." The list of those which can be connected in a similar way with his proposals for the development of "civil knowledge" is nearly as long. To begin with, while it is not likely that Bacon meant to refer to writings of his own when he remarked, apropos of the "wisdom of conversation," that "this part of civil knowledge hath been elegantly handled, and therefore I cannot report it for deficient" (III, 447), it is perhaps worth noting that two of the essays published in 1597—"Of Discourse" and "Of Ceremonies and Respects"—treated themes belonging unmistakably to this branch of the subject. Moreover, at least three other essays of the same date—"Of Negotiating," "Of Followers and Friends," and "Of Faction"—dealt with subjects mentioned specifically by Bacon in the same general section of the Advancement (III, 447, 456, 462, 474). As these essays, however, were already in existence several years before the program with which we are concerned was set forth, they can hardly be said, with any certainty, to have been inspired by it.

The case is obviously different with essays first published in 1612 or 1625, and it is noteworthy that several of these developed topics indicated as "deficient" in the Advancement or the De Augmentis. Thus the essay "Of Counsel" (1612) reads like a deliberate contribution to what Bacon called (III, 448) the "wisdom of counsel and advice in private causes":[5] it is illustrated, as he says treatises on this subject should be, by fable and history (III, 453), and it contains in the first paragraph a commentary on a proverb of Solomon not unlike those which he had introduced into the same section of the Advancement "to give authority to this part of knowledge" (III,

448–52). Similarly, the essays "Of Vain-glory" (1612), "Of Dispatch" (1612), "Of Boldness" (1625), "Of Delays" (1625), and "Of Simulation and Dissimulation" (1625) would appear to have had their origin in a passage of the Advancement in which Bacon set forth the "heads" of a series of possible treatises on the "doctrine of advancement in life."[6] And finally, it seems to me fairly clear that the essays "Of Seditions and Troubles" (written, 1607–12; [VI, 535–6, 589] first published in an expanded form, 1625), "Of the True Greatness of Kingdoms and Estates" (1612; enlarged in 1625), "Of Empire" (1612; enlarged in 1625), and "Of Plantations" (1625) were either written or enlarged by Bacon in deliberate fulfilment of his program, sketched in 1605 and greatly elaborated in 1623, for the development of that branch of "civil knowledge" that had to do particularly with the art of government. To become convinced that this is true in the case of "Of Seditions and Troubles," one has only to read Bacon's statement in the Advancement (III, 474) that "unto princes and states . . . , the natures and dispositions of the people, their conditions and necessities, their factions and combinations, their animosities and discontents, ought to be . . . in great part clear and transparent," and then turn to the opening sentence of the essay in which the motive for its composition is indicated: "Sheapards of people had neede knowe the Kalenders of Tempests in State" (VI, 589). In the case of "Of the True Greatness of Kingdoms and Estates," the evidence is even more striking. This essay as it appeared in the volume of 1625 was identical, language excepted, with a long discourse which Bacon had introduced into the De Augmentis two years before as an "example of a summary treatise touching the extension of empire" (I, 792–802), and which in turn represented the enlargement of a short essay published in 1612 (VI, 586–8). The revision, in short, if not the original composition of the essay, was the result of preoccupations intimately connected with the development of Bacon's scheme for the advancement of "civil knowledge." That a similar relationship existed between this scheme and the essays "Of Empire" and "Of Plantations" cannot perhaps be so clearly demonstrated. Both essays, however, have much in common with "Of the True Greatness of Kingdoms and Estates," and both treat subjects listed in the same chapter of the De Augmentis which contains the Latin version of that essay.[7]

Such, then, are the chief parallels in theme between Bacon's later essays and his previously formulated program for the improvement of "moral" and "civil" knowledge.[8] In view of the fact that these correspondences involve more than half of the pieces written in 1612 and 1625, and extend in a number of cases to details of their substance, it is hard to escape the conclusion that one of the principal influences on the composition of the later essays was precisely those "conceptions of the proficiency and advancement of knowledge" of which it has been customary to suppose the Essays independent. I say "one of the principal influences"; for I believe that Bacon's choice of subjects in the later Essays can be fully explained only by taking into account a number of other causes. Chief among these, no doubt, was the orientation given to his reflections by his youthful practice of collecting commonplaces. One of the results of this practice—a series of "Antitheta Rerum," or groups of contrasting maxims on general topics, compiled by him when he was a young man—is preserved for us in the De Augmentis;[9] in it may be found the subjects and a considerable number of the detailed ideas or images of at least nineteen of the essays published in 1612 and 1625.[10] Again, several of the Essays clearly had their ultimate origins in episodes of Bacon's career as a publicist and statesman. Thus "Of Unity in Religion" (1612; revised and enlarged, 1625) obviously grew out of the preoccupations that had inspired his pamphlet entitled An Advertisement touching the Controversies of the Church of England (1589) (VIII, 74 ff.); "Of the True Greatness of Kingdoms and Estates" (1612, 1625) had its inception in a speech on the Union with Scotland delivered by Bacon in the House of Commons in February 1607, and developed the following year in a tract called Of the True Greatness of the Kingdom of Britain (VII, 39–40, 47–64); and "Of Usury" (1625) embodied, with but few changes, the greater part of a memorial on the same subject drawn up in April 1623 for presentation to the King (XIV, 410, 414–9). The Essays, in short, exhibit traces of various other influences besides those which form the special subject of this paper. To admit this, however, is not to lessen one's conviction that one of Bacon's primary motives in composing a majority of the pieces contained in his second and third collections was a desire to supply some of the deficiencies in morality and policy of which he had become aware while engaged in the "general and faithful perambulation of learning" which constituted the first stage in his great philosophical undertaking. Certainly all of the evidence which has been assembled points to some such interpretation of his purpose as this;[11] and it is perhaps not altogether fanciful to assume that it was his consciousness of this purpose that dictated his choice of subtitle for the volume of

1625. For assuredly if the preceding remarks have not been entirely beside the point, no phrase could have been more appropriate, under the circumstances, than Counsels Civil and Moral (VI, 535).

II

Whoever has taken the pains to read the Essays in the order and form of their original publication must inevitably have been struck, on passing from the essays of 1597 to those of 1612 and then to those of 1625, by several outstanding differences in method and style.[12] In the first place, as compared with the essays of 1597, those of 1612 and 1625 exhibit a marked tendency toward greater fullness and coherence in the development of particular ideas, so that instead of being mere collections of juxtaposed maxims without connective elements, they are now for the most part closely articulated compositions. How great a difference this is may be seen from the following passages representing Bacon's manner in the three successive stages of his work:

OF DISCOURSE (1597)

> ¶ If you dissemble sometimes your knowledge of that you are thought to knowe, you shall bee thought another time to know that you know not. ¶ Speech of a mans selfe is not good often, and there is but one case, wherin a man may commend himselfe with good grace, and that is in commending vertue in another, especially if it be such a vertue, as whereunto himselfe pretendeth. ¶ Discretion of speech is more than eloquence, and to speake agreably to him, with whome we deale is more thē to speake in good wordes or in good order. ¶ A good continued speech without a good speech of interlocution sheweth slownesse: and a good reply or second speech without a good set speech sheweth shallownesse and weaknes, as wee see in beastes that those that are weakest in the course are yet nimblest in the turne. ¶ To vse too many circumstances ere one come to the matter is wearisome, to use none at all is blunt (VI, 526).

OF DEFORMITY (1612)

Whosoeuer hath any thing fixed in his person, that doth induce contempt; hath also a perpetuall spurre in himselfe, to rescue and deliuer himself from scorne. Therefore all deformed persons are extreme bold: first, as in their owne defence, as being exposed to scorne; but in processe of time, by a generall habite. Also, it stirreth in them industrie, and specially of this kinde, to watch and obserue the weaknesse of others, that they may haue somewhat to repay. Againe in their superiours, it quencheth ielousie towards them, as persons that they thinke they may at pleasure despise; and it layeth their competitors and emulators asleepe: as neuer beleeuing they should bee in possibility of aduancement, till they see them in possession. So that vpon the whole matter, in a great wit, deformity is an aduantage to rising (VI, 571).

OF BOLDNESS (1625)

It is a trivial grammar-school text, but yet worthy a wise man's consideration. Question was asked of Demosthenes, what was the chief part of an orator? he answered, action: what next? action: what next again? action. He said it that knew it best, and had by nature himself no advantage in that he commended. A strange thing, that that part of an orator which is but superficial, and rather the virtue of a player, should be placed so high, above those other noble parts of invention, elocution, and the rest; nay almost alone, as if it were all in all. But the reason is plain. There is in human nature generally more of the fool than of the wise . . . (VI, 401–2).

Another difference, closely related to this one, between the earlier and later essays is the increasing frequency among the latter of essays exhibiting a formal and explicit plan. Only one of the pieces in the collection of 1597—"Of Honor and Reputation"—and that only in part, can be said to have any clearly marked structure at all. The proportion is somewhat greater in the edition of 1612,[13] but here also the prevailing type of composition, for all the increase in coherence, is aphoristic rather than methodical. In 1625, on the other hand, while the short planless type of essay is still to be found, though always in a more developed form than in 1597,[14] the number of pieces exhibiting a clear and explicit organization by points is greatly increased.[15]

But after all what most clearly distinguishes the later essays of Bacon from those in his first volume is a greater concreteness of style, resulting from the multiplication in 1612 and still more in 1625 of various means of illustration and adornment almost entirely lacking in 1597—metaphors and comparisons, historical "examples," "sentences" from the classics and the Bible, and here and there personal reminiscences and observations.[16] A comparison of the passage quoted above from "Of Discourse" (1597) with the following from the 1625 version of "Of Riches" will give an idea of the character and direction of the change:

> Seek not proud riches, but such as thou mayest get justly, use soberly, distribute cheerfully, and leave contentedly. Yet have no abstract nor friarly contempt of them. But distinguish, as Cicero saith well of Rabirius Posthumus, In studio rei amplificandæ apparebat, non avaritiæ prædam, sed instrumentum bonitati quæri. Hearken also to Salomon, and beware of hasty gathering of riches; Qui festinat ad divitias, non erit insons. The poets feign, that when Plutus (which is Riches) is sent from Jupiter, he limps and goes slowly; but when he is sent from Pluto, he runs and is swift of foot. Meaning that riches gotten by good means and just labour pace slowly; but when they come by the death of others (as by the course of inheritance, testaments, and the like), they come tumbling upon a man. But it mought be applied likewise to Pluto, taking him for the devil. For when riches come from the devil (as by fraud and oppression and unjust means), they come upon speed. . . . The improvement of the ground is the most natural obtaining of riches; for it is our great mother's blessing, the earth's; but it is slow. And yet where men of great wealth do stoop to husbandry, it multiplieth riches exceedingly. I knew a nobleman in England, that had the greatest audits of any man in my time; a great grazier, a great sheep-master, a great timber man, a great collier, a great

> corn-master, a great lead-man, and so of iron, and a number of the like points of husbandry. So as the earth seemed a sea to him, in respect of the perpetual importation.[17]

The problem of how to account for the changes which have just been described has naturally presented itself to more than one of the many students of the Essays. Of the solutions which have been offered I shall mention only two. The first—that of Macaulay[18]—is essentially a psychological explanation: if the style of the later essays—for example, "Of Adversity" (1625)—is superior "in eloquence, in sweetness and variety of expression, and in richness of illustration" to that of the earlier—for example, "Of Studies" (1597)—the primary reason is that with Bacon the usual order of mental development was reversed, so that his "fancy" came to maturity late, long after his "judgment" had been fully formed. The second explanation—that of M. Pierre Villey[19]—attributes the new elements in the later essays, particularly the increase in coherence and in the number of images, "examples," and personal reminiscences, to an external influence—the Essais of Montaigne. This is how M. Villey sums up the matter for the essays of 1625:

> Ces trois élements nouveaux, souvenirs personnels, exemples, procédés de style et tours de phrase capables de nuancer et de préciser les idées, révèlent une transformation radicale dans la manière de Bacon. Le système qui avait présidé à la construction des premiers Essais est maintenant abandonné. . . . Bacon a passé lentement du genre des maximes au genre de la méditation. Bien qu'il ne soit pas fourni dans les Essais de Montaigne d'exemples et d'images, ma conviction est que Montaigne est pour beaucoup dans cette transformation. Quiconque songera que, depuis la traduction de Florio, le livre de Montaigne était devenu très populaire en Angleterre, sera tout disposé à le croire. Par le titre qu'il avait adopté d'ailleurs, l'essayiste Anglais n'avait-il pas marqué son admiration? Ne s'était-il pas montré enclin à subir l'influence de son devancier?[20]

Both of these explanations I believe to be incorrect, and for much the same reason: both err through assuming that the elements which distinguished the later from the earlier essays constituted a manner of writing not before practiced by Bacon. The truth of the matter, on the contrary, is that all of these elements, in varying proportions, are to be found in works of Bacon antedating not only the essays of 1612 but also those of 1597. Whoever will read such productions as An Advertisement touching the Controversies of the Church of England (1589) (VIII, 74–95), the famous letter to Burleigh (circa 1589) (VIII, 108–9) and Certain Observations made upon a Libel (1592) (VIII, 146–208), to say nothing of the Meditationes Sacræ and the Colors of Good and Evil, published with the Essays of 1597 (VII, 77–92, 233–54), will find abundant evidence that the habit of writing coherent, well-planned discourses, enriched with figures, "sentences," and "examples," so far from being a comparatively late development, the result of a psychological change or of the reading of Montaigne, was in reality an essential part of Bacon's literary equipment from the first.

How, then, are we to account for the fact that it was not until 1612, and then only in part, that this manner found its way into the Essays, and that even as late as 1625 Bacon continued to compose occasionally in the aphoristic style characteristic of the essays of 1597?

An answer to these questions has been given by Villey in the study already referred to,[21] and so far as it goes, it is, I believe, correct. Briefly, it is this: that the Essays of 1597 were conceived, not as essays in the sense which Montaigne had already given to the term, but as collections of maxims or "sentences," a genre whose popularity throughout Europe in the sixteenth century is well known;[22] that in composing them Bacon utilized to a great extent collections of generalized maxims, both original and borrowed, already recorded in his note-books;[23] and that, not having exhausted these materials in his first volume and perhaps being encouraged by the success which this volume attained, he continued the practice in a number of the later essays, several of which are demonstrably little more than rearrangements of "sentences" which by his own acknowledgment he had had by him since his youth.[24]

All this is plausible enough, and the evidence, though not as complete as one could wish, is nevertheless sufficient. Villey, however, has overlooked another factor, quite as important, I believe, in explaining Bacon's continued use of the method of aphorisms in 1612 and 1625 as the success of his first volume or as the existence of unutilized maxims in his note-books; and that is his clearly formulated belief, expressed in 1605 and reaffirmed without change in 1623, that for certain purposes "writing in aphorisms" is to be preferred to a more methodical and fully developed type of composition. The passage forms part of his discussion of the "Method of Tradition" in the Second Book of the Advancement of Learning:

> Another diversity of Method, whereof the consequence is great, is the delivery of knowledge in Aphorisms, or in Methods; wherein we may observe that it hath been too much taken into custom, out of a few Axioms or observations upon any subject to make a solemn and formal art; filling it with some discourses, and illustrating it with examples, and digesting it into a sensible Method; but the writing in Aphorisms hath many excellent virtues, whereto the writing in Method doth not approach.
>
> For first, it trieth the writer, whether he be superficial or solid: for Aphorisms, except they should be ridiculous, cannot be made but of the pith and heart of sciences; for discourse of illustration is cut off; recitals of examples are cut off; discourse of connexion and order is cut off; descriptions of practice are cut off; so there remaineth nothing to fill the Aphorisms but some good quantity of observation: and therefore no man can suffice, nor in reason will attempt, to write Aphorisms, but he that is sound and grounded. But in Methods,
>
> Tantum series juncturaque pollet,
> Tantum de medio sumptis accedit honoris,
>
> as a man shall make a great shew of an art, which if it were disjointed would come to little. Secondly, Methods are more fit to win consent or belief, but less fit to point to action; for they carry a kind of demonstration in orb or circle, one part illuminating another, and therefore satisfy; but particulars, being dispersed, do best agree with dispersed directions. And lastly, Aphorisms, representing a knowledge broken, do invite men to enquire farther; whereas Methods, carrying the shew of a total, do secure men, as if they were at furthest (III, 405; cf. I, 665–6).

It ought now perhaps to be clear why Bacon used "aphorisms" rather than "methods" in writing his first essays, and why having once chosen this medium he continued to employ it, though in a modified form, and with decreasing frequency, until the end. So intelligible, indeed, is his procedure in the light of what has been said that the real problem is not to account for the persistence of the aphoristic style, but rather to explain the gradual emergence alongside it, in the essays of 1612 and 1625, of a style in which "discourse of illustration," "recitals of examples," and "discourse of connexion and order" were no longer "cut off," but on the contrary multiplied until they became the most striking elements in the general effect.

The problem in the nature of things is not susceptible of an entirely satisfactory solution; but it is possible, I believe, to indicate one of the most important factors. As I have tried to show in the first part of this paper, many of the essays of 1612 and 1625 are intimately related in purpose and substance to the *Advancement of Learning*. Now, no one, it seems to me, can turn from the most characteristic of these essays to the *Advancement* without becoming aware of the essential similarity of the style—a similarity much more striking than that already pointed out between the same essays and such early productions as *An Advertisement touching the Controversies of the Church*. The *Advancement*, like the essays, abounds in figures and in "sentences" and "examples"; like at least some of the essays, too, it exhibits a high degree of attention to coherence and plan. Significantly enough, the resemblance of the *Advancement* to the later essays appears to be closest in those passages of the former in which Bacon undertook to furnish specimens of the kind of inquiries he would wish to see carried out in the fields of "moral and civil knowledge." These passages, though indistinguishable in style from the rest of the work, form in reality separate essays, complete in themselves, on such themes as the roots of good and ill (III, 420–4), good active and passive (424–8), custom and habit (438–40), studies (440–1), the choice of good ends (441–3), the wisdom of conversation (445–7), and the architecture of fortune (457–71). How closely the style of these passages approaches that of the essays published in 1612 and 1625, as described above, may be seen from the following typical extract, which it is instructive to contrast with the 1597 version of "Of Discourse":[25]

The wisdom of Conversation ought not to be over much affected, but much less despised; for it hath not only an honour in itself, but an influence also into business and government. The poet saith,

Nec vultu destrue verba tuo:

a man may destroy the force of his words with his countenance: so may he of his deeds, saith Cicero; recommending to his brother affability and easy access; Nil interest habere ostium apertum, vultum clausum; it is nothing won to admit men with an open door, and to receive them with a shut and reserved countenance. So we see Atticus, before the first interview between Cæsar and Cicero, the war depending, did seriously advise Cicero touching the composing and ordering of his countenance and gesture. And if the government of the countenance be of such effect, much more is that of the speech, and other carriage appertaining to conversation; the true model whereof seemeth to me well expressed by Livy, though not meant for this purpose; Ne aut arrogans videar, aut obnoxius; quorum alterum est alienæ libertatis obliti, alterum suæ: the sum of behaviour is to retain a man's own dignity, without intruding upon the liberty of others. On the other side, if behaviour and outward carriage be intended too much, first it may pass into affection, and then quid deformius quam scenam in vitam transferre, to act a man's life? But although it proceed not to that extreme, yet it consumeth time, and employeth the mind too much. And therefore as we use to advise young students from company keeping, by saying, Amici fures temporis, so certainly the intending of the discretion of behaviour is a great thief of meditation. Again, such as are accomplished in that honor of urbanity please themselves in name, and seldom aspire to higher virtue; whereas those that have defect in it do seek comeliness by reputation; for where reputation is, almost every thing becometh; but where that is not, it must be supplied by puntos and compliments. Again, there is no greater impediment of action than an over-curious observance of decency, and the guide of decency, which is time and season. For as Salomon sayeth, Qui respicit ad ventos, non seminat;

> et qui respicit ad nubes, non metet; a man must make his opportunity, as oft as find it. To conclude; Behaviour seemeth to me as a garment of the mind, and to have the conditions of a garment. For it ought to be made in fashion; it ought not to be too curious; it ought to be shaped so as to set forth any good making of the mind, and hide any deformity; and above all, it ought not to be too strait or restrained for exercise or motion (III, 445–7).

Images, quotations and allusions, connective words and phrases: here are all of the traits which, as we have seen, combined to give to the pieces in the two later collections their distinctive physiognomy. And what is true of this passage is true of all the others which I have listed. The mystery, in short, of Bacon's changed manner in his later essays is now revealed: in writing these essays he merely adopted, more and more completely, the style which he had used in the *Advancement of Learning*.[26]

The motives which prompted him to do this are not hard to conjecture. For one thing, many of the later essays, as we have seen, bore the same relation to the program formulated in the *Advancement* and the *De Augmentis* as the passages just studied; and two of them in particular were made up, in whole or in part, of material already utilized as examples of possible treatises in one or the other of these works. What more natural, then, than that in composing the essays thus inspired Bacon should have selected as the medium most appropriate to their subject-matter the style, not of his *Essays* of 1597, but of the specimen treatises which he had introduced into the *Advancement*?

Again, it is not impossible that his adoption in the essays of at least one feature of the style used in the *Advancement* was the result of conscious conviction. In several passages in the section of the latter work devoted to "moral and civil knowledge," Bacon laid particular stress upon the value of history and poetry as sources of precepts and illustrations. Thus, apropos of the neglect of the "part of knowledge touching the several characters of natures and dispositions," he wrote that ". . . this kind of observations wandereth in words, but is not fixed in inquiry . . . ; wherein our fault is the greater, because both history, poesy, and daily experience are as goodly fields where these observations grow; whereof we make a few posies to hold in our hands, but no man bringeth them to the confectionary, that receipts might be made of them for use of life."[27] Similarly, for "the inquiry touching the affections," he thought that the "best doctors" were "the poets and writers of histories": in them "we may find painted forth with great life, how affections are kindled and incited; and how pacified and refrained; and how again contained from act and further degree; how they disclose themselves, how they work, how they vary, how they gather and fortify, how they are inwrapped one within another, and how they do fight and encounter one with another, and other like particularities: amongst the which this last is of special use in moral and civil matters . . . (III, 438). And again, in the course of his treatment of "civil knowledge" he remarked that "the form of writing which of all others is fittest for this variable argument of negotiation and occasions is that which Machiavel chose wisely and aptly for government; namely, *discourse upon histories or examples*. For knowledge drawn freshly and in our view out of particulars, knoweth the way best to particulars again" (III, 453). After these declarations, it is not difficult to understand the prominence which he gave to "examples" from historians and poets in such later essays as "Of Seditions and Troubles," "Of Empire," "Of Counsel "Of Friendship," "Of the True Greatness of Kingdoms and Estates," "Of Prophecies," "Of Vain-glory," and "Of Vicissitude of Things."

Finally, we must not forget that when Bacon began to prepare the second edition of the *Essays* toward 1607, the memory of his work on the *Advancement* was still sufficiently fresh in his mind so that even if he had desired to do so, he would doubtless have found it difficult to escape entirely the influence of its style.

In view of these considerations we are perhaps justified in concluding that the change of manner in Bacon's later essays was due chiefly, not to any external influence or to any fundamental change in their author's mental constitution, but rather to the renewed momentum given to writing in "methods" by his labors on the *Advancement of Learning*—a momentum which all the more easily carried over into the essays written after 1605 because of the close relationship in purpose and theme which existed between many of these essays and the work in which the distinguishing features of their style were most clearly foreshadowed.

NOTES

1 *A Harmony of the Essays, etc., of Francis Bacon* (Westminster, 1895), p. xxvii.

2 "As for my Essays, and some other particulars of that nature, I count them but as the recreations of my other studies, and in that sort purpose to continue them; though I am not ignorant that those kind of writings would, with less pains and embracement (perhaps), yield more lustre and reputation to my name, than those other which I have in hand" (XIV, 374).

3 Notably by F. G. Selby in the notes to his editions of the Essays (London, 1895) and of the Advancement (London, 1898), and by Pierre Villey in his Montaigne et François Bacon (Paris, 1913), pp. 39–40. By far the most complete list of parallels between the Essays and Bacon's other works—a list to which I am much indebted in this paper—is to be found in an unpublished Master's thesis by one of my former students, Mrs. Frank Hawley, of La Grange, Illinois.

4 III, 417–45 and 445–76. For the corresponding portions of the De Augmentis, see I, 713–828. Hereafter I shall give page references to the De Augmentis only when its text differs in substance from that of the Advancement.

5 The essays "Of Cunning" (1612) and "Of Wisdom for a Man's Self" (1612) exhibit a similar inspiration.

6 III, 456–71. The following passages contain the germs, and in several cases, some of the illustrative material, of the essays mentioned in the text: 462–3 ("Of Vain-glory"); 463–4 ("Of Boldness"); 465–6 ("Of Delays"); 466–8 ("Of Simulation and Dissimulation"); 469 ("Of Dispatch").

7 Cf. I, 792: "Cum Artes Imperii tria Officia Politica complectantur; primo, ut Imperium conservetur; secundo, ut beatum efficiatur et florens; tertio, ut amplificetur finesque ejus longius proferantur. . . ."

8 At least one of the later essays, it may be noted in passing, owes its general inspiration and some of its illustrative details, to another section of Bacon's program—that dealing with "divine knowledge." Compare the 1625 text of "Of Unity in Religion" (VI, 381–4) with a passage in the De Augmentis (I, 833–4), in which he sets down among the deficients a treatise on the "degrees of unity in the kingdom of God." The same idea is expressed in a less definite form in the Advancement (III, 482).

9 I, 689–706. The period of compilation is fixed by the following passage (I, 706): Atque hæc Antitheta . . . fortasse tanti non fuerint; sed cum jam olim parata et collecta a nobis essent, noluimus diligentiæ nostræ juvenilis fructum perire. . . . In illo autem adolescentiam plane spirant, quod sint in Morali sive Demonstrativo genere uberiora; in Deliberativo et Judiciali perpauca."

10 The list is as follows: (1) 1612: "Of Death," "Of Marriage and Single Life," "Of Nobility," "Of Empire," "Of Friendship," "Of Superstition," "Of Riches," "Of Beauty," "Of Love," "Of Custom and Education," "Of Fortune," "Of Praise," "Of Judicature"; (2) 1625: "Of Revenge," "Of Simulation and Dissimulation," "Of Envy," "Of Boldness," "Of Delays," "Of Innovations." Cf. Villey, Montaigne et François Bacon, pp. 30–1.

11 Villey (Montaigne et François Bacon, p. 40) reaches a similar conclusion, but confines its application merely to a few of the essays published in 1625. He contributes a valuable point, however, by calling attention to the analogy, from the point of view of their relation to his program for the advancement of knowledge, between these essays and Bacon's Historia Ventorum, Historia Vitæ et Mortis, and Historia Densi et Rari, which form "modèles des études d'histoire naturelle qu'il demande" in the Advancement and the De Augmentis (cf. III, 370 ff.; I, 501–2), and his collection of Apophthegms (VII, 121 ff.), which are "modèles de ces recueils qu'il désire voire extraire des histoires" (cf. III, 342). To these parallels we may add the History of the Reign of King Henry VII (1625) and the fragment of a History of the Reign of King Henry VIII (published by Rawley in 1629), both of which would seem to have been written in fulfilment of a suggestion made in the Advancement (III, 336–7).

12 These differences have been noted by many students of Bacon, from Macaulay to the present day. See, for example, M. A. Scott, The Essays of Francis Bacon (New York, 1908), pp. lxx–lxxi; Hugh Walker, The English Essay and Essayists (London, 1915), pp. 17–20; G. P. Krapp, The Rise of English Literary Prose (New York, 1915), p. 535; and Bryan and Crane, The English Familiar Essay (Boston, 1916), pp. xvi–xix. By far the fullest treatment of the subject in print is that of Pierre Villey, Montaigne et François Bacon, Ch. II.

13 Four essays: "Of Great Place," "Of Counsel," "Of Dispatch," and "Of Judicature." To these may be added "Of Seditions and Troubles," which, though not published until 1625, was written before 1612 (see VI, 589).

14 E.g., "Of Revenge," "Of Adversity," "Of Delays," "Of Innovations," "Of Suspicion."

15 E.g., "Of Truth," "Of Simulation and Dissimulation," "Of Envy," "Of Friendship," "Of Usury," "Of Building," "Of Gardens," "Of Anger," "Of Vicissitude of Things." To the same class belong certain essays published in 1612 but more or less altered in 1625: "Of Unity in Religion," "Of Goodness and Goodness of Nature," "Of Nobility," "Of Empire," "Of the True Greatness of Kingdoms and Estates."

16 All of these last are to be found either in essays written in 1625 or in passages added in 1625 to essays which had appeared in earlier collections. See "Of Cunning," "Of the True Greatness of Kingdoms and Estates," "Of Riches," "Of Prophecies," "Of Custom and Education," and "Of Usury."

17 VI, 460–1. Everything after the quotation from Cicero was added in 1625 (cf. VI, 567). On the sources of the concrete elements in the *Essays*, see Scott, *The Essays of Francis Bacon*, pp. lxxxvii–xciv.

18 "Lord Bacon" (1837), in *The Life and Works of Lord Macaulay*, Edinburgh edition, VI, 240–2.

19 *Montaigne et François Bacon*, Ch. II. This study originally appeared in the *Revue de la Renaissance* during 1911 and 1912.

20 *Ibid.*, pp. 38–9. See also the same writer's "Montaigne en Angleterre," in *Revue des deux mondes*, Ier septembre 1913, pp. 126–7.

21 Pp. 28–9, 30–1.

22 See Villey, *Les sources et l'évolution des Essais de Montaigne* (Paris, 1908), II, 8–19; W. F. Bryan, in *Mod. Lang. Notes*, XXXI (1916), 350–1; and J. Zeitlin, in *Journal of Eng. and Ger. Philology*, XIX (1920), 47–65.

23 Two of the essays in the edition of 1597—"Of Ceremonies and Respects" and "Of Followers and Friends"—contain material

already included in Bacon's Promus of Formularies and Elegancies, a commonplace book compiled between 1594 and 1596. See Durning-Lawrence, Bacon is Shake-speare (New York, 1910), pp. 198, 200, 202, 209. These borrowings are not noted by Villey.

24 Cf. Villey, pp. 30–1, completed by note 10, p. 290, above, and by the following reminiscences of the Promus in the essays of 1612 (the references in parentheses are to the text of the Promus as printed by Durning-Lawrence, op. cit.): "Of Goodness and Goodness of Nature" (238), "Of Dispatch" (199), "Of Friendship" (209), "Of Riches" (196), "Of Beauty" (196), and "Of Nature in Men" (196, 217).

25 See above, p. 279. No less striking is the difference between the passage on "studies" (III, 440–1) and the 1597 essay on the same subject.

26 His borrowing extended even to particular allusions, figures, and turns of expression. The greatest number of these reminiscences are to be found in the essays of 1612; the list includes the opening metaphor in "Of Wisdom for a Man's Self" (cf. III, 454), a fable from Æsop and a Biblical "sentence" in "Of Goodness and Goodness of Nature" (cf. III, 319, 443), a quotation from Solomon in "Of Empire" (cf. III, 280), a simile in "Of Praise" (cf. III, 291–2), three similes in "Of Nature in Men" (III, 415, 439), a "sentence" and an "example" in "Of Fortune" (cf. III, 454), a "sentence" in "Of Death" (cf. III, 427), and a "sentence" in "Of Love" (cf. III, 328).

27 III, 435. The point is made even more emphatic in the De Augmentis. Cf. I, 733–4.

"ALL COLOURS WILL AGREE IN THE DARK.": A NOTE ON A FEATURE IN THE STYLE OF FRANCIS BACON

R. Tarselius

In his monumental edition of the works of Francis Bacon, James Spedding[1]—who so indefatigably devoted most of his life to pleading his hero's cause against any calumniator—makes some arresting comments in the summary of Bacon's character at the end of the last volume: ". . . he was a very favourable judge of other men's abilities, *and formed a very modest estimate of his own* . . . *he attached little importance to himself, except as an instrument for their* (referring to ideas, principles, etc.) *accomplishment* . . . *This absence of self-importance was in one respect—to the world, if not to himself—a disadvantage* . . . *The habit of self-assertion was not at his command*" (14.568; my italics).

It is interesting to compare this picture of modesty and self-denial with testimonies given by some of Bacon's contemporaries. Thus Ben Jonson's vivid description in the quite well-known lines "*His language* . . . *was nobly censorious. No man ever spake more neatly, more pressly, more weightily or suffered less emptiness, less idleness in what he uttered* . . . *He commanded where he spoke, and had his judges angry and pleased at his devotion*,"[2] does not seem to coincide altogether with Spedding's conception. The poet's observations are confirmed rather than contradicted by Dr. Rawley,[3] who had, perhaps, ampler opportunities to watch Bacon in his lifetime than anyone else and who states in his *Life of the Right Honourable Francis Bacon*[4]: "His opinions and assertions were for the most part binding and, not contradicted by any, *rather like oracles than discourses* . . ." (my italics).

Can a modern reader of his prose draw any conclusions or come to any decision in this respect? Can a close study of his language—for it is after all from the pages of his books that his spirit still

Reprinted from *Studia Neophilologica*, Vol. 25 (1958), pp. 155–60, by permission of the author and the publisher.

speaks to us—reveal with any certainty which of the interpretations is the correct one? Personally, having examined his writings in their entirety, I admit that I can deduce no humble attitude, no lack of self-importance from his presentation of his matter; on the contrary, I would rather be inclined to state that it is very seldom that a writer—even of purely didactic literature—manages to impart to the reader the force and the validity of his theses in such an unmistakable way purely and exclusively by his manner of expression.

To illustrate this I quote at random from his Essays[5]:

> Men create oppositions which are not; and put them into new terms so fixed, as whereas the meaning ought to govern the term, the term in effect governeth the meaning. There be also two false peaces or unities: the one, when the peace is grounded but upon an implicit ignorance; for all colours will agree in the dark: the other, when it is pieced upon a direct admission of contraries in fundamental points. For truth and falsehood, in such things, are like the iron and clay in the toes of Nabuchadnezzar's image; they may cleave, but they will not incorporate. ("Of Unity of Religion," VI, 383)

> But leaving these curiosities, (though not unworthy to be thought on in fit place,) we will handle, what persons are apt to envy others; what persons are most subject to be envied themselves; and what is the difference between public and private envy. A man that hath no virtue in himself, ever envieth virtue in others. For men's minds will either feed upon their own good or upon other's evil; and who wanteth the one will prey upon the other; and whoso is out of hope to attain to another's virtue, will seek to come at even hand by depressing another's fortune. ("Of Envy," VI, 393)

> Above all, those are most subject to envy, which carry the greatness of their fortunes in an insolent and proud manner; being never well but while they are shewing how great they are, either by outward pomp, or by triumphing over all opposition or competition; whereas wise men will rather do sacrifice to envy, in suffering themselves sometimes of purpose to be crossed and overborne in

> things that do not much concern them. Notwithstanding so much is true, that the carriage of greatness in a plain and open manner (so it be without arrogancy and vain glory) doth draw less envy than if it be in a more crafty and cunning fashion. (*Ibid.*, VI, 395)

> They that deny a God destroy man's nobility; for certainly man is of kin to the beasts by his body; and, if he be not of kin to God by his spirit, he is a base and ignoble creature. It destroys likewise magnanimity, and the raising of human nature; for take an example of a dog, and mark what a generosity and courage he will put on when he finds himself maintained by a man; who to him is instead of a God or *melior natura*; which courage is manifestly such as that creature, without that confidence of a better nature than his own, could never attain. ("Of Atheism," VI, 414–5)

In trying to analyse what particular features help to convey the serene, almost majestic conviction that his sentences carry, I feel a very conspicuous one to be his inclination to use what might be called the characterizing *will*[6] in statements of a general or generalizing kind. For by coining a phrase like, *e.g., all colours will agree in the dark*, he has stated a *universal* truth rather than given his personal view or presented an observation of his own. And by underlining the typical tendency of colours or their particular disposition under certain circumstances, he has saved himself from further discussion, this characterization of colours being beyond any contradiction. To maintain simply that *colours agree in the dark* may not be convincing enough; to refer to the well-known fact that they are apt to do so or tend to do so by nature or habit, renders the argument indisputable.

Some further examples (with "will" italicized) are:

(1) Salomon hath pronounced that *in counsel is stability*. Things *will* have their first or second agitation: if they be not tossed upon the arguments of counsel, they *will* be tossed upon the waves of fortune. ("Of Counsel," VI, 423)

(2) A wise man *will* make more opportunities than he finds. ("Of Ceremonies and Respects," VI, 501)

(3) It was truly said, *optimi consiliarii mortui*: books *will* speak plain when counsellors blanch. ("Of Counsel," VI, 426)

(4) It appeareth in nothing more, that atheism is rather in the lip than in the heart of man, than by this; that atheists *will* ever be talking of that their opinion, as if they fainted in it within themselves. ("Of Atheism," VI, 413)

(5) For the last inconvenience, that men *will* counsel with an eye to themselves; certainly *non inveniet fidem super terram* is meant of the nature of times, and not of all particular persons. ("Of Counsel," VI, 425)

(6) These things are but toys to come amongst such serious observations. But yet, since princes *will* have such things, it is better they should be graced with elegancy than daubed with cost. ("Of Masques and Triumphs," VI, 467)

Nowhere is his predilection for this *will* more manifest than in explanatory phrases starting with *for*.[7] His method appears to be this: he presents his subject, states his view, pleads his cause, gives his advice or proves his matter, thus proceeding all the more confidently as there follows in the explanatory clause a general statement of the kind described above, which, containing this *will*, gives to his thesis the ultimate proof of universal applicability:

(7) As for talkers and futile persons, they are commonly vain and credulous withal. For he that talketh what he knoweth, *will* also talk what he knoweth not. ("Of Simulation and Dissimulation," VI, 388)

(8) Deformed persons, and eunuchs, and old men, and bastards, are envious. For he that cannot possibly mend his own case *will* do what he can to impair another's. ("Of Envy," VI, 393)

(9) But let not a man trust his victory over his nature too far; for nature *will* lay buried a great time, and yet revive upon the occasion or temptation. ("Of Nature in Men," VI, 469–70).

(10) Unmarried men are best friends, best masters, best servants . . . A single life doth well with churchmen; for

charity will hardly water the ground where it must first fill a pool. ("Of Marriage and Single Life," VI, 391–2)

(11) Discern of the coming on of years, and think not to do the same things still; for age will not be defied. ("Of Regiment of Health," VI, 453)

So much for a modern reader's reflexions on coming across this abundance of will in sentences which have nowadays attained an almost proverbial ring. But then, of course, there always remains the problem whether Bacon himself conceived will as transmitting this particular meaning, and there the modern reader feels somewhat baffled in his efforts, well knowing that the interpretation of shall and will in this period of Early Mod. English is too elusive a task to be solved with absolute certainty. A collation of the text of 1625 with the earlier ones of 1597 and 1612 gives no clue; there is no difference in the wording, which means that there is nothing to indicate hesitation and final decision. A comparison with Bacon's Latin edition of his Essays[8]—generally a practicable manner of procedure when trying to interpret his meaning[9]—is of equally little avail here, there being no exact equivalent in Latin to the will-construction in English. As can be inferred from the Latin translation,[10] Bacon has, in rendering the eleven cases quoted above, chosen the present tense for three of them, cases (3), (4), and (10), and—what might seem striking—used the future for six[11] of them. His use of the future need not, however, be taken as evidence that he conceived them as purely futuric. And—to go back to the original question—the tinge of futurity that this characterizing will undoubtedly contains, does not make it less suited to convey the author's intention, as I comprehend it, for, if he asserts that phenomena are given or wont to appear or react in a certain manner, he can presume with equally great conviction that the same thing will be valid in the future as well.

NOTES

1 See D. N. B., Vol. XVIII, pp. 723 ff., and prefaces to the individual volumes in Spedding's edition.

2 Discoveries Made upon Men and Matter; Dominus Verulamis, in The Works of Ben Jonson, ed. C. H. Herford and P. Simpson (Oxford, 1925–52), VIII, 590–2.

3 William Rawley was Bacon's chaplain till he ceased to be Lord Chancellor in 1621, and remained his close confidant for the rest of his life. Rawley was also entrusted with the editing of Bacon's manuscripts after his death. See D. N. B., Vol. XVI, p. 768.

4 This biography served as an introduction to the Resuscitatio or bringing into public light several pieces of the works . . . of Francis Bacon (1657).

5 For my choice of the Essays and the MS from which the quotations have been taken, see my paper on Would as an Exhortative Auxiliary in Stockholm Studies in Modern Philology, Vol. XVIII, Uppsala 1953, text and footnotes.

6 This will is well-known to every reader of English literature from phrases like "Fooles will be fooles styll" (Gammer Gurton's Needle), "Crabs move sideling, Lobsters will swim swiftly backward," "Men, by their nature, are prone to fight, they will fight for any cause, or for none" (the last two quotations are taken from NED, Will, B, 8). "But what can you do, Bicket? They will have it." (Galsworthy, The White Monkey), etc. It has been defined in different ways, according to which of the elements, reiteration, volition, natural bent or futurity, etc., is the most strongly felt. But it seems to me that since the element of characterization is an all-pervading one in all these cases, this definition may safely be adopted here. See further Jespersen, A Modern English Grammar, Part IV, § 15.3 (5) ff., Kruisinga, English Accidence and Syntax, I, 5th ed. p. 481 ff., Curme, A Grammar of the English Language, III, § 38.4.

7 On the whole, Bacon shows an obvious tendency to sum up his argumentation in conclusive observations starting with for. Thus the Essay "Of Envy," containing 76 head clauses in all, has 21 explanatory clauses starting with for. In the Essay "Of Nobility" the proportions are 29 to 8. Compare also the excerpts of his style given above.

8 Posthumously published by Dr. Rawley in 1638.

9 It is well known that Bacon was constantly changing and augmenting the text of the Essays, and although one need not go as far as Spedding: ". . . wherever the English and the Latin differ, the Latin must be regarded as the later and the better

authority" (foot-note 4, I, 10) it should be borne in mind that Bacon himself regarded his Latin edition as his legacy to posterity: ". . . I do conceive that the Latin Volume of them (being in the universal language) may last as long as books last." (The epistle dedicatory to the Duke of Buckingham, 1625; VI, 366.)

10 The Latin versions of the above sentences run as follows:

(1) Res humanae proculdubio, aut primam, aut secundam Agitationem subibunt.
(2) Prudens Opportunitates plures faciet, quam inveniet.
(3) Libri Veritati non parcunt . . .
(4) . . . quod Athei Opinionem suam saepe praedicent et defendant, ac si ipsi sibi diffiderent.
(5) Quantum ad postremum Incommodum; Consiliarios nimirum, in Consilio dando, suae rei prospecturos, non Domini . . .
(6) — — —
(7) Qui enim eloquitur quae scit, effutiet etiam quae nescit.
(8) qui Conditionem suam emendare nullo modo potest, Conditionem alterius pro Viribus suis labefactabit.
(9) Natura enim, ad longum tempus, sepulta jacebit et tamen occasione data reviviscet.
(10) Non enim facile quis eriget Solum, si prius Stagni alicujus Receptaculum interveniat.
(11) Considera Aetatem ingruentem, neque confide eadem perpetuo continuare: Non enim Bellum indicendum Senectuti.

11 There is no translation of the Essay of Masques and Triumphs (case (6)) in the edition of 1638. As for the remaining case (11), Bacon has here apparently altered the shape of his thoughts altogether.

FRANCIS BACON

Anne Righter

It was the fate of the Roman Colosseum to serve for many centuries as a quarry. Innumerable tons of stone were carted away to be incorporated into later and quite diverse structures, to support the roofs, comprise the walls, or be lost to sight among the foundations of buildings whose purpose, scale and form were utterly different from those of Vespasian's amphitheatre. That the relentless pillaging of ages should nevertheless leave standing a wreck so gigantic, and essentially so coherent, testifies eloquently both to the magnitude of the original, and to the diminished aspirations of later men. There is a sense in which the work of Francis Bacon also has served the centuries as a quarry. One piece is mortised into the Royal Society. Others help to compose the post-medieval structure of English prose, of English historiography, of English law. Fragments of Baconian architecture turn up on all sides: in Hobbes and in Locke, Descartes, Leibniz, Voltaire, Mill, Kant, Shelley, Coleridge and Marx. Technology, the experimental method, inductive reasoning, linguistic analysis, psychology: all of them appear to incorporate some elements of Bacon's thought, although it is usually difficult to identify these elements precisely, or to determine their real importance. Equally tenacious is the transferred life of those Baconian phrases in which, miraculously, abstract ideas become available to the senses without relinquishing their basic character and precision: the clear and equal glass, the idols of cave, tribe, market-place and theatre, the instances of the lamp, the doctrine of scattered occasions, the branching candlestick of lights. Separated from their original context, they continue not only to live, but to articulate hypotheses and discoveries of which Bacon himself never dreamed.

Reprinted from The English Mind: Studies in the English Moralists Presented to Basil Willey, edited by Hugh Sykes Davies and George Watson (Cambridge University Press, 1964), pp. 7–29, by permission of the author and the publisher.

This gradual dismemberment of the *Instauratio magna*, and of the works clustered around it, is nothing to which Bacon, in principle at least, would have objected. In fact, he had foreseen it. Over and over again he refers the ultimate realization of his thought to the future. His published work is a bell to call other wits together, a collection of sparks flying out in all directions to kindle a general conflagration or, most memorably of all, an instrument which the craftsman can tune but upon which he cannot perform.

> And being now at some pause, looking back into that I have passed through, this writing seemeth to me (*si nunquam fallit imago*), as far as a man can judge of his own work, not much better than that noise or sound which musicians make while they are in tuning their instruments: which is nothing pleasant to hear, but yet is a cause why the music is sweeter afterwards. So have I been content to tune the instruments of the Muses, that they may play that have better hands (III, 476).

Whether Bacon ever suspected that the music of the future, indebted to him as it is in so many ways, would nevertheless reject that unifying Method by which he set such store is hard to determine. There were moments in which he himself seemed troubled by the fact that his marvellous mechanism for discovery seemed disinclined to desert "the braver gate (of ivory)" for the practical gate of horn. Certainly, however, he was aware that his ideas in general were incomplete, as abbreviated and hastily roughed out as most of the writings in which they were embodied. Time was short; it was a question of indicating directions and, perhaps even more important, of persuading posterity to try.

What would have appalled Bacon is the extent to which his influence has been seen as pernicious. He could never have guessed that his efforts to establish the Kingdom of Man would come to be regarded as destructive by precisely those generations which at last inhabit it. Like the father of Salomon's House in the *New Atlantis* (1627), Bacon genuinely "pitied men"; that he should be regarded—frequently by writers also concerned to deny his positive contributions—as the architect of the dilemmas of the twentieth century, the man who effected an unholy and lasting divorce between science and poetry, reason and the imagination, Christian ethics and the way of the world, is a species of tragic irony. Yet Bacon has persistently appeared for our time in the role of false prophet, a Moses who leads not to the Promised Land of Cowley's adulatory poem, but to the wilderness of materialism. He is the villain of that moment of indecision between the medieval and the modern worlds, which other artists (Donne, Ralegh, Marlowe, or even Leonardo da Vinci) have been praised for reflecting; the man who cut through and reduced a fertile richness of choice and ambiguity to what C. S. Lewis (speaking of the Essayes) has described as a metallic-looking cactus raised on the edge of a desert, "sterile, inedible, cold and hard to the touch."[1]

It is a commonplace of Bacon criticism to refer to his inconsistency, and to the astonishing measure of disagreement which exists among his commentators. On a personal level there is the disparity between Spedding's misunderstood man of integrity and feeling, and the more popular image of the "meanest of mankind." As for conflicting interpretations of the work and its influence, they are so numerous that it sometimes seems impossible to find out the truth at all.[2] Certainly Bacon was a complicated man, given to self-contradiction. Considering the scope of his thought, together with its emphasis upon continuous growth and correction, these inconsistencies are scarcely surprising. Even more important, however, is the fundamental fact that Bacon's work is not only unfinished: it was by its very nature impossible to finish. Moving from one fragmentary statement to another with a kind of desperate urgency, he himself clearly thought that time, isolation and his civil employments were the impediments, the remorae of his beloved image, that kept the great ship from sailing. It does not seem to have occurred to him that the task itself was impractical: basically contradictory in that it lay beyond any single man's accomplishment, yet utterly dependent as a whole upon his own creating imagination. It is, perhaps, only with the triumph of modern science that it has become possible to see how Faustian a figure Bacon was and how paradoxical the plan of the Instauratio magna. Despite his insistence upon the anonymity of science, the independence of the Method from the special abilities and characteristics of those who employ it, this is an intensely individual dream. The unity of the Instauratio magna, its true form, is that of a various, enormously inclusive but nevertheless particular mind. One is brought back to it at every step. Whatever the practical consequences of those pieces of Bacon's work which have been taken up by later men, the architecture of the whole is that of the imagination, not of fact: the unfinished cathedral at Beauvais rather than the

Colosseum. What is attempted outreaches the capacities of the material, the form, and the creator by whom they are utilized. It is a strange situation, and one which should condition response to the prose as inevitably as it does the reaction to that fantastic choir and transept without a nave which is all of Beauvais that could be made to stand. It is also perhaps more promising than that weary discussion about the treatment of the imagination in the De Augmentis (1623) and The Advancement of Learning (1605) as a way into the consideration of Bacon as an artist.

"Lord Bacon," Shelley declared firmly in the Defence of Poetry, "was a poet." The remark is all too familiar. What is usually forgotten is that Shelley went on to explain precisely why.

> His language has a sweet and majestic rhythm, which satisfies the sense, no less than the almost super-human wisdom of his philosophy satisfies the intellect; it is a strain which distends, and then bursts the circumference of the reader's mind, and pours itself forth together with it into the universal element with which it has perpetual sympathy.

There is much in the expression of this with which it is fashionable, or has been until recently, to find fault. Yet Shelley is neither indulging here in that woolly, uncritical thinking of which he has so often been accused, nor is he simply referring vaguely to the splendours of Bacon's prose. He is saying something about Bacon's qualities as a writer which is both intelligent and perceptive. Bacon's prose succeeds for Shelley not merely in gratifying both the intellect and the senses, but in bringing them together for a purpose. His is a style of persuasion which forces a kind of greatness upon the mind of the reader, an enlargement which, working through mind and emotions both, enables the reader to break through his ordinary attitudes and comprehend that Truth which Bacon's language serves.

Shelley's claims for Bacon are large ones, but no greater than those of Coleridge. For Coleridge, Bacon was one of the four great English geniuses, and he expended considerable effort in an attempt to prove that "the Athenian Verulam and the British Plato," as he called them, were twinned and kindred spirits. Coleridge is less concerned than Shelley with Bacon's language, and more with the extractable core of his thought. He does, however, note at one point that

> faulty verbal antitheses [are] not unfrequent in Lord Bacon's writings. Pungent antitheses, and the analogies of wit in which the resemblance is too often more indebted to the double or equivocal sense of a word than to any real conformity in the thing or image, form the dulcia vitia of his style, the Dalilahs of our philosophical Samson.[3]

In a note, Coleridge offers an example taken from The Advancement of Learning: "As for the philosophers, they make imaginary laws for imaginary commonwealths, and their discourses are as the stars, which give little light because they are so high" (III, 475). Coleridge's objection to this sentence is based upon his observation that the word "high" means "deep or sublime" in the one case, and "distant" in the other. He concedes that Bacon's meaning is clear and evident; nevertheless he is offended by the play on words. Conditioned as we are by "metaphysical" poetry, by the serious and sympathetic approach to Donne and his school, it is hard to agree with Coleridge. We no longer believe that Shakespeare threw away the world for a quibble. Similarly, the multiple meanings involved in Bacon's word "high" justify themselves not only because they are perfectly controlled, but because they demand to be seen as an integral part of the economy and vitality of the sentence. Bacon intends to marry the two ideas of remoteness and of depth and sublimity. The star image allows him tersely and suggestively to do so. He is not exercising his wit at the expense of the thing he has to say, as Coleridge thought: he is saying exactly what he means in a fashion which associates his prose with some of the techniques of seventeenth-century poetry.

The ambiguities and misunderstandings of Baconian criticism can perhaps be illustrated nowhere more clearly than in the fact that this very sentence from The Advancement of Learning, which Coleridge castigates for its "metaphysical" qualities, forms part of Professor L. C. Knights' attack upon Bacon as the early representative and guiding spirit of that "dissociation of sensibility" under which we still labour but from which "metaphysical" poetry of course, and the great Elizabethans, were blissfully free:

> The great majority of his figures of speech are simple illustrations of the ideas that he wishes to convey . . . the function of the images is not to intensify the meaning, to make it deeper or richer, but simply to make more

> effective a meaning that was already fully formed before the application of the illustrative device.[4]

And Knights goes on to assert that Bacon uses language like a lawyer, for narrowly forensic purposes, rather than as a complex means of expression. For him, that comparison of the philosophers of imaginary commonwealths with the stars, which Coleridge found insufficiently direct and referential, is an example of imagery introduced into the sentence mechanically, to prove a point, and thereby debased. Coleridge complains that the wit and detachable life of Bacon's image detract from the clarity and logic of the point being made: Knights that it is a dead figure of speech, introduced solely as an illustration of the argument. Both views seem to do Bacon less than justice. It would be more accurate to say, surely, that the star image is employed in the sentence neither as a bit of verbal gymnastics, nor as a legal rhetorician's means of expressing contempt for the witness. The philosophers of Utopia are to be sent away, but sadly, like Plato's poets. The association with the stars deliberately confers upon them a dignity and splendour which is as much a part of Bacon's judgement as his rejection—a rejection which proceeds from the fact that they are too far from the earth to light it. After all, Bacon himself did not despise the task of framing imaginary laws for an imaginary commonwealth, even though he felt obliged in the end to leave the _New Atlantis_ unfinished in favour of the weary but (as he saw it) more necessary task of collecting data for a natural history.

Knights is of course as aware as Coleridge that Bacon sometimes plays on the multiple meanings of words, although he cannot approve of the way in which, as it seems to him, it is done. "For the truth is, that time seemeth to be of the nature of a river or stream, which carrieth down to us that which is light and blown up, and sinketh and drowneth that which is weighty and solid" (III, 292–3). It is one of Bacon's favourite images, the visual formulation of an idea which appears over and over again in his work with little verbal change. For Knights, this play upon "light" and "solid" is illegitimate and the image deceitful, because "although the analogy appears to clinch the argument, it does not in fact prove anything. The comparison is _imposed_, and instead of possessing the validity that comes from the perception of similarity, it is simply a rhetorical trick." It is not easy to see why Bacon's river is any more _imposed_ than Donne's in that beautiful analogy beginning "As streames are, Power is" with which the argument of the "Third Satyre" concludes. Both in fact are attempts to embody a thoroughly abstract and at the same time very particular idea in physical terms. As for that false clinching of the argument which makes Knights indignant, as though he were listening to the sophistries of some smooth-tongued lawyer defending a dubious cause, Bacon might have replied that he was scarcely more interested in proving anything by his analogy than Donne in his "Third Satyre," or his good friend George Herbert in "The Pulley." He would not have denied that he intended to persuade, in a sense by no means alien to the poetry either of Herbert or of Donne. Here the work done in recent years on Bacon's view of rhetoric and the imagination speaks against Knights.[5] Bacon did not, as Knights affirms, regard rhetoric as fundamentally a "deceitful art." That it could be such, and all too often was, he was as well aware as Plato in the Gorgias; Bacon's own work entitled Of the Coulers of Good and Evill (1597) was intended as a touchstone in this respect, a means of arming the listener or reader against the legerdemain of language used in the service of specious proof. Both by precept and example, he was concerned to advance an idea of rhetoric as a marriage between reason and the imagination for the purpose of moving the will, which was strictly bound to the service of truth and right action. Emblems, fables, similitudes and other figures of speech are for Bacon anything but mechanically imposed ornaments: they are the indispensable means of transforming "conceits intellectual to images sensible, which strike the memory more" (III, 399), becoming more vivid and available to the understanding precisely because they appeal to the whole man, not simply to his intellect. Certainly, Bacon does not believe that he is proving a point when he says that in the river of Time things of worth are known to sink and be lost to sight, while the trivial floats and eddies with the current. He is trying essentially to persuade his reader to break through that crippling subservience to tradition which venerates Aristotle and passes over Heraclitus, imitates Cicero and forgets about Tacitus, simply in accord with the valuation placed upon these writers by the past. He is, as Shelley understood, concerned to kindle the imagination of his audience in order to erlarge the circumference of its mind, to shatter barriers and conventional attitudes with an individual combination of reason and poetry which enfranchises rather than restricts. Here, as in that great passage about the spiderous nature of scholasticism—the dangers of knowledge divorced from objective reality—which Knights links with the "river of Time" sentence in his attack, Bacon is employing imagery neither in the service of false argument, nor simply for decoration: it is a precise and subtle means of expression linked tightly to the great English tradition of imaginative prose.

Knights further insists that Bacon's images, as mere demonstrations or supports for arguments, display none of that "vivid feeling for both sides of the analogy such as we find in more representative Elizabethans." This poverty of response, he implies, betrays itself particularly in Bacon's references to the natural world. Only in one isolated passage is he able to feel any consciousness in Bacon of "the creative life behind the natural phenomena that he observes." Otherwise, in his view, we are face to face with a wholly pragmatic and insensitive observer. J. B. Leishman, in The Monarch of Wit (1951), has queried Knights' "both sides of the analogy," not merely with respect to Bacon's alleged insufficiency but in itself, as a doubtful characteristic of seventeenth-century poetry. As for Bacon's indifference to the non-human life of nature, one does not need to go as far as Spedding (who found in Bacon's translation of the Psalmist's fatalism,

> Or as the grass, that cannot term obtain
> To see the Summer come about again,

a tenderness of expression and sensitive sympathy with nature tantamount to a "poet's faith") to feel that Knights' observation is unjust. Professor D. G. James has pointed out how instinctively Bacon's mind recoiled from that colourless, mechanistic world which at one point it approached, taking refuge instead in an outworn vitalism which bestowed "perception" and "election" upon objects in a fashion familiar to us in the poetry of Shakespeare.[6] Even when Bacon happens to be arguing for the reconstitution of First Philosophy, for the recognition of unity in diversity, his prose preserves both the individuality of the things he is concerned to link, and his own delight in their separate natures:

> Is not the precept of a musician, to fall from a discord or harsh accord upon a concord or sweet accord, alike true in affection? Is not the trope of music, to avoid or slide from the close or cadence, common with the trope of rhetoric of deceiving expectation? Is not the delight of the quavering upon a stop in music the same with the playing of light upon the water? Splendet tremulo sub

> lumine pontus. [Beneath the trembling light glitters the sea.] Are not the organs of the senses of one kind with the organs of reflection, the eye with a glass, the ear with a cave or strait, determined and bounded? Neither are these only similitudes, as men of narrow observation may conceive them to be, but the same footsteps of nature, treading or printing upon several subjects or matters (III, 348–9).

This passage from the second book of The Advancement of Learning is of further interest in that it seems flatly to contradict Knights' assertion that "although the Advancement, like the Essays, is studded with literary quotations and allusions, their purpose is invariably to point a moral or illustrate an argument: there is never any indication that Bacon has been moved by poetry." No one could say, surely, that the lovely line from the Aeneid which Bacon has set in the midst of his own prose was introduced either to point a moral or to illustrate an argument. It is useless for either purpose. Nor is it the kind of line which anyone remembers in the first place, or enters into a commonplace book with an eye to such future service. This Virgilian glittering of light on the sea must be valued for itself or not at all. As for its presence in Bacon's mind, and on his page at this particular moment, it has clearly been evoked by that sensuous procession of love, music, the arts of language, and the beauty of the natural world which it crowns. Whatever his critics (the "brushers of noblemen's clothes," as he liked to call them) may say, the senses were always for Bacon far more than a simple mechanism for perceiving, in order to master, facts. They were also, in his own experience, the points at which the abstract and the palpable, the intellect and the responses of the body, met and gave delight. One may search in vain through Bacon's work for any shamefaced confession of emotion of the sort that Sidney has given us with regard to the old ballad of Percy and Douglas, but this scarcely means that he was insensitive to poetry. No man who was could have summoned up that line of Virgil in those circumstances, nor felt impelled at that precise moment to pass from highly charged prose to verse.

Knights' account of Bacon's actual statements about the role of poetry and the value to be placed upon the activity of the imagination has been so well and convincingly amended that it is needless to refer to the issue more than briefly. If Bacon's discussion of poetry in The Advancement of Learning is brief and unimportant by comparison with the time he devotes to other matters, there is a good and valid reason for such summary treatment. Poetry, as Bacon is at pains to affirm, is not one of the "deficient arts" which his book aims to rescue from neglect. It is, in fact, flourishing. (The Advancement of Learning was published in 1605; considering the verse, both dramatic and nondramatic, produced just before that time, and what was still to come, it would be hard to contest Bacon's judgement.) Bacon was a man able to foresee the problems which poets would encounter in that world of the future in which science should finally have come into its own. It was in order to save poetry from dismissal, once that whole medieval-Renaissance conception of the micro-macrocosm to which it was bound had crashed into pieces, that Bacon handled it as he did:

> If man is incapable of the true "image of the universal world," then he can no longer be regarded as a microcosm any more than nature can be proved a macrocosm, and the poet cannot mirror this fractured world; it is not his function to deal with irreconcilables. Bacon's answer was definite and final: he cannot. Therefore discard the pretense that the poet is a mirror of nature, cry aloud that he is not and never can be the world's philosopher (in the Baconian sense), and define his task anew in terms of fashioning for the delectation and profit of man "a more ample greatness, a more exact goodness, and a more absolute variety, than can be found in the nature of things" (The Advancement of Learning, III, 343). The poet can no longer pretend to mirror the scientists' world-as-it-is; accept the dualism and save poetry as a mirror of reality-as-moral/aesthetic pattern. Alas that the misinterpretation of doctrine should have resulted in the parochialisms of Davenant's epics of manners.[7]

Harrison claims that Bacon's separation of poetry from philosophical knowledge gave poetry a credit different in kind, not merely in degree, from science. Also, that his treatment of the imagination authorized its importance in political and ethical matters, while in his respect for and understanding of allegory and myth he anticipated some important modern attitudes.

Knights often seems to castigate Bacon unfairly for beliefs which scarcely represented any special pragmatic wickedness of his own, but were the common coin of the period. Bacon's immersion in his historical moment, the Elizabethan quality of his mind, is at least as striking as the extent to which his individuality separated itself from the beaten paths of the age. Much of what Bacon says about poetry as illustration or moral guide can be paralleled in Sidney. Between Bacon's assertion that poetry has "some participation of divineness, because it doth raise and erect the mind, by submitting the shows of things to the desires of the mind; whereas reason doth buckle and bow the mind unto the nature of things" (III, 344), and Sidney's famous distinction between the golden world of poetry and the brazen world of fact, there would seem to be little difference. As for Bacon's failure to perceive the value of poetry as a means "of deepening and refining the emotions," such a perception would have been a surprising part of any Elizabethan aesthetic. Writers like Sidney, Jonson, or Montaigne—whose sensibilities presumably were not "dissociated"—do not approach such an evaluation any more clearly than Bacon. For Knights, however, Bacon's whole attitude towards the emotions is repressive, inadequate, and "makes against wholeness of living." Here again, it is hard to see how Bacon's belief that a man should not be "passion's slave," but should keep his emotions under the control of his reason, or noblest faculty, sets him apart from his contemporaries. It is true that Elizabethan tragedy presents us with a whole gallery of heroes who fail to act in accordance with this principle, but then the behaviour of Hamlet, Lear, Brachiano, Hieronymo or Vindice is scarcely for imitation in any off-stage world. As for Bacon's treatment of the dangers of love, in a work intended for the guidance of statesmen and princes, it seems neither as pernicious as Knights suggests, nor as far from the meditations of a man like Burton on the same subject. "They do best, who if they cannot but admit love, yet make it keep quarter, and sever it wholly from their serious affairs and actions of life, for if it check once with business, it troubleth man's fortunes." This sentence from the essay "Of Love" which Knights singles out for special opprobrium is, of course, simply a conventional Renaissance prudential counsel, and one perhaps as relevant to the Cabinet Ministers of the present day as to those of Bacon's own time.

That Knights' final plea for a reason that "recognizes the claims of the sensibility as a whole and tries to work in harmony with it" is moving and urgent, no one could deny. He speaks eloquently about the inner schism of the twentieth century, the emotional poverty that has been the unexpected companion of Bacon's Kingdom of Man. One is led to disagree with him only in his assessment of Bacon himself as the villain of the piece, and in the distortion of Bacon's prose so as to make it the progenitor of our most serious modern ills. In point of fact, Eliot's phrase "dissociation of sensibility" is inescapably modern, and describes a modern dilemma—one from which Knights himself (and all of us, in that we belong to the age we do) cannot completely escape. But it is a mistake to project this dilemma on to the past, particularly when by doing so the real nature of thought and writing which might be of inestimable service is obscured and falsified. Bacon is by no means a negative figure, a disintegrator and destroyer. More accurately, he is a man who foresaw both some of the achievements and some of the ills of the future, and whose wholeness of thought, a welding together of reason and the imagination, the individual and the impersonal, the abstract and the sensuous, still possesses a positive power.

In his essay on "Style," Pater speaks of the delicate line separating mere fact from something which must be recognized as different in quality and degree:

> In Pascal, for instance, in the persuasive writers generally, how difficult to define the point where, from time to time, argument which, if it is to be worth anything at all, must consist of facts or groups of facts, becomes a pleading—a theorem no longer, but essentially an appeal to the reader to catch the writer's spirit, to think with him, if one can or will—an expression no longer of fact but of his sense of it, his peculiar intuition of a world, prospective, or discerned below the faulty conditions of the present, in either case changed somewhat from the actual world.

It might be a description of The Advancement of Learning, or indeed of Bacon's work as a whole. It is for his sense of fact, the colours and the peculiar unity of a single mind mirrored in a prose responsive to the slightest demands made upon it that Bacon must be regarded, in Shelley's sense, as a poet. He may have believed in his own famous image of man's mind as a clear and equal glass, lending no dimension or colour of its own to that external reality which it reflected: he himself was fortunately incapable of such impersonality. Even in the "scientific" collections of data, the Historia Vitae et Mortis, or the Historia Densi et Rari, the presence everywhere of an individual shaping mind preserves some value in the work for an age scarcely able to separate Bacon's supposition that lions lose their teeth because their breaths are so strong from the fantastic lore of medieval bestiaries, or to ponder seriously over his announcement that "Wine and beer in frost lose their vigour; yet in thaws and south winds they revive, relax, and as it were ferment again." The strange animism of this latter remark, in which the single technical term is handled far more diffidently than those which seem to endow the inanimate with a soul, is altogether characteristic of Bacon, and worlds away from what we ordinarily regard as dispassionate, scientific observation.

The astonishing variety of Bacon's prose has often been remarked, even Knights pointing with approval to passages in the Historie of the Raigne of Henry VII (1622) which, he claims, might have been written by Nashe. In accordance with his own rhetorical precepts, Bacon seems to have adjusted his English style anew in every major work, fitting it as perfectly as possible to the subject-matter, the purpose and the audience addressed. The masques and entertainments, the great parliamentary and legal speeches, the historical work, The Advancement of Learning, New Atlantis and Essayes have each a manner appropriate to them. Yet all are bound together by a common concern for the inseparability of thought and expression which involves more than a simple reaction against the verbal excesses of Ciceronian style. All of them, in their different ways, appeal to the reader to catch not simply fact but that peculiar and individual sense of fact of which Pater speaks. It is in this manner, rather than as the fountainhead of Royal Society plain prose of the last quarter of the seventeenth century, that Rawley's account of Bacon's belief that words should be "subservient or ministerial to matter, and not the principle" asks to be understood. What he was enunciating is a principle of good prose in any period, whether it is that of Sir Thomas Browne at his best, or of Flaubert.

It would be hard to deny that when he picked up his pen, Bacon himself was probably unconscious of the degree to which he reflected his own inner landscape, as well as that of the external world. It was certainly not his purpose to do so. Nothing, in fact, is more obvious than the care with which he avoids introducing any of those "personal" touches in his writing which make other Elizabethans so much more immediately appealing. At least four factors, however, worked to make him an artist in spite of himself: his isolation, the need to persuade, a sense of devouring time, and the fact that abstract ideas stubbornly presented themselves to him through the medium of the senses. "I may truly say, my soul hath been a stranger in the course of my pilgrimage," Bacon wrote sadly in his old age. It is a point that he touches upon more than once, in private meditations and in those Latin appeals to various European scholars through which he hoped, vainly, to gather support beyond England for his great work. All his life Bacon was surrounded by people (from Ben Jonson to the unhappy Essex) who genuinely admired him and held his friendship in high regard. Yet there was no one really to comprehend his thought and aims. James I accepted the dedication of The Advancement of Learning, but remarked privately that Bacon's work was like the peace of God, that passeth all understanding. Harvey, Bacon's personal physician, appears to have thought highly of his employer's wit and style. For the plans and conclusions of Bacon the philosopher-scientist, on the other hand, the true man of science had only the slightest respect. From the very beginning, Bacon faced a unique problem of communication:

> For that knowledge which is new, and foreign from opinions received, is to be delivered in another form than that that is agreeable and familiar; and therefore Aristotle, when he thinks to tax Democritus, doth in truth commend him, where he saith, "If we shall indeed dispute, and not follow after similitudes, &c." For those whose conceits are seated in popular opinions, need only but to prove or dispute; but those whose conceits are beyond popular opinions, have a double labour; the one to make themselves conceived, and the other to prove and demonstrate. So that it is of necessity with them to have recourse to similitudes and translations to express themselves. And therefore in the infancy of learning, and in rude times, when those conceits which are now trivial were then new, the world was full of parables and similitudes; for else would men either have passed over without mark, or else rejected for paradoxes that which was offered, before they had understood or judged (III, 406–7).

It is, in effect, Bacon's explanation of the nature of his own prose. His thought was both complicated and unfamiliar; its expression was not easy. Furthermore—although here we reach the borders of a region where Bacon's own judgement and self-awareness cannot be relied upon—it was to a very large extent the child of the imagination, a "dream of learning," and therefore asked naturally for the services of the imagination in order to declare itself.

Bacon needed desperately to persuade. He had to make a whole series of ideas and convictions not merely clear but convincing to a world which seemed slow and reluctant to think, but whose co-operation was nevertheless essential to the success of his enterprise. Even had he really wanted, he could not have used the mechanical, impersonal prose of later scientists. Moreover, he was pressed by mortality. "Time groweth precious with me," he was writing even in 1606. Bacon was as obsessed with the brevity of human life as Shakespeare, by the bitter contradiction between man's potentialities and the span of time allotted for their realization. This is the urgency which drives so many of his sentences to a conclusion in which the claims of emotion, of the footsteps treading behind, and of reason (man's mind as a clear and equal glass) achieve a balance by no means alien to Elizabethan tragedy, yet peculiarly Bacon's own. For "it is the duty and virtue of all knowledge to abridge the infinity of individual experience, as much as the conception of truth will permit, and to remedy the complaint of vita brevis, ars longa" (III, 356).

Bacon, as Caroline Spurgeon once noted, tended to represent all good things, and in particular all desirable forms of mental activity, under the form of light.[8] The light and darkness patterns in his work are everywhere visible, and almost invariably charged with an emotion which seems to spring equally from the idea expressed by the individual passage, and from Bacon's curious sensitivity to varying degrees of obscurity and brilliance. Miss Spurgeon's account of Bacon's imagery was primarily concerned to distinguish it from Shakespeare's, and it was not perhaps altogether fair to Bacon. Certainly she was right in pointing out the extent to which he relied upon Biblical reference. But then his dependence upon myth, anecdote of the kind collected in his Apophthegms, and fantastic natural history of the sort that the writer knows to be false in itself, is equally striking. He was fond of many comparisons which proclaim him a man of his period—the world as a stage or a garden, man's life as a journey, analogies with music, and the like—but it is particularly noticeable how many of his most characteristic similitudes and metaphors are concerned not merely to render the abstract palpable to the senses, but to suggest that like the things of the green and growing world, these abstract ideas partake somehow of those organic principles of growth and change which we associate with trees, plants, and the development of streams from their source to the sea.

This characteristic of Bacon's imagery suggests a comparison with Elizabethan drama. That Bacon was interested in the stage is apparent from the frequency with which he refers to it and invokes its terminology. He was well aware that men react differently—and often more strikingly—as part of a theatre audience and as individuals, aware also that the evil which comes upon a man from his own fault, and not simply from fortune, "strikes deadly inwards" and is essential to tragedy. It is true that he also believed these facts had been insufficiently exploited owing to what he described as the plain neglect of drama as a discipline in his own time. He was not, however, the only Elizabethan who suffered from a neoclassical blindness; his failure to recognize what was directly in front of him does not mean that he was unable to understand what the theatre was all about. Certainly, there would seem to be a profound and subtle relationship between Shakespearian drama and Bacon's attitude towards Truth.

Professor Basil Willey has observed how genuinely Bacon seems at times to approach the spirit of Keats' "negative capability." "Nothing," he writes, "is more characteristic of Bacon than his distrust of the 'meddling intellect,' which interposes too soon with its abstractions and distorts nature instead of explaining her."[9] A double impulse, a need to discover and establish Truth on the one hand, and to prevent thought from settling and assuming a fixed form on the other, lies at the heart of all of Bacon's work. It is a measure, perhaps, not only of his greatness but also of his weakness as a practical man of science. Even as he could never sacrifice, as Gilbert or Harvey did, the wholeness and impossible scope of his thought in favour of some small area of knowledge which could have been mastered, so he could not resolve the contradiction involved in his desire both for Truth and for a state of continuous potentiality, except by imaginative means. It is on some such rock that the Method, with its insistence upon a complicated double movement between experiment and axiom, particular and general idea, foundered. Despite all of Bacon's hopes, it must always have looked more like Richard II's flight of fancy about the two buckets filling one another than a genuinely utilitarian process. It is the imagination in the end, an imagination clandestinely escaped from the place to which Bacon assigned it, and not reason, which cements together the structure of his thought.

Hence the importance of those image patterns referred to earlier, in which abstract ideas are expressed by means of similitudes in which possibilities of growth and change are implicit. The favourite idea of light as a form or symbol for Truth also explains itself in these terms. Fluid, changing, measurably present and yet impossible to circumscribe, light is the obvious imaginative guise under which the contradictions of Bacon's twin impulses could be caught up and resolved. Imagery, however, could scarcely bear the entire burden. In Henry VII Bacon can be observed working on his material in such a way that the structure of the book as a whole declares the quality of its author's mind. A delicate balance between facts and events in all their complexity and essential irrationality, and the degree of order imposed upon them by a mind concerned to create some significant form of Truth—without limiting the material falsely, or reducing it to the deadness of paraphrasable content—makes the account not only a complete success of its kind, but also the blood-brother of Shakespeare's history plays. Bacon's Henry VII stands brilliantly between the shapeless, helter-skelter records of the chroniclers, and that medieval impoverishment of history which reduced it to man's idea of God's will. It is exactly the position that Shakespeare's Henry V occupies between the inconsequential jumble of the anonymous Famous Victories of Henry V (a play that might have been written by Bardolph and Pistol) and the relentless historical propagandizing of Bale's King John. These two works by Bacon and Shakespeare are, despite difference of genre, fundamentally alike in their reconciliation by means of the imagination of an idea of order with the natural heterogeneity of experience.

Historical writing obviously presents a special problem, and also a special means of solution. It is a definable form, as most of the rest of Bacon's writing was not, possessed of both ancient and Italian, if not of English, models. Also, it is inevitably limited by what has happened to survive as record of the past, and by the judgement of the individual observer. Timeless, inhuman nature, on the other hand, recognizes no such limits. Even human nature, once divorced from specific instance and circumstance, or from the frank bias and experience of the writer, becomes difficult to discuss in any way that escapes both the vague and the dogmatic. It was in these two areas, however, that Bacon felt his major task of interpretation lay. Not surprisingly, he felt the need of some instrument for both discovery and continuous search—and found it in the aphorism:

> As young men, when they knit and shape perfectly, do seldom grow to a further stature; so knowledge, while it is in aphorisms and observations, it is in growth; but when once it is comprehended in exact methods, it may perchance be further polished and illustrate and accommodated for use and practice; but it increaseth no more in bulk and substance (III, 292).

Aphorisms, he remarked elsewhere, "representing a knowledge broken, do invite men to inquire further; whereas methods, carrying the show of a total, do secure men, as if they were at furthest" (III, 405). Given his peculiar dilemma between the desire for truth and the distrust of certainty, the need to generalize and abridge and the fear of violating the individuality of facts, no form could have suited him better.

At the moment, Bacon's Essayes, the single English work in which his conception of the aphorism can be adequately studied, seems to be generally undervalued. Knights finds the traditional reputation of the book exaggerated; Lewis quotes with approval Professor Douglas Bush's remark that "everyone has read them, but no one is ever found reading them."[10] In point of fact, that cosy image of short, discursive pieces full of their author's personal charm, reading suitable for drowsy winter evenings beside the fire, which Lamb and other nineteenth-century writers have succeeded in imposing upon the form, is the worst possible approach to Bacon's essays. Equally disserviceable is the habit of referring to them as though they formed an homogeneous whole. Everyone knows about the way in which the essays gradually increased in number from the ten of the original 1597 edition to the fifty-eight of the 1625 version; and about both the stylistic change involved and the position of the work with regard to Bacon's plea in The Advancement of Learning for a collection of civil and moral knowledge. Yet the 1625 edition is not a tidy knitting together of various ideas which interested Bacon; it is an accumulation of disparate pieces as difficult to generalize about, or to connect internally, as Donne's

Songs and Sonets, and it is to be read in a not dissimilar fashion. No one would attempt to talk about Donne's *jeu d'esprit* "The Bait," or "The Flea," in the same language, and as though they were poems quite compatible in quality and intent with "The Extacie" or "A Valediction, Forbidding Mourning." Yet essays as dissimilar as those "Of Gardens," "Of Seditions" and "Of Truth" are commonly blanketed under the same generalizations, described in the same terms, as though there were not all the difference in the world between them.

In general, Bacon's essays fall into three classes. The first is concerned to give straightforward advice in the most economical and memorable form possible, whether for the building of houses, the planning of masques and gardens, or the proper attitude towards studies. They are characteristically terse, but on the whole can be read much as one reads ordinary prose. The second group weaves together a series of shrewd observations, examples from the past, and hints of general principles in such a way as to indicate directions and provide materials for assessing individual situations without assuming any form or point of view which could be considered as final, complete, and beyond further growth. An essay like "Of Dispatch," or "Of Empire," demands a more active co-operation from the reader than those of the first group, a combined effort of reason and imagination based upon the realization that what Bacon has provided on the page is a series of interacting half-statements, rather than a conclusion. By far the most interesting, however, are those pieces in which, characteristically, the need to realize and yet not to inhibit certain abstract ideas forces Bacon to the limit of his powers, and to a use of the aphorism in which prose approaches perhaps as closely as is possible in its compression and suggestiveness to the condition of poetry:

> Since aphorisms (unlike maxims or reflections) are not simply true or untrue, but illuminate reality in an indirect way: since, in other words, they always mean what they "mean" *and* something more . . . it follows that even if a number of aphorisms could be grouped in such a way that from one set of meanings a coherent system might be constructed, yet their second (equally important) meanings would still remain defiant of system, each pointing in a different direction.[11]

Dr. Stern is here thinking primarily of the aphorisms of Lichtenberg, but his words are equally appropriate to the collections of aphorisms which make up the greater part of the essays in this third group.

An essay like "Of Truth" asks to be read partly as a "metaphysical" poem is read, and partly in a peculiar fashion imposed upon it by the aphorism as a form. "What is Truth; said jesting Pilate; And would not stay for an Answer" (VI, 377). The rifle-shot of this opening, the little imaginative explosion, is a familiar Baconian technique and frequently imitated. Less imitable, however, is the curious configuration of the space which separates this first sentence from the one which follows. "Certainly there be, that delight in Giddinesse; And count it a Bondage, to fix a Beleefe; Affecting Free-Will in Thinking, as well as in Acting." It is not merely that these are two sentences of a markedly different kind: the second simply does not move forward from the first in any fashion which we normally associate with the logic of prose. The movement performed is deliberately oblique in a way that forces the reader in part to create the link himself. A passive attitude here, or even a very rapid perusal of the page, is fatal to the essay. The sentences will indeed seem, as they have to one of Bacon's critics, to lie together end to end as stiffly as logs. Agree to the special demands of Bacon's prose on the other hand, here and throughout the essay, and a vast and complex building—the joint creation of author and reader, of reason and the imagination, completely individual and yet never either exhausted or quite the same twice—begins to arise from the sentences.

It is the nature of the aphorism to mean more than one thing. In the words themselves, not merely in the progression of the sentences, Bacon contrives to gather together a whole series of different and sometimes contradictory meanings and emotions; to hold them in suspension in such a way that they react upon one another; and to explore without dictating. It is characteristic of Bacon, for instance, that his value of Truth does not exclude a sense of the splendour of illusion, and that he can manage to pay "the lie" a handsome tribute with the very same words which on another level are concerned to emphasize its failings.

> This same truth, is a Naked, and Open day light, that doth not shew, the Masques, and Mummeries, and Triumphs of the world, halfe so Stately, and daintily, as

> Candlelights. Truth may perhaps come to the price of a Pearle, that sheweth best by day: But it will not rise, to the price of a Diamond, or Carbuncle, that sheweth best in varied lights (VI, 377).

The man who wrote those sentences not only had a feeling for both sides of the analogy: he was capable of recognizing and expressing a complexity of experience which only Shakespeare perhaps among his contemporaries handled with greater skill. And Bacon did not have, as Shakespeare did, the services of actors, stage, and drama as a form to help him illuminate ideas from many sides simultaneously.

All things considered, it is remarkable how frequently Bacon's language approaches that of the contemporary stage. From the point of view of verbal similarities, the wonder is not so much that the Bacon-Shakespeare controversy has never ended, as that it has not been found necessary to prove that he was not Webster, Marlowe, Chapman, Marston, nor yet the unknown author of the interpolations in *The Spanish Tragedy*. The very terseness and pointed quality of his sentences, particularly in the *Essayes*, doubtless has something to do with this. His is a much less elaborate and implacably *written* style than many of the period, and it possesses some of the directness and immediacy of dramatic speech:

> And therefore Velleius the Epicurean needed not to have asked, why God should have adorned the heavens with stars, as if he had been an *aedilis*, one that should have set forth some magnificent shows or plays. For if that great work-master had been of an human disposition, he would have cast the stars into some pleasant and beautiful works and orders, like the frets in the roofs of houses; whereas one can scarce find a posture in square, or triangle, or straight line, amongst such an infinite number; so different a harmony there is between the spirit of man and the spirit of nature (III, 396).

Even in a passage like this, where Bacon is concerned to tear down the whole fabric of the Elizabethan world picture, to say something exactly opposite from Shakespeare, his means of expression are so closely allied as to make it seem as though some ghostly anti-Hamlet were speaking. Reason still requires the services of the imagination in order to express itself: the new and the old stand together for a last moment on the brink of a world which Bacon had in some measure foreseen, but in which he would have remained a stranger.

NOTES

1 English Literature in the Sixteenth Century, Excluding Drama (Oxford, 1954), p. 538.

2 An amusing balance-sheet of opinion on Bacon can be found in Rudolph Metz, "Bacon's Part in the Intellectual Movement of his Time," in Seventeenth-Century Studies Presented to Sir Herbert Grierson (Oxford, 1938) and in Elizabeth Sewell, The Orphic Voice (London, 1960), pp. 59–60.

3 The Friend (London, 1818), section II, essay viii.

4 "Bacon and the Seventeenth-Century Dissociation of Sensibility," in Knights, Explorations (London, 1946), pp. 98–9.

5 Cf. Karl R. Wallace, Francis Bacon on Communication and Rhetoric (Chapel Hill, N.C., 1943); John L. Harrison, "Bacon's View of Rhetoric, Poetry and the Imagination," Huntington Library Quarterly, XX (1957).

6 The Dream of Learning (Oxford, 1951), p. 18.

7 Harrison, op. cit., p. 119.

8 Caroline F. E. Spurgeon, Shakespeare's Imagery and What It Tells Us (Cambridge, 1935), pp. 16–29.

9 The Seventeenth Century Background (London, 1934), p. 36.

10 Bush, English Literature in the Earlier Seventeenth Century (Oxford, 1962) (revised), p. 197.

11 J. P. Stern, Lichtenberg: a Doctrine of Scattered Occasions (Bloomington, Ind., 1959), pp. 262–3.

ADDITIONAL ARTICLES FOR FURTHER STUDY

Adams, R., "The Social Responsibilities of Science in *Utopia, New Atlantis* and after," *Journal of the History of Ideas*, Vol. 10 (1949), pp. 374–98.

Andrewes, J., "Bacon, Hazlitt, and the 'Dissociation of Sensibility,'" *Notes & Queries*, Vol. 199 (1954), pp. 484–6, 530–2.

Bierman, J., "Science and Society in the *New Atlantis* and Other Renaissance Utopia," *PMLA*, Vol. 78 (1963), pp. 492–500.

Blodgett, E., "Campanella and the *New Atlantis*," *PMLA*, Vol. 46 (1931), pp. 763–80.

Broad, C.D., *The Philosophy of Francis Bacon* (Cambridge, 1926), reprinted in *Ethics and the History of Philosophy* (London, 1952), pp. 117–43.

Cochrane, R.C., "Francis Bacon and the Architect of Fortune," *Studies in the Renaissance*, Vol. 5 (1958), pp. 176–95.

Cochrane, R. C., "Bacon in Early Eighteenth Century English Literature," *Philological Quarterly*, Vol. 37 (1958), pp. 58–79.

Cohen, M.R., "Bacon and Inductive Method," *Studies in Philosophy and Science* (New York, 1949), pp. 99–106.

Colie, R.L., "Cornelius Drebbel and Salomon de Caus: Two Jacobean Models for Salomon's House," *Huntington Library Quarterly*, Vol. 18 (1954), pp. 245–60.

Davis, W.R., "The Imagery of Bacon's Late Work," *Modern Language Quarterly*, Vol. 27 (1966), pp. 162–73.

Ducasse, C.J., "Francis Bacon's Philosophy of Science," *Structure, Method and Meaning*, ed. P. Hensle *et al*. (New York, 1951), pp. 115–44.

Farrington, B., "On Misunderstanding the Philosophy of Francis Bacon," *Science, Medicine and History*, ed. E. A. Underwood (Oxford, 1953), Vol. 1, pp. 439–50.

Fisch, H., "Bacon and Paracelsus," *Cambridge Journal*, Vol. 5 (1952), pp. 752–8.

ADDITIONAL ARTICLES FOR FURTHER STUDY

Harrison, C.T., "Bacon, Hobbes, Boyle, and the Ancient Atomists," Harvard Studies and Notes Philological and Literary, Vol. 15 (1933), pp. 191–218.

Kocher, P., "Bacon and his Father," Huntington Library Quarterly, Vol. 21 (1957), pp. 133–58.

Larsen, R.E., "The Aristotelianism of Bacon's Novum Organum," Journal of the History of Ideas, Vol. 23 (1962), pp. 435–50.

Luciani, V., "Bacon and Machiavelli," Italica, Vol. 24 (1947), pp. 26–40.

Luciani, V., "Bacon and Guicciardini," PMLA, Vol. 62 (1947), pp. 96–113.

McCabe, B., "Francis Bacon and the Natural Law Tradition," Natural Law Forum, Vol. 9 (1964), pp. 111–21.

Macrae, R., "Unity of Sciences: Bacon, Descartes, Leibniz," Journal of the History of Ideas, Vol. 18 (1957), pp. 27–48.

Metz, R., "Bacon's Part in the Intellectual Movement of his Time," Seventeenth Century Studies presented to Sir Herbert Grierson (Oxford, 1938), pp. 21–32.

Snow, V., "Francis Bacon's Advice to Fulke Greville on Research Techniques," Huntington Library Quarterly, Vol. 23 (1960), pp. 369–78.

Vickers, B.W., "Swift and the Baconian Idol," in The World of Jonathan Swift, ed. Brian Vickers (Oxford, 1968).

Wheeler, T., "Bacon's Purpose in Writing Henry VII," Studies in Philology, Vol. 54 (1957), pp. 1–13.

White, H.B., "Bacon's Imperialism," The American Political Science Review, Vol. 52 (1958), pp. 470–89.

Zeitlin, J., "The Development of Bacon's Essays and Montaigne," Journal of English and Germanic Philology, Vol. 27 (1928), pp. 496–519.